FRIEDRICH SCHILLER

Poet of Freedom

Volume III

Schiller Institute
Washington, D.C.
1990

The translators wish to acknowledge the help of two native German-speaking members of the Schiller Institute, for their work in ensuring the accuracy of the translations in this volume, and for their continuing encouragement and support for this effort—Wolfgang Lillge and Ralf Schauerhammer.

© 1990 Schiller Institute
ISBN: 0-9621095-2-5
Library of Congress:
90-62731

Cover design: Alan Yue
Book design: Paul Arnest
Project editors: Christina Huth, Marianna Wertz
Composition: World Composition Services, Inc., Sterling, Virginia

Please direct all inquiries to the publisher:
Schiller Institute, Inc.
P.O. Box 66082
Washington, D.C. 20035-6082

CONTENTS

Foreword v
by Helga Zepp-LaRouche
Chairman, Schiller Institute

Introduction:
Brief Is the Pain, the Joy Shall Be Eterne xi
by William F. Wertz, Jr.

POETRY 1

DRAMA

The Virgin of Orleans 33
Homage to the Arts 163

HISTORY

Introduction to *The History of the Revolt
of the United Netherlands Against
Spanish Rule* 177

AESTHETICS AND PHILOSOPHY

Love, Virtue, Friendship 195
Philosophical Letters 197
On the Pathetic 227
On the Sublime 255
Thoughts Concerning the Use of the Common
and Base in Art 273
On the Necessary Limits in the Use of
Beautiful Forms 281
On Naïve and Sentimental Poetry 307
On the Moral Use of Aesthetic Manners 399
On Epic and Dramatic Poetry 409

FOREWORD

Schiller Institute Chairman Helga Zepp-LaRouche, West German political leader and wife of the American statesman Lyndon H. LaRouche, Jr., wrote this foreword as an international call for Freedom Demonstrations to be held on November 10, 1989, the 230th birthday of Friedrich Schiller. On November 9, one day earlier, the great, historic opening of the Berlin Wall occurred. Millions of East German citizens poured into the West, with "tears of joy" in their eyes, to launch a process of liberation that continues as this volume goes to print.

The Schiller Institute is itself a major player in these events, as it has, since its inception in 1984, advocated and campaigned for the Berlin Wall to come down, and for the reunification of Germany as one sovereign state, within the free West. In November 1988, Lyndon LaRouche, accompanied by his wife, traveled to West Berlin, where he held a major press conference, to outline a series of proposals for the West to develop the economies of East Germany, Poland, and other East bloc nations, in exchange for their freedom from Soviet tyranny—called Food for Peace. The impact of those proposals can be felt today throughout Europe, East and West.

This volume of translations is part of that effort by the Schiller Institute. By reacquainting Americans with the writings of Germany's "Poet of Freedom," we hope thereby to enhance support in the United States for the rebirth of freedom in the poet's native land. Thus will we, too, regain the true freedom, which, as Schiller himself says, only the greatest of classical culture can give to man.

FREEDOM FOR ALL PEOPLE ON THIS EARTH!

BY HELGA ZEPP-LAROUCHE
CHAIRMAN OF THE SCHILLER INSTITUTE

> No, there's a limit to the tyrant's power,
> When the oppressed can find no justice, when
> The burden grows unbearable—he reaches
> With hopeful courage up unto the heavens
> And seizes hither his eternal rights,
> Which hang above, inalienable
> And indestructible as stars themselves—
> The primal state of nature reappears,
> Where man stands opposite his fellow man—
> As last resort, when not another means
> Is of avail, the sword is given him—
> The highest of all goods we may defend
> From violence.—We stand before our country,
> We stand before our wives, before our children.
> —*Friedrich Schiller*
> *Wilhelm Tell*

For a long time, it seemed that the idea of freedom no longer possessed that value which would make it worth fighting for—at least in the so-called free West, where the materialism of the prosperous society had long been dissociated from any lofty ideal, for which men would once have been ready to give their lives. And then, seemingly out of the blue, in 1989, the 230th birthday of Friedrich Schiller, the ideas of the Poet of Freedom are becoming the vital foundation of freedom movements in many parts of the world all at once!

When the students in Beijing, in May of this year, demonstrated for democracy for weeks on end, at the Square of Heavenly Peace, they erected the Statue of Liberty as a symbol of their struggle, and they chose the chorus from Beethoven's Ninth Symphony—composed to Schiller's "Ode to Joy"—as the hymn of their movement. It turns out that the best people, in times of great crisis, turn to the profound conceptions and ideas that really constitute the dignity of man. The fact that the brutal massacre of the Deng regime could not break this revolutionary spirit, is shown by the growing movement of Chinese students throughout the world. On the contrary, the more inhuman the communist dictators show themselves to be, the more intense become the movements of the soul, which are responsible for all progress in human history. As it says at the end of the "Ode to Joy":

> Courage firm in grievous trial,
> Help, where innocence doth scream,
> Oaths which sworn to are eternal,
> Truth to friend and foe the same,
>
> Manly pride 'fore kingly power—
> Brothers, cost it life and blood—
> Honor to whom merits honor,
> Ruin to the lying brood!
>
> Closer draw the holy circle,
> Swear it by this golden wine,
> Faithful to the vow divine,
> Swear it by the Judge celestial!

But also throughout the East bloc, people are trying to throw off their yoke. A crisis such as has not been seen for decades over food and basic necessities, is certainly the driving factor for why various nations and ethnic groups are rejecting the central power in Moscow. But for people in Armenia and Azerbaijan, in Ukraine, in Georgia, Moldavia, the Baltic republics, Hungary, Poland, East Germany, and Czechoslovakia, there are other elements mixed in—the unquenchable thirst for freedom, which even the long years of dictatorship could not break! And so one can recall what Schiller wrote in the introduction to his description of the collapse of another dictatorship, namely the revolt of the Netherlands against Spain:

"Great and comforting is the reflection, that against the defiant usurpations by monarchic force, in the end a remedy is still at hand, that their most calculated designs against human freedom can be spoiled, that a bold-hearted resistance can bend low even the outstretched hand of a despot, heroic perseverance can finally exhaust his terrifying resources. Never did this truth pierce me so vividly as the history of that memorable revolt, which severed the United Netherlands forever from the Spanish crown—and on that account, I regarded it as not unworthy of the effort to set before the world this beautiful memorial of common citizens' strength, to awaken in the breast of my reader a joyful sense of his own individual self, and to give a new undismissible example, of what human beings can dare to hazard for the cause, and what they may accomplish by uniting."

And these days in East Berlin *William Tell* is being performed—that work of Schiller which already during the Nazi period was the play of the resistance—and is being repeatedly interrupted by stormy applause. It is as though Schiller, in this drama, had the fate of Germany before his eyes, when he wrote in the famous Ruetli scene:

Now let us take the oath of this new league.
—We will become a single land of brothers,
Nor shall we part in danger and distress.

—We will be free, just as our fathers were,
And sooner die, than live in slavery.
—We will rely upon the highest God
And we shall never fear the might of men.

Why is it that the music of Beethoven and the poetry of Schiller have such a powerful effect on the souls of men, in just such times of violent upheaval as these? Because at the foundation of their work is the human ideal that places human dignity on the highest plane. It is the idea of the unassailable, inalienable rights of all men, and therefore the concept of man, that unifies the freedom movements throughout the world.

Human history has come to a *punctum saliens*, a point of decision. Both the communist dictatorships and the hitherto-existing form of the Western alliance have come to an end, and it is still unclear whether the historic opportunity will be grasped, and whether a free world order can be built, or whether these upheavals will end in chaos and war.

In either case, the fate of men is now, for the first time in history, so closely interlinked, that developments will lead either to a global disaster or a worldwide renaissance. The choice lies with us, to a great extent: Will we make use of this great moment to help to bring about Schiller's dream of an Age of Reason?

Throughout the world, therefore, men are called upon, on Schiller's 230th birthday, to express their support for the idea of Freedom, in the form of freedom demonstrations wherever that be possible, or, where circumstances prevent that, perhaps instead to participate in this worldwide movement by listening to Beethoven's Ninth Symphony.

—November 9, 1989

INTRODUCTION

BY WILLIAM F. WERTZ, JR.

> "Brief is the pain, the joy shall be eterne."
> —*Friedrich Schiller*
> *The Virgin of Orleans*

This third volume of translations issued by the Schiller Institute of the writings of Friedrich Schiller, is being published on the occasion of the 230th birthday anniversary of the great Poet of Freedom. During the course of this year, 1989, the world has seen, on the one hand, the outrageous "legal" railroading of the leadership of the republican movement in the West—Lyndon H. LaRouche, Jr. and several of his colleagues, including this writer; and on the other hand, the beginnings of a worldwide republican revolution, the high point of which, at this writing, has been the mass strike for political freedom in China.

The Schiller Institute, inspired by the republican outlook of its namesake, has been in the forefront of efforts to fight tyranny throughout the world, including in China. It is therefore no accident of history that the students in Tiananmen Square in Beijing chose as their theme-song Ludwig van Beethoven's Ninth Symphony, the concluding movement of which is a choral setting of Schiller's poem "To Joy."

When news of the Chinese revolution began to be reported in the West, Lyndon LaRouche and his six codefendants had been sentenced to prison terms ranging from three to fifteen years, and were already in prison, having been denied bond pending appeal. The same Henry Kissinger, who would later publicly apologize for the brutal Communist Chinese dictatorship of Deng Xiaoping after the massacre of thousands of students, had sufficiently influenced elements of the Bush administration and the Department of Justice, so as to effect, at least temporarily, a no less brutal persecution of the LaRouche political movement, albeit by judicial rather than the overt military means used in China.

And yet, despite the temporary setback to the cause of freedom that both persecutions represent, the potential for positive revolutionary change globally is perhaps greater now than ever before. As Lyndon LaRouche has pointed out, an anti-Bolshevik revolution is now sweeping both China and the Soviet Union, at the same time that the desire for sovereign economic development is gaining strength throughout the developing sector, and in particular Central and South America. In this context, even the United States and Western Europe will not long remain unaffected by this republican upsurge, particularly in the context of the global financial and economic crisis.

It is in this context that the Schiller Institute's effort to promote a community of principle among nations, based upon the political principles of the American Revolution and the German classics, has gained increasing moral authority internationally. What better reflection could there be of the cultural power of the ideas promoted by the Schiller Institute since its founding in 1984, than the dual image of the "Ode To Joy" being sung in Tiananmen Square, as a replica of the Statue of Liberty was being erected!

The very fact that the Communist Chinese regime temporarily held onto its tyrannical power through bloody suppression, or that Kissinger and other proponents of a global power-sharing arrangement with Moscow and Beijing have perpetrated injustices against Lyndon LaRouche and the movement associated with him, will only contribute to their more rapid political demise. Already, the evil perpetrated by these political circles on behalf of their own self-interest has resulted in their loss of any legitimate moral mandate to continue to govern. In life, the apparent victories of evil can and must be transformed by human effort to the advantage of the good.

The translations that appear in this volume represent just such an effort on the part of this writer and a number of his colleagues in the Schiller Institute, to transform the injustice of his and his codefendants' incarceration to the cultural benefit of the current global revolutionary upsurge against tyranny of every sort. All the works translated in this volume by this writer, including *The Virgin of Orleans*, *The Philosophical Letters*, *On the Pathetic*, *On the Sublime*, and *On Naïve and Sentimental Poetry*, were translated in the Alexandria County Detention Center in Virginia during the first six months of 1989. It is the hope of this writer, that the circulation of these translations, completed under adverse conditions, which, like the massacre in Tiananmen Square, are designed to discourage and intimidate those who believe in freedom, will help to ensure that the revolution abroad in the world today will not fail to bring about real, durable political freedom for humanity as a whole.

Just as the translating of these works by Schiller helped morally and culturally to sustain this writer, and to reenforce his commitment to truth and beauty during the inception of his incarceration, so the reading of these and other works by Schiller will give you, the reader, consolation in the face of adversity, and the strength to persevere in giving the world the direction of the good.

SCHILLER AND BEETHOVEN

In the course of doing these translations, this writer was fortunate to have read Thayer's *Life of Beethoven*. One of the things that becomes clear in reading this work is the tremendous effect Schiller had on Beethoven over as much as three decades, and, specifically, how much Beethoven personally identified with Schiller's Johanna d'Arc. Because this writer's translation of *The Virgin of Orleans* benefitted from being done, as it were, through the eyes of Beethoven, Schiller's impact on Beethoven is important for the reader to understand.

Although Beethoven never personally met Schiller (though they were contemporaries), as early as 1793, when Beethoven was yet a young man in Bonn, an associate of his, Bartolomäus Ludwig Fischenich, was in correspondence with Schiller's wife Charlotte. In a letter, Fischenich reported that Beethoven was already intent upon setting Schiller's poem "To Joy" to music. Of course, it was nearly thirty years later, that Beethoven composed the Ninth Symphony, which thus makes it the result of a lifelong preoccupation on Beethoven's part.

Beethoven did not set many of Schiller's works to music, compared, for instance, to the number of pieces by Goethe which he set. He explained, in a statement quoted by his student Carl Czerny (1791-1856), "Schiller's poems are very difficult to set to music. The composer must be able to lift himself far above *the poet;* who can do that in the case of Schiller? In this respect, Goethe is much easier."[1]

In line with this assessment, Beethoven in 1810 indicated his intention to compose an overture to Schiller's *Wilhelm Tell*, but, after much intriguing to persuade him otherwise, he instead wrote the overture to Goethe's *Egmont*. Besides the "Ode to Joy," Beethoven set to music only two other pieces by Schiller: the "Song of the Monks" in *Wilhelm Tell* (Act 4, scene 3), which he composed on the occasion of the death of his old friend the violinist Wenzel Krumpholz, on May 3, 1817, as a reflection on human mortality; and a canon he wrote, based upon the last line of *The Virgin of Orleans:* "Brief is the pain, the joy shall be eterne."

---

1. Thayer, Alexander Wheelock, *Life of Beethoven*, Elliot Forbes editor, Princeton University Press, p. 472.

Nonetheless, Beethoven's identification with Schiller was fundamental. Thayer reports, for instance, that Beethoven kept the following words from Schiller's *The Mission of Moses*, describing the Supreme Being, on his writing table: "I am that which is. I am all, what is, what was, what will be; no mortal man has ever lifted my veil."[2]

Moreover, it is absolutely clear that Beethoven personally identified with Johanna d'Arc, as represented in Schiller's play, for in his correspondence, he makes numerous allusions to the drama. Once, when asked why he always carried a notebook with him, Beethoven replied, as did Johanna in Schiller's play, "Without my banner dare I not to come." For Beethoven, his music was a divine mission and thus his true identity. Like Johanna, he could not face his Maker were he for a moment to abandon his vocation.

In a particularly difficult moment in his life, having lost his hearing, in failing health, and embroiled in a bitter fight with his sister-in-law—whom he called "raven-mother" after Queen Isabeau—over the custody of his nephew Karl, Beethoven writes to a friend, quoting Johanna again: "May God be gracious to me." In *The Virgin of Orleans*, Johanna offers this prayer just as she breaks loose from her chains and flies to the battlefield to achieve victory for the fatherland.

But undoubtedly the most poignant reflection of Beethoven's personal identification with Johanna is the canon he wrote, referred to above. Like her, Beethoven dedicated his life to a divine mission, the immortal effects of which can be seen centuries after his death, in today's struggle for freedom. (That Beethoven was politically a republican fighter can be seen by his comment, quoted in Thayer, on seeing a French officer during the Napoleonic occupation of Germany: "If I, as general, knew as much about strategy as I the composer know of counterpoint, I'd give you something to do!"[3] Of Napoleon himself, Beethoven expressed

---

2. Thayer, *ibid*. p. 481.
3. Thayer, *ibid*. p. 466.

tremendous anger at his betrayal of the republican cause: "Is he [Napoleon] then, too, nothing more than an ordinary human being? Now he, too, will trample on all the rights of man and indulge only his ambition. He will exalt himself above all others, become a tyrant!"[4]

Like Johanna, to achieve his purpose Beethoven had to overcome tremendous adversity. Yet his conclusion, like Johanna's, was that whatever suffering one must undergo for a higher purpose, that pain will be brief in comparison to the joy of having been faithful to one's divine mission, which is eternal.

The Virgin of Orleans

Undoubtedly, the reader will be struck by this translation of the title of the play, because the play has previously been translated as *The Maiden of Orleans*. However, Schiller did not entitle the play *Das Mädchen von Orleans*, which means *maiden*, but rather *Die Jungfrau von Orleans*, which means *virgin*. Moreover, this translation of *Die Jungfrau* is central to the content of the play, and any other translation is an obfuscation.

Johanna is divinely inspired by God, through the intercession of the Virgin Mary. In the prologue, the question is raised as to whether she is divinely inspired, as were Moses and the shepherd David, or whether her powers are Satanic, as were those of the Whore of Babylon. In fact, her father has a vision of her with "a sparkling diadem of seven stars upon her head," which is an allusion to the Whore of Babylon in the Book of Revelation.

In the first act, Johanna reveals that when she prayed to the Virgin Mary before "an ancient image of God's mother," the Holy One came to her and urged her to assume her banner and annihilate France's foe:

---

4. Thayer, *ibid.* p. 349.

> . . . a Virgin pure can bring
> About each thing that's glorious on earth,
> If only she resisteth earthly love.
> Just look on *me!* A maiden chaste like thou
> Have I the Lord, the Godly, given birth,
> *Act I, scene 10*

The banner that Johanna is urged to carry has depicted upon it the Virgin Mary and the child Jesus, hovering above an earthly sphere, so as to contrast divine love with earthly love.

Thus, from the beginning of the drama, Johanna is portrayed as in the image of the Virgin Mary. Her power to accomplish her God-given mission to save the French nation is based upon her renouncing earthly love, and acting instead on the basis of divine love. This distinction between *eros* and *agapē*, between the Whore of Babylon and the Virgin Mary, is the central theme of the drama. As long as she is faithful to divine love, Johanna is invincible; she is capable of performing miracles militarily, in defeating the foe on the battlefield, and politically, in uniting the deeply divided French people.

In the third act, for instance, Johanna succeeds in uniting the French noblemen Burgundy and Du Chatel, who had been divided by the fact that Du Chatel murdered Burgundy's father. In an allusion to Christ's injunction in the Sermon on the Mount, to love thine enemy, Schiller's Johanna says:

> A kindly master opens up his portals
> For all the guests, no one doth he exclude;
> Free, as the firmament contains the world,
> So must his grace enclose both friend and foe.
> The sun emits its beams of light alike
> To all the spaces of infinity;
> Like measuring the Heaven pours its dew
> Out on all of the thirsting vegetation.
> *Act III, scene 4*

To Burgundy's accusation that her powers are Satanic, Johanna offers an effective metric in judging the source of her power:

> ... in making peace, is hate
> Resolving an affair of Hell? And from
> The eternal pool doth harmony come forth?
> What is there guiltless, holy, humanly good,
> If not the battle for the fatherland?
> Since when is nature so in struggle with
> Itself, that Heaven doth the righteous cause
> Desert and that the devil it defends?
> But if that, which I say to thee, is good—
> Where else than from above could I it draw?
> *Act II, scene 10*

The fact that Johanna's power to accomplish the impossible is heavenly, and based upon her rejection of earthly pleasures, is not understood whatsover by those whom she aids. Thus, Dunois and La Hire both contend for the virgin's hand in marriage, and both King Charles and Agnes Sorel encourage her in this direction, having no idea that such a secondary concern was contrary to her primary mission.

After an encounter with the Black Knight, Johanna does indeed disobey her vow to resist earthly love. She is thus tempted by "a phantom form from out of Hell." Her heart is then seduced by pity for her country's foe, Lionel. As a result of thus abandoning her divine mandate, Johanna is rendered powerless.

When she is accused by her father, Thibaut, of being possessed by the devil, she remains silent, rather than defend herself, and is consequently banished by the King. Captured by the English, she rejects Lionel's proposal of earthly love. He imprisons her, and launches an offensive against the French, who, no longer defended by Johanna, are on the verge of total defeat.

Under these circumstances, Johanna asks: "O hath the Heaven not an angel more!" Praying, "So be gracious God to me!" like Samson, she breaks her chains and seizes victory out of the jaws of defeat.

In the last scene of the play, mortally wounded, she is depicted as an "angel" and "a transfigured spirit." Before she dies, she asks for her banner:

> Without my banner dare I not to come:
> It was entrusted to me by my Master,
> Before His throne I must needs lay it down—
> I may display it, for I bore it true.
> *Act V, scene 14*

Then with the banner in hand, Johanna, like the Virgin Mary, ascends to heaven:

> What comes o'er me—Light clouds are lifting me—
> The heavy armor doth to wingèd garments turn
> Upward—upward—The earth doth backward flee
> Brief is the pain, the joy shall be eterne!
> *Act V, scene 14*

Schiller's View of Women

Although Schiller rarely treated Christian themes explicitly, the coherence of Schiller's philosophy and Christianity could not be clearer than in this play. This is particularly true in respect to Schiller's view of womanhood, but also of man's purpose more generally.

Unlike today's radical feminist, who might attempt to coopt Johanna d'Arc for her own purposes, Schiller rejects the image of woman reflected in the Satanic Whore of Babylon, and instead adopts the revolutionary Christian image of woman expressed in the Virgin Mary. The significance of the Virgin is that she is the first human being to believe in the divinity of Christ. She freely decides to accept the task of giving birth to the Redeemer of Mankind. In doing so, in contrast to Eve, who acted disobediently out of *eros*,

Mary acts out of *agapē*. Her state of mind is thus closest among human beings to that of Christ, to whom she gives birth.

It is for this reason, that in the *Paradiso* of his *Divine Comedy*, Dante stresses that if one wants to be like Christ, one must first rise to the level of the Virgin Mary, for it is the Virgin Mary, who among mortals most resembles Christ, in terms of promethean charity. In that sense, although the Virgin Mary is particularly significant in terms of the positive Christian view of womanhood, her voluntaristic acceptance of responsibility for saving the human species is an example to be emulated by all, both men and women.

Mary is not a member of the Christian Trinity—Father, Son, and Holy Spirit—and therefore not God, in opposition to the gnostic notion of the Trinity, but she is the mediation of the Word become flesh.

In today's hedonistic world, the idea that someone might subordinate earthly love to a divine mission is about as foreign as the idea of the immaculate conception itself. And yet, Schiller, who writes *The Virgin of Orleans* after the French Revolution has failed to achieve its potential, due to the smallness of mind of the population, develops in Johanna those divine qualities of mind, which are necessary to achieve republican liberty.

Just as the Virgin Mary is the mediation of the incarnation of God, so Johanna represents the instrument of divine love. In contrast to her father, Thibaut, who argues stoically in the prologue,

> Obeying quietly let us await
> Whom victory will give us as a king
> Success in battle is but God's decree,
> And he's our *master*, who the holy chrism
> Receiveth and puts on the crown at Rheims.
> *Prologue, scene 3*

Johanna voluntaristically declared: "Yes, miracles still happen!"

> His trembling creature will He then elect,
> And through a tender virgin He will choose
> To glorify Himself, for He's almighty!"
> *Prologue, scene 3*

As in the play *Wilhelm Tell*, where he causes Walter Fürst to say, "God must help us through our own arm," Schiller's view is coherent with the Christian notion of the *filioque*, especially as that concept is expressed in the Transfiguration.[5] In Christianity, it is believed that the Holy Spirit flows both from the Father *and from the Son, filioque* in Latin. Since Christ is both God and man, by imitating Him, man is capable of participating in and expressing divine charity himself. As Christ said to His apostles after His Transfiguration, to those who believe in His divinity and their own God-given power to imitate Him, nothing is impossible. However, at that moment the apostles lacked such faith. Echoing Christ after the Transfiguration, Johanna says in Act III,

> Ye blinded hearts! O ye of little faith!
> The Heaven's majesty around you shines,
> Before your eye it doth unveil its miracles
> And ye perceive in me nought but a woman.
> *Act III, scene 4*

Even the least of God's children, by imitating Christ and by freely accepting God's mission, as does the Virgin Mary ("Be it unto me according to thy word"), is capable of contributing to the Good. This is not arrogance, as Thibaut charges:

> 'Tis arrogance, whereby the angels fell
> Whereby the spirit of Hell takes hold of man.
> *Prologue, scene 2*

Rather, it is a humble acceptance of God's will, as opposed to the pursuit of one's own self-centered will. As such, it is

---

5. Wertz, et al., *Friedrich Schiller, Poet of Freedom*, Vol. II.

God Himself, as in Mary's Magnificat ("My soul doth magnify the Lord"), who is glorified by the power He gives individual man for His purpose.

Johanna does indeed momentarily falter in the play. However, this does not confirm, as her father charges in the fourth act of the play, that she has employed the devil's art. The opposite is the case. Her victories are indeed divinely inspired. She falters merely because she has violated her oath to the Virgin Mary in expressing earthly love for Lionel.

She reflects at this moment what Schiller refers to, in *On the Pathetic*, as the sublime of disposition. Up to this point, she has acted merely out of obedience. In violating her oath, she is conscious of her guilt, and while not *acting* sublimely, is all the more determined to atone for this failure. The sublimity of her disposition at this moment is made greater by the fact that she is wrongfully maligned by her own father as a witch, and banished by the very French court and nation she has helped to save.

In the fifth act, Johanna, having thus suffered due to her human frailty, engages in what Schiller refers to as the sublime of action. She morally atones for her violated duty and now acts not out of mere obedience, but rather out of free will. She rejects Lionel's offer of earthly love and chooses to free her fatherland, even if it should lead to her own destruction. Her ascension at the end of the play, in imitation of the Virgin Mary's ascension to Heaven, reflects Schiller's view, that to be free, man must be capable of triumphing even over death.

When Johanna, after having asked, "O hath the Heaven not an angel more!" breaks her own chains with the grace of God and flies like an angel to the battlefield to save her fatherland, she, like Samson, freely accepts the termination of her own mortal existence, in the furtherance of a higher divine purpose. She thus demonstrates that man is more than his mere physical existence. She demonstrates man's absolute moral freedom. The reader is urged to contrast

Johanna's sublimity with the responses of other characters in the play, all of whom reflect Schiller's criticism of the unresponsiveness of the French people, at the time of the French Revolution, to what Schiller described as a great moment, a *punctum saliens*, in human history.

Thus, in writing *The Virgin of Orleans*, Schiller was intervening to further the global fight for political freedom, which had been sparked by the successful American Revolution of 1776, but which had been set back by the Jacobin Terror of 1789. At a moment such as today, when there is a potential once again for a revolutionary struggle based on the principles of 1776, Schiller's play has special importance.

Schiller Transcends History

Johanna is the living image of the fighting qualities required today. As such, the play and her character transcend actual history.

In writing the play, Schiller departed from the actual history of Johanna d'Arc in several crucial ways. History records that Johanna, who was born in 1412, had a vision of St. Michael, at age thirteen, and then again at age fifteen. In 1429, at age seventeen, she defeats the English at Orleans and leads the Dauphin to Rheims, where he is crowned Charles VII. After the Dauphin's coronation, she is taken prisoner during the defense of Compiegne, sold by her captor to the Duke of Burgundy, and by the Duke to the English. After a year's imprisonment, she is tried and convicted by an ecclesiastical court, of sorcery and heresy. She is sentenced to life imprisonment; however, under pressure from the English, she is burned at the stake. At no time does the King make the smallest attempt to effect her release.

Rather than focus on her imprisonment, trial, and burning at the stake, Schiller deliberately chooses to alter history, so as to represent poetically the central theme of the play—the triumph of divine love. Thus, instead of being visited by St. Michael, she receives her inspiration in the play from the Virgin Mary. In the actual history, Johanna appeals to Charles in writing, after his coronation in Rheims, to be allowed to return home, believing her mission complete. When Charles refuses, she continues to fight for France, but no longer with the same invincibility. In the play, on the other hand, Schiller's Johanna loses her divine power before the coronation in Rheims, after she violates her vow to renounce earthly love.

By ending the play with her miraculous escape from prison and victorious effort on the battlefield, to defeat the English and consolidate the coronation of Charles by saving his life, Schiller emphasizes the *potentiality* of the divine love, which Johanna musters, to *transform* history, as we know it. In that sense, the alterations Schiller makes in the actual history merely serve to underscore the principle of human freedom. If one acts on the basis of divine love, one can accomplish miracles and do the impossible. By transforming actual history, a history well known to the general public, Schiller establishes the poetic truth, that man in a sublime state is not bound by so-called reality, and through his labor can effect changes in universal history.

This point is worth underscoring. As Schiller emphasizes in *On the Pathetic*, "it is the poetic, not the historical truth, upon which all aesthetical effect is grounded. The poetic truth does not exist therein, that something has actually occurred, but rather therein, that it could occur, therefore in the inner possibility of the matter."

It is this "inner possibility" of sublime action, of which we are all capable and which is required of us all, which Schiller captures in his portrayal of Johanna. In departing from actual history in the play, Schiller thus poetically portrays the living image of God, which can be found and developed in each and every one of us. This is the genius of *The Virgin of Orleans* and its importance to the cause of human freedom today.

Moral Beauty

This third volume of translations of works by Friedrich Schiller also contains several aesthetical writings, the *Philosophical Letters*, the Introduction to *The Revolt of the Netherlands*, the lyrical drama *Homage to the Arts* and selected poetry. In this Introduction, I shall concentrate particularly on the importance of two aesthetical pieces, *On the Pathetic* and *On the Sublime*.

After writing *Don Carlos* in 1787, Schiller refrained from writing another drama until he wrote the *Wallenstein* trilogy in 1796. During this period, his poetic output was also considerably reduced, as he undertook a thorough study of aesthetics, in order to base his later productions on his own thought-out theory of beauty.

As indicated in the introduction to Volume II, Schiller's theory of aesthetics was based upon a refutation of Immanuel Kant's *Critique of Judgment.* Kant, whose theories gave rise to German romanticism, rejected the idea that beauty could be objectively determined. Insisting that beauty is merely a matter of subjective taste, he denied the intelligibility and therefore the reproducibility of creativity, i.e., he denied that there is a science of the human mind and a science of the mind's ability to produce works of art.

In contrast, Schiller, unique among great artists, elaborated at length in his writings on aesthetics, both on the state of mind necessary to produce great art and upon what constitutes true art and what its role is.

With the translations in this volume, combined with those in Volumes I and II, all of the critical aesthetical writings of Schiller are now available in new translations to the English-speaking reader. It is therefore possible, through a thorough study of these writings, for the reader to replicate in his own mind the process which Schiller himself underwent during the years 1788–95, in not only refuting Kant and romanticism, but in developing the theoretical underpinnings of classical art.

The starting point for Schiller's theory of aesthetics is the state of mind necessary to produce beauty. In numerous locations, Schiller makes it clear that the artist must have a beautiful soul in order to produce beautiful art, and that such a soul is characterized by freedom from compulsion. Moreover, Schiller further identifies such freedom as proceeding from love.

In reading Schiller, one is reminded of St. Augustine's dictum, that "the law of freedom is the law of love." Is such a Christian interpretation of Schiller's theory of aesthetics appropriate? The reader is referred to two of Schiller's works to answer this question for himself.

First, consider the *Philosophical Letters* and Schiller's treatment of love in this work, which is translated in this volume. In her ground-breaking essay, "Poetry and Agapē," published in Volume II, Helga Zepp-LaRouche quotes extensively from the *Philosophical Letters* to support her thesis that Schiller is the poet of *agapē*. As Schiller writes in the section on "God," "love is the ladder, whereby we climb aloft to divine likeness." In a direct reference to Christ's injunction to man in the Sermon on the Mount, Schiller continues:

> Be perfect, as your Father in heaven is perfect, says the founder of our belief. Weak humanity grew pale at this command, therefore He explained Himself more clearly: Love one another.

Secondly, the reader is referred to Schiller's discussion of Christ's parable of the Good Samaritan, in *Kallias, or, On the Beautiful*, published in Volume II. Schiller employs this parable as the empirical proof for the truth of his theory of beauty. He describes five variations of the help offered to an injured person lying on the side of the road. Only in the case of the very last passerby, a truly good Samaritan, is the moral deed of aiding the injured man at the same time beautiful. Only in the last case does the passerby act not out of external compulsion, but rather out of inner freedom. Charity is his inner nature. He helps "without being called upon and without debate with himself." His moral action is beautiful, because "it appears as an effect of nature arising from itself. . . . Duty has become nature to him."

Thus, Schiller describes his own conception of "moral beauty" in opposition to the Kantian conception of morality, which is externally imposed. In so doing, he affirms and elaborates upon the Christian conception of *agapē* or charity, which Kant, who was a gnostic, rejects in favor of his categorical imperative or moral law.

For Schiller, moral beauty is charity that is expressed with freedom, because the inner nature of man, his will, has been transformed, such that in the image of God, he himself is charity. It is in this sense that Schiller's theory of beauty reflects the above-cited Augustinian comment, that "the law of freedom is the law of love."

This distinction between "moral beauty," which is a "free action," and Kantian morality, which is compelled and therefore not beautiful, should be borne in mind when considering Schiller's aesthetic writings, which are translated in this volume, *On the Pathetic* and *On the Sublime*.

In these two works, which should be viewed together, Schiller stresses that the species characteristic of man is freedom of the will. However, by no means is man free, if there is even one exception to this characteristic; specifically, if he is unable to overcome death. His freedom is absolutely nothing, if he is bound by death.

However, as Schiller emphasizes, man is capable of overcoming the violence which death would otherwise do to his freedom, either through the moral concept of resignation to necessity or the religious concept of submission to divine counsel. Man annihilates the capacity of death to do violence to his freedom, by freely subjecting himself to a higher purpose, a purpose which is immortal. This, of course, is precisely what Johanna d'Arc does in *The Virgin of Orleans*. She "freely" submits her will to divine counsel and, though mortally wounded, she gains eternal life.

As Schiller writes in *On the Pathetic*, the ultimate end of art is to represent the supersensuous, which he otherwise refers to as man's "moral freedom" or the "free principle" in man. As he says, art must delight the mind and be pleasing to freedom. Therefore, art is neither the mere representation of sensuous nature, nor is it the representation of moral law. Both the sensuous in itself, and morality as defined by Kant, oppress the principle of freedom in man.

For this reason, an artist should not represent pathos or suffering, except insofar as the overcoming of the pathetic indirectly represents the existence of the supersensuous. In other words, to be aesthetic, the pathetic must be sublime. Everything that is sublime springs from reason or intelligence and is noble.

As Schiller writes, he who follows his sensuous instinct is common; he who follows his instinct in regard to the law is decent; and he who follows reason alone acts nobly. Such noble actions, as in the case of Johanna d'Arc, stem from a pure mind, that is internally free. This state of mind, this supersensuous capacity, Schiller otherwise describes as *agapic* love.

This supersensuous reality, which defines man, can not be directly represented sensuously, because its conditions do not derive from the world of the senses. It is above nature and cannot be derived from natural causes, even though it is accomplished through natural forces. Therefore, it can only be represented negatively or indirectly.

In *On the Pathetic*, Schiller employs the example of Laocoön to demonstrate how suffering is represented sensuously in such a way as to indirectly represent the supersenuous in man. Attacked by two monstrous serpents, Laocoön, instead of seeking to escape, remains, in an effort to save his two defenseless sons from the snakes' fangs, and in the process is himself destroyed.

As Schiller points out, Laocoön neither follows the law of nature, self-preservation, nor does he act merely out of regard for moral law. Rather, he acts freely, out of love for his children. Our sympathy for him is stronger, because it is sympathy that we feel for the sympathy he has for his children. He acts out of love, even if it means his own destruction. He gives himself up to destruction of his own free will and his death becomes an act of will. He thus overcomes death and establishes indirectly the "moral freedom" in man, which characterizes man as a species. Moreover, as in the case of Johanna d'Arc, this principle of freedom is identical with the expression of charity. Only to the extent that man is willing to act out of love for humanity, even if it may mean his own destruction, does he affirm a higher purpose to life than mortal existence. Only to the extent that man acts thus nobly, even in the face of death, is he truly free.

According to Schiller in *On the Sublime*, the sublime is distinct from beauty, in that it is the state of mind which elevates us above the power of nature. The feeling of beauty derives from the harmonization of the sensuous instinct with the law of reason, whereas in the sublime, reason and sensuousness do not harmonize. Thus, the feeling of the sublime is a mixed feeling of pain and joy. This union of two contradictory sentiments ("Brief is the pain, the joy shall be eterne") in a single feeling, proves our moral independence, in that the state of our mind does not necessarily conform to the state of the senses, and that we have in us a principle independent of all sensuous emotions.

Since beauty is only the experience of the harmony of sensuousness with reason, we would never learn from it alone, of our moral freedom as beings of reason. Only in the face of sensuous adversity, most emphatically death, does man exhibit a moral freedom from the merely sensuous. If man still feels joy, while experiencing sensuous pain, as does Johanna at the end of the play, he thus demonstrates an absolute moral capacity.

As Schiller stresses, the role of the pathetic in art is to foster absolute independence in one's soul through identification with the sublime state of mind of the character, who overcomes suffering, who is joyful even in the face of pain. The more frequently we renew our minds through contemplation of the sublime in art, the more able do we become to resolve actual suffering into a sublime emotion when it occurs. The sublime overcoming of the pathetic in art is thus a kind of inoculation against "unavoidable fate." As Schiller writes, "The pathetic is an artifical misfortune and, like the true misfortune, it places us in *direct contact* with the spiritual law, that rules in our bosom."

In *On the Pathetic*, Schiller further elaborates his notion of the proper role of poetry:

> Poetry can become to man, what love is to the hero. It can neither advise him, nor strike for him nor otherwise do work for him; but it can educate him as a hero, it can summon him to deeds and to all that he should be, equip him with strength.

What attracted Beethoven to Schiller's Johanna, what attracts all who read *The Virgin of Orleans* with an open heart to her example, and what Schiller set out to accomplish in writing this play, should now be clear. Johanna d'Arc, as Schiller conceived her and represented her poetically, embodies the inner possibility of freedom and nobility in man. By reading the play or seeing it performed, we are educated by the character of Johanna to be heroes, we are equipped with the strength required to accomplish the miraculous and the impossible, we are prepared by the misfortune and its heroic resolution represented artificially on the stage to resolve actual suffering in our own lives in a sublime manner.

If in respect to Laocoön our capacity for sympathy is enhanced because we feel sympathy for the sympathy he has for his children, so is our commitment to devote our lives to a divine mission strengthened by the love we feel for Johanna's love of humanity. She improves us, by elevating our intellectual capacity above the self-centered common concerns of the prevailing *Zeitgeist* [spirit of the times]. Her very frailty gives us faith that we, too, with our own limitations, are capable of liberating ourselves absolutely from the violence of sensuous adversity, by submitting our wills to the will of divine providence, not blindly, but with intellectual force.

When Schiller wrote, after the American Revolution, he believed the world to be on the verge of an Age of Reason. With the failure of the French Revolution, the possibility of such an epoch was deferred to the distant future. Schiller assigned to art the role of aesthetically educating man to be capable of the moral beauty necessary to achieve that epoch.

Today, mankind is once again filled with the Spirit of 1776. The image of Johanna carrying her banner into battle on behalf of the fatherland reminds us of the qualities required of us all, if today's potential for an Age of Reason is not to be lost, as it was during Schiller's time.

The critical question each and every one of us must be able to answer affirmatively, when unavoidable mortality finally comes, is whether we shall be able, like Johanna, to display our banner before God's throne, having borne it truly during our brief lives. If the answer is yes, then we too can sing with Beethoven and Schiller, "Brief is the pain, the joy shall be eterne."

Petersburg, Virginia
August 19, 1989

FRIEDRICH SCHILLER
Poet of Freedom

POETRY

POETRY

From the Early Years (1776–1781)
　Amalia

From the Anthology of 1782
　Friendship
　Group from Tartarus

Classical Poetry (1788–1805)
　Genius
　The Antique to the Northern Wanderer
　The Singers of Antiquity
　The Diver
　The Antiques at Paris
　The Glove
　The Ring of Polycrates
　The German Muse
　Longing
　Cassandra

From the Early Years (1776–1781)

AMALIA

Fair as angels with Walhalla's passion,
Fair before all mortal youths was he,
Heav'nly mild like May's sun did his vision,
Beam as from the bluish mirror-sea.

And his kisses—paradise-like feeling!
Like two flames entwining lovingly,
Like the harptone's inter-winding playing
To the Heaven-laden Harmony—

Hurlèd, tumbled, melted soul and soul together,
Lips and cheeks did burn and shiver fair,
Spirit flowed in Spirit—swam the Earth and Heaven
As if faded 'round the loving pair!

He is gone—so vainly, O so vainly
Moans to him the anxious, mournful cry!
He is gone, and all delight so lively
Whimpers off in one forsaken sigh.

Lance Rosen

From the Anthology of 1782

FRIENDSHIP
From the Letters of Julius to Raphael

Friend! how frugal is all being's guide—
On small-minded thinkers shame abide,
Who so anxiously the laws would know—
Throng o'th' bodily world and realm o'th' soul
On *one* flywheel, toward their purpose roll,
Here my Newton saw it go.

Spheres it teaches, slaves of but *one* rein,
Round the heart o'th' mighty world domain
Labyrinthine paths to rise—
Spirits in embracing systems run
Toward the *mighty spiritual sun,*
As the brook to th' ocean flies.

Was't not this omnipotent desire,
That in love's eternal happy fire
Did *our* hearts unto each other force?
Raphael, upon *thine* arm—delight!
Venture I to th' spiritual sun so bright
Joyful on perfection's course.

Happy! happy! *Thee* have I thus found,
Have from out of millions *thee* wound round,
And from out of millions, *thou* art *mine*—
Let the savage chaos come once more,
Let the atoms in confusion pour,
For eternity our hearts entwine.

Must I not from out *thy* flaming eyes
Draw th' reflection of *my* paradise?
But in *thee* I wonder at myself—
Fairer does th' fair earth to me appear,
In the friend's demeanor shines more clear,
Lovelier the Heaven itself.

Melancholy drops the tearful weight,
Sweetly th' storm of passion to abate,
In the breast of charity;—
Seeks not e'en the tortuous delight,
Raphael, within thy spirit's sight,
A voluptuous grave impatiently?—

Stood i'th' all o' Creation I alone,
Do I dream of souls i'th' rocky stone
And embracing them I kiss—
My complaints I moan into the sky,
I enjoy'd, the chasm did reply,
Fool enough! sweet sympathetic bliss.

Lifeless groups are we, whene'er we hate,
Gods, when lovingly we do relate!
Yearning for the gentle shackle's force—
Upwards through the thousandfold gradation
Of the countless spirits in creation,
Does this urge divinely course.

Arm in arm, e'er freer still and freer,
From barbarism to Grecian seer,
Who unto the last Seraph is near,
Of one mind in coiling dance we flow,
Till there in the sea of everlasting glow
Time and measure dying disappear.—

Friendless was the Lord o'th' world so great,
Lack he felt, thus spirits did create,
Mirrors blest of *his* felicity!—
Though the highest Being no equal found,
From the cup of all of being's round
To *him* foams—Infinity.

William F. Wertz, Jr.

GROUP FROM TARTARUS

Hark—as murmurs of the seas rebelling,
As through shallow rocky basins whines a stream,
Moans a stifled, heavy, empty-knelling,
Anguish-driven scream!

    Pain distorteth
How they look, and woe reporteth
    From their throats in curse-filled wrath.
Hollow are their eyes then, and their glances
Seek for Coc'tus Bridge in fearful trances,
    Tears then follow on their mournful path.

And they ask each other mutely, fearful:
    If or not this be the end?—
'ternity swings high above their circle,
    Saturn's reaper it in two doth rend.

Lance Rosen

Classical Poetry (1788–1805)

GENIUS

"Trow I,"say'st thou, "the word, which wisdom's master doth teach me,
    Which the neophyte host surely and read'ly affirms?
Unto genuine peace can only knowledge transport me,
    Is then the system upheld only by fortune and law?
Must I the urge mistrust, which softly doth warn of the precept,
    Which thou, Nature, thyself, into my bosom impressed,
Till on the e'erlasting scroll the school her ensign imprinted
    And the formula's rule shackles the fugitive soul?
Tell me then this, thou hast into these depths descended,
    Out of the moldering grave cam'st thou, returning unscathed,
'Tis to thee known, what the vault of darksome sayings is guarding,
    If with mummies doth dwell life's consolation thereby.
Must I then wander the nocturnal path? I shake, I confess it,
    Walk it *will* I despite, leads it to justice and truth."
Friend, thou know'st yet the era of gold—as have all the poets
    Many legends of it childlike and movingly told—
Such a time, when holiness still in living form wandered,
    When as virgin and chaste, feeling still guarded itself,
When still the glorious law, which over the sun's orbit governs
    And concealed i' th' egg moveth the jumping off point,

Still did necessity's quiet command, continuous, changeless,
   Too i' th' bosom of man freer the billows bestir,
When unerring the mind and true, as the hand of the clockwork,
   But to the truthful did point, to the eternal alone?
Then was no profaner, no initiate was seen there,
   What one did livelily feel, was not there sought 'mongst the dead;
Equally clear to every heart was the e'erlasting precept,
   Equally hidden the spring, whence it enlivening flowed.
But that fortunate age has gone hence! Presumptuous whimsy
   Has the peace so divine of faithful nature disturbed.
That emotion profaned is no more voice of the godly,
   And grows the oracle mute in the dishonorèd breast.
Save in the quieter self the harkening spirit's perceived still,
   And the mystical word safeguards the hallowèd mind.
Here the searcher evokes it, with heart unsullied descending,
   And by the Nature forlorn wisdom to him is restored.
Hast thou, happy one, ne'er the guardian angel foresaken,
   Ne'er of instinct revered forfeited warnings beloved,
If be the truth portrayed in pure eyes still true and unsullied,
   If it ringeth still bright in thy childlike breast,
If doubt's rebellion is silenced within thy soul so contented,
   Will it, knowst thou for sure, silent be e'er as today,
Then will the strife of the sentiments never require a judge,
   Ne'er the malevolent heart darken the intellect bright—

O, then, goest thou hence, in thine own innocence
    precious.
    Knowledge can teach to thee naught—let it then
        learn from thee!
That very law which with rod wrought of bronze directs
    the rebellious,
    Naught means to thee. What thou dost, what thou
        lik'st, is the law,
And to all generations is issued a godly commandment:
    What thou with hallowèd hand buildest, with
        hallowèd mouth
Utter'st, will move the astonished mind with almighty
    power;
    But thou perceivest not the God, who rules within
        thine own breast,
Nor the force of the ensign, which bends all spirits
    before thee,
    Simply go'st thou and still throughout the conquerèd
        world.

Dennis Speed

THE ANTIQUE TO THE NORTHERN WANDERER

Over torrents wert thou trav'ling and oceans wert
    swimming,
    Over the range of the Alps bore thee the dizzying
        bridge,
That thou be near me to see and be exalting my beauty,
    Which an inspirited fame spreads through the
        wondering world;
And now stand'st thou 'fore me, thou can'st me, Holy,
    be touching,
    But art thou to me now nearer, and am I to you?

Susan Bowen

THE SINGERS OF ANTIQUITY

Say, where are the excellent ones, where find I the singers,
  Who with their word so alive, hearkening people delight,
Who from Heaven of God, to Heaven of mankind were singing
  And transported the mind up on the wings of their song?
Ah, yet live still the singers, but lacking are actions, the lyre
  Joyful to waken, we lack, ah! a most resonant ear.
Fortunate poets o' th' fortunate world! from speaker to speaker
  Flew, from gen'ration to th' next your own e'er sensitive word.
As one receiveth the gods, so devoutly each one was greeted,
  Which did Genius in him, speaking and forming, create.
In the glow of the song aroused were the hearer's emotions,
  In the hearer's response nourished the singer the glow,
Fed and purified it! The fortunate, he in the people's
  Voices still clear to whom rang back the soul of the song,
To whom from outside appeared, in this life, the heavenly Godhead,
  Whom the modern one scarce, scarce yet perceives in his heart.

Ernest Schapiro and Marianna Wertz

THE DIVER

"Which knight or esquire, which one will dare
To dive down in this deep gulf?
A golden goblet I throw now down there,
Devour'd it already the swarthy mouth.
Who can the goblet to me be returning,
He may thus possess it, it is his earning."

The King thus speaks it, and hurls from the height
O'th' cliff so abrupt and steep,
Which hangs o'er the sea stretched endless in sight,
The goblet in Charybdis' howling deep.
"Who will be the brave one, again I wonder,
To dive far into these depths down under?"

And the knights and the vassals 'round him be,
They listen, but silent remain,
Looking below to the savage sea,
And none doth the goblet desire to gain.
And the King, for the third time his question bareth;
"To go down under then no one dareth?"

But all remain mute, knight and esquire,
And a noble squire, meek and rash,
Steps from the timorous vassals choir,
And his mantle throws he, tosses his sash,
And all of the men around him and women,
On the glorious youth their stunned gazes fasten.

And as he steps to the rocky slope
And looks in the gulf below,
The waters that she so deeply did gulp,
Does Charybdis now howling backwards throw,
And as with the distant thunder's uproaring,
They burst from her ominous womb outsoaring.

And it bubbles and boils and hisses and booms,
Like when water with fire doth blend,
To the heavens splutter the vaporous foams
And flood on flood doth press without end,
And wants to be drained and empty never,
As would yet the sea one more sea bear ever.

Yet fin'lly, the power so wild has left,
And black from the argent swell
Opens downward a dark yawning cleft,
Boundless, as though to the realms of Hell,
And raging sees one the surge of the billows,
Beneath in the twist of the rotating funnels.

Now swift, ere the breakers reappear,
The stripling to God doth pray,
And—is heard all around him a shriek of fear,
And already the whirlpool has washed him away
And clandestinely over the daring swimmer
Locketh the jaws, appeareth he never.

And stillness falls over the water's gulf,
In the deep doth a hollow roar swell,
And trembling hears one from mouth to mouth:
"Magnanimous stripling, fare thee well!"
And one hears it howling duller and duller,
And they wait still with worry, with moments of horror.

And should'st thou thy crown itself down there fling
And say: "Who e'er brings me the crown,
He shall then wear it, and be the King"—
For this precious reward I no longing do own.
What the howling there deep down under concealeth,
To no fortunate soul of the living revealeth.

Well many a craft, by whirlpool held fast,
Shoots quick to the depths of the wave,
Yet while shattered to pieces, the keel and mast
Emerge from the e'er inextricable grave.—
And like tempest's howling, clearer and clearer,
One hears its raging, e'er nearer and nearer.

And it bubbles and boils and hisses and booms,
Like when water with fire doth blend,
To the heavens splutter the vaporous foams,
And wave on wave doth press without end,
And as with the distant thunder's uproaring,
It bursts from her ominous womb outpouring.

And lo! from the ominous womb atide,
Something rises white as a swan,
And an arm and a glistening neck are espied,
And it paddles with strength and with diligence on,
And 'tis he, and in his left hand swinging,
Waves he the goblet, so joyfully bringing.

And breathed he long and breathed he well
And he greeted the heavenly light.
With joyfulness each to the other did call:
"He lives! He is there! It stopped not his flight!
From the grave, from the eddying water's shiv'ring,
Hath this brave one rescued his own soul living."

And he comes, now encircles the crowd joyous so,
To the feet of the King he falls,
The goblet he offers him kneeling low,
And the King to his daughter enchanting calls,
Who fills it with wine to the border glist'ning,
And the youth doth then turn to the King who's list'ning:

"Long life to the King! Rejoice in full,
Who do breathe in the rose-colored light!
For down below it's horrible;
And let man not tempt the divinities' might,
And desire never and ne'er to uncover
What they kindly by night and by fear do cover.

"It ripped me down under with speed of light—
Then thrust me in crag-covered shaft,
Wild flooding a spring rushed with all of its might:
It seized me in double stream's furious wrath,
And like as a gyro gets dizzily twisted
Drove me 'round, I could no longer resist it.

"Then God showed to me, to Him I did cry
In that terrible need so great,
In the deepness a rocky reef did lie,
Which I grasped at quickly and from death escaped—
And there hung too the goblet on coral appalling,
Else would it in bottomless waters be falling.

"For 'neath me still lay it, mountain deep,
In darkness of deep purple hue,
And though to the ear 'tis like lasting sleep,
The eye did with shudd'ring to the depths view,
How the salamanders and dragons and monsters
Do stir in the jaws of a Hell of terrors.

"A horrible mixture did swarm there in black,
All balled up in hideous clumps,
The rock fish, the ray fish with thorny back,
The hammer's dreadfully shapeless lumps,
And threatening me with teeth all in motion
The terrible shark, the hyena o'th' ocean.

"And there hung I and was with great horror possessed,
From the succor of man far apace,
Among specters, the singular sensitive breast,
Alone in this hideous, lonely place,
Deep under the ring of man's conversation,
'Mid the monsters' melancholy desolation.

"And shudd'ring I thought, it's crawling near,
Moved a hundred limbs at once alive,
While snapping at me—in nightmarish fear,
I let loose from the coral I'd clutched to survive;
Was seized by the whirlpool with furious raving,
And it threw me back up, it was thus my saving."

The King is now taken by wonderment,
And speaks: "The goblet's thine own,
And to grant thee this ring's my intent,
Adorned with this exquisite most precious stone,
Attempt thou yet once more and bring me tidings,
What thou saw'st of the sea in the depths of thy divings."

The daughter did hear this, with softness of heart,
And with flattering words made her plea:
"Leave, Father, enough with thine hideous sport!
He hath just surmounted what none dared for thee
And canst thou thy heart's appetites not be taming,
Then maybe the knights can the esquire be shaming."

Then the King doth grasp for the goblet in haste,
In the whirlpool he flings it aright:
"And bring'st thou the goblet and here be it placed,
Thou shalt be to me the most excellent knight.
And shalt her today as thy loving wife marry,
Who now doth thee mercy in tender pray'r carry."

Then a heavenly force overcomes his soul there,
And a boldness shines forth from his eye,
And he sees as a blush paints her features so fair,
And sees her then whiten, and sinking lie,—
It drives him to capture the prize he doth cherish,
And he dives down under to live or to perish.

Well hear all the breakers, well do they return,
They're proclaimed in a thundering call—
They bow themselves under with gazes that yearn;
They're coming, they're coming the waters all
They rush on upwards, they rush on ever,
The stripling they bring back never.

Sheila Anne Jones

THE ANTIQUES AT PARIS

What the Grecian Art created,
Wants the Frank with weapons laden
To transport to Seine's yon strand.
And within museums glor'ous
He displays his spoils victor'ous
To th'astonished Fatherland!

They'll be silent to him ever,
Climbing from their pillars never
To where life's fresh circle's known.
He'll alone possess the Muses,
Who in warm breast them infuses,
To the Vandals they are stone.

Susan Bowen

THE GLOVE

Before his lion court waiting,
The games anticipating,
King Francis sat,
And round him the kingdom's great powers,
And round on balcony towers
The ladies in fair éclat.

And as with finger he beckons,
A cage in the distance opens,
And inside with deliberate strides
A lion glides,
And without sound
Looks 'round,
With long yawns making
And his mane is shaking,
And his limbs he's plying,
And down is lying.

And the King further beck'ning,
There opens with ease
A second door,
From which flees
So wildly sprung out
A tiger to th' fore,
When he the lion espies,
Loud he cries,
Strikes with his tail
A frightening flail,
And sticks his tongue out,
And in circles shy
Round th' lion goes by
Fiercely purring,
He stretches out murm'ring
By his side lying.

At the King's further beck'ning,
Then speweth the twice-open'd house thereabout
Two savage leopards at once thereout,

They plunge forth with stout-hearted battle-lust
On the tiger beast,
He grasps them with his claws so ferocious,
And the lion with roar
Standeth upright, sounds no more,
And round in a knot,
From bloodlust hot,
Lay down the cats so atrocious.

Then falls from the terrace above,
From a beautiful hand a glove,
In between tiger and lion it lay
Just at midway.

And to Knight Delorges, mockingly
Turneth now Lady Cunigund daring,
"Sir Knight, if your love is so hot for me,
As you each hour to me are swearing,
Why, then get me my glove now back."

And the knight in celerious tack
Climbeth down in the cage truly scaring,
With steady pacing,
And from the monstrous middle racing,
Grabs he the glove now with finger daring.

And with amazement and with horror
Knights and ladies all watch him with terror,
And the glove he returns without fear.
Then from every mouth his praises shower,
But to me the loving glance most dear—
Which promises him his bliss is near—
Receives he from Cunigund's tower.
And he throws in her face the glove he's got:
"Your thanks, Lady, I want that not,"
And he leaves her that very hour.

Marianna Wertz

THE RING OF POLYCRATES

He stood upon his castle's turret,
He gazed out with delighted spirit
O'er mastered Samos down below.
"The whole of this to me is subject,"
Began he to the King of Egypt,
"That I am fortunate, avow."

"Thou hast enjoyed the godly favor!
Those formerly thine equals ever,
Bend now beneath thy scepter's might.
Yet one still lives, their vengeance seeking,
Thy bliss my lips cannot be speaking
So long the foeman's eye has sight."

And ere the King had barely ended,
A herald, from Miletus wended,
Before the tyrant made his bow.
"Let, Lord, arise the sweet oblation
And with the laurel's gay vernation
Encircle now thy splendid brow.

"By spear thy foe was stricken under,
I'm with the happy news sent hither
By thy true Gen'ral Polydor—"
And taking from a black container,
Still bloody, to the both men's terror,
A well-known head he brings to th' fore.

The King steps back with trepidation:
"Trust not in fortune, thee I caution,"
Replies with anxious look to him.
"Reflect, upon the faithless welling,
How simply can the storm be quelling,
Thy fleet's uncertain fortunes swim."

And ere he has these words yet spoken,
His speech by jubilation's broken,
Which from the port rejoicing blasts.
Beladen with their foreign riches,
Return now to their native beaches
The teeming wood of vessels' masts.

The royal guest was much bewildered:
"Today thy fortune is good humored,
Yet fear thou its inconstancy.
The Grecian troops expert in weapon
With battle's peril would thee threaten,
Already near this shore they be."

And ere did he these words but utter,
One hears from out the ships now flutter,
A thousand voices: "Vic'try!" roar.
"From foe's affliction we're unfettered,
The Cretans by the storm are scattered,
'Tis over, ended is the war!"

With terror doth the guest-friend beckon:
"Indeed, thee fortunate I reckon,
Yet," said he, "for thy good I shake.
Before gods' envy I am frightful,
The joy of life so pure and rightful
Were not for mortals to partake.

"For me all things have also prospered,
In every kingly thing endeavored
The grace of heaven by me stayed;
Though once I had an heir to cherish,
God took from me, I saw him perish,
To fortune has my debt been paid.

"Thus, wouldst thou from all grief be shielded,
To the Unseen thy plea be wielded,
That they thy fortune lend some woe.

For saw I none yet ending happ'ly,
On whom with hands e'er laden fully
The gods their blessings do bestow.

"If this the gods have not conceded,
A friend's advice then must be heeded
And call upon thyself this woe,
And from what out of all thy treasure
Thy heart derives the highest pleasure,
Take that and in this ocean throw."

By fear persuaded speaks the other:
"Of all, that doth this island harbor,
My highest blessing is this ring.
To th' Furies be it dedicated,
That my luck be exonerated."
And in the flood the gem did fling.

And in the next day's morning gleaming,
There strides forth with a visage beaming
A fisherman before the King:
"My Lord, this fish I have just captured,
As no more in my net have ventured,
It as a gift to thee I bring."

And as the cook the fish was slashing,
Confounded comes he hither dashing
And with astonished look cries out:
"Look, Lord, the ring, which thou hast carried,
I found it in the fish maw buried,
O, limits hath thy fortune not!"

At this the guest turned 'round with horror:
"Thus here can I reside no longer,
My friend canst thou no longer be.
The gods thy ruination cherish,
Forth haste I, not with thee to perish."
And spoke't and swiftly sailed to sea.

Melanie Morris

THE GERMAN MUSE

No Augustan era flow'ring,
None of Medici's kind show'ring
Smiled on the German Art.
Fostered not in Glory's power,
She unfolded not her flower
In the rays good kings impart.

By the greatest German children,
By King Friedrich's great dominion,
Went she shieldless, honored not.
Praise unto the German's owing,
May his heart be overflowing:
From *himself* her worth he wrought.

Therefore climbs in arches higher,
Therefore flows in billows fuller
German poets' hymnal source;
And in its abundant swelling
And from out the heart's deep welling,
Mocketh it the ruling force.

Lance Rosen

LONGING

Ah! from out this valley's floorage,
By the chilling mists oppressed,
Could I only find the passage,
Ah! I'd feel myself as blessed!
Yonder glimpse I hilled dominions,
Ever young and green for aye!
Had I wings with supple pinions,
Thither to the hills I'd fly.

Dulcet concords hear I ringing,
Strains of sweet celestial calm,
And the tranquil breeze is bringing
Of its fragrance, to me balm.
Golden fruits do I see glowing,
Bobbing 'midst the foliage dark,
And the flowers yonder growing
Will not be the winter's mark.

Oh, how lovely, sure, to wander
There in ever summertide,
And the air in highlands yonder,
Ah! how cordial must it bide!
Yet the current's rage doth daunt me,
Which betwixt doth grimly roar,
And the torrent's waves are risen,
That my soul is harrowed o'er.

I descry a shallop drifting,
Ha, but look! no helmsman's nigh.
Dive in swiftly! No more shifting!
Sylphidine her sails now hie.
Go with faith and go with daring,
Gods accord no note of hand.
But a wonder can thee carry
To the lovely wonderland.

Steve Riegelhaupt

CASSANDRA

Joy in Trojan halls abounded,
Ere the high feast fell away,
Jubilation's hymns resounded
In the music's golden play.
All the wearied hands now rested
From the sad and tearful feud,
Meanwhile Peleus, so splendid
Priam's pretty daughter wooed.

And with laurel wreaths attiring,
Festive troop on troop did pour
In the gods' high home retiring,
To the Thymbrian altar there.
Through the streets in muffled madness
Danced the baccanalian lust,
And forsaken in her sadness
Was but *one* unhappy breast.

Joyless in the joyful fulness,
Solitary did she rove,
There Cassandra walked in stillness
In Apollo's laurel grove.
In the forest's deepest winding
Refuge took the seer there,
And she cast the priestly binding
To the earth in angry flare:

"All are here so freely joyful,
Ev'ry heart is truly blessed,
And the elder parents hopeful,
And the sister's smartly dressed.
I alone must mourn so lonely,
For the sweet dream flies from me,
And, bewinged, to these walls only
Ruin drawing nigh I see.

"One lone torch I see aglowing,
But 'tis not in Hymen's hand,
To the clouds I see it growing,
But 'tis not an altar brand.
Feasts I see them cheerful spreading,
Yet, in my foreboding heart
I now hear the godly treading,
Which with woe rips them apart.

"And they chide my lamentation,
And my grief can but disdain,
Lonely in this desolation
Must I bear my heart in pain,
Shunned by those in fortune sharing
And to cheerfulness a blot!
I'm thy heavy burden bearing,
Pythias, thou angry god!

"Wherefore hast thou cast me down here,
In this land forever blind,
Of thine oracle a seer,
With a wholly opened mind?
Wherefore gave'st thou me as vision,
What to alter I can ne'er?
The ordained bears no revision,
The most feared approaches e'er.

"Profits it in face of terror,
To unveil the human brow?
Life itself is naught but error,
And it is but death to know.
Take, O take this lucid sadness,
Let me bloody shine not see!
Frightful is it, as the witness
Mortal of thy truth to be.

"Give to me again my blindness
And the happy mind that's numb!
Never sang I songs of kindness,
Since *thy* voice I have become.
Future thou hast given to me,
Yet thou took'st the present day,
Took'st the hours that make life merry—
Take thy false gift now away.

"Ne'er with bridal decoration
Have I decked my fragrant brow,
Since thy duty's consecration
Bound me to a mournful vow.
All my youth was only crying,
And I knew alone but pain,
Ev'ry bitter need descrying
Struck my heart with passioned strain.

"Joyful saw I loved ones playing,
Each one lives and loves in full
In youth's pleasureful arraying,
Only my heart pounded dull.
Spring to me appears but vainly,
When the earth's adorned in bliss:
Who can joy in life when plainly
Staring in its dark abyss!

"Polyxena, blest I find thee
In delusion's drunken heart,
For the best of Greece would bind thee
As his bride and never part.
Proudly is her breast uplifted,
Scarce contains its joyful lot,
E'en you, heav'nly powers gifted,
In her dream she envies not.

"And he too I did envision,
Whom my longing heart desired,
His fair glances do petition,
By a loving glow inspired.
Gladly would I him be wedding
And in homely dwelling be,
But a Stygian shade is treading
Ev'ry night twixt him and me.

"All her pallid spectres yonder
Doth Persephone send here,
Where I flutter, where I wander,
Do the ghosts before me rear.
In the joy of youthful pleasure
Press they horribly on me,
An atrocious throng their measure—
Never can I joyful be.

"And I see the death-steel gaping
And the eye of Murder glow,
Neither right nor left escaping,
Can I from this terror go;
Knowing, shudd'ring, never moving,
From its glance I may not hie
Must my destiny be proving,
In a foreign land to die."

And still as her words are ringing—
Hark! a muddled sound does spread
From the temple's gate it's springing:
Thetis' mighty son lay dead!
Eris is her serpents tumbling,
All the gods from there have flown,
And the thunderclouds are rumbling
Heavily o'er Ilion.

Sheila Anne Jones

DRAMA

THE VIRGIN OF ORLEANS

A ROMANTIC TRAGEDY

TRANSLATED BY WILLIAM F. WERTZ, JR.

DRAMATIS PERSONÆ

CHARLES THE SEVENTH, King of France
QUEEN ISABEAU, *his mother*
AGNES SOREL, *his beloved*
PHILIP THE GOOD, *Duke of Burgundy*
COUNT DUNOIS, *Bastard of Orleans*

Royal officers
LA HIRE
DU CHATEL
ARCHBISHOP OF RHEIMS
CHATILLON, *a Burgundian Knight*
RAOUL, *a Lorrainean Knight*
TALBOT, *Field Marshal of the Englanders*

Schiller began work on *The Virgin of Orleans*, the dramatic account of the life of Joan of Arc, on July 1, 1800, just one month after completing his drama *Maria Stuart*. The play was first performed in September 1801 in Leipzig, in honor of the Weimar Court. It appeared in print for the first time in October 1801, in the *Calendar of the Year 1802*, published by Schiller's friend Unger in Berlin.

English leaders
LIONEL
FASTOLF
MONTGOMERY,
  a Welshman
COUNCILMEN OF ORLEANS
AN ENGLISH HERALD

THIBAUT D'ARC, *a rich countryman*

  His daughters
MARGOT
LOUISON
JOHANNA

  Their suitors
ETIENNE
CLAUDE MARIE
RAIMOND

BERTRAND, *another countryman*
THE APPARITION OF A BLACK KNIGHT
CHARCOAL-BURNER *and* CHARCOAL-BURNER'S WIFE

SOLDIERS AND PEOPLE. *Royal Crown-servants, Bishops, Monks, Marshals, Magistrates, Courtiers and other non-speaking persons in the retinue of the Coronation Procession.*

PROLOGUE

A country region.

Front to the right a holy image in a chapel; to the left a tall oak tree.

SCENE I

THIBAUT D'ARC, *his three daughters.*
Three young shepherds, their suitors.

THIBAUT: Yes, beloved neighbors! To this day are we
Still Frenchmen, still free citizens and masters
O' th' ancient soil, the which our fathers plowed;
Who knows, who over us commands tomorrow!
For everywhere the Englishman doth let
His victory-laden banner fly, his steeds
Are trampling on the blooming fields of France.
Paris hath him as victor now received,
And with the ancient crown of Dagobert
Adorns the offspring of a foreign stem.
The grandchild of our King must wander round
In flight and dispossessed through his own realm,
And 'gainst him fights i' th' army of the foe
His closest cousin and his foremost peer,
Yes, his own raven-mother it commands.
Around burn hamlets, cities. Nearer still
And nearer rolls the smoke of devastation
Into these valleys, which still rest in peace.
—Thus, beloved neighbors, I've resolved by God,
Because today it's still within my power,
To have the daughters cared for; for the woman
I' th' throes of warfare needeth a protector,
And true love helps to lessen every burden.
(to the first shepherd)
—Come, Etienne! My Margot do you court.
The acres come together neighborly,
The hearts are in agreement—that endows

A happy marriage! *(to the second)*
                    Claude Marie! You're silent,
And my Louison casts her eyes to th' ground?
Shall I divide two hearts, that found themselves,
Since you no treasures have to offer me?
Who now *hath* treasures? House and barns are both
The spoils of nearest enemy or fire—
The faithful breast o' th' upright man alone
Is a firm shelter in these stormy times.
LOUISON: My father!
CLAUDE MARIE: My Louison!
LOUISON *(embracing* JOHANNA*):*   Beloved Sister!
THIBAUT: I give to each one thirty acres land
And stall and farmhouse and a herd—For God
Hath blessed me, and so doth he bless you too!
MARGOT *(embracing* JOHANNA*):*
Delight our father. Follow our example!
Let us this day conclude three happy bonds.
THIBAUT: Go! Make the plans. Tomorrow is the wedding;
I want all in the town to join the feast.

(The two couples exit wound arm in arm.)

SCENE II

THIBAUT. RAIMOND. JOHANNA.

THIBAUT: Jeanette, thy sisters now are getting married,
I see them happy, they delight mine age;
But thou, my youngest, giv'st me grief and pain.
RAIMOND: What are you up to? Why do you scold your daughter?
THIBAUT: Here this brave youth, with whom no other can
Compare in all the town, th' excellent one,
He hath to thee his inclination turned
And sues for thee, already the third autumn,

With quiet wish, with heartfelt energy;
But thou dost him reject, reserved and cold,
And yet not any other of the shepherds
May win away from thee a kindly smile.—
I see thee in thy youthful fullness shine,
Thy spring is here, it is the time of hope,
Unfolded is the flower of thy body;
Yet e'er in vain I tarry, that the flower
Of tender love shall break from out its bud
And joyful ripen to the golden fruit!
O that doth please me nevermore and points
To grievous error in the ways of nature!
The heart doth please me not, that stern and cold
Locks up itself i' th' very years of feeling.

RAIMOND: Enough now, Father Arc! Let her alone!
The love of my most excellent Johanna
Is but a noble, tender heav'nly fruit,
And quietly by steps the precious ripens!
Now she still loves to dwell upon the mountains,
And from the free and open heath she fears
To climb down here beneath the lowly roof
Of men, where none but narrow sorrows dwell.
Oft see I her from this deep vale with still
Astonishment, when she on lofty mead
I' th' middle of her herd stands towering,
With noble body, and her earnest look
Sends down upon the little lands o' th' earth.
Then seems to me she points to something higher,
And oft methinks, she stems from other times.

THIBAUT: That is just it, which is not pleasing to me!
She flees her sisters' joyous company,
The desert mountains she seeks out, deserts
Her nightly bed before the call o' th' cock,
And on the hour of terror, when the man
So gladly joins with men in confidence,
She sneaks, just like the bird with hermit traits,
Off to the grayish gloomy spirit realm
Of night, treads home upon the crossroads, and

Holds secret dialogue with mountain air.
Wherefore selects she always *this* location
And drives her herd directly hitherward?
I see her pondering entire hours
Sit underneath the yonder Druid tree,
From which all happy creatures run away.
For monstrous is it here: an evil being
Hath had its habitat beneath this tree
Already since the old, gray heathen times.
The eldest in the village tell themselves
About this tree such dreadful, shocking tales:
Miraculous sounds of most peculiar voices
One often hears from out its gloomy branches.
E'en I myself, when once i' th' later twilight
The way was leading me near to this tree
Have seen a ghostly woman sitting here.
She slowly stretched from out the wide-spread pleats
Of her attire, a barren hand to me,
As if she were to beckon; but I hied
On by, commended unto God my soul.

RAIMOND *(pointing to the holy image in the chapel):*
The blessed nearness of this gracious image,
That here bestrews the Heaven's peace around it,
Not Satan's work, doth guide your daughter here.

THIBAUT: O no! no! Not in vain it shows itself
To me in dreams and anxious countenances.
On three occasions have I her beheld
To sit at Rheims upon our Monarch's throne,
A sparkling diadem of seven stars
Upon her head, the scepter in the hand,
From which three pure white lilies did spring forth,
And I, her father, both her sisters too
And all the princes, counts, archbishops and
The King himself did bow in front of her.
How comes to me such luster in my cottage?
O that doth indicate a deep fall!
Symbolically this warning dream presents
To me the futile strivings of her heart.

She is ashamed of her own lowliness—
Since God bejeweled her body with rich beauty,
With high and wondrous presents her did bless
Above all shepherd-maidens of this vale,
So feeds she sinful arrogance i' th' heart.
'Tis arrogance, whereby the angels fell,
Whereby the spirit of Hell takes hold of man.

RAIMOND: Who nurses a more modest, virtuous mind
Than your own pious daughter? Is't not she,
Who serves her older sisters joyfully?
She is most highly gifted of them all,
And yet you see her as a lowly maid
Perform the hardest tasks in still obedience
And through her very hands so wonderful
The herds and crops as well do thrive for you;
Around all, that she doth create, pours forth
An inconceivable effusive bliss.

THIBAUT: Indeed! An inconceivable bliss—O'er me
Comes a peculiar horror at this blessing!
—No more thereof. I'm mum. I'll say no more;
Shall I accuse my very own dear child?
I can do nought but warn her, pray for her!
Yet I must give a warning: Flee this tree,
Do not remain alone and dig no roots
At midnight, do not there prepare a potion
And write not any symbols in the sand!
'Tis easy to tear ope the realm of spirits,
They lie in waiting 'neath a scanty cover,
And hearing quietly they storm up here.
Do not remain alone, for in the desert
Came Satan's angel to the Lord of Heaven.

SCENE III

BERTRAND *enters, a helmet in the hand.*

THIBAUT. RAIMOND. JOHANNA.

RAIMOND: Still! Here comes Bertrand back from out the city.

    See, what he bears!
BERTRAND: You gaze at me, you are
    Astonished by the implement so strange
    Here in mine hand.
THIBAUT: Indeed we are. Announce,
    How came you by the helm, why bring you us
    That evil symbol in this peaceful region?

(JOHANNA, *who in both preceding scenes stood aside in silence and without taking any interest, grows attentive and steps nearer.*)

BERTRAND: Scarce I myself can say, just how the thing
    Hath fallen in mine hand. I had bought up
    Some iron implements at Vaucouleurs;
    A mighty crowd I found there in the market,
    For fleeing people had just then arrived
    From Orleans with evil war reports.
    In uproar crowded all the town together,
    And as I make my way through all the bustle,
    There steps a brown Bohemian woman toward
    Me with this helm in hand, looks sharply in mine eyes
    And speaks: "Comrade, you're looking for a helm,
    I know, you're seeking one. So here! Take this!
    For but a trifling it is yours to buy."
    "Go to the mercenaries," tell I her,
    "I am a farmer, do not need the helmet."
    But she did not let up and stated further:
    "No man is able to assert, if he
    Not need the helm. A steel roof for one's head
    Is worth more now than is a house of stone."
    So drove she me through all the lanes, on me
    The helmet urging, which I did not want.
    I saw the helm, that was so bright and fair
    And worthy of the head of any knight,
    And as I doubting weighed it in mine hand,
    Reflecting on the strangeness of th' adventure,
    Then was the woman quickly from my sight,
    The stream of people had her swept away,

And in mine hands the helmet did remain.
JOHANNA *(quickly and eagerly grasping thereafter):*
  Give me the helm!
BERTRAND: What doth it you avail?
  That is no jewel for a virgin's head.
JOHANNA *(seizes the helmet from him):*
  Mine is the helm, and it belongs to me.
THIBAUT: What's happ'ning to the maid?
RAIMOND: Grant her the wish!
  This warlike jewel doth befit her well,
  For in her breast is locked a manly heart.
  Reflect, how she o'ercame the tiger wolf,
  The fiercely savage beast, that did our herds
  So devastate, the dread of every herdsman.
  She all alone, the lion-hearted virgin,
  Fought with the wolf and wringed the lamb from him,
  That he already bore in bloody throat.
  Whatever valiant head this helmet covers,
  It can adorn none that's more worthy!
THIBAUT *(to* BERTRAND*):* Speak!
  What new calamity of war's occurred?
  What tidings brought those fugitives?
BERTRAND: God help
  The King and with this land commiserate!
  We have been beaten in two mighty battles,
  The enemy stands in the midst of France,
  Abandoned are all lands up to the Loire—
  Now hath he brought together his whole might,
  Wherewith he doth beleaguer Orleans.
THIBAUT: May God protect the King!
BERTRAND: Immeasurable
  Artillery is brought up from all sides,
  And as the dark'ning squadrons of the bees
  Swarm round the basket in the summer days,
  As from the blackened air the locust clouds
  Descend and cloak the fields for miles on end
  In an incalculable teaming swarm,
  So hath a cloud of war from many nations

Poured forth upon the fields of Orleans,
And from the unintelligible mix
Of tongues, the camp in dull confusion roars.
For even mighty Burgundy, the lands'
Authority, hath brought up all his men,
Those from Liege and those from Luxembourg,
Those from Hainaut, and from the land Namur,
And those who live in fortunate Brabant,
The opulent Ghentians, who in silk and velvet
Strut proudly, those from Zeeland, whose clean city
Arises from the waters of the sea,
And the herd-milking Hollanders, and those
From Utrecht, yes from outermost West Friesland,
Who look toward the ice-pole—they follow all
The power-wielding Burgundy's command
To arms and wish to conquer Orleans.

THIBAUT: O the unholy pitiful disunion,
That turns the arms of France against the French!

BERTRAND: Her too, the agèd Queen, proud Isabeau,
The princess of Bavaria, one sees,
Bedecked in steel go riding through the camp,
With poison prickled words to instigate
To rage all of the nations 'gainst her son,
Whom she had borne in her maternal womb!

THIBAUT: A curse upon her! And may God one day
Destroy her as He did proud Jezebel!

BERTRAND: The terrible Earl Salisbury, the wall-
Destroyer, leads the forces of the siege,
With him the lion's brother Lionel
And Talbot, who with homicidal sword
Mows down entire nations in the battles.
In brazen spirit they have sworn an oath,
To consecrate all virgins to disgrace
And, who hath borne the sword, to th' sword to
  sacrifice.
Four lofty watch towers have they constructed,
To tower o'er the town; above spies out
Earl Salisbury with murder-eager look

And counts the speedy wand'rers on the lanes.
Full many thousand balls of hundredweight
Are slung into the city, churches lie
Below in ruin and the royal tower
Of Notre Dame bows its exalted head.
They have as well dug powder passages,
And thus above a hellish kingdom stands
The anxious city, waiting every hour,
As it becomes inflamed with thunderclap.
(JOHANNA *listens with tense attention and puts the helmet on.*)

THIBAUT: However where were then the valiant swords
Saintrailles, La Hire and France's parapet,
The hero-minded Bastard, that the foe,
All powerful, so tearing forward pressed?
Where is the King himself, and looks he idly on
The kingdom's need and downfall of its cities?

BERTRAND: At Chinon now the King doth hold his court,
In need of men, he can not hold the field.
What use the leader's pluck, the hero's arm,
When pallid fear doth paralyze the army?
A terror, as if sent down here by God,
Hath even seized the bosom of the bravest.
In vain the princes' summons doth resound.
Just as the sheep uneasy crowd together,
Whene'er the howling of the wolves is heard,
So seeks the Frank, forgetting his old fame,
Alone the safety of the citadel.
A single knight alone, do I hear tell,
Hath brought a feeble troop of men together
And goes unto the King with sixteen ensigns.

JOHANNA (*quickly*):
Who is the knight?

BERTRAND: He's Baudricour. Yet scarce
Can he escape the foe's reconnaissance,
Who follows with two armies on his heels.

JOHANNA: Where halts the knight? Inform me, if you know.

BERTRAND: He stands but scarcely one day's trip away
   From Vaucouleurs.
THIBAUT *(to* JOHANNA*)*:
                   What troubles thee? Thou ask'st
   Of matters, Maiden, which befit thee not.
BERTRAND: Since now the foe's so mighty and no help
   Is longer hoped for from the King, they have
   At Vaucouleurs adopted with one mind
   A resolution, to give up to Burgundy.
   So we shall bear no foreign yoke and stay
   With th' ancient royal stock—indeed perhaps
   Shall we return once more to our old crown,
   If Burgundy once reconciles with France.
JOHANNA *(with inspiration)*:
   Nought of agreements! Nought of giving up!
   The savior nears, he arms himself for combat.
   At Orleans shall the fortune of the foe be wrecked,
   His measure's full, for harvest is he ripe.
   The virgin with her sickle shall arrive
   And shall mow down the seeds of his pride;
   Down from the Heaven she shall tear his fame,
   Which he hath hung up high upon the stars.
   Despond not! Do not flee! For ere the rye
   Turns yellow, ere the lunar disc is full,
   No English steed will longer drink from waves
   Of the magnificently streaming Loire.
BERTRAND: Ah! Miracles no longer do occur!
JOHANNA: Yes, miracles still happen!—A white dove
   Will fly and will attack with eagle's boldness
   These vultures, who the fatherland tear up.
   It will beat down this proud Burgundian,
   Who hath betrayed the realm, and then this Talbot,
   The heaven-storming hundred-handed one,
   And Salisbury, the raper of the temples,
   And also all these brazen island-dwellers
   Just like a herd of lambs she'll chase before her.
   The Lord will be with her, the God of battles.
   His trembling creature will He then elect,

And through a tender virgin He will choose
To glorify Himself, for He's Almighty!
THIBAUT: What spirit taketh o'er the wench?
RAIMOND: It is
The helm, that so inspires her martially.
Look at your daughter now! Her eyes do flash,
And glowing fire flashes in her cheeks.
JOHANNA: This realm shall fall? This land of such renown,
The fairest, that th' eternal sun doth see
Throughout its course, the paradise of lands,
That God loves as the apple of His eye,
Shall bear the fetters of a foreign people?
—Here ran the heathen's might aground. Here was
At first the cross, the form of mercy raised,
Here rest the ashes of the holy Louis,
From out of here Jerusalem was conquered.
BERTRAND (*astonished*):
Just listen to her talk! Whence did she draw
This lofty revelation?—Father Arc,
To you gave God a daughter wonderful!
JOHANNA: No more shall we have monarchs of our own,
Nor shall we have a master native born—
The King, who never dies, shall vanish from
The world—he who protects the holy plow,
Who the flock protects and fruitful makes the earth,
Who the bonded serf leads to his liberty,
Who the cities joyfully puts round his throne,
Who standeth by the feeble and the evil scares,
Who of envy nought doth know—for he's the greatest—
Who a man is and an angel of compassion
Upon this earth so hostile.—For the throne
Of monarchs, which with gold doth shimmer, is
The lodging of th' abandoned ones—here stand
Both might and heartfelt charity—here quakes
The guilty one, with trust the righteous one comes near

And jesteth with the lions round the throne!
The foreign monarch, who comes from abroad,
Whose Fathers' holy bones do not repose
In this ancestral land, can he it love?
He who was never young among our youth,
Unto whose heart our words will never ring,
Can he a father be to his offspring?

THIBAUT: God fend for France and for its King! We are
A peaceful country folk, who know not how
To wield the sword nor romp on martial steed.—
Obeying quietly let us await,
Whom victory will give us as a king.
Success in battle is but God's decree,
And he's our *master*, who the holy chrism
Receiveth and puts on the crown at Rheims.
—Come to the labor! Come! And think each one
But on the one that's next! And let the grand,
The princes of the earth draw lots for land;
The devastation we can calmly spy,
For firm in storm the soil we till doth lie.
In flames our villages may burn to th' ground,
The horses' steps may trample down the rye—
But the new spring will bring new crops thereby,
And quickly do our fragile huts rebound!

(*All except the* VIRGIN *exit.*)

SCENE IV

JOHANNA *alone.*

Farewell, ye mountains, ye beloved swards,
Ye quiet and familiar vales, farewell!
Johanna will now no more o'er you wander,
Johanna says forever fare you well.
Ye meadows, which I watered, and ye trees,
Which I have planted, green forth merrily!
Farewell, ye grottoes and ye cooling springs!

Thou echo, lovely voice upon this vale,
Which oft an answer gave to my refrain—
Johanna goes, and she ne'er comes again!

Ye places of mine every silent pleasure,
You do I leave behind for evermore!
Disperse yourselves, ye lambs, amid the heather,
Ye are a flock without a herdsman more,
For there's another herd which I must pasture,
On danger's yonder field of bloody gore:
So hath the spirit's call to me been given,
I'm not by idle earthly longing driven.

For Who on Horeb's summits once descended
To Moses in a fiery bush of flame
And 'fore the Pharoah him to stand commended,
Who one time Jesse's boy of pious fame,
The shepherd, as His champion intended,
Who e'er His grace to shepherds did proclaim,
He spake to me from branches of this tree:
"Go forth! Thou shalt bear witness on the earth for
 me.

In rugged ore shalt thou thy limbs enlace,
With steel thou shalt bedeck thy tender breast,
Nor love of men thine heart may e'er embrace
With sinful flames of idle earthly zest.
The bridal wreath thy locks will never grace,
No darling child will blossom at thy breast,
Yet thee with military honors I
Shall o'er all earthly women glorify.

For when i' th' fight the bravest do despair,
When France's final destiny draws nigh,
Then thou mine oriflamme wilt onward bear
And, as the rapid reaper cuts the rye,
Shalt thou the haughty conqueror impair;
Thou wilt his wheel of fortune now defy,
To France's hero sons salvation bring
And Rheims set truly free and crown thy King!"

A signal hath the Heaven promised me—
He sendeth me the helm, it comes from Him,
With godly strength His iron touches me,
And through me flames the pluck o' th' Cherubim!
Into the martial throng it urges me,
It drives me forth with stormy vim,
The field-call hear I to me strongly pound,
The war horse rears, and all the trumpets sound.
(She exits.)

ACT I

SCENE I

Court encampment of KING CHARLES *at Chinon.*

DUNOIS *and* DU CHATEL.

DUNOIS: No, this no longer I'll endure. I say
I've had it with this King, who infamously
Forsakes himself. Within my bosom bleeds
My valiant heart, and glowing tears I'd like to weep,
That robbers in the royal realm of France
Are sev'ring with the sword, the noble cities,
Which with the monarchy have agèd grown,
Deliver to the foe their rusty keys,
While here in idleness of rest and peace
We waste the precious noble rescue time.
—I hear that Orleans is menaced now,
I fly down here from distant Normandy,
The King I think in warlike manner armed
I'll find already at his army's head,
And find him—here! Surrounded by his jugglers
And troubadours, resolving subtle riddles
And giving Sorel gallant festivals,
As if profoundest peace ruled in the realm!
The field commander leaves, he can no longer
Behold the horror.—I forsake him too

And give him over to his evil fate.
DU CHATEL: Here comes the King!

SCENE II

KING CHARLES *to the preceding.*

CHARLES: The field commander sends me back his sword
  And doth renounce his service.—In God's name!
  So are we rid of one disgruntled man,
  Who quarrelsome wished but to master us.
DUNOIS: *One* man is of much worth in such dear times,
  I'd fain not lose him so light-mindedly.
CHARLES: That say'st thou but through joy in contradiction;
  While he was here, thou never wert his friend.
DUNOIS: He was a proud, annoying grievous fool
  And knew ne'er when to finish—but this time
  He knows. He knows the time is right to leave,
  When no more honor is to be obtained.
CHARLES: Thou art in thy most amiable mood,
  I'll not disturb thee in it.—Du Chatel!
  Here there are envoys from the agèd King
  Renè, commended master of refrains
  And widely famed.—One must regale them well
  And offer each of them a golden chain.
  (*to the* BASTARD)
  What art thou laughing at?
DUNOIS: That golden chains
  Thou shakest from thy mouth.
DU CHATEL: My Sire! There is
  No longer money in thy treasury.
CHARLES: So then produce some.—Noble singers may
  Not go away unhonored from my court.
  They make our barren scepter flower forth,
  They weave the never-dying verdant branch
  Of life into the unproductive crown,

> They rulingly appear as rulers do,
> From gentle wishes they construct their throne,
> And not in space their harmless kingdom lies:
> Hence shall the singer with the Monarch go,
> They both on mankind's pinnacle reside!

DU CHATEL: My regal Master! I have spared thine ear,
So long as there was counsel and support,
But now the urgent need doth loose my tongue.
—Thou hast nought more to offer, ah! thou hast
No more, wherefrom thou can'st tomorrow live!
The high tide of thy riches hath run out,
And deepest ebb is in thy treasury.
The soldiers have not yet received their pay,
They threaten grumbling to desert.—Scarce do
I know, how thine own royal domicile
But scantily, not princely, to maintain.

CHARLES: Take out a mortgage on my royal tolls
And let thee borrow money from the Lombards.

DU CHATEL: My Sire, thy royal revenues, thy tolls
Are pledged already three years in advance.

DUNOIS: And meanwhile are the pledge and land both lost.

CHARLES: To us remain still many rich, fair lands.

DUNOIS: So long it pleases God and Talbot's sword!
When Orleans is taken, mayest thou
Then with thy King Renè the sheep protect.

CHARLES: Thou ever try'st thy wit upon this King.
And yet is it this very landless prince,
Who just today endowed me regally.

DUNOIS: But hopefully not with his crown of Naples,
For God's sake no! For it is up for sale,
Thus have I heard, since he's been grazing sheep.

CHARLES: That is a joke, a cheerful game, a feast,
Which he gives to himself and his own heart,
To found himself an innocent pure world
In this barbaric, harsh reality.
Yet what he that is great and regal wants—
He wants to bring again the ancient times,

When tender courtly love did rule, when love
Did lift the great heroic heart o' th' knight
And noble ladies sat in judgment seats,
With gentle sense all subtleties resolving.
In former ages dwells the gay old man,
And as they still in olden ballads live,
So would he set it up on earth, just like
A heav'nly city in the golden clouds.
Established hath he there a court of love,
Whereto the noble knights shall go as pilgrims,
Where ladies chaste shall be in glory throned,
Where purest courtly love shall come again,
And he hath me selected Prince of Love.
DUNOIS: I am not so much stricken from my kind,
That I'd revile the mastery of love.
I take my name from her, I am her son,
And all my heritage lies in her realm.
My father was the Prince of Orleans;
To him no woman's heart was invincible,
Yet was no hostile fort for him too fast.
Wilt thou be worth'ly called the Prince of Love,
Then be the bravest of the brave!—As *I*
Have read from out those olden books, then love
Was always paired with lofty, knightly acts,
And heroes, had one so instructed me,
Not shepherds sat down at the table round.
Who can not beauty valiantly protect,
Deserveth not her golden prize.—Here is
The battleground! Fight for thy Fathers' crown!
Defend now with thy mighty, knightly sword
Thy property and noble ladies' honor—
And hast thou from the streams of foeman's blood
Made conquest bold of thine ancestral crown,
Then is it time and thee it princely suits,
To crown thee with the myrtle wreath of love.
CHARLES *(to a* SQUIRE, *who enters)*:
  What is it?
SQUIRE: Councilmen of Orleans request

A hearing.
CHARLES: Lead them in.
(SQUIRE *exits.*)
                          They'll ask for help—
What can I do, who helpless is himself!

SCENE III

Three COUNCILMEN *to the preceding.*

CHARLES: Be welcome, my much loyal citizens
  Of Orleans! How is my goodly city?
  Doth it continue, with accustomed courage
  To stand against the foe, who it beleaguers?
COUNCILMAN: Ah Sire! The highest need doth press, and hourly grows,
  Destruction swelleth onward toward the city.
  The outer works are now destroyed, the foe
  Wins over new terrain with every storm.
  The walls are now stripped naked of defenders,
  For fighting restlessly the men attack;
  Yet few will see their native gates again,
  The city's threatened too by hunger's plague.
  Hence hath the noble Count of Rochepierre,
  Who here commands, in this the highest need
  Contracted with the foe, by ancient custom,
  To yield himself up on the twelfth day hence,
  If in this time no army on the field
  Appears, that's large enough, to save the city.
  (DUNOIS *makes a violent movement of anger.*)
CHARLES: The term is brief.
COUNCILMAN: And so now are we here
  With foe's escort, that we thy princely heart
  Implore, thee to take pity on thy city
  And to send help to us within this time.
  Else he surrenders it on the twelfth day.
DUNOIS: Saintrailles was really able to agree

ACT I, SCENE III   THE VIRGIN OF ORLEANS

  To such a shameful contract!
COUNCILMAN: No, my Lord!
  So long as that brave man did live, there could
  Ne'er be such talk of peace and of surrender.
DUNOIS: So is he dead!
COUNCILMAN: Upon our wall did sink
  The noble hero for his Monarch's cause.
CHARLES: Saintrailles dead! O in this single man
  Mine army sinks!

*(A KNIGHT comes and speaks a few words softly with the
       BASTARD, who starts up disconcerted.)*

DUNOIS: That too!
CHARLES: Now! What occurs?
DUNOIS: Count Douglas sends us news. The Scottish people
  Are in revolt and threaten to desert,
  If they today still don't receive arrears.
CHARLES: Du Chatel!
DU CHATEL *(shrugs his shoulders):*
              Sire! I know no counsel.
CHARLES: Pledge,
  Yes mortgage, what thou hast, e'en half my realm—
DU CHATEL: Nought helps! They have too often been put off!
CHARLES: They are the finest soldiers in mine army!
  They shall not now, not now abandon me!
COUNCILMAN *(falling at his feet):*
  O King, assist us! To *our* need give thought!
CHARLES *(full of despair):*
  Can I create an army out of nought?
  Will cornfields grow for me in my flat hand?
  Tear me in pieces, tear mine heart from me,
  Mint it instead of gold! My blood have I
  For you, not silver do I have nor soldiers!
*(He sees SOREL enter and hurries to her with
  outstretched arms.)*

SCENE IV

AGNES SOREL, *a casket in her hand,
to the preceding.*

CHARLES: O my dear Agnes! My belovèd life!
 Thou com'st, to tear me from my desperation!
 I have thee now, I flee unto thy breast—
 Nought hath been lost yet, for thou art still mine.
SOREL: My precious Monarch!
 (looking around with anxiously questioning glance)
   Dunois! Is it true?
 Du Chatel?
DU CHATEL: Sadly!
SOREL: *Is* the need so great?
 There's lack of pay? The troops would be withdrawn?
DU CHATEL: Yes, sadly is it so!
SOREL *(pressing the casket on him):*
   Here, here is gold,
 Here are the jewels—Melt my silver down—
 And sell, or mortgage all my castles—Put
 A lien upon my holdings in Provence—
 Turn all to cash and satisfy the troops.
 Depart! There is no time to lose!
 (Urges him to depart.)
CHARLES: Now, Dunois? Now, Du Chatel! I'm still poor
 To you, when I the crown of womanhood
 Possess?—As noble as myself hath she
 Been born, the royal blood of Valois is
 Itself not purer; she would decorate
 The foremost throne o' th' world—yet she disdains it,
 My love alone she'll be and so be called.
 Did she permit me e'er to make a gift
 Of higher value than an early bloom
 In winter or a seldom fruit? From me,
 Takes she no sacrifice and brings me all!
 Risks her entire riches and possessions
 Magnanimously on my sinking fortune.

DUNOIS: Indeed, she is a maniac like thou
  And casts her all into a burning house
  And scoops into Danaïde's leaky cask.
  Thee she will never rescue, but herself
  Will she with thee destroy—
SOREL: Believe him not.
  He's risked his very life ten times for thee—
  And now is angered, that I risk my gold.
  How? Have I not all sacrificed for thee
  With joy, what's more esteemed than gold and pearls,
  And should I now retain for me my fortune?
  Come! Let us cast all superficial ornaments
  Of life away from us! Let me give thee
  A noble example of renunciation!
  Transform thy courtly finery to soldiers,
  Thy gold to iron; all, that thou dost have,
  Cast it away determined for thy crown!
  Come! Come! We'll share the danger and the want!
  The steed prepared for war let us now mount,
  The tender bodies to the glowing shaft
  O' th' sun expose, the clouds above ourselves
  Receive as blanket and the stone as pillow.
  The rugged warrior will endure his woe
  In patience, if he sees his King just like
  The poorest persevere and do without!
CHARLES *(smiling)*:
  Yes, now's fulfilled in me an olden word
  Of prophecy, that once a nun to me
  In Clermont in prophetic spirit spake,
  A woman, did the nun declare, would make
  Me victor over all mine enemies
  And would regain my Fathers' crown for me.
  Far off I seek her in the foeman's camp,
  I hope to reconcile the mother's heart—
  Here stands the heroine, who leads to Rheims,
  Through love mine Agnes renders I shall win!
SOREL: Thou shalt it do through thy friends' valiant
    sword.

CHARLES: I hope much too from discord twixt my foes—
    For to me sure intelligence hath come,
    That twixt these haughty lords of England and
    My cousin Burgundy not all still stands
    As formerly. And hence have I dispatched
    La Hire with messages unto the Duke,
    If I might it attain, in leading back
    The angered peer to olden faith and duty—
    With every hour I wait for his arrival.
DU CHATEL *(at the window)*:
    The knight's now galloping into the court.
CHARLES: O welcome messenger! Now, so shall we
    Soon know, if we shall yield or we shall win.

SCENE V

LA HIRE *to the preceding.*

CHARLES *(goes toward him)*:
    La Hire! Dost thou bring hope to us or none?
    Explain in brief. What have I to expect?
LA HIRE: Expect nought more, except from thine own
        sword.
CHARLES: The haughty Duke will not be reconciled!
    O speak! What answer gave he to my message?
LA HIRE: Above all things, and e'en before he could
    Unto thee lend an ear, he did demand,
    That o'er to him be handed Du Chatel,
    Whom he doth name the murd'rer of his father.
CHARLES: And were we to decline this shameful term?
LA HIRE: Then be the bond ripped up, before it starts.
CHARLES: Hast thou thereon, as I commanded thee,
    Then challenged him to fight me on the bridge
    In Montereau, just where his father fell?
LA HIRE: I threw thy gauntlet down to him and spake,
    Thou would'st thy very noble rank give up
    And as a knight would battle for thy realm.

But he replied: To him there ne'er were need,
To fight for that, which he already held;
Yet if thou didst desire so for a fight,
So then would'st thou him find at Orleans,
Whereto it be his will to go tomorrow.
Therewith he laughing turned his back to me.

CHARLES: Did not arise within my parliament
The undefiled pure voice of righteousness?

LA HIRE: It hath grown dumb before the parties' rage.
An action of the parliament declared
Divested of the throne, thee and thy race.

DUNOIS: Ha, brazen pride of citizens turned lords!

CHARLES: Hast thou about my mother nought assayed?

LA HIRE: About thy mother!

CHARLES: Yes! And what did she declare?

LA HIRE *(after he reflects a few moments)*:
'Twas just the feast o' th' royal coronation,
When I arrived at Saint Denis. Adorned
Were the Parisians as if for a triumph,
In every alley arcs of honor rose,
Through which the King o' th' Englishmen did march.
Bestrewn with flowers was the way, and cheering,
As if our France its fairest victory
Had won, the rabble sprang around his coach.

SOREL: They cheered—and cheered, that they upon the heart
Of their most loving, gentle Monarch trod!

LA HIRE: I saw the youthful Harry Lancaster,
The boy, sit down upon the royal chair
Of our Saint Louis, and his haughty uncles
Bedford and Gloucester stood alongside him,
And our Duke Philip knelt down at the throne
And took the oath of fealty for his lands.

CHARLES: O honor-forgetting peer! Unworthy cousin!

LA HIRE: The child was terrified and stumbled, when
The high steps to the throne he did ascend.
"An evil omen!" murmured all the people,
And there arose a peal of ringing laughter.

> Then stepped the agèd Queen, thy mother, up
> To him, and—it enrages me to say!

CHARLES: Now?

LA HIRE: In her arms she took hold of the boy
> And placed him on thy father's chair herself.

CHARLES: O Mother! Mother!

LA HIRE: E'en the raving mad
> Burgundians, the murder-wonted bands,
> Grew glowing hot with shame to look at this.
> She did perceive it, and to th' people turned
> Cried she with a loud voice: "Thank me, ye Frenchmen,
> That I the sickly stem with a pure branch
> Ennoble, you defend before the mis-
> Begotten son of a derangèd father!"

(The KING covers himself, AGNES hurries to him and clasps him in her arms, all those standing around express their abhorrence, their horror.)

DUNOIS: The she-wolf! the rage-foaming old Megaere!

CHARLES *(after a pause to the COUNCILMEN)*:
> Ye now have heard, how stand the matters here.
> Delay no longer, go to Orleans
> Again and notify my faithful city:
> That I release it from its oath to me.
> It may its welfare take unto its heart
> And yield itself to the Burgundian's mercy—
> He's called the *Good*, and he will be humane.

DUNOIS: How, Sire? Thou wouldst forsake thine Orleans!

COUNCILMAN *(kneels down)*:
> My royal Lord! Do not withdraw thine hand
> From us! Do not give up thy faithful town
> Unto the cruel mastery of England.
> It is a noble stone upon thy crown,
> And none hath to our kings, thine ancestors,
> The faith more sacredly preserved.

DUNOIS: Are we
> Defeated? Is't allowed, to leave the field,

Before one sword's been thrust to save the city?
  With one small facile word, before the blood
  Hath flowed, dost thou intend to give away
  The best towns from the heart of France?
CHARLES: Enough
  Of blood hath flowed already and in vain!
  The heavy hand of Heaven is against me:
  Defeated is mine army in all battles,
  My parliament rejecteth me, my capital,
  My folk receive my foe with exultation,
  Those who by blood are nearest me, forsake,
  Betray me—mine own mother nourishes
  The foreign foeman's brood at her own breasts.
  —We will withdraw to th' other side o' th' Loire
  And yield unto the mighty hand of Heaven,
  Which now is with the English people.
SOREL: God wills it not, that we, of our own selves
  Despairing, turn our back upon this realm!
  This word came not from out thy valiant breast.
  The mother's most unnatural cruel act
  Hath broke my Monarch's own heroic heart!
  Thou'll find thyself again, and manly be,
  Resist that destiny with noble courage,
  Which grimly fights against thee now.
CHARLES *(lost in a gloomy state of mind)*:
                                                    Is it not true?
  A darksome, terrifying fate prevails
  Through Valois' family, it is rejected
  Of God. The mother's vicious actions led
  The Furies here into this very house:
  My father laid in madness twenty years,
  Three older brothers death before me hath
  Mowed down—it hath by Heaven been concluded,
  The House of Charles the Sixth shall be o'erthrown.
SOREL: In thee it will arise made young anew!
  Have faith in thine own self.—O! not in vain
  Hath gracious destiny reserved but thee
  Of all thy brothers, thee the youngest one

Hath summoned to the undesired throne.
Within thy gentle soul the Heaven hath
Prepared itself a doctor for all wounds,
Which parties' rage inflicted on the land.
The flames of civil war wilt thou extinguish,
Mine heart tells me, that thou shalt plant the peace,
O' th' Frankish kingdom be the new creator.

CHARLES: Not I. The turbulent, harsh, stormy time
Demands a helmsman more endowed with strength.
I could have made a peaceful people happy;
A wild rebelling one I can not tame,
Nor open with the sword to me their hearts,
Which locked in hatred are from me estranged.

SOREL: The folk are blinded, a delusion stuns them.
But yet this giddiness will pass away,
Awaken will, the day no more is distant,
The love for their hereditary king,
Which in the Frankish breast is deeply planted,
The ancient hate, the jealousy will waken,
Which hostilely divides both folk eterne;
His very fortune fells the haughty victor.
Hence do not leave with overhastiness
The battlefield, fight for each foot of earth,
Defend, as if it were thy very breast,
This Orleans! Let all the ferries rather
Be sunk, let all the bridges be burnt down,
Which over this divider of thy realm,
The Stygian waters of the Loire, lead thee.

CHARLES: What I could do, so have I done. I have
Made offer of myself in knightly contest
For mine own crown.—This they do me refuse.
In vain I squanderèd my people's lives,
And now my cities sink into the dust.
Shall I just like that unnatural mother
Let mine own child be ripped up with the sword?
No, I shall abdicate, that he may live.

DUNOIS: How, Sire? Is that the language of a king?
Doth one *so* give a crown away? The worst

Of all thy people stakes his land and blood
Upon his point of view, his hate and love;
The party's all, whene'er the bloody sign
Of civil war hath been hung out to see.
The husbandman deserts the plow, the wife
Her distaff, children, old men arm themselves,
The townsman his own town ignites, with his
Own hands the countryman his growing crops,
To injure thee or to promote thy welfare
And to assert the wishes of his heart.
Nought spareth he and he doth not expect
Forbearance, when his honor calls, when he
Doth battle for his gods or for his idols.
Hence out with this effeminate compassion,
That is not fitting to a regal breast.—
Let thou the war rave on, as it's begun!
Thou hast not lightly kindled it thyself.
The folk must sacrifice itself for its own King,
That is the destiny and law o' th' world.
The Frank knows not, nor wills it otherwise.
Worth nothing is the nation, which will not
Its all stake joyfully upon its honor.

CHARLES (*to the* COUNCILMEN):
Expect from me no different decision.
God shelter you. I can no more.

DUNOIS: Then turn
The victory god his back on thee forever,
As thou hast on thy father's realm. Thou hast
Thyself forsaken, so forsake I thee.
Not Burgundy's and England's might united,
Thine own small spirit throws thee from the throne.
The kings of France are heroes at their birth,
But thou art not thus martially begotten.
(*to the* COUNCILMEN)
The King surrenders you. But I will throw
Myself to Orleans, my father's city,
And underneath its ruins dig my grave.
(*He wants to go.* AGNES SOREL *detains him.*)

SOREL *(to the* KING*):*
  O let him not in anger go from thee!
  His mouth speaks brutal words, and yet his heart
  Is true as gold; he is indeed the same,
  Who loves thee warm and for thee oft hath bled.
  Now come, Dunois! Confess, that 'twas the heat
  Of noble wrath led you too far—But thou
  Forgive thy faithful friend his fervent speech!
  O come, come! Let me rapidly unite
  Your hearts again, before this hasty wrath
  Unquenchable, the ruinous, inflames!
  (DUNOIS *stares fixedly at the* KING *and seems to await an answer.*)
CHARLES *(to* DU CHATEL*):*
  We shall now cross over the Loire. Let all
  My goods be brought aboard the ship!
DUNOIS *(quickly to* SOREL*):*   Farewell!
     (turns quickly and goes, COUNCILMEN *follow.*)
SOREL *(wrings her hands full of despair):*
  O if he goes, so are we quite forsaken!
  —Chase him, La Hire. O seek him to appease.

(LA HIRE *exits.*)

SCENE VI

CHARLES. SOREL. DU CHATEL.

CHARLES: Is then the crown such a unique possession?
  Is it so bitter hard, therefrom to part?
  I know that which still harder is to bear:
  To let oneself by these defiantly
  O'erbearing spirits be controlled, to live
  By grace of haughtily self-centered vassals,
  That is the hard thing for a noble heart
  And bitterer than to succumb to fate!
  (to DU CHATEL, *who still hesitates)*
  Do, what I thee commanded!

Du Chatel *(throws himself at his feet):*
>> O my King!
Charles: It now hath been decided. No more words!
Du Chatel: Make peace then with the Duke of
> Burgundy,
> Else see I no salvation more for thee.
Charles: Thou counselest me this, and *thine own blood*
> It is, wherewith I shall seal up this peace?
Du Chatel: Here is mine head. I have it ventured oft
> For thee in battles, and I lay it now
> For thee with joy upon the bloody scaffold.
> Let's pacify the Duke. Deliver me
> To th' total sternness of his wrath and let
> My flowing blood resolve the ancient hate!
Charles *(looks at him for some time, moved and silent):*
> Is it then true? Is it so bad with me,
> That mine own friends, who look right through mine heart,
> Show me the road of shame for my salvation?
> Yes, now I realize how deep's my fall,
> For in mine honor confidence is gone.
Du Chatel: Bethink—
Charles: >> Speak no word more! Arouse me not!
> Had I ten realms to look at with my back,
> I will not save myself with my friend's life.
> —Do, what I thee commanded. Go and let
> Mine armament embark.
Du Chatel: >> It shall with speed
> Be done.

(Stands up and goes, AGNES SOREL cries violently.)

SCENE VII

CHARLES *and* AGNES SOREL.

Charles *(grasping her hand):*
>> O be not sorrowful, mine Agnes.

Beyond the Loire lies also still a France,
We travel to a much more happy land.
There laughs a milder, ne'er-beclouded Heaven,
And lighter breezes blow, and gentler customs
Receive us there, where singing doth abide,
And fairer blossom forth both life and love.
AGNES: O must I look upon this day of misery!
The King must go away in banishment,
The son must wander from the father's house
And look upon his cradle with his back.
O pleasant country, that we are forsaking,
Ne'er shall we enter thee again with joy.

SCENE VIII

LA HIRE *comes back.* CHARLES *and* SOREL.

SOREL: You come alone. You do not bring him back?
(Whilst she looks at him more closely.)
La Hire! What's wrong? What says your look to me?
A new misfortune hath occurred!
LA HIRE: Misfortune
Hath been exhausted, sunshine comes again!
SOREL: What is't? I beg you.
LA HIRE *(to the* KING*):*   Call the envoys back
From Orleans!
CHARLES: Wherefore? What hath occurred?
LA HIRE: Recall them now. Thy luck hath turned around,
A battle hath occurred—thou hast *prevailed*.
SOREL: Prevailed! O heavenly music of the word!
CHARLES: La Hire! A fabulous report deceives thee.
Prevailed! I've no more faith in victory.
LA HIRE: O thou wilt soon believe in greater wonders.
Here comes the Archbishop. He leads the Bastard
Into thine arms again—
SOREL: O beauteous flower

Of triumph, which like noble Heaven's fruit
Bears peace and harmony!

SCENE IX

ARCHBISHOP OF RHEIMS. DUNOIS. DU CHATEL *with*
RAOUL, *an armored knight, to the preceding.*

ARCHBISHOP (*leads the* BASTARD *to the* KING *and lays their hands in one another's*):
   Embrace, ye Princes! Let all the grudge and quarrel vanish now,
   Since Heaven doth proclaim itself for us.
   (DUNOIS *embraces the* KING.)
CHARLES: Pull me from mine astonishment and doubt.
   What doth this solemn earnestness announce?
   What brought this rapid change about?
ARCHBISHOP (*leads the knight forward and places him before the* KING): Report!
RAOUL: We had brought up some sixteen companies,
   Folk from Lorraine, to join unto thine host,
   And Bandricour, the knight from Vaucouleurs,
   Was our commander. When we now the heights
   At Vermanton attained and in the vale,
   Through which the Yonne did stream, hereunder climbed,
   There stood the foe before us on th' extended plain,
   And weapons flashed, when we looked to our rear.
   We saw ourselves surrounded by both armies,
   There was no hope, to triumph nor to flee;
   Then sank the most courageous heart, and all,
   Full of despair, already would lay down their arms.
   Now while our leaders with each other still
   Sought counsel and none found—behold, there did appear
   A wonder most peculiar to our eyes!
   For suddenly from out the forest's depths

Stepped forth a virgin, with behelmèd head
Like to a martial goddess, fair at once
And dreadful to behold; around her neck
In darksome ringlets fell her hair; a glance
From Heav'n seemed to 'luminate her highness,
As she raised up her voice and thus did speak:
"What fear ye, valiant Frenchmen! At the foe!
And were there more of them than sand i' th' sea—
God and the Holy Virgin lead you on!"
And quickly from the ensign bearer's hand
She tore the banner, and before the train
With daring manner strode the mighty one.
We, dumb with wonder, without willing, follow
The lofty banner and its carrier,
And at the foe we storm without delay.
Who, highly stricken, standeth motionless,
With wide-eyed fixèd look amazed to see
The wonder, that unfolds before his eyes—
Yet swiftly, as if fear of God had him
Affected, now he turns around to flee,
And casting arms and armor from himself
Disbandeth the whole army through the field;
Then helps no strict command, no leader's call,
'Fore terror senseless, without looking back,
Plunge man and steed into the river's bed
And let themselves be choked without resistance—
A slaughter was it, call it not a battle!
Two thousand enemies did deck the field,
Those not included, whom the stream devoured,
And of our own there was no missing man.

CHARLES: Quite strange, by God! Most wonderful and strange!

SOREL: And did a virgin work this miracle?
Whence came she here? Who is she?

RAOUL: Who she be,
Will she alone unto the King reveal.
She calls herself a seeress and God-
Dispatchèd prophetess and promises,

To rescue Orleans, before the moon doth change.
The folk believe her and doth thirst for combat.
The host she follows, soon will she be here.
(One hears bells and a clashing of weapons, which are striking against one another.)
Hear ye the riot? The pealing of bells?
She is't, the people greet the one dispatched by God.
CHARLES *(to* DU CHATEL*):*
Conduct her in—
(to the ARCHBISHOP*)*
      What shall I think thereof!
A maiden brings me triumph and just now,
When but a godly arm can rescue me!
That doth not happen in the course of nature,
And dare I—Bishop, dare I miracles believe?
MANY VOICES *(behind the scene):*
Hail, Hail the Virgin, the Deliveress!
CHARLES: She comes!
 (to DUNOIS*)* You occupy my place, Dunois!
We want to test this Maid of miracles:
Is she inspired and by God dispatched,
Then she will know how to discern the King.

*(*DUNOIS *seats himself, the* KING *stands to his right, next to him* AGNES SOREL, *the* ARCHBISHOP *with the others opposite, so that the middle space remains empty.)*

SCENE X

The preceding. JOHANNA, *accompanied by the* COUNCILMEN *and many knights, who fill up the background of the scene; with noble manner she steps forward and looks at the bystanders one at a time.*

DUNOIS *(after a profound, solemn stillness):*
Art thou the one, most wondrous Maiden—

JOHANNA *(interrupts him, looking at him with clarity and highness):*
Bastard of Orleans! Thou wilt tempt God!
Rise from this place, which thee doth not befit,
Unto this greater one have I been sent.

(She goes with decisive step up to the KING, *bows a knee before him and stands back up at once, stepping back. All those present express their astonishment.* DUNOIS *leaves his seat, and space is created before the* KING.*)*

CHARLES: Thou see'st my countenance for the first time
Today—From whence then to thee comes this knowledge?
JOHANNA: I saw thee, where thee no one saw but God.
(She approaches the KING *and speaks mysteriously.)*
In recently departed night, recall thee!
When all around thee lay in deepest sleep
Interred, then didst thou rise from thine own bed
And mad'st a heated prayer unto thy God.
Let *these* go out from here, and I'll name thee
The content of thy prayer.
CHARLES: What I to Heaven
Confide, I do not need to hide from men.
Disclose to me the content of my plea,
So doubt I no more, that thee God inspires.
JOHANNA: There were then three entreaties, which thou mad'st;
Give heed now, Dauphin, if I thee them name!
At first thou didst entreaty make to Heaven:
If unjust wealth adheres unto this crown,
If any other heavy guilt, not yet
Atoned for, even from thy father's time,
Had called this tearful war into existence,
Thee to accept as off'ring for thy folk
And to pour out upon thine head alone
Th' entire vial of its wrath.
CHARLES *(steps back in consternation):*
Who art thou, mighty being? Whence comst thou?

(All show their astonishment.)
JOHANNA: Thou mad'st to Heaven then this second plea:
   If its high will and resolution be,
   To wrest away the scepter from thy stock,
   All to remove from thee, which thine own Fathers,
   The monarchs in this kingdom, did possess—
   Three goods alone thou didst entreat of Him
   To preserve for thee: the contented breast,
   The heart o' th' friend and then thine Agnes' love.
   (KING *conceals his face, weeping violently. Great
      emotion of astonishment among those present. After
      a pause.*)
   Shall I thy third request thee now still name?
CHARLES: Enough! Thee I believe! So much no man
   Can do! Thee hath the highest God dispatched.
ARCHBISHOP: Who art thou then, most holy wondrous
      Maiden?
   What happy land did bear thee? Speak! Who are
   The God-belovèd parents, who begot thee?
JOHANNA: Most reverend Lord, Johanna is my name,
   I am only a shepherd's lowly daughter
   From out my Monarch's townlet Dom Remi,
   Which lies within the diocese of Toul,
   And I have tended there my father's sheep
   From childhood on.—And heard I much and oft
   Them tell about the foreign island folk,
   Who've come across the sea, to make of us
   Their servants and to force on us the lord,
   Who's foreign born, who doth not love the folk;
   And that already the great city Paris
   They've occupied and now control the realm.
   Then called I to God's mother pleadingly,
   To turn from us the foreign chains of shame,
   And to preserve for us our native King.
   And 'fore the village, in which I was born,
   Doth stand an ancient image of God's mother,
   To which came many pious pilgrimages,
   And nearby there doth stand an holy oak,

Through many miracles of blessing's power famed.
And in the oak tree's shade I gladly sat,
The herd there grazing, for mine heart impelled me.
And did I lose a lamb i' th' desert mountains,
My dream would always point it out to me,
When I i' th' shadow of this oak tree slept.
—And one time, as I through a lengthy night
In pious meditation underneath this tree
Had sat and had resisted sleepiness,
Then came the Holy One to me, a sword
And banner bearing, otherwise like I
Dressed as a shepherdess, and she did speak to me:
"It's I. Stand up, Johanna. Leave the herd,
The Lord calls thee unto another business!
Assume this banner! Gird thee with this sword!
Therewith annihilate my people's foe
And lead thy Master's son thereunto Rheims
And crown him yonder with the royal crown!"
However then I spake: "How can I such
An action dare to take, a tender maid,
Unlearnt in the pernicious means of combat!"
And she replied: "A virgin pure can bring
About each thing that's glorious on earth,
If only she resisteth earthly love.
Just look on *me!* A maiden chaste like thou
Have I the Lord, the godly, given birth,
And godly art myself!"—And then she touched
Mine eyelid, and as I looked up above,
There was the Heaven full of angel boys,
Who carried pure white lilies in their hands,
And dulcet tone did float throughout the air.
—And so three nights one following the other
The Holy One appeared and called: "Stand up, Johanna!
The Lord calls thee unto another business."
And as she in the third night did appear,
Then she was wroth, and scolding she did speak these words:

ACT I, SCENE X   THE VIRGIN OF ORLEANS

"Obedience is woman's task on earth,
Severe forbearance is her heavy fate.
Through rigid service she must be refined—
Who here hath given service, there above is great."
And speaking in this way she let the robe
O' th' herdsmaid fall, and as the Queen of Heaven
I' th' brilliance of the sun did she there stand,
And golden clouds transported her above,
Receding slowly, to the blissful land.

(All are moved, AGNES SOREL crying violently conceals her face on the KING's breast.)

ARCHBISHOP *(after a long silence)*:
I' th' face of such divine accreditation
Must every doubt of earthly craft be silent.
The action proveth, that she speaks the truth:
But God alone can work such miracles.
DUNOIS: Not in her wonders, in her eyes I do believe,
The virgin innocence upon her face.
CHARLES: And am I sinner worthy of such grace?
Unerring and all searching eye, thou seest
Mine innermost and know'st mine humbleness!
JOHANNA: Above the humbleness o' th' high shines brightly,
Thou didst bow down, hence He hath raised thee highly.
CHARLES: So shall I give resistance to my foes?
JOHANNA: Subjected do I France place at thy feet!
CHARLES: And Orleans, thou sayst, will not surrender?
JOHANNA: Thou'll sooner see the Loire flow in reverse.
CHARLES: Shall I as conqueror then march to Rheims?
JOHANNA: I'll lead thee thither through a thousand foes.

(All the knights present cause a din with their lances and shields and give signs of courage.)

DUNOIS: Assign the Virgin to the army's head!
We follow blindly, where the godly one
Us leads. Her seer eye shall be our guide,

And this courageous sword shall her preserve!
LA HIRE: Not e'en a world in weapons do we fear,
When she is marching in before our troops.
The God of triumph walketh at her side:
In strife doth she, the mighty one, us guide!

(The knights cause a great din of weapons and advance.)

CHARLES: Yes, holy Maiden, lead thou now mine host,
And all its princes shall attend to thee.
This sword of highest martial power, that
The crown's field marshal angrily sent back
To us, hath found a far more worthy hand.
Receive it now, thou holy prophetess,
And be henceforth—
JOHANNA: No, not thus, noble Dauphin!
Not through this instrument of earthly power
Is victory lent to my Lord. I know
Another sword, through which I shall succeed.
I will describe it thee, just as the spirit
Taught it to me; send forth and have it fetched.
CHARLES: Name it, Johanna.
JOHANNA: Send to th' ancient city,
Fierbois, there, in Saint Catherina's churchyard,
There is a vault, wherein much iron lies,
Heaped up from olden loot of victory.
The sword's thereunder, that shall service me.
By the three golden lilies is it known,
Which on its very blade have been impressed:
This sword have fetched, for through it thou wilt
 triumph.
CHARLES: Send someone forth and do, as she doth say.
JOHANNA: And a white banner let me carry forth,
Encompassed with a seam of purple hue.
Upon this banner be the Heaven's Queen
Presented with the beauteous Jesus-boy,
She hovers up above an earthly sphere.
For thus the Holy Mother showed it me.
CHARLES: So be it, as thou sayest.

JOHANNA (*to the* ARCHBISHOP): Reverent Bishop,
Upon me lay your sacerdotal hand
And speak the blessing over your own daughter!
(*Kneels down*)
ARCHBISHOP: Thou hast come to us, blessings to dispense,
Not to receive them—Go i' th' strength of God!
Yet we are but unworthy ones and sinners!
(*She stands up.*)
SQUIRE: A herald comes from England's field commander.
JOHANNA: Let him come in, for God hath sent him here!

(*The* KING *beckons to the* SQUIRE, *who goes out.*)

SCENE XI

The HERALD *to the preceding.*

CHARLES: What bring'st thou, herald? Say what is thy mission.
HERALD: Who is it, who for Charles of Valois,
The Count of Ponthieu, is the spokesman here?
DUNOIS: Unworthy herald! Thou degraded knave!
Art thou so impudent, to disavow
The King of France upon his own domain?
Thy coat of arms protects thee, else thou shouldst—
HERALD: France recognizes but a single king,
And this one dwelleth in the English camp.
CHARLES: Be silent, cousin! Now, thy mission, herald!
HERALD: My noble Marshal, who laments the blood,
That hath already flowed and still shall flow,
Still holds his warrior's sword inside its sheath,
And ere collapses Orleans in storm,
Still offers thee a kindly compromise.
CHARLES: Let's hear it!
JOHANNA (*steps forward*):
                Sire! Allow me in thy stead

   To talk unto this herald.
CHARLES: Do that, Maiden!
   Thou shalt decide, if there be war or peace.
JOHANNA *(to the* HERALD*):*
   Who sendeth thee and speaketh through thy mouth?
HERALD: The British Marshal, Count of Salisbury.
JOHANNA: Herald, thou liest! The lord speaks not
     through thee.
   Alone the living speaketh, not the dead.
HERALD: My Marshal lives i' th' fullness of good health
   And strength, and lives to bring you all destruction.
JOHANNA: He lived, when thou departedst. But this
     morning
   A shot from Orleans stretched him to th' ground,
   As he looked down from tower La Tournelle.
   —Thou laugh'st, since I thee distant things reveal?
   Believe then not my speech, but thine own eyes!
   His corpse's train will then encounter thee,
   When thine own feet transport thee back again.
   Now, herald, speak and say what is thy mission!
HERALD: If thou know'st how what's hidddden to unveil,
   So knowst thou it, before I tell it thee.
JOHANNA: I have no need to know it, but now hear
   Thou that of mine! and then these words make known
   Unto the princes, who have sent thee here!
   —Monarch of England and ye also, Dukes
   Bedford and Gloucester, who direct the realm!
   Give your account unto the King of Heaven
   For all the blood that hath been spilt! And give
   To us the keys of all the towns, which ye
   Have overcome against the law of God!
   The Virgin cometh from the King of Heaven,
   To offer to you peace or bloody war.
   Choose! For I tell you this, that ye may know it:
   This beauteous France is not assigned to you
   By blessed Mary's Son—but rather Charles,
   My Lord and Dauphin, whom God's given it,
   Will regally make entry into Paris,

Accompanied by all the great men of his realm.
—Now, herald, go and get thee quick from here,
For ere thou may'st attain thy camp once more
And bring this message, is the Virgin there
And victory doth in Orleans secure.

(She goes, everything is in motion, the curtain falls.)

ACT II

Region bordered by rocks.

SCENE I

TALBOT *and* LIONEL, *English army officers.*
PHILIP, DUKE OF BURGUNDY, *Knights* FASTOLF *and*
CHATILLON *with soldiers and banners.*

TALBOT: Here underneath these rocks now let us come
Unto a halt and make a solid camp,
If we perchance our fleeing folk can reassemble,
Who in th' initial terror were dispersed.
Establish a good sentry, man the heights!
Indeed the night secures us from pursuit,
And if th' opponent hath not wings as well,
So fear I no surprise attack. But still
There's need for caution, for we have to do
With an audacious foe—and are defeated.

(KNIGHT FASTOLF exits with the soldiers.)

LIONEL: Defeated! General, say that word no more.
I can't permit myself to think, that Frenchmen
Today have seen the backs of Englishmen.
—O Orleans! Orleans! Grave of our fame!
Upon thy fields doth England's honor lie.
Insultingly ridiculous defeat!
Who will believe it in the coming times?
The victors at Poitiers, Crecy

And Agincourt o'ertaken by a woman!
BURGUNDY: That must console us: we are not by men
　Defeated, we are conquered by the devil.
TALBOT: The devil of our folly.—Burgundy,
　Affrights this ghost o' th' rabble princes too?
　This superstition is a wicked cloak
　For your own cowardice—Your folk fled first.
BURGUNDY: No one held firm. The flight was universal.
TALBOT: No, Sir! Upon your flank it did begin.
　You plunged straight into our encampment, shouting:
　"Hell's broken loose, and Satan fights for France!"
　And thus you brought our folk into confusion.
LIONEL: You can't it disavow. Your flank was first
　To yield.
BURGUNDY: Because the first assault was there.
TALBOT: The Maiden knew the weak point of our camp:
　She knew, just where our fear was to be found.
BURGUNDY: Shall Burgundy bear guilt for this
　　misfortune?
LIONEL: We English people, were we all alone,
　By God! we would not Orleans have lost!
BURGUNDY: No—for *you* ne'er had Orleans beheld!
　Who cleared the way for you into this realm,
　Reached unto you the loyal hand of friendship,
　When you did climb this hostile foreign coast?
　Who placed the crown in Paris on your Henry
　And did subject to him the Frenchmen's heart?
　By God! If this strong arm had never led
　You in, then you would never have beheld
　The smoke from out one Frankish chimney rise.
LIONEL: If mighty words could make it happen, Duke,
　Then you alone had subjugated France.
BURGUNDY: You are not pleased, since Orleans escaped
　From you, and now you vent your anger's bile
　On me, the union's friend. Wherefore from us
　Did Orleans escape except your greed?
　It was prepared, to yield itself to me—
　You, your own envy only hindered it.
TALBOT: Not just for you have we beleaguered it.

ACT II, SCENE II   **THE VIRGIN OF ORLEANS**   77

BURGUNDY: How would it be, did I withdraw mine host?
LIONEL: Not worse, believe me, than at Agincourt,
  Where we were finished both with you and with all
    France.
BURGUNDY: Yet of our friendship were you in much
    need,
  And dearly your imperial regent purchased it.
TALBOT: Yes, dearly, dearly we today have paid
  For it at Orleans with our own honor.
BURGUNDY: Press it no further, Lord, you could regret
    it!
  Abandoned I my master's righteous banner,
  Upon mine head did load the traitor's name,
  To suffer from the foreigner such things?
  Why am I here in battle fighting France?
  If I must render service to the ingrate,
  So would I have it be my native king.
TALBOT: You are in conversation with the Dauphin,
  We know of it; yet we shall find the means,
  To shelter us from treason.
BURGUNDY: Death and hell!
  Encounters one me so?—Chatillon!
  Let all my folk make ready to depart.
  We are returning to our land.

(CHATILLON *exits.*)

LIONEL: Luck on the way!
  Ne'er was the fame o' th' Briton more resplendent,
  Than when, entrusting to his goodly sword
  Alone, he fought without accomplices.
  Let every one his battle fight alone,
  For it is true eternally: French blood
  And English can ne'er honestly be mixed!

SCENE II

QUEEN ISABEAU, *accompanied by a page, to the
preceding.*

ISABEAU: What must I hear, Field Marshals! Call a halt!
  What sort of mentally delirious planet

Doth so entangle your else wholesome senses?
Now, when but harmony can you preserve,
Do you in hatred want to separate
And warring ready for your own destruction?
—I beg you, noble Duke. Recall your rash
Command.—And you, our Talbot, full of fame,
Conciliate the 'furiated friend!
Come, Lionel, help me persuade to peace
The haughty souls and make them reconcile.
LIONEL: I not, my Lady. All's the same to me.
Thus do I think: whatever can not stand
Together, doth the best, if it dissolve.
ISABEAU: How? Doth the juggler's art of Hell, which was
To us so ruinous in the fight, here too
Still, sense-confusing us infatuate?
Who did the row commence? Speak!—Noble Lord!
(*to* TALBOT)
Is't you, who so forgot his own advantage,
As to offend the worthy union partner?
What wish you to create without this arm?
He did construct unto your King his throne,
He holds it still and throws it, when he wills;
His army strengthens you, still more his name.
All England, pours it all its people out
Upon our coasts, would not be able to
Subdue the realm, if it be unified:
The French alone could overcome the French.
TALBOT: We know that we should honor loyal friends,
To guard 'gainst falsehood is discretion's duty.
BURGUNDY: Who faithlessly will gratitude deny,
He lacketh not the liar's brazen brow.
ISABEAU: How, noble Duke? Could you so very much
Renounce your princely honor and your shame,
Into that hand, which murdered your own father,
To lay your own? Were you enraged enough,
To think of honest reconciliation
E'en with the Dauphin, whom unto the edge
Of his destruction you yourself have slung?

So near unto his fall would you sustain him
And your own work insanely ruin yourself?
Here do your friends all stand. Your benefit
Doth rest alone in the firm bond with England.
BURGUNDY: Far is my mind from making peace with Dauphin,
And yet the disrespect and wantonness
Of haughty England I can not endure.
ISABEAU: Come! Make allowance for a hasty word.
Grave is the grief, which presses on the General,
And, as you know, misfortune makes unjust.
Come! Come! Now both embrace, let me this rift
Quick healing close, ere it becomes eternal.
TALBOT: What think you, Burgundy? A noble heart
Confesses gladly when o'ercome by reason.
The Queen hath spoken a sagacious word;
So let this handshake heal the injury,
The which my tongue did hastily inflict.
BURGUNDY: The Madame uttered a judicious word,
And my just wrath yields to necessity.
ISABEAU: Well! Let's then seal the reestablished bond
With one fraternal kiss, and may it be
The winds will blow away what hath been spoken.

(BURGUNDY *and* TALBOT *embrace one another.*)

LIONEL: (*contemplates the group, to himself*):
Luck to the peace, which Furies do bestow!
ISABEAU: A single battle have we lost, Field Marshals,
Luck was opposed to us; but don't therefore
Allow your noble pluck to sink. The Dauphin
Despaireth of the Heaven's shield and calls
For help from Satan's art; but yet he hath
In vain surrendered unto his damnation,
And Hell itself shall not deliver him.
A conquering maiden leads the host o' th' foe—
I will lead that of yours, I'll be for you
A substitute for prophetess and virgin.
LIONEL: Madame, go back to Paris. We intend

To win with goodly weapons, not with women.
TALBOT: Go! Go! Since you are in the camp, all's in
Retreat, there's no more triumph in our weapons.
BURGUNDY: Yes go! Your presence here creates nought good,
The warrior taketh but offense at you.
ISABEAU: *(looks with astonishment at one after the other):*
You also, Burgundy? You're taking sides
Opposed to me with these ungrateful lords?
BURGUNDY: Now go! The soldier loses his good courage,
When he believes he's fighting for your cause.
ISABEAU: I've scarcely reestablished peace 'tween you,
So you already are allied against me?
TALBOT: Go, go with God, Madame. We shall not fear
The devil more, so soon as you are gone.
ISABEAU: Am I not your own loyal union partner?
Is not your cause the same as that of mine?
TALBOT: But yours is not the same as ours. We are
Engaged here in an honest goodly strife.
BURGUNDY: I will avenge my father's bloody murder,
The pious filial duty sanctifies my weapons.
TALBOT: But out with it! What you to th' Dauphin do,
Is neither humanly good, nor divinely right.
ISABEAU: A curse shall meet him to ten generations!
He hath transgressed against his mother's head.
BURGUNDY: He did avenge a father and a husband.
ISABEAU: He set himself up to adjudge my morals!
LIONEL: That was quite disrespectful of the son!
ISABEAU: And he hath sent me into banishment.
TALBOT: That was to consummate the public's voice.
ISABEAU: A curse meet me, if I e'er him forgive!
And ere he governs in his father's realm—
TALBOT: You'd sooner sacrifice his mother's honor!
ISABEAU: You know not, feeble souls,
What an offended mother's heart can do.
I love, whoever doth me good, and hate,

Who injures me; and is it mine own son,
Whom I have borne—the more deserving hate.
To whom I being gave, will I it rob,
If he with wicked, brazen wantonness
Doth harm the very womb, which carried him.
You, who your war are waging 'gainst my son,
You have no right nor grounds, to rob from him.
What heavy debt against you hath the Dauphin
Incurred? What duties to you did he break?
The search for honor, common envy drive you—
I am allowed to hate him, I have borne him.

TALBOT: Well, in your vengeance he doth feel his mother!

ISABEAU: You wretched hypocrites, how I despise you,
Who lie unto yourselves as to the world!
Ye Englishmen stretch forth your robber hands
To seize this France, where you have neither right
Nor valid claim to even so much earth,
As any horse's hoof doth cover.—And this Duke,
Who lets the good man be rebuked, sells out
His fatherland, his forebears' heritage,
Unto the kingdom's foe and foreign lord.
—Yet is your every third word righteousness.
—Hypocrisy I scorn. Just as I am,
So doth the eye o' th' world see me.

BURGUNDY: 'Tis true!
That fame you have maintained with forceful spirit.

ISABEAU: I have my passions and mine ardent blood
As any other, and I came as Queen
Into this land, to live, and not to seem.
Should I to joy be dead, because the curse
Of fate hath joined my lively happy youth
Unto a husband who is quite insane?
More than my life I love my liberty,
And he who wounds me here—And yet wherefore
Should I dispute with you about my rights?
The viscous blood flows heav'ly in your veins,

You know not of the pleasures, just the rage!
And this Duke here, who throughout his whole life
Hath wavered 'tween both bad and good, can hate
Not from the heart nor from the heart can love.—
I go to Melun. Give me this man here,
(pointing to LIONEL*)*
Who pleases me, for company and entertainment,
And then do what you will! I question nought
Regarding English nor Burgundians.
(She beckons her page and wants to leave.)

LIONEL: Rely on it. The fairest Frankish boys,
Whom we shall capture, we'll send to Melun.

ISABEAU *(coming back)*:
You are quite capable, to strike with sword,
The Frank alone can speak what's delicate.
(She exits.)

SCENE III

TALBOT. BURGUNDY. LIONEL.

TALBOT: O what a woman!
LIONEL: Your opinion, Generals!
Shall we fly further still or shall we turn
Around, and through a rapid daring stroke
Extinguish the disgrace o' th' present day?
BURGUNDY: We are too weak, the people are dispersed,
The terror in the host is still too new.
TALBOT: A blinding fright alone hath conquered us,
The quick impression of a single moment.
This awful image of the scared imagination,
When closer seen, will vanish into nought.
Thus is my counsel: we shall lead the army
Across the stream again at break of day,
Against the foe.
BURGUNDY: Reflect thereon—

LIONEL: With your
  Permission. Here is nothing to consider.
  We must win back with speed what hath been lost,
  Or we're disgraced throughout eternity.
TALBOT: It is resolved. Tomorrow we shall strike.
  And to destroy this fantasy of terror,
  The which our people blinded and unmanned,
  Let us in personal engagement measure
  Ourselves against this virgin-acting devil.
  Stands she before our valiant swords, well then,
  So hath she damaged us for the last time;
  But stands she not—and to be sure, she'll shun
  The earnest fight—the host is disenchanted.
LIONEL: So be it! And to me, my General, leave
  This easy battle play, where flows no blood.
  For I intend to catch that ghost alive,
  And 'fore the Bastard's eyes, her paramour's,
  I'll carry her upon these arms across
  Into the British camp, to th' host's delight.
BURGUNDY: But promise not too much.
TALBOT: Obtain I her,
  I don't intend so softly to embrace her.
  Come now, to quicken enervated nature
  By means of a refreshing, careless slumber,
  And then to the departure with the dawn!
  (They exit.)

SCENE IV

JOHANNA *with the banner, in helmet and breast armor, but otherwise dressed as a woman,* DUNOIS, LA HIRE, *knights, and soldiers show themselves above upon the rocky road, pass by quietly, and appear at once thereafter on the stage.*

JOHANNA *(to the knights, who surround her, whilst the train above continues):*

Ascended is the wall, we are i' th' camp!
Now cast away the cloak of secret night
From you, which hath concealed your silent train,
And make known to the foe your dreadful nearness
Through clam'rous battle cry—God and the Virgin!
ALL *(cry aloud amidst the wild din of weapons)*:
God and the Virgin!
(drums and trumpets)
SENTRY *(behind the scene)*:
              Th' foe! The foe! The foe!
JOHANNA: Now torches here! Cast fire in their tents!
The flames of rage intensify the fright,
And threat'ning round let death surround them!
(Soldiers hasten forth, she wants to follow.)
DUNOIS *(holds her back)*:
Thou hast thy part accomplished now, Johanna!
I' th' midst o' th' camp hast thou conducted us,
Thou hast the foe into our hands delivered.
However from the contest now stay back,
Leave unto us the bloody resolution.
LA HIRE: The road of triumph show thou to the host,
The banner bear in your pure hand before us;
But take the sword, the deadly, not thyself,
Tempt the deceitful God of battle not,
For blind and with no sparing holds he sway.
JOHANNA: Who dares command me halt? Who doth prescribe
To th' spirit, who me leads? The shaft must fly,
Whereto its archer's hand impelleth it.
Where there is danger, must Johanna be.
Not now, not here am I ordained to fall:
The crown must I behold upon my Monarch's head—
No foe will tear this life away from me,
Till I complete, what God doth order me.
(She exits.)
LA HIRE: Come, Dunois! Let's pursue the heroine
And lend the valiant breast to her as shield!
(Exit.)

SCENE V

English soldiers flee across the stage. After that TALBOT.

FIRST: The Maiden! In the midst o' th' camp!
SECOND: Not possible! Ne'er more! How came she to the camp?
THIRD: Through the air! The devil helps her!
FOURTH AND FIFTH: Flee! Flee! We are all doomed to death!
(*Exit.*)
TALBOT (*comes*):
   They hearken not—they will not stand with me—
   Dissolved are all obedience's bonds!
   As if all Hell its legion of damned souls
   Spit out on us, a reeling madness drags
   The valiant and the coward brainlessly
   Away; not e'en a little band can I
   Put up against the flood-tide of the foe,
   Which waxing, surging penetrates the camp!
   —Am I the only sober one, and must
   Around me all in fever's fervor rage?
   Before these Frankish weaklings to escape,
   Whom we in twenty battles have o'ercome!—
   Who is she then, the unsubduable,
   The terror-goddess, who the battle's luck
   At once reverses and a timid host
   Of coward roes transformeth into lions?
   A conjurer, who plays her studied role
   Of heroine, shall terrorize true heroes?
   A woman snatched from me all triumph's fame?
SOLDIER (*rushes in*):
   The Maiden! Flee! Flee, General!
TALBOT (*strikes him down*):
                              Flee to Hell
   Thyself! This sword shall bore him through,
   Who speaks to me of fear and coward's flight!
(*He exits.*)

SCENE VI

The prospect opens. One sees the English camp stand in complete flames. Drums, flight, and pursuit. After a while MONTGOMERY *comes.*

MONTGOMERY (*alone*):
 Where shall I flee to? Foes are all around and death!
 Here our enraged Field Marshal, who with threat'ning sword,
 Escape obstructing drives us toward our death.
 There the dreadful one, who ruinously round herself
 Like the lust of fire rages—And around no bush,
 Which can conceal me, nor a hollow of safe space!
 O were I never shipped across the sea to here,
 I, most unlucky! Vain delusion dazzled me,
 To seek cheap glory in the Frankish war,
 And now pernicious destiny conducteth me
 Into this bloody, murd'rous fight.—Were I away
 From here, at home still on the Severn's blooming bank,
 I' th' safety of my father's house, wherein my mother
 In grief remained and my sweet, tender fiancée.

(JOHANNA *appears in the distance.*)

 Woe's me! What see I! There appears the dreadful one!
 From flaming fires, dimly shining, doth she rise,
 As from the jaws of Hell a specter of the night.
 —Whereto can I escape! Already doth she seize
 Me with her eyes of fire, casts from afar
 At me the never-failing glance's snares.
 Around my feet the magic coil is, firm and firmer
 Entangled, that so fettered they deny
 Me flight! Must I look yonder, though mine heart
 Against it struggles, at that deadly form!

(JOHANNA *takes a few steps toward him and remains standing again.*)

She nears! I will not wait, until the grim one
Attacks me first! Imploringly will I her knees
Embrace, her for my life entreat—she is a woman—
If I perhaps through tears can soften her!

(Whilst he wants to go up to her, she steps toward him quickly.)

SCENE VII

JOHANNA. MONTGOMERY.

JOHANNA: Thou art condemned to death. A British
  mother thee begot.
MONTGOMERY *(falls at her feet):*
  Desist, thou dreadful one! The undefended man
  Do not transfix. I've cast away my sword and shield,
  I sink down at thy feet defenselessly, imploring.
  Leave me the light of life, accept a ransom payment.
  Rich in possessions lives my father still at home
  I' th' beauteous land of Wales, there where the
    serpentine
  Severn doth roll its silver stream through verdant
    pastures,
  And fifty villages acknowledge his dominion.
  With ample gold he'll ransom his beloved son,
  When he hath learned I'm still alive i' th' Frankish
    camp.
JOHANNA: Deluded fool! Lost one! Into the Virgin's hand
  Art thou now fallen, the pernicious one, wherefrom
  No rescue nor redemption more is to be hoped for.
  If in the crocodile's control misfortune thee
  Hath given or into the spotted tiger's claws,
  If thou hast robbed the lion mother's youthful brood,
  Thou couldst then have discovered pity and
    compassion—
  But deadly is't, the Virgin to encounter.
  For to the spirit realm, the strict, inviolable,

Am I by dreadful binding contract duty bound,
With the sword to murder every living thing, the which
The god of battle fatefully doth send toward me.
MONTGOMERY: Frightful is thy discourse, yet thy look is soft,
Not dreadful art thou in proximity to see,
Mine heart doth draw me unto thy delightful form.
O by the gentleness of thy most tender sex
I beg of thee: Take pity on me in my youth!
JOHANNA: Do not implore me by my sex! Don't call me woman!
Just as the incorporeal spirits, who don't woo
In earthly wise, I join myself unto no sex
Of humans, and this armor covers up no heart.
MONTGOMERY: O by the holy ruling law of love,
To which all hearts pay homage, I implore thee.
At home I've left behind a lovely fiancée,
Fair, just like thou art, blooming in the charm of youth.
She tarries weeping for her loved one to return.
O if thou ever even hop'st to love, and hop'st
Through love to be made happy—part not cruelly
Two hearts, which by the holy bond of love are tied!
JOHANNA: Thou dost invoke mere earthly foreign deities,
Who to me are not holy nor revered. I know
Nought of the bonds of love, with which thou dost implore me,
And never shall I learn to know its idle service.
Prepare now to defend thy life, for death calls thee.
MONTGOMERY: O so take pity on my parents in their misery,
Whom I have left at home. Yes, certainly thou too
Hast left thy parents, who for thee are pained with sorrow.
JOHANNA: Unhappy man! And thou remind'st me now thereof,
How many mothers of this land are childless now,

How many tender children fatherless, how many
Expectant brides have widows now become through
  you!
Now England's mothers also may experience
Despair and make acquaintance with the tears,
Which France's wives in their great misery have shed.
MONTGOMERY: O, hard is it, on foreign soil to die
  unwept.
JOHANNA: Who called you to this foreign land, to
  devastate
The blooming labor of the fields, to chase us from
The native hearth and throw the fire brands of war
Into the peaceful sanctuaries of the cities?
Ye dreamed already in your heart's vain mania,
To plunge the freeborn Frenchman into servitude's
Disgrace and this great land, as if it were a boat,
To firmly fasten to your haughty ocean ship!
Ye fools! The royal coat of arms of France hangs on
The throne of God; and sooner do ye tear a star
From Heaven's carriage than a village from this realm,
Inseparably forever unified!—The day
Of vengeance hath arrived; while living ye no more
Shall e'er again take measure of the holy sea,
Which God as land's divider 'tween both you and us
Hath set and which ye have transgressed outrageously.
MONTGOMERY *(lets her hand loose):*
  O I must perish! Shudd'ring death now seizes me.
JOHANNA: Die, friend! Why tremble thus so timidly 'fore
  death,
The inescapable fate? —Behold me! Look!
A virgin am I merely, born a shepherdess;
Not to the sword accustomed is this hand,
Which bore the innocent and pious shepherd's staff.
Yet separated from the meadows of mine home,
From father's bosom, from the sister's loving breast,
Must I here, I must—the godly voice impels me, not
Mine own desires—a bitter harm for you, for me
No joy, a ghost of consternation, strangling go,

Death spread abroad and be at last its sacrifice!
For I'll ne'er see the day of joyous going home:
To many of your folk shall I still fatal be,
Still many widows shall I make, but in the end
I shall myself be killed and shall my fate fulfill.
—Fulfill thou also thine. Now seize thy sword afresh,
And for the sweetest prize of life we shall contend.

MONTGOMERY (*stands up*):
Now, if thou mortal art as I and weapons can
Thee injure, it can also to mine arm be destined,
By sending thee to Hell, to finish England's woe.
Within God's gracious hands I lay my destiny.
Call thou condemnèd one upon thine hellish spirits,
To stand by thee! Now ready to defend thy life!

(*He seizes shield and sword and presses in on her, martial music resounds in the distance, after a brief duel* MONTGOMERY *falls.*)

SCENE VIII

JOHANNA *alone*.

Thy foot transported thee to death—Depart!
(*She steps away from him and remains standing thoughtfully.*)
Exalted Virgin, thou work'st mighty things in me!
Thou dost supply to mine unwarlike arm its strength,
This heart thou armest with inexorability.
My soul melts with compassion and mine hand doth shake,
As if it broke into a temple's holy frame,
The blooming body of th' opponent to do harm;
Already 'fore the iron's shining edge I shudder,
Yet if there's need, at once the strength is there for me,
And never erring in my trembling hand the sword
Doth reign itself, as if it were a living spirit.

SCENE IX

A KNIGHT *with closed visor.* JOHANNA.

KNIGHT: Accursèd one! Thine hour hath arrived,
   I sought thee on th' entire field of battle.
   Injurious deception, travel back
   To Hell, from whence thou hast ascended here!
JOHANNA: Who art thou, whom his evil angel sent
   To challenge me? Just like a prince's is
   Thy manner, nor a Briton seemest thou to me,
   For the Burgundian band thee designates,
   Before which my sword's tip is pointed down.
KNIGHT: Rejected one, deserv'st thou not to fall
   Beneath a prince's noble hand. The axe
   O' th' hangman ought to sever from thy trunk
   Thy damnèd head and not the valiant sword
   Held by the royal Duke of Burgundy.
JOHANNA: So art thou then this noble Duke himself?
KNIGHT *(opens his visor):*
   I'm he. O wretch, now tremble and despair!
   Satanic arts shall shelter thee no more:
   Thou hast till now but weaklings overcome—
   A man stands 'fore thee.

SCENE X

DUNOIS *and* LA HIRE *to the preceding.*

DUNOIS: Turn thee, Burgundy!
   Contest with men, but not with virgin women.
LA HIRE: We'll guard the prophetess's holy head,
   First must thy dagger penetrate this breast—
BURGUNDY: 'Tis not this amorous Circe that I fear,
   Nor you, whom she's so shamefully transformed.
   O blush now, Bastard, shame on thee, La Hire
   That thou the ancient bravery to arts
   Of Hell degrad'st, and the contemptible

Shield-bearer makest of a devil's whore.
Come here! I bid you all! He doth despair
O' th' shield of God, who flees unto the devil.

(They prepare themselves to fight, JOHANNA *steps between them.)*

JOHANNA: Hold up!
BURGUNDY: Thou tremblest for thy paramour?
  Before thy very eyes shall he—
  (presses in on DUNOIS*)*
JOHANNA: Hold up!
  Part them, La Hire—No Frankish blood shall flow!
  Not by the sword this strife shall be decided.
  Another way is in the stars resolved—
  Now separate, say I—Hear and revere
  The spirit, which moves me, which through me speaks!
DUNOIS: Why dost thou mine uplifted hand restrain
  And stem the bloody judgment of the sword?
  The iron hath been drawn, it strikes the blow,
  Which shall avenge and reconcile our France.
JOHANNA *(places herself in the middle and separates both parties by a wide space in between them; to the* BASTARD*)*:
  Step to the side!
  (to LA HIRE*)*   Remain in fetters standing!
  I have to speak a word now with the Duke.
  (after all is quiet)
  What willst thou, Burgundy? Who is the foe,
  For whom thine homicidal glances seek?
  This noble prince is France's son as thou,
  This valiant is thy friend in arms and countryman,
  I am myself the daughter of thy fatherland.
  We all, whom thou dost strive t' annihilate,
  Belong among thine own—our outstretched arms
  Are open wide to welcome thee, our knees
  Are ready thee to venerate—our sword
  Against thee hath no tip. And venerable

Thy face is to us, e'en in hostile helm,
Which bears the precious features of our King.
BURGUNDY: With the cajoling tone of thy sweet speech
Wilt thou, O Siren! lure thy sacrifice.
Thou, crafty one, delude me not. Mine ear's
Secure against the snares of thy remarks,
And fiery arrows of thine eyes slide off
Upon the goodly armor of my bosom.
Now to arms, Dunois!
With blows and not with words let us contest.
DUNOIS: First words and later blows. Art thou afraid
I' th' face of words? That too is cowardice
And the betrayer of an evil cause.
JOHANNA: 'Tis not imperious need that driveth us
Unto thy feet; and not as supplicants
Do we before thee come.—Around thee look!
In ashes doth the English camp now lie,
And your dead ones are strewn across the field.
Thou hear'st the Frankish battle trumpets sound:
God hath decided, victory is ours.
The freshly broken branch of beauteous laurel
We are prepared to share with all our friends.
—O come o'er here! Come, noble fugitive!
O'er here, where there is right and victory.
E'en I, the God-sent one, extend to thee
The hand, just like a sister. Rescuing
I wish to draw thee o'er to our pure side!—
The Heaven is for France. And Heaven's angels—
Thou see'st them not—they're fighting for the King,
With lilies is each one of them adorned;
Clear white just like this banner is our cause,
The faultless Virgin is its spotless emblem.
BURGUNDY: Ensnaring is the lie's deceptive word,
And yet her speech is like that of a child.
If evil spirits lend the words to her,
So they triumphant copy innocence.
I will not listen further. To your weapons!
Mine ear, I feel, is weaker than mine arm.

JOHANNA: Thou nam'st me an enchantress, blamest me
　For hellish arts—Is making peace, is hate
　Resolving an affair of Hell? And from
　Th' eternal pool doth harmony come forth?
　What is there guiltless, holy, humanly good,
　If not the battle for the fatherland?
　Since when is nature so in struggle with
　Itself, that Heaven doth the righteous cause
　Desert and that the devil it defends?
　But if that, which I say to thee, is good—
　Where else than from above could I it draw?
　Who would have come to join with me upon
　My shepherd's sward, the childish shepherd's maid
　T' initiate to royalty's affairs?
　I've never stood before exalted princes,
　The art of speech is foreign to my mouth.
　Yet now, since I'm in need of moving thee,
　Possess I insight, knowledge of high things,
　Before my childlike view lies sunny fair
　The destiny of countries and of kings,
　And in my mouth a thunderbolt I bear.
BURGUNDY (*vividly moved, opens his eyes in her
　　direction and observes her with astonishment and
　　emotion*):
　What's wrong? What's happ'ning to me? Is't a god,
　Who in my deepest bosom turns mine heart!
　She never doth deceive, this touching form!
　No! No! I am through *magic's* power blinded,
　So hath it been by a celestial power:
　Mine heart tells me, she hath been sent by God.
JOHANNA: He hath been moved, he hath! I have not pled
　In vain; the thunder-cloud of anger melts
　Away from off his brow like dewy tears,
　And from his eyes, emitting beams of peace,
　The golden sun of feeling breaketh forth.
　—Off with the weapons—clasp now heart to heart—
　He weepeth, he is overcome, he's ours!

(Sword and banner sink from her, she hastens to him with outstretched arms and embraces him with passionate impetuosity. LA HIRE *and* DUNOIS *let their swords fall and hasten to embrace him.)*

ACT III

Court camp of the KING *at Chalons on the Marne.*

SCENE I

DUNOIS *and* LA HIRE.

DUNOIS: We were both friends o' th' heart and armèd brothers,
 To serve a single cause we raised our arm
 And held together fast in need and death.
 Let not the love of women rip the band,
 That hath endured each change of destiny.
LA HIRE: Prince, hark to me!
DUNOIS: You love the wondrous Maiden,
 And 'tis well known to me, what you intend.
 Unto the King you think immediately
 To go now and request the Virgin as
 A present to you—for your bravery
 He can't refuse the well-deservèd prize.
 But know—before I in another's arms
 Behold her—
LA HIRE: Hear me, Prince!
DUNOIS: It's not the eye's
 Swift fleeting pleasure that attracts me to her.
 Mine own unconquered sense a woman ne'er
 Hath stirred, until I saw the wondrous one,
 Whom the decree of God doth designate
 As savior to this realm and wife to me,
 And in the moment to myself I swore

An holy oath, to lead her home as bride.
For only she who's strong can be the friend
O' th' man who's strong, and this mine ardent heart
Doth yearn, to rest upon an equal breast,
That can encompass and endure its strength.

LA HIRE: How could I dare it, Prince, my weak deserts
To measure with your name's heroic fame!
Where'er Count Dunois standeth at the gate,
Must every other competition yield.
But yet a lowly shepherdess can not
Stand worthily as consort at your side:
The royal blood, that runs throughout your veins,
Doth show disdain for such a lowly mixture.

DUNOIS: She is the godly child of holy nature
As I, and is of equal birth to me.
Shall she dishonor any prince's hand,
Who is herself a bride unto pure angels,
Who doth her head with godly radiance
Surround, which brighter beams than earthly crowns,
Who sees the greatest, highest of this earth
Lie insignificant beneath her feet?
For all the princes' thrones, placed one upon
The other, till unto the stars built up,
Could not attain the height, where *she* doth stand
In her angelic majesty!

LA HIRE: The Monarch may decide.

DUNOIS: No, she herself
Must it decide! She hath the French made free,
And she herself must freely give her heart.

LA HIRE: Here comes the King!

SCENE II

CHARLES. AGNES SOREL. DU CHATEL, *the* ARCHBISHOP
and CHATILLON *to the preceding.*

CHARLES (*to* CHATILLON):
He comes! He wishes me to recognize

As his own King, you say, and pay me homage?
CHATILLON: Here, Sire, within thy royal town Chalons,
The Duke desires, my Governor, to cast
Himself unto thy feet.—He ordered me,
To greet thee as my Master and my King;
He follows on my heels, soon draws he near himself.
SOREL: He comes! O beauteous sunshine of this day,
Which joy doth bring and peace and harmony!
CHATILLON: My Lord will come here with two hundred knights,
He'll at thy feet bend down upon his knees,
Yet he expects, that thou wilt *not* endure it,
As thine own cousin friendly wilt embrace him.
CHARLES: Mine heart doth glow, to beat against his own.
CHATILLON: The Duke requests, that of the ancient strife
Upon the first return with not a word
There be a mention!
CHARLES: Sunk eternally
Let be the past i' th' Lethe. We now desire
To see but cheerful days in future times.
CHATILLON: Those who have fought for Burgundy, shall all
I' th' reconciliation be included.
CHARLES: I shall, this way, my royal kingdom double!
CHATILLON: And Isabeau, the Queen, if she accepts it,
Shall also be included in the peace.
CHARLES: She wages war with *me*, not I with *her*.
Our strife is through, so soon as she herself it ends.
CHATILLON: Twelve knights shall be the surety for thy word.
CHARLES: My word is holy.
CHATILLON: And the Archbishop
Shall share an holy host 'twixt thee and him
As pledge and seal of honest harmony.
CHARLES: So be my portion of eternal weal,
As heart and handshake are with me as one.
What other pledge demands the Duke as well?

CHATILLON (*with a glance at* DU CHATEL):
   Here see I *one*, whose very presence here
   Could poison the initial greeting.

   (DU CHATEL *goes silently.*)

CHARLES: Go,
   Now Du Chatel! Until the Duke thy sight
   Can tolerate, may'st thou remain concealed!
   (*He follows him with the eyes, then hastens after him
      and embraces him.*)
   Friend of justice! Thou wishest to do more
   Than this for my repose!

   (DU CHATEL *exits.*)

CHATILLON: The other points this instrument doth
      name.
CHARLES (*to the* ARCHBISHOP):
   Bring it in order. We approve of all,
   For us no price is too high for a friend.
   Go, Dunois! Take a hundred noble knights
   With you and cordially o'ertake the Duke.
   All of our soldiers shall bewreathe themselves
   With branches, that they may receive their brothers.
   Th' entire city for the feast adorn itself,
   And all the bells shall it aloud proclaim,
   That France and Burgundy unite anew.

   (A SQUIRE *comes. One hears trumpets.*)

   Hark! What's the meaning of the trumpet's call?
SQUIRE: The Duke of Burgundy now makes his entrance.
   (*Exits.*)
DUNOIS (*goes with* LA HIRE *and* CHATILLON):
   Up! Go to meet him!
CHARLES (*to* SOREL):
   Agnes, thou weepst? I also almost lack
   The fortitude, to suffer through this scene.
   How many of death's victims had to fall,
   Until we peacefully could meet again!

Yet every storm abates its rage at last,
The day grows into thickest night, and comes
The time, so ripen too the latest fruits.
ARCHBISHOP *(at the window):*
The Duke can hardly in the thronging crowd
Himself set free. They hoist him from his horse,
They kiss his very mantle, and his spurs.
CHARLES: It is a goodly people, in its love
Quick-blazing just as in its wrath.—How swift
Is it forgotten, that this very Duke
Defeated both their fathers and their sons!
The moment swallows an entire life.
—Compose thyself, Sorel! Thine ardent joy
Might be for him a prickle in his soul;
Nought shall him here aggrieve and make ashamed.

SCENE III

The preceding. DUKE OF BURGUNDY. DUNOIS. LA HIRE.
CHATILLON *and two other knights from the Duke's
retinue. The* DUKE *remains standing at the entrance, the*
KING *moves toward him, at once* BURGUNDY *approaches,
and at that moment, when he wants to lower himself
upon a knee, the* KING *receives him in his arms.*

CHARLES: You have surprised us—You to overtake,
Had been our thought—Yet you have speedy steeds.
BURGUNDY: Unto my duty brought they me.
(He embraces SOREL *and kisses her upon the brow.)*
With your
Permission, Cousin. That's our lordly right
In Arras, and no beauteous woman dares
Deny the custom.
CHARLES: Your court household is
The seat of courtly love, 'tis said, and mart,
Where all that's beautiful must be in stock.
BURGUNDY: We are a merchandizing folk, my King.

> Whate'er delicious grows in all the Heaven's regions,
> For show and for enjoyment is displayed
> Upon our mart at Bruges, the highest though
> Of all the many goods is woman's beauty.

SOREL: A woman's faith is still a higher prize,
> Yet on the market it is never seen.

CHARLES: You are in bad repute and standing, Cousin,
> That you defame a woman's fairest virtue.

BURGUNDY: Such heresy's its own worst penalty.
> Hail you, my Monarch! Early hath your heart,
> What me a savage life but lately, taught!
> *(He notices the* ARCHBISHOP *and extends his hand to him.)*
> Most venerable man of God! Your blessing!
> One meets you always in the right location,
> Who wants to find you, must in goodness walk.

ARCHBISHOP: My Master calls, whene'er He wills; this heart
> Is full of joy, and I can gladly part,
> Since mine own eyes have now this day beheld!

BURGUNDY *(to* SOREL*):*
> 'Tis said, you've of your noble stones deprived
> Yourself, in order to forge arms therefrom
> Against me? How? Are you so martially
> Intent? Was it so grave to you, to ruin me?
> But now our quarrel is foreby; and found
> Again is everything, which had been lost,
> Your jewelry even hath its way found back:
> For war against me was it once prescribed—
> Take it from mine hand as a sign of peace.
> *(He receives from one of his attendants the jewel casket and hands it over to her opened.* AGNES SOREL *looks disconcerted at the* KING*.)*

CHARLES: Receive the gift, it is a twofold precious pledge
> Of beauteous love to me and reconciliation.

BURGUNDY *(whilst he inserts a diamond rose in her hair):*

Wherefore is it not France's royal crown?
I would with equally disposèd heart
Upon this beauteous head it firmly place.
(seizing her hand meaningfully)
And—count on me, if you sometime should need
To have a friend!

(AGNES SOREL, *breaking out in tears, steps to the side, also the* KING *struggles against a great emotion, all bystanders, moved, look at both princes.*)

BURGUNDY *(after he hath looked at all of them by turns, throws himself into the arms of the* KING*)*:
    O my dear Sovereign!

(*In the same moment the three Burgundian knights hasten to* DUNOIS, LA HIRE *and the* ARCHBISHOP *and embrace one another. Both princes lie for a time speechless in one another's arms.*)

 I could despise you! You I could renounce!
CHARLES: Still! Still! No further!
BURGUNDY: And this Englander
 Could I crown! Swear loyalty unto this stranger!
 You, mine own King, into destruction plunge!
CHARLES: Forget it! All is now forgiven. All
 This single moment hath effaced. It was
 Our destiny, a most unhappy star!
BURGUNDY *(seizes his hand)*:
 I'll make amends! Believe me, that I will.
 For all your suff'ring you should be restored,
 Your entire royal realm you shall receive
 Again—and not one village shall be lacking!
CHARLES: We are now one. I fear no foeman more.
BURGUNDY: Believe me, I with happy heart did not
 Bear arms against you. O if you but knew—
 Wherefore have you this one not sent to me?
 (pointing toward SOREL*)*
 I would not have been able to resist her tears!
 —Now shall no might of Hell again divide

    Us, since we've clasped each other breast to
      breast!
    Now have I found my very own true place,
    Upon this heart my wand'ring journey ends.
ARCHBISHOP *(steps between both):*
    You are united, Princes! France doth rise
    A newly youthful Phoenix from its ashes,
    Upon us doth a beauteous future smile.
    The country's grievous injuries shall heal,
    The villages, which we've laid waste, the cities
    From their debris shall rise more splendidly,
    The fields shall deck themselves afresh with green—
    Yet, who hath fallen victim to your discord,
    The dead will stand up nevermore; the tears,
    Which from your strife have flowed, *are wept* and so
    Remain! The coming generation soon
    Will blossom, yet the past was misery's theft,
    The grandchild's bliss awakes no more the fathers.
    These are the fruits of your fraternal discord!
    Let it serve as a lesson to you! Fear the sword's
    Divinity, ere from the sheath you draw it.
    The mighty one can let loose war; yet not
    Made docile, as the hawk returneth from
    The air unto the hunter's hand, heeds not
    The savage god the call of human voice.
    Not twice in the right moment as today
    Comes forth the hand o' th' Savior from the clouds.
BURGUNDY: O Sire! An angel dwelleth at your side.—
    Where is she? Why do I not see her here?
CHARLES: Where is Johanna? Why is she not here
    With us in this most festive beauteous moment,
    Which *she* us granted?
ARCHBISHOP: Sire! The holy Maiden
    Loves not the quiet of an idle court,
    And if divine command doth not her call
    Into the light o' th' world, so she avoids
    Abashedly the idle gaze of common eyes!
    She certainly confers with God, when she

For France's benefit is not employed;
For blessings follow every step she takes.

SCENE IV

JOHANNA *to the preceding. She is in armor, but without helmet, and bears a wreath in her hair.*

CHARLES: Thou comest as a priestess decked, Johanna,
To consecrate the bond, that thou hast made?
BURGUNDY: How dreadful was the Virgin in the battle,
And how doth peace around her beam with grace!
—Have I my word absolved, Johanna? Art thou
Content, and do I thine applause deserve?
JOHANNA: To thee thyself hast thou the greatest favor shown.
Now thou dost shimmer in the blessèd light,
Since just now thou in blood-red gloomy shine
A dreadful moon didst in this heaven hang.
(looking around)
I found here many noble knights assembled,
And all their eyes are shining bright with joy—
A *single* sad one only have I met,
Who must conceal himself, where all rejoice.
BURGUNDY: And who is conscious of such heavy debt,
That of our favor he must needs despair?
JOHANNA: May he approach? O answer, that he may!
Thy merit make complete. A reconciliation
There's not, which doth not free the heart in full.
One drop of *hate*, which in the cup of joy
Remaineth, turns the blessèd drink to poison.
—No crime so bloody be, that Burgundy
Upon this day of joy it won't forgive!
BURGUNDY: Ha, thee I understand!
JOHANNA: And wilt forgive?
Thou wilt it, Duke?—Come in here, Du Chatel!

(She opens the door and leads DU CHATEL *in, the latter remains standing in the distance.)*

The Duke is with all of his enemies
Now reconciled, he's with thee too.

(DU CHATEL *walks a few steps nearer and seeks to read the*
DUKE'S *eyes.*)

BURGUNDY: What makest thou
Of me, Johanna? Know'st thou, what thou askest?
JOHANNA: A kindly master opens up his portals
For all the guests, no one doth he exclude;
Free, as the firmament contains the world,
So must his grace enclose both friend and foe.
The sun emits its beams of light alike
To all the spaces of infinity;
Like measuring the Heaven pours its dew
Out on all of the thirsting vegetation.
Whate'er is good and comes from up above,
Is universal and without reserve,
And yet within the folds the darkness dwells!
BURGUNDY: O she can switch with me, just as she wills,
Mine heart is yielding wax within her hand.
—Embrace me, Du Chatel! I pardon you.
Ghost of my father, be not wroth, if I
The hand, which murdered thee, in friendship seize.
Ye gods of death, account it not to me,
That I now break mine awful vengeance vow!
With you thereunder in th' eternal night,
Here beats no heart more, here is all eternal,
All stands immovably fast—yet otherwise
Is it up here above i' th' solar light:
The man, who is both lively and hath feeling,
Is easy victim of the mighty moment.
CHARLES (*to* JOHANNA):
What have I not to thank thee for, high Virgin!
How beauteously hast thou thy word fulfilled!
How quickly my whole fate is turned around!
Thou hast my friends won back to me, my foes
Hast plunged into the dust and from my cities
The foreign yoke dispensed with.—Thou alone

Achievest all.—Now speak, how pay I thee!
JOHANNA: Be always human, Lord, in luck, as thou
　In ill luck wast—and on the peak of greatness
　Forget not, what a friend doth weigh in need;
　In thine humiliation thou hast learnt it.
　Deny thy mercy and thy justice not
　To th' last one of thy folk; for from the herd
　God calls the savioress to thee—thou wilt
　Assemble all of France beneath thy scepter,
　The father and forefather of great princes be;
　Those after thee who come, shall brighter shine,
　Than those who went before thee on the throne.
　Thy stem will bloom, so long as it preserves
　Its love within its people's heart;
　But arrogance can lead it to its fall,
　And from the lowly huts, whence to thee now
　Hath come the savior, threatens mystically
　Destruction to thy guilt-bestained grandchildren!
BURGUNDY: Enlightened Maiden, whom the Spirit
　　inspires,
　If thine eyes penetrate into the future,
　So tell me too of mine own stem! Will it
　Expand majestically, as it's begun?
JOHANNA: Burgundy! To the level of the throne
　Hast thou thy chair raised up, and higher strives
　The haughty heart, it lifts into the clouds
　The daring house.—Yet from above a hand
　Will promptly order that its growth be stopped.
　Yet do not fear therefore thine house's fall!
　It lives on in a virgin brilliantly,
　And scepter-bearing monarchs, shepherds of
　Their folk shall blossom forth from out her womb.
　They then shall govern on two mighty thrones,
　The laws compose of all the world that's known
　And of a new one, which the hand of God
　Still hides behind unnavigated seas.
CHARLES: O speak, if it the Spir't reveals to thee,
　Will this new bond of friendship, which we've now

Revived, our sons' grandchildren also still
Unite in later times?
JOHANNA *(after a silence):*
                      Ye kings and rulers!
Fear have of discord! Waken not Dispute
Out of its cavern, where it sleeps; for once
Aroused, restrains it late itself again!
Grandchildren it begets, an iron race,
The fire ignites itself upon the fire.
—Demand no more to know! Take joy now in
The present, let me quietly conceal
The future!
SOREL: Holy Maiden, thou explorest
Mine heart, thou know'st, if it toward greatness vainly strives;
To me give too a pleasing oracle.
JOHANNA: The Spirit shows me but great world events—
Thy destiny doth rest in thine own breast!
DUNOIS: And yet what will be thine own destiny,
Exalted Maiden, whom the Heaven loves?
For sure the fairest bliss o' th' earth doth bloom for thee,
Since th' art so holy and devout.
JOHANNA: One's bliss
Dwells yonder in the lap of the eternal Father.
CHARLES: Thy fortune henceforth be thy Monarch's care!
For I will make thy name magnificent
Throughout all France; the latest generations
Shall call thee blessèd—and at once shall I
Accomplish it.—Kneel down!
(He draws the sword and touches her with the same.)
And now stand up
As one who's noble! I, thy King, do raise
Thee from the dust of thine own darksome birth—
Within their graves thy fathers I ennoble—
Thou shalt the lily wear i' th' coat of arms,
Thou shalt of equal birth be with the best
In all of France; alone the royal blood

Of the Valois be nobler than thine own!
The greatest of the great shall feel himself
Through thine own hand esteemed; mine be the care,
To marry thee unto a noble husband.
DUNOIS *(steps forth):*
Mine heart elected her, when she was lowly;
The recent honor, which shines round her head,
Increases not her merit nor my love.
Here in the countenance of mine own King
And of this holy Bishop I extend
To her the hand as to my princely consort,
If she would hold me worthy, to receive her.
CHARLES: Irresistible Maiden, wonder heapest thou
On wonder! Yes, I now believe, that nought's
To thee impossible. Thou hast o'ercome
This haughty heart, that until now spoke scorn
To love's omnipotence.
LA HIRE *(steps forth):*
                          Johanna's fairest jewel,
Know I her rightly, is her modest heart.
The homage of the greatest she is worth,
Yet ne'er will she her wish raise up so high.
She strives not dizzily for earthly highness,
The faithful inclination of an honest mind
Suffices her, as doth the silent lot,
That I do offer to her with this hand.
CHARLES: Thou too, La Hire? Two first-rate challengers,
Alike in martial fame and hero's virtue!
—Wilt thou, who reconciles my foes to me,
My kingdom doth unite, my dearest friends
Divide? But *one* of you can her possess,
And I esteem each worthy of such prize.
So speak thou now, thine heart must here decide.
SOREL *(steps nearer):*
The noble Virgin is surprised I see,
And modest shame puts color in her cheeks.
Now give her time, to question her own heart,
To trust a female friend and to unloose

The seal of her securely fastened breast.
Now is the moment come, when even I
May sisterly approach this virgin stern,
To her present my faithful silent bosom.—
Now let us womanly first think thereon
That which is womanly and then await,
What we shall here decide.

CHARLES *(about to go):* So be it then!

JOHANNA: Not thus, my Sire! What gave my cheeks their color,
Was not confusion of a silly shame.
I've nothing to confide unto this noble lady,
Of which I'd be ashamed i' th' face of men.
The choice of these good knights doth highly honor me;
But I did not desert my shepherd's mead,
To hunt for worldly, idle majesty,
Nor yet, to braid a bride's wreath in my hair,
Did I put on this brazen armament.
I have been called to quite another work—
The virgin pure alone can it achieve.
I am the warrioress o' th' highest God,
And to no man can I become a spouse.

ARCHBISHOP: To be the loving partner of a man
Is woman born—when she obeyeth nature,
She serveth Heaven then most worthily!
And hast thou satisfied the orders of
Thy God, who summons thee into the field,
So shalt thou lay thy weapons far from thee
And turn again unto the gentler sex,
Which thou hast disavowed, the which is not
Called on to do the bloody work of arms.

JOHANNA: Most reverend Lord, I know not yet to say,
What will the Spirit order me to do;
Yet when the time doth come, his voice will not
Be silent to me, and I'll it obey.
But now he calls me to complete my work.
The forehead of my Master hath not yet

Been crowned, the holy oil hath not yet wet
His head, nor is my Master yet called King.
CHARLES: We are about to go on th' way to Rheims.
JOHANNA: Let's not stand still, for all around our foes
Are working busily, to close thy way.
Yet I shall lead thee through their very midst!
DUNOIS: And yet when everything hath been achieved,
When we triumphant now to Rheims have marched,
Wilt thou then not permit me, holy Maiden—
JOHANNA: Doth Heaven will, that I in vict'ry crowned
Return from out this battle to the death,
So is my work completed—and the shepherdess
Hath no more business in the Monarch's house.
CHARLES (*seizing her hand*):
The Spirit's voice is now impelling thee,
Love is now silent in thy God-filled breast.
It will not always silent be, believe me!
Our weapons shall soon rest, for victory
Leads by the hand to peace, then joy returns
Once more to every breast, and tenderer
Emotions do awaken in all hearts.
They will awaken also in thy breast,
And tears of such sweet longing wilt thou weep,
As never have thine eyes them shed—this heart,
Which Heaven wholly now fulfills, will then
Unto an earthly friend in love be wending.
Now saving hast thou thousands brought to joy,
And, to bring joy to *one*, shalt thou thus end!
JOHANNA: Dauphin! Art thou of the divine appearance
Already tired, that thou its form destroy,
The virgin pure, whom God to thee hath sent,
Wilt downward drag into the common dust?
Ye blinded hearts! O, ye of little faith!
The Heaven's majesty around you shines,
Before your eye it doth unveil its miracles,
And ye perceive in me nought but a woman.
May any woman 'close herself with martial ore,
And interfere into the strife of men?

Woe's me, if I my God's avenging sword
   Bore in the hand and in the idle heart
   Did bear the inclination for the earthly man—
   'Twere better for me, were I never born!
   Such words no more, I say to you, if you
   Would not arouse to wrath the spirit in me!
   The eye of men, that longs for me, already
   To me is horror and a desecration.
CHARLES: Break off. It is in vain, her to bestir.
JOHANNA: Command, that one the warlike trumpets blow!
   I'm pressed and grow alarmed when arms are still,
   It chases me from out this restful state
   And drives me forth, that I my work fulfill,
   Commandingly reminding of my fate.

SCENE V

A KNIGHT *hastily to the preceding.*

CHARLES: What is't?
KNIGHT: The foe hath gone across the Marne
   And readies for engagement.
JOHANNA *(inspired):*   Fight and battle!
   Now is my soul delivered from its bonds.
   Equip yourselves, while I deploy the troops.
   (She hastens out.)
CHARLES: Follow her, La Hire!—E'en at the gates of Rheims
   They wish to make us battle for the crown!
DUNOIS: True courage drives them not. It is the last
   Attempt of feeble raging desperation.
CHARLES: Burgundy, I spur you not. Today's the day,
   To make amends for many evil days.
BURGUNDY: You shall be satisfied with me.
CHARLES: Myself,
   I'll go before you on the road of fame

And in the face o' th' coronation city
Will battle for my crown.—Now my dear Agnes!
Thy knight declares farewell to thee!
AGNES *(embraces him)*:
I do not weep, I tremble not for thee,
My faith grasps trustingly into the clouds!
So many pledges of its favor Heaven
Did not bestow, that we i' th' end should mourn!
With vict'ry crowned I shall embrace my Lord,
Mine heart tells me, in Rheims' o'ertaken walls.

(Trumpets resound with courageous tone and go, while the scene is being transformed, over into a wild martial turmoil; the orchestra joins in at the scene's opening and is accompanied by martial instruments behind the scene.)

The scene changes into an open region, which is bordered by trees.

During the music one sees soldiers rapidly draw away across the background.

SCENE VI

TALBOT, *supported by* FASTOLF *and accompanied by soldiers. At once thereafter* LIONEL.

TALBOT: Here underneath these trees now set me down,
And you betake yourself back into battle;
I do not need assistance, for to die.
FASTOLF: O most unhappy miserable day!

(LIONEL appears.)

To what a sight you're coming, Lionel!
Here lies the General wounded unto death.
LIONEL: That God forbid! O noble Lord, stand up!
Now is't not time, to sink down wearily.
Yield not to death, be master over nature
With your commanding will, that it may live!

TALBOT: In vain! The day of destiny hath come,
  The which shall overthrow our throne in France.
  In vain in battle full of desperation
  I bet my very last, it to avert.
  Crushed by the stroke of swordblade here I lie,
  No more to rise again.—Rheims hath been lost,
  So rush, to rescue Paris!
LIONEL: Paris hath made a treaty with the Dauphin,
  A messenger hath just brought us the news.
TALBOT (*pulls the bandage off*):
  So stream away, ye brooklets of my blood,
  For over-weary am I of this sun!
LIONEL: I can not stay here.—Fastolf, bring the General
  To a secure location, we can not
  Much longer hold ourselves in this position.
  Our forces flee already on all sides,
  The Maid doth push forth irresistably—
TALBOT: Nonsense, thou winnest, and I must succumb!
  Against stupidity e'en gods contend in vain.
  Exalted Reason, brightly shining daughter
  Of godlike head, thou wise establisher
  Of the world edifice, guide of the stars,
  Who art thou then, if thou, unto the tail
  Of foolishness' racing charger bound,
  And vainly calling, with the drunken one
  Must seeing plunge thyself into th' abyss!
  Accursèd be, who turns his life to what
  Is great and worthy and makes thought-out plans
  With sapient spirit! To the King of Fools
  Belongs the world—
LIONEL: Mylord! You have yet but
  A few more moments worth of life—now think
  Of your Creator!
TALBOT: Were we as brave men
  By other brave men overcome, we could
  Console ourselves with universal fate,
  Which always-altering revolves its sphere—
  Yet to succumb to such crude witch's play!

Was our industriously earnest life
Not worthy of a much more earnest exit?
LIONEL *(extends his hand to him):*
Mylord, farewell! The duty due of tears
I'll pay you honestly, when battle's through,
If I am then remaining still. But now
The Fate doth call me forth, that on the battlefield
Still judging sitteth and its lots doth shake.
I'll see you later in another world!
Brief is the parting for the lengthy friendship.
(Exit.)
TALBOT: Soon is it over, and I'll give to th' earth,
To the eternal sun the atoms back,
Which as delight and pain had joined in me—
And of the mighty Talbot, who the world
Did fill with his war fame, remains nought else
Except a handful of light dust.—So goes
The man unto his end—and the unique
Advantage, which from our life's struggle we
Take with us, is the insight into nought
And heartfelt scorn for everything thereof,
Which seemed to us exalted and worth wishing—

SCENE VII

CHARLES. BURGUNDY. DUNOIS. DU CHATEL
and SOLDIERS *enter.*
TALBOT *and* FASTOLF.

BURGUNDY: The bulwark hath been stormed.
DUNOIS: The day is ours.
CHARLES *(noticing* TALBOT*):*
See, who it is, who yonder from the light
O' th' sun takes grave involuntary leave?
His armor shows me not a wicked man—
Go, spring to him, if help avail him still.

    *(*SOLDIERS *from the King's retinue go thereto.)*

FASTOLF: Back! Keep away! Respect have 'fore the dead,
  Whom ye in life have never wished to near!
BURGUNDY: What see I! Talbot lies in his own blood!

(*He goes up to him.* TALBOT *looks at him staringly and dies.*)

FASTOLF: Away, Burgundy! Let the sight o' th' traitor
  Not poison be to th' final glance o' th' hero!
DUNOIS: The frightful Talbot! The unconquerable!
  Dost thou make do with such a narrow space,
  And the extensive earth of France could not
  Suffice the striving of thy giant spirit.
  —'Tis only now I greet you, Sire, as King:
  The crown was wavering upon your head,
  So long as in this body lived a spirit.
CHARLES (*after he hath silently contemplated the dead*):
  A Higher One hath him o'ercome, not we!
  He lies on France's earth, like to the hero
  Upon his shield, which he would not let go.
  Bring him away!

(SOLDIERS *lift up the dead body and carry it away.*)

  Peace be unto his dust!
  To honor him a monument shall rise:
  Here in the midst of France, where he his course
  As hero ended, shall his bones repose!
  So far as he no hostile sword did thrust—
  His epitaph shall be the place, where he is found.
FASTOLF (*hands over the sword*):
  Lord, I am now thy prisoner.
CHARLES (*gives him back his sword*):
                    Not so!
  Cruel war doth also honor pious duty:
  Free shall you follow to your master's grave.
  Now hasten, Du Chatel—Mine Agnes trembles—
  Release her from her fear for us—Bring her
  The message, that we live, that we o'ercame,
  And her in triumph lead to Rheims!

(DU CHATEL *exits.*)

SCENE VIII

LA HIRE *to the preceding.*

DUNOIS: La Hire!
Where is the Virgin?
LA HIRE: What? That ask I you.
I left her fighting at your side.
DUNOIS: I thought she was defended by your arm,
When hastened I to give the King mine aid.
BURGUNDY: Amid the thickest hostile swarm I saw
Not long ago her pure white banner wave.
DUNOIS: Woe's us, where is she? Evil me forebodes!
Come, hasten we to set her free.—I fear,
Her daring courage her too far hath led,
Surrounded by the foe she battles all alone,
And helpless she's o'ercome now by the throng.
CHARLES: Hie, rescue her!
LA HIRE: I follow, come!
BURGUNDY: We all!

(They hasten forth.)

Another deserted region of the battle field.

One sees the towers of Rheims in the distance, illuminated by the sun.

SCENE IX

A KNIGHT *in all black armor, with closed visor.* JOHANNA *pursues him up to the front of the stage, where he stands quietly and awaits her.*

JOHANNA: Thou cunning one! Now I discern thy malice!
Deceiving me hast thou by feigned escape
Lured me from battlefield and death and fate
Removed from many heads of British sons.
Yet now destruction catches thee thyself.

BLACK KNIGHT: Why dost thou me pursue and cling thyself
  So rage-inflamed unto my heels? It's not
  To me determined, by thine hand to fall.
JOHANNA: Abhorred art thou within my deepest soul,
  Just like the night, whose color is thine own.
  Thee to extinguish from the light of day
  Invincible desire impelleth me.
  Who art thou? Open up thy visor.—Had
  I not beheld the warlike Talbot fall
  In battle, so I'd say, that thou wert Talbot.
BLACK KNIGHT: Is thy prophetic spirit's voice now silent?
JOHANNA: It speaks aloud within my deepest breast,
  That at my side misfortune now doth stand.
BLACK KNIGHT: Johanna d'Arc! Up to the gates of Rheims
  Hast thou pressed forward on the wings of victory.
  Suffice thee now acquired fame. Dismiss
  The fortune, that hath served thee as a slave,
  Ere it in wrath itself sets free: it hates
  Fidelity, and till the end serves none.
JOHANNA: What mean'st thou that i' th' middle of my course
  I should stand still and all my work forsake?
  I'll it perform and thus fulfill my vow!
BLACK KNIGHT: Thee nothing can, thou mighty one, withstand,
  In every fight thou conquerest.—But go
  Into no battle more. Hark to my warning!
JOHANNA: This sword I shall not lay from out mine hands,
  Until the haughty England hath succumbed.
BLACK KNIGHT: Look there! There Rheims arises with its towers,
  The aim and purpose of thy drive—the cupola
  O' th' high cathedral thou beholdest shine,
  There wilt thou enter in triumphant pomp,

To crown thy King and thus fulfill thy vow.—
Go not therein. Turn round. Hark to my warning.
JOHANNA: Who art thou, double-tongued, deceitful being,
That wishes to alarm and me confuse?
How darest thou, deceitful one, announce
False oracles to me?
(The BLACK KNIGHT *wishes to depart, she steps in his way.)*
        No, thou dost give
Reply to me or perish by mine hands!
(She wishes to strike a blow at him.)
BLACK KNIGHT *(touches her with the hand, she remains standing motionless):*
Kill but what mortal is!
(Night, lightning, thunder clap. The KNIGHT *sinks.)*
JOHANNA *(stands astonished at the beginning, but soon composes herself again):*
It was nought living.—'Twas a phantom form
From out of Hell, a stubborn-minded spirit,
Who hath ascended from the fiery pool,
To shock my noble heart within my bosom.
Whom fear I with the sword of mine own God?
Triumphant shall I now complete my course,
And came e'en Hell itself into th' arena,
My courage shall not waver and not yield!
(She wants to exit.)

SCENE X

LIONEL. JOHANNA.

LIONEL: Accursèd one, prepare thee for the fight!
Not both of us shall leave this place alive.
The best of all my people hast thou killed,
The noble Talbot hast his mighty soul
Exhaled into my bosom.—I'll avenge
The valiant one or share his destiny.

And that thou knowest, who lends thee thy fame,
Though he may die or triumph—I am Lionel,
The last among the princes of our host,
And still not overcome is this mine arm.
(He presses in on her, after a brief duel she takes the sword from his hand.)
Unfaithful fortune!
(He struggles with her.)

JOHANNA *(seizes him from behind by the plume of his helmet and tears his helmet down violently, so that his face is exposed; at the same time she draws her sword with her right hand):*
                      Suffer, what thou soughtest,
Through me the Holy Virgin sacrifices thee!
(At this moment she looks at him in the face, his sight seizes her, she remains standing motionless and then slowly lets her arm sink.)

LIONEL: Why waitest thou and check'st the stroke of death?
Now take my life as well, thou took'st my fame—
I'm in thine hand, I do not wish forbearance.
(She gives him a sign with her hand, to withdraw.)
Shall I escape? Shall I owe thanks to thee,
That I'm alive?—I'd sooner die!

JOHANNA *(with averted face):*   Preserve thyself!
I wish to know nought of it, that thy life
Into my power had been given.

LIONEL: I hate thee and thy gift—I do not wish
Forbearance—Kill thine enemy, who thee
Abhors, who wished to kill thee.

JOHANNA: Kill me then—
And flee!

LIONEL: Ha! What is that?

JOHANNA *(conceals her face):* Woe unto me!

LIONEL *(steps nearer to her):*
Thou killest, it is said, all Englishmen,
Whom thou i' th' fight o'ercom'st—Wherefore spare me
Alone?

JOHANNA (*raises her sword with a quick motion over him, but lets it quickly sink again, as she looks him in the face*):
       O, Holy Virgin!
LIONEL: Wherefore nam'st thou
  The Holy One? She knoweth *nought* of thee,
  For the Heaven hath no part in thee.
JOHANNA (*in the most violent anxiety*):
                              What have
  I done! I have my promise broken now!
  (*She wrings her hands despairingly.*)
LIONEL (*observes her with sympathy and steps nearer to her*):
  Unhappy Maiden! I lament for thee,
  Thou movest me, thou hast been generous
  To me alone; I feel, that now mine hate
  Doth vanish, I must sympathize with thee!—
  Who art thou? Whence com'st thou?
JOHANNA: Away! Escape!
LIONEL: Thy youth, thy beauty cause me to lament!
  Thine aspect penetrates mine heart. I'd like
  To rescue thee—But tell me, how can I?
  Come! Come! Renounce this terrible
  Connection.—Cast away from thee, these arms!
JOHANNA: I am unworthy, them to bear!
LIONEL: Then cast
  Them from thee, quick, and follow me!
JOHANNA (*with horror*):   Thee follow!
LIONEL: Thou canst indeed be rescued. Follow me!
  I wish to rescue thee, but don't delay.
  A monstrous pain takes hold of me for thee
  And an unnameable longing, thee to rescue—
  (*takes hold of her arms*)
JOHANNA: The Bastard nears! It's they! They're seeking me!
  If they discover thee—
LIONEL: I'll shelter thee!
JOHANNA: I'll die, if by their hands thou wert to fall.
LIONEL: Am I then dear to thee?

JOHANNA: O Saint of Heaven!
LIONEL: Shall I see thee again? Or hear from thee?
JOHANNA: No! Never!
LIONEL: This thy sword as pledge, that I
See thee again!
(He tears her sword from her.)
JOHANNA: Thou, madman, darest it?
LIONEL: Now I shall yield to force, I'll see thee once
again!
(He exits.)

SCENE XI

DUNOIS *and* LA HIRE. JOHANNA.

LA HIRE: She lives! 'Tis she!
DUNOIS: Johanna, have no fear!
Thy friends are standing at thy side in force.
LA HIRE: Flees there not Lionel!
DUNOIS: Let him escape!
The righteous cause, Johanna, overcomes,
Rheims opens up its gates, and all the folk
Exultingly stream forth to meet their King—
LA HIRE: What ails the Virgin? She grows pale, she
sinks!
(JOHANNA becomes dizzy and wants to sink.)
DUNOIS: She hath been wounded—Tear her armor off—
It is her arm, and slight's her injury.
LA HIRE: Her blood escapeth.
JOHANNA: Let it with my life
Stream hence!
(She lies unconscious in LA HIRE'S arms.)

ACT IV

A festively decorated hall.

The columns encircled with festoons, behind the scene flutes and oboes.

SCENE I

JOHANNA:
>The weapons rest, the storm of war abates,
>On bloody battle follow song and dance;
>Through all the streets gay singing resonates,
>The church and altar shine with festal glance,
>And out of verdant boughs are built the gates,
>And winding wreaths the columns do enhance;
>Wide Rheims contains not each and every guest,
>Who seething streams unto the people's fest.
>
>And exultation of one joy bursts into flame,
>And but one thought now strikes in every breast;
>What bloody hatred recently did maim,
>That shares o'erjoyed the universal zest;
>He's only proudly conscious of his name,
>Who's to his Frankish heritage confessed:
>The glow o' th' ancient crown is now made new,
>And to its royal son France pays his due.
>
>But me, who for this glory hath contended,
>The universal bliss doth me not sway;
>In me the heart is altered and is wended,
>From this festivity it flees away—
>Into the British camp it now hath wended,
>O'er there unto the foe my glances stray,
>And from the ring of joy must I now steal,
>The heavy guilt o' th' bosom to conceal.
>
>Who? I? Within mine own pure breast
>The image of a man do bear?
>This heart, which Heaven's glow hath blest,
>To risk an earthly love shall dare?

I, mine own country's savioress,
The highest God's own warrioress,
For mine own country's foe inflame!
Dare I to the chaste sun it name,
And I not be destroyed by shame!
*(The music behind the scene passes over into gentle,
    melting melody.)*
Woe is me! Woe's me! What tones!
How they do seduce mine ear!
Each one doth recall his voice,
Conjures up his image here!

Would the storm o' th' battle seize me,
Whizzing spears around me sound
In the burning struggle's roar!
I'd my courage find once more!

O these voices, O these tones,
How they do ensnare mine heart,
Every power in my bosom
They dissolve in soft desire,
Melt to tears in sorrow's fire!
(after a pause, more lively)
Should I have killed him? Could I, since I looked
Into his eyes? Kill him! I'd sooner have
The murd'rous steel upon mine own breast drawn!
And am I culpable, since I was human?
Is pity sinful?—Pity! Didst thou hear
The voice of pity and humanity
From others too, whom thy sword sacrificed?
Why was it silent, when the Welshman thee,
The tender stripling, for his life implored?
Deceitful heart! Thou liest to th' light eterne,
The pious voice of pity thee did spurn!

Why had I to behold him in the eyes,
To see the features of his noble face!
'Twas with thy glance that thine offense began,
Unhappy one! A sightless tool demandeth God,

With sightless eyes thou hadst it to attain!
So soon thou saw'st, God's shield did thee forsake,
The snares of Hell did thee at once enchain!
(The flutes repeat, she sinks into a silent melancholy.)
Pious staff! O had I never
Battle-sword exchanged for thee!
Had it never in thy branches,
Holy oak tree, rustled me!
Wert thou present to me never,
Lofty Queen of Heaven's sphere!
Take, I can't deserve it ever,
Thine own crown, it take o'er there!

Ah, I saw the Heaven ope
And the Blessed's countenance!
Yet on earth is all mine hope,
And i' th' Heaven is it hence!
Must thou me then with this burden,
This so terrifying trade?
Could I this mine heart then harden,
Which the Heaven feeling made?

Wilt thou thine own might proclaim,
Choose but those, who free of blame
Stand in thine eternal home:
Thine own spirits send to roam,
Who is pure, who will not die,
Who feels not, who doth not cry!
Not the tender virgin hail,
Not the herdmaid's spirit frail!

Care I for the lot of battles,
Or the discord of the kings?
Guiltless did I drive my lambs
On the silent mountain heights.
Yet thou rip'st me into living,
In the haughty Princes' hall,
Unto guilt my life thus giving,
Ah! 'twas not my choice at all!

SCENE II

AGNES SOREL. JOHANNA.

SOREL (*comes in lively emotion; when she catches sight of the* VIRGIN, *she hastens up to her and falls upon her neck; suddenly she remembers herself, she lets her loose and falls down before her*):
No! Not so! Here i' th' dust 'fore thee—
JOHANNA (*wants to lift her up*): Stand up!
What ails thee? Thou forgettest thee and me.
SOREL: Let me! It is the press of joy, which casts
Me down unto thy feet—I must pour forth
My boiling-over heart before my God.
I worship the Invisible in thee.
Thou art the angel, who hath led my Lord
To me at Rheims and with the crown adorned,
What I had never dreamt to see, it is
Fulfilled! The coronation train's prepared,
The Monarch stands in festive robes arrayed,
Assembled are the peers, the mighty ones
O' th' crown, to bear th' insignia of office;
To the cathedral flowing streams the people,
The roundelay doth sound, the bells resound.
O fullness of this bliss I cannot bear!
(JOHANNA *lifts her gently up.* AGNES SOREL *pauses for a moment, whilst she looks the* VIRGIN *more closely in the eye.*)
Yet thou remain'st e'er grave and stern; thou can'st
Good luck create, yet sharest thou it not,
Thine heart is cold, thou feelest not our joys.
Thou hast the Heaven's majesty beheld—
No earthly fortune moveth the pure breast.
(JOHANNA *seizes her hand with vehemence, but quickly lets it go again.*)
O could'st thou be a woman and be feeling!
Lay off this armament, there's no more war,
Confess that thou art of the gentler sex!

My loving heart flees shyly back from thee,
So long as thou art like the stringent Pallas.
JOHANNA: What askest thou of me!
SOREL: Disarm thyself!
Lay off this armament, for love doth fear
To draw near to this steel-becladden breast.
O be a woman and thou shalt feel love!
JOHANNA: Now shall I me disarm! Right now! To death
Will I in battle lay my bosom bare!
Not now—O would that seven folds of ore
Defend me 'fore your feasts, before myself!
SOREL: Count Dunois loveth thee. His noble heart,
To fame but opens and to hero's virtue,
It glows for thee in holy sentiment.
O it is fair, to see oneself belovèd by
A hero—'tis still fairer, him to love!
(JOHANNA *turns away with aversion.*)
Thou hatest him!—No, no, thou canst but him
Not love—however how shalt thou him hate!
One hates but him, who tears from us the one
Beloved, but none is the beloved to thee!
Thine heart is tranquil.—If it could but feel—
JOHANNA: Lament for me! Bemoan my destiny!
SOREL: What could be absent still unto thy bliss?
Thou hast thy word fulfilled: now, France is free,
Into the crowning city hast thou led
The King in triumph and attained high fame;
A happy people thee embrace, thee praise,
From every tongue doth inundating flow
Thy praise, thou art the goddess of this feast;
The King himself with his own crown beams not
More gloriously than thou.
JOHANNA: O could I but
Conceal myself i' th' deepest womb o' th' earth!
SOREL: What ails thee? What peculiar agitation!
Who'd dare to freely look upon this day,
If thou shouldst cast thy glances down to th' ground!
Let me blush red, me, who nearby to thee

>   So little feel, myself cannot advance
>   To thine heroic strength, unto thine height!
>   For shall I my whole weakness unto thee
>   Confess?—Not glory of the fatherland,
>   Not the refurbished splendor of the throne,
>   Not popular delight nor joy in triumph
>   Engageth this my fragile heart. There is
>   But one, who wholly it fulfills, it hath
>   Room only for this solitary feeling:
>   He is the one adored, the people cheer him,
>   Him do they bless, for him they strew these flowers,
>   'Tis he who's mine, he's my belovèd one.
> JOHANNA: O thou art happy! Bliss exalteth thee!
>   Thou lovest, where all love! Thou may'st thine heart
>   Unlock, express aloud thine own delight
>   And frankly bear it 'fore the gaze of men!
>   This feast o' th' kingdom is thy feast of love,
>   All of the people here, the infinite,
>   Who throng into these walls as in a flood,
>   They do thy feeling share, they hallow it;
>   Thee they do cheer, they weave a wreath for thee,
>   Thou with the universal bliss art one,
>   Thou lovest what brings joy to all, the sun,
>   And thy love's luster is, what thou dost see!
> SOREL (*falling around her neck*):
>   O thou enchantest me, thou knowest me full well!
>   Yes, I mistook thee, thou art cognizant of love,
>   And what I feel, thou speakest mightily.
>   Mine heart's released from its own fear and shyness,
>   It seethes with confidence to meet with thee—
> JOHANNA (*tears herself from her arms with vehemence*):
>   Forsake me. Turn thyself from me! Pollute
>   Thyself not with my pestilential nearness!
>   Be happy, go, let me in deepest night
>   My horror, my misfortune, my disgrace
>   Conceal—
> SOREL: Thou dost alarm me, I do not
>   Thee grasp; yet have I ne'er thee understood.

And always was thy dark deep being veiled to me.
Who would conceive, of what thine holy heart,
Thy pure soul's tender feeling is afeard!
JOHANNA: Thou art the holy one! Thou art the pure!
Saw'st thou mine innermost, thou shuddering
Didst thrust the foe from thee, the traitoress!

SCENE III

The preceding. DUNOIS. DU CHATEL *and* LA HIRE *with the banner of* JOHANNA.

DUNOIS: We search for thee, Johanna. All is now
Prepared, the King doth send us, he desires,
That thou 'fore him the holy banner bearest;
Thou shalt attach thyself to th' princes' ranks,
The closest to him thou thyself shalt go!
For he denies it not, and all the world
Shall witness it, that he to thee alone
Awardeth all the honor of this day.
LA HIRE: Here is the banner. Take it, noble Virgin,
The princes wait, and all the people tarry.
JOHANNA: I march before him! I the banner carry!
DUNOIS: Whom else doth it befit! Which other hand
Is pure enough, to bear the sanctuary!
Thou swang'st it in the fighting; carry it
As ornament now on this road of joy.
(LA HIRE *wants to hand the banner over to her, she recoils from it shuddering.*)
JOHANNA: Away! Away!
LA HIRE: What ails thee? Th' art afraid
I' th' face of thine own banner!—Look at it!
(*He unfurls the banner.*)
It is the same, which thou in triumph swang'st.
Thereon depicted is the Queen of Heaven,
Who hovers up above an earthly sphere;
For thus the Holy Mother taught it thee.

JOHANNA (*looking thither with horror*):
   'Tis she! Herself! Just as she came to me.
   See, how she looks this way and knits her brow,
   With glowing ire looks from her dark eyelashes!
SOREL: O she's beside herself! Come to thyself!
   Know thyself, thou seest nothing that is real!
   That is her earthly imitated form,
   She walks herself in the celestial choirs!
JOHANNA: Dreadful one, com'st thou to punish thy creature?
   Destroy me, punish me, thy lightning take
   And let it fall upon my guilty head.
   My bond I've violated—desecrated,
   And thy most holy name have I profaned!
DUNOIS: Woe's us! What is that! What unblessèd speech!
LA HIRE (*astonished, to* DU CHATEL):
   Do you this strange emotion understand?
DU CHATEL: I see, what I do see. A long time have
   I feared it.
DUNOIS: How? What do you say?
DU CHATEL: That which,
   I think, I dare not say. Would God, it were
   Now over, and the Monarch had been crowned!
LA HIRE: How? Hath the terror, which from out this banner
   Went forth, reverted back upon thyself?
   Before this symbol let the British quake,
   To enemies of France it's terrible,
   But to her faithful citizens it's gracious.
JOHANNA: Yes, thou say'st right! To friends it is propitious,
   And to the enemy it sendeth dread!
   (*One hears the coronation march.*)
DUNOIS: So take the banner! Take it! They begin
   The march, there's not a moment to be lost!

(*They force the banner upon her, she seizes it with violent resistance and exits, the others follow.*)

The scene changes into an open place before the cathedral.

SCENE IV

Spectators fill the background, from them emerge
BERTRAND, CLAUDE MARIE *and* ETIENNE *and come
forward. The coronation march resounds muffled from
the distance.*

BERTRAND: Hear the music! 'Tis they! They near already!
  What is the best to do? Shall we ascend
  Onto the platform or shall we press through
  The folk, that we lose nought of the procession?
ETIENNE: There is no way of getting through. All streets
  Are fully thronged by men, on steed and coaches.
  Let us approach up close unto these houses;
  Here we conveniently can see the march,
  When it comes passing by.
CLAUDE MARIE: But 'tis, as if
  One half of France were found together here!
  So overpow'ring is the flood, that it
  Us too hath lifted up and washed up here
  In the remote Lorrainian land!
BERTRAND: Who will
  At leisure sit within his corner, when
  I' th' fatherland that which is great transpires!
  It hath as well cost sweat and blood enough,
  Until the crown came to its rightful head!
  And our own Monarch, he who truly is,
  To whom we now present the crown, shall be
  Escorted no more meanly than Parisians' theirs,
  Whom they at Saint Denis have crowned! He is
  Not well-disposed, who from this feast remains
  Away nor shouts with us: Long live the King!

SCENE V

MARGOT *and* LOUISON *join the preceding.*

LOUISON: We shall again behold our sister, Margot!
  Mine heart doth throb.

MARGOT: We shall behold her both
In brightness and in majesty and tell
Ourselves: It is Johanna, it's our sister!
LOUISON: I can it not believe, till with mine eyes
I've seen her, that this mighty one, whom one
The Virgin calls of Orleans, our sister
Johanna is, who had to us been lost.
(The march comes ever closer.)
MARGOT: Thou doubtest still! Thou wilt with eyes it see!
BERTRAND: Give heed! They're coming!

SCENE VI

Flute players and oboists open the procession. Children follow, clothed in white, with branches in their hands, behind these two heralds. Thereafter a train of halberdiers. Magistrates follow in robes. Hereafter two marshals with their staffs, the DUKE OF BURGUNDY, *carrying the sword,* DUNOIS *with the scepter, other grandees with the crown, the imperial orb and the staff of justice, others with offerings; behind these knights in their order's decoration, choir boys with the censer, then two bishops with the sacred ampoule,* ARCHBISHOP *with the crucifix;* JOHANNA *follows him with the banner. She goes with sunken head and uncertain steps, her sisters give signs of astonishment and joy at her sight. Behind her comes the* KING, *under a canopy, which four barons carry; courtiers follow, soldiers conclude. When the procession is inside the church, the march is silent.*

SCENE VII

LOUISON. MARGOT. CLAUDE MARIE. ETIENNE.
BERTRAND.

MARGOT: Saw'st thou our sister?
CLAUDE MARIE: Who i' th' golden armor,

Who with the banner went before the King!
MARGOT: 'Twas she. It was Johanna, 'twas our sister!
LOUISON: And she did know us not! She did surmise
  The nearness not o' th' bosoms of her sisters.
  She looked to th' earth and did appear so pale,
  And trembling did she walk beneath her banner—
  When I beheld her, I could not rejoice.
MARGOT: So have I now our sister seen in both
  Her brightness and her majesty.—Who had
  So much as thought or in his dreams surmised,
  When she was driving herds upon our mountains,
  That we would ever see her in such splendor.
LOUISON: Our father's dream hath been fulfilled, that we
  At Rheims before our sister would bow down.
  That is the church, which father in his dreams
  Beheld, and everything is now fulfilled.
  Yet our father also saw aggrievèd faces—
  Ah, I'm disturbed, her to behold so grand!
BERTRAND: Why stand we idly here? Come in the church,
  To watch the holy rituals!
MARGOT: Yes, come!
  Perhaps, that we shall meet our sister there.
LOUISON: We have already her beheld—let us
  Return into our village.
MARGOT: What? Ere we
  Have greeted and addressed her?
LOUISON: She belongs
  To us no more, her place is with the kings
  And princes—Who are we, that we should crowd
  Ourselves with idle pride into her splendor?
  Strange was she to us, when she still was ours!
MARGOT: Will she of us be 'shamed and us despise?
BERTRAND: The King himself is not ashamed of us,
  He greeted friendly e'en the lowliest.
  Be she so highly risen, as she will—
  The King is greater still!

(Trumpets and kettle drums resound from the church.)
CLAUDE MARIE: Come to the church!

(They hasten to the background, where they lose themselves among the people.)

SCENE VIII

THIBAUT *comes, clothed in black,* RAIMOND *follows him and wishes to hold him back.*

RAIMOND: Stay, Father Thibaut! Stay back from the throng!
  Here do you see but men of cheerful mind,
  And your affliction doth offend this feast.
  Come! Let's flee from the town with rapid steps.
THIBAUT: Didst thou see mine unhappy child? Hast thou
  Observed her well?
RAIMOND: O, I implore you, flee!
THIBAUT: Didst thou take notice, how her paces wavered,
  How pale and how disturbed her visage was?
  The most unhappy one feels her condition;
  This is the moment now, to save my child,
  I will employ it.
  (He wishes to go.)
RAIMOND: Stay! What will you do?
THIBAUT: I'll take her by surprise, will hurl her down
  Out of her idle fortune, yes with force
  Will I conduct her back unto her God,
  Whom she renounces.
RAIMOND: Ah! Consider well!
  Do not plunge your own child into destruction!
THIBAUT: If but her soul doth live, her frame may die.

(JOHANNA rushes out of the church, without her banner; the people press forward, adore her and kiss her clothing, she is held up in the background by the crowd.)

She comes! 'Tis she! She rushes palely from the
  church,
Her anguish drives her from the sanctuary—
That is the heavenly tribunal, that
Reveals itself to her!—
RAIMOND: Farewell!
  Demand not, that I longer escort you!
  Full of hope I came, and go now full of pain.
  I have your daughter once again beheld
  And feel, that I have lost her now anew!

(*He exits,* THIBAUT *removes himself on the opposite side.*)

SCENE IX

JOHANNA. *The people. Thereafter her sisters.*

JOHANNA (*hath defended herself from the people and
  comes forward*):
  I can not stay—The spirits follow me,
  The organ's tones resound to me like thunder,
  Th' cathedral's vault collapses over me—
  The Heaven's free expanses must I seek!
  I left the banner in the sanctuary,
  This hand shall touch it never, nevermore!
  —To me it was, as had I my belovèd sisters,
  Margot and Louison, as in a dream
  Beheld to glide in front of me.—Alas!
  It was but a deceiving apparition!
  They're far, far and unreachably remote,
  As my childhood's, my innocence's bliss!
MARGOT (*stepping forward*):
  'Tis she, it is Johanna.
LOUISON (*hastens toward her*):
                    O, my sister!
JOHANNA: So was't no fancy—it is you—I clasp you,
  Thee, my Margot! And thee, my Louison!
  Here in the foreign, populated desert

I do embrace the trusting sisters' breast!
MARGOT: She knows us still, is still the goodly sister.
JOHANNA: And still your love conducts you here to me
So far, so far! You're wroth not at your sister,
Who loveless without leave departed you!
LOUISON: Thee God's dark providence conducted forth!
MARGOT: The fame of thee, which moveth all the world,
Which carrieth thy name on every tongue,
Hath us awakened in our tranquil village
And led unto this feast's festivity.
We come, that we behold thy majesty,
And we are not alone!
JOHANNA *(quickly):* Our father is with you!
Where, where is he? Why doth he hide himself?
MARGOT: Our father is not with us.
JOHANNA: Not? He doesn't want
To see his child? You bring me not his blessing?
LOUISON: He knows not, that we're here.
JOHANNA: He knows it not!
Wherefore then not?—You are confused? You're silent
And look to th' earth! Now say, where is our father?
MARGOT: Since thou art gone—
LOUISON *(beckons her):* Margot!
MARGOT: Our father hath
Become depressed.
JOHANNA: He is depressed!
LOUISON: Take comfort!
Thou knowest Father's e'er foreboding soul!
He will compose himself, he'll rest content,
When we convey to him, that thou art happy.
MARGOT: But art thou happy? Yes, thou must be so,
Since thou so great art and esteemed!
JOHANNA: I am,
Since I behold you once again, your voice
Do recognize, belovèd tone, I am
Reminded of paternal fields once more.
There did I drive the herds upon our summits,

There was I happy as in Paradise—
Can I be not again, nor so become once more!
(She conceals her face on LOUISON'S *breast.* CLAUDE MARIE, ETIENNE *and* BERTRAND *appear and remain standing timidly in the distance.)*

MARGOT: Come, Etienne! Bertrand! Claude Marie!
Our sister is not proud, she is so mild
And speaks so friendly, as she ne'er hath done,
When she still in the village lived with us.
(The former step nearer and want to extend their hands to her, JOHANNA *looks at them with a staring glance and falls into a deep astonishment.)*

JOHANNA: Where was I? Speak to me! Was it all but
A lengthy dream, and am I now awake?
Am I away from Dom Remi? Is't not!
I fell asleep beneath the magic tree
And am awake, and you stand round me here,
The well-beknown familiar characters?
I have about these sovereigns and these fights
And deeds of warfare merely dreamt—they were
But shadows, which passed by in front of me,
For vividly one dreams beneath this tree.
How came you unto Rheims? How came I here
Myself? Ne'er, ne'er forsook I Dom Remi!
Confess it frankly and mine heart give joy.

LOUISON: We are in Rheims. Thou hast not merely dreamt
About these deeds, thou hast them all indeed
Accomplished.—Know thyself, look round thee here,
And feel thy glowing golden armament!
*(*JOHANNA *moves her hand towards her breast, reflects and is startled.)*

BERTRAND: From mine own hand you did receive this helm.

CLAUDE MARIE: It is no wonder, that you think you dream,
For what you have accomplished and have done,
Can not occur more wondrous in a dream.

JOHANNA *(quickly)*:
   Come, let us flee! I'll go with you, I'll go
   Back to our village, to our father's lap.
LOUISON: O come! Come with us!
JOHANNA: All these people do
   Extol me far beyond what I deserve!
   You have beheld me childish, small and weak:
   You love me, yet you do not worship me!
MARGOT: Thou would'st forsake all this magnificence?
JOHANNA: I cast it from me, the detested finery,
   The which your heart divideth from mine heart,
   And I'll become once more a shepherdess.
   Just like a lowly maid will I serve you,
   And I'll repent with strictest penitence,
   That I have vainly raised myself o'er you!
   (Trumpets resound.)

SCENE X

The KING *steps out of the church; he is in the coronation robes.* AGNES SOREL, ARCHBISHOP, BURGUNDY, DUNOIS, LA HIRE, DU CHATEL, *knights, courtiers, and the people.*

ALL VOICES *(shout repeatedly, during which the* KING *comes forward)*:
   Long live the King! Our Sovereign Charles the
      Seventh!
   (Trumpets join in. On a signal, which the KING *gives, the heralds impose silence with lifted staffs.)*
KING: My goodly people! Thank you for your love!
   The crown, which God hath placed upon our head,
   It was obtained and conquered by the sword,
   With noble blood of citizens 'tis wet,
   Yet peaceful shall the olive branch grow green
   Around it, thanked be all, who for us fought,
   And all of those, who did resist us, be
   Forgiven, for God hath us mercy shown,

And our initial royal word be—Mercy!
PEOPLE: Long live the King! Our Sovereign Charles the
   Good!
KING: From God alone, the Highest Ruling One,
Do France's kings receive their royal crown.
But we have in a way that can be seen
Received it from His hand.
(turning to the VIRGIN*)*
Here stands the one dispatched by God, who gave
You once again your own ancestral King,
The yoke of foreign tyranny hath broken!
Her name shall equal be to Saint Denis,
Who is protector of this land of ours,
And to her fame an altar shall arise!
PEOPLE: Hail, Hail the Virgin, the Deliveress!
(trumpets)
KING *(to* JOHANNA*):*
If thou by mankind art begot as we,
So say, what fortune can make thee rejoice;
Yet if thy fatherland is there above,
If thou the brilliance of celestial nature
Within this virgin body dost conceal,
So take away the fetters of our senses
And let us thee behold in thy bright form,
As Heaven seeth thee, that we adoring
Shall in the dust thee honor.
(A universal silence, every eye is directed toward the
   VIRGIN*)*
JOHANNA *(suddenly crying out):*
                    God! My father!

SCENE XI

The preceding. THIBAUT *steps from the crowd and
stands directly opposite* JOHANNA.

SEVERAL VOICES: Her father!
THIBAUT: Yes, her miserable father,

    Who the unhappy one begot, whom God's
    Tribunal driveth, his own daughter to accuse.
BURGUNDY: Ha! What is that!
DU CHATEL: Now doth it dreadful dawn!
THIBAUT *(to the* KING*)*:
    Thinkst thou, thou wilt be rescued by God's might?
    Deluded prince! Ye blinded Frankish folk!
    Thou hast been rescued by the Devil's art.
    (All step back with horror.)
DUNOIS: Doth this man rave?
THIBAUT: Not I, but thou dost rave,
    And this one here, and also this wise Bishop,
    Who do believe, the Lord of Heaven would
    Proclaim Himself through such a wretched maid.
    Let's see, if she e'en in her father's brow
    Maintains the conjury of daring lies,
    Wherewith she did deceive both folk and King.
    Respond to me i' th' name o' th' Trinity:
    Dost thou belong to th' Holy and the Pure?
    (Universal silence, all glances are drawn toward her; she stands motionless.)
SOREL: God, she grows dumb!
THIBAUT: That must she 'fore the dreadful name,
    That in the very depths of Hell
    Is to be dreaded!—She a holy one,
    By God dispatched!—Upon a cursèd place
    It was conceived, beneath the magic tree,
    Where e'en from olden times the evil spirits
    Conducted Sabbath—here she bartered her
    Immortal part unto the foe of man,
    That he extol her with brief worldly fame,
    Let her lay bare her arm, behold the points,
    Wherewith she hath received the mark of Hell!
BURGUNDY: Atrocious!—Yet one must believe the father,
    Who testifies against his very daughter!
DUNOIS: No, one should not believe the raving one,
    Who in his very child reviles himself!

SOREL *(to* JOHANNA*):*
O speak! Break through this most unhappy silence!
We've faith in thee! Our trust is firm in thee!
A word from out thy mouth, a single word
Shall us suffice—However speak! Destroy
This ghastly accusation—Just declare,
Thou art not guilty, and we've faith in thee.
(JOHANNA *stands motionless,* AGNES SOREL *steps away from her with horror.)*

LA HIRE: She is afraid. Astonishment and dread
Lock up her mouth.—Before such horrible
Indictment innocence itself must quake.
(He draws near to her.)
Compose thyself, Johanna. Feel thyself.
The guiltless hath a tongue, a victor's view,
Which strikes down slander with the force of lightning!
In noble wrath arouse thyself, look up,
Rebuke and put to shame unworthy doubt,
Which doth abuse thine holy virtue.
(JOHANNA *stands motionless.* LA HIRE *steps back in shock, the commotion increases.)*

DUNOIS: What fears the folk? Why tremble even princes?
She is not guilty—I will vouch for that,
Myself, for her with all my princely honor!
Here do I cast my knightly gauntlet hence:
Who dares, to name her as a guilty one?
(A violent thunder clap, all stand in dread.)

THIBAUT: Give answer by the God, who up there thunders!
Speak, thou art guiltless. Disavow it, that the foe
Is in thine heart, and give the lie to me!
(A second, stronger clap; the people flee to all sides.)

BURGUNDY: Protect us God! O what a dreadful sign!

DU CHATEL *(to the* KING*):*
Come! Come, my Sovereign! Flee from out this place!

ARCHBISHOP *(to* JOHANNA*):*
I' th' name of God I ask thee: Art thou silent

From out of feeling innocence or guilt?
If doth this voice of thunder speak for thee,
So seize this crucifix and give a sign!

(JOHANNA *remains motionless. New violent thunder
claps. The* KING, AGNES SOREL, ARCHBISHOP,
BURGUNDY, LA HIRE *and* DU CHATEL *exit.*)

SCENE XII

DUNOIS. JOHANNA.

DUNOIS: Thou art my wife—I have believed on thee
Upon first sight, and just so think I still.
I've faith in thee more than in all these signs,
Than in this thunder e'en, which speaks above.
In noble wrath th' art mute, disdainest it,
Embedded in thine holy innocence,
So scandalous suspicion to refute.
—Disdain it, but entrust thyself to me,
Upon thine innocence have I ne'er doubted.
Tell me no word, thine hand alone give me
As pledge and token, that thou dost rely
Upon mine hopeful arm and thy good cause.
(*He extends his hand to her, she turns away from him
with a convulsive motion; he remains standing in
rigid terror.*)

SCENE XIII

JOHANNA. DU CHATEL.
DUNOIS. *Finally* RAIMOND.

DU CHATEL (*coming back*):
Johanna d'Arc! The Monarch will permit,
That you depart the city unimpaired.
The gates stand open to you. Have no fear
Of an offense. The Monarch's peace protects you.—

Count Dunois, follow me! You have no honor,
To tarry longer here.—O what an ending!

(He leaves. DUNOIS *starts up from his numbness, casts another glance at* JOHANNA *and exits. The latter stands all alone for a moment. Finally* RAIMOND *appears, remains standing a while in the distance and looks at her with quiet pain. Then he steps up to her and seizes her by the hand.)*

RAIMOND: Take hold o' th' moment. Come! O come! The streets
Are clear. Give me your hand. I'll lead you hence.

(At his sight she gives a first sign of feeling, she looks at him stiffly and glances to the Heaven; then she seizes him violently by the hand and exits.)

ACT V

A wild forest.

In the distance charcoal-burners' huts. It is entirely dark, violent thunder and lightning, shooting therebetween.

SCENE I

CHARCOAL-BURNER *and* CHARCOAL-BURNER'S WIFE.

CHARCOAL-BURNER:
That is a gruesome, murd'rous thunderstorm!
The Heaven threatens to pour down on us
In fiery brooks, and in the brilliant day
It's night, that one the stars above might see.
As if all Hell had been let loose the storm
Doth fume, the earth doth quake, and trees of ash
Grown old with years bend low their cracking crowns.
And this horrific war up there above,
Which even teaches gentleness to savage beasts,

That makes them tamely hide themselves within their
      caves,
   Among mankind can not establish peace—
   From out the howling of the winds and storm
   You hear the thunder clap of cannon fire;
   Both of the armies stand so near the other,
   That but the forest parts them, and each hour
   It can explode in bloody dreadfulness.
CHARCOAL-BURNER'S WIFE:
   God stand by us! Our enemies indeed
   Already were defeated and dispersed—
   How comes it, that they frighten us anew?
CHARCOAL-BURNER:
   That is, because they fear the King no more.
   E'er since the Maid became a witch at Rheims,
   The evil foe no longer helpeth us,
   All now goes backwards.
CHARCOAL-BURNER'S WIFE: Hark! Who neareth here?

SCENE II

RAIMOND and JOHANNA to the preceding.

RAIMOND: Here see I shelters. Come, here do we find
   A lodging 'fore the raging storm. You can't
   Endure much longer, for three days already
   You've wandered 'round, escaping human eyes,
   And savage roots were your sole nourishment.
   (The storm abates, it becomes clear and calm.)
   They're friendly charcoal-burners. Come inside.
CHARCOAL-BURNER:
   You seem to be in need of rest. Come in!
   Whate'er our wretched roof provides, is yours.
CHARCOAL-BURNER'S WIFE:
   What doth the tender virgin want with arms?
   Of course! The present is a grievous time,
   Where e'en the woman puts herself in armor!

The Queen herself, Dame Isabeau, 'tis said,
Is seen in armor in the foeman's camp,
As well a virgin, maiden of a shepherd,
Hath for the King, our Lord, engaged in battle.

CHARCOAL-BURNER:
What do you say? Go in the cottage, bring
A beaker of refreshment to the virgin.
(CHARCOAL-BURNER'S WIFE *goes to the cottage.*)

RAIMOND (*to* JOHANNA):
You see, not every human being's cruel,
E'en in the wilderness dwell gentle hearts.
Now lighten up! The storm hath ceased its raging,
And beaming peacefully the sun doth set.

CHARCOAL-BURNER:
I think you wish to join our Monarch's host,
Since you set out in arms—Be on your guard!
The Englishmen have set up camp nearby,
And troops of theirs patrol throughout the woods.

RAIMOND: Woe's us! How are we to escape?

CHARCOAL-BURNER: Remain,
Until my boy returneth from the city.
He shall conduct you forth on hidden paths,
So that there's nought for you to fear. We know
The by-ways.

RAIMOND (*to* JOHANNA):
        Lay the helm off and the armor;
They make you known and give you no protection.
(JOHANNA *shakes her head.*)

CHARCOAL-BURNER:
The virgin is quite sad—Be still! Who comes there?

SCENE III

The preceding. CHARCOAL-BURNER'S WIFE *comes out of the cottage with a beaker. The* CHARCOAL-BURNER'S BOY.

CHARCOAL-BURNER'S WIFE:
It is the boy, for whose return we wait.

(to JOHANNA*)*
  Drink, noble Virgin! May God bless it you!
CHARCOAL-BURNER *(to his* SON*):*
  Com'st thou, Anet? What bringst thou?
CHARCOAL-BURNER'S BOY *(hath looked the* VIRGIN *in the eye, who just then raises the beaker to her mouth; he recognizes her, steps up to her and tears the beaker from her mouth):* Mother! Mother!
  What do you do? Whom do you host? That is the witch
  of Orleans!
CHARCOAL-BURNER *and his* WIFE:
  God grant us mercy!

(They cross themselves and flee.)

SCENE IV

RAIMOND. JOHANNA.

JOHANNA *(composed and gentle):*
  Thou see'st, the curse pursues me, and all flees me;
  Care for thyself and also me forsake.
RAIMOND: I you abandon! Now! And who should your
  Companion be?
JOHANNA: I am not unaccompanied.
  Thou hast the thunder clapping heard o'er me.
  My fate conducteth me. Care not, I shall
  Attain my goal, without my seeking it.
RAIMOND: Where will you go? Here stand the Englishmen,
  Who to you swore a wrathful, bloody vengeance—
  There stand our forces, who have you expelled,
  Have banished—
JOHANNA: Nought occurs to me, but what must be.
RAIMOND: Who shall seek out your food? Who you protect
  From savage beasts and still more savage men?

You care for, if you're ill and miserable?
JOHANNA: I know all of the herbs, all of the roots;
From mine own sheep I learned how to discern
The healthy from the poisonous—I know
The orbits of the stars and drift o' th' clouds,
And I do hear the rush of hidden springs.
A man needs little, and all nature's rich
In life.
RAIMOND *(seizes her by the hand):*
        Will you not look into yourself?
Will you not reconcile with God—return
Repenting to the Holy Church's womb?
JOHANNA: E'en thou dost hold me guilty of grave sin?
RAIMOND: Must I not? Your own taciturn confession—
JOHANNA: Thou, who hast followed me into my misery,
The only being, who to me stayed true,
To me did chain himself, when all the world
Me did expel—thou too holdst me an outcast,
Who disavows her God—
(Raimond is silent.)   O that is hard!
RAIMOND *(astonished):*
You were then really not a sorceress?
JOHANNA: I a sorceress?
RAIMOND: And these miracles
You had performed them with God's power and
That of his holy saints?
JOHANNA: How otherwise!
RAIMOND: And you kept silent to this terrible
Indictment?—You are speaking now, and 'fore the King,
Where speaking would have mattered, you were silent!
JOHANNA: I did submit in silence to my fate,
That God, my Master, over me decreed.
RAIMOND: You could give no reply unto your father!
JOHANNA: Since it from father came, so came't from God,
And fatherly will also be the proof.

RAIMOND: The Heav'n itself attested to your guilt!
JOHANNA:
  The Heaven spake, hence I was silent.
RAIMOND: How? You could
  Have cleansed yourself with but a word, and left
  The world in this unfortunate mistake?
JOHANNA: 'Twas no mistake, it was a dispensation.
RAIMOND: You innocently suffered all this shame,
  And no complaint did issue from your lips!—
  I am amazed at you, I stand in shock,
  Mine heart takes heed within my deepest bosom!
  O gladly do I take your word for truth,
  For hard it were for me, to think you guilty.
  Yet could I dream, that any human heart
  Would bear in silence this monstrosity!
JOHANNA: Do I deserve, to be the one dispatched,
  If blindly I did not my Master's will esteem?
  And I am not so wretched, as thou thinkst.
  I suffer want, yet that is no misfortune
  For my condition; I'm in flight and banned,
  Yet in the desert learn to know myself.
  There, where the glow of honor circled me,
  There was the strife within my breast; I was
  The most unhappy one, when to the world
  I seemed the one most to be envied—Now
  I have been healed, and this strong storm in nature,
  Which threatened its destruction, was my friend,
  It hath the world made pure and also me.
  In me is peace—Now come, whatever will,
  I am no longer conscious of my weakness!
RAIMOND: O come, come, let us hie, your innocence
  Loud, loud 'fore all the world to manifest!
JOHANNA: Who this confusion did dispatch, will it dispel!
  Save when it's ripe, doth fall the fruit of fate!
  A day will come, which will me purify.
  And who've me now rejected and condemned,
  They shall become aware of their delusion,
  And tears will flow then for my destiny.

RAIMOND: I should endure in silence, till perchance—
JOHANNA (*seizing him softly by the hand*):
  Thou seest but the naturalness of things,
  For by the earthly band thy view is veiled.
  I have what is undying with mine eyes
  Beheld—without the gods no hair doth fall
  From head of man—Dost thou the sun see there
  Descending in the heavens? So indeed
  It will return i' th' morning in its clarity,
  So shall the day of truth come ineluctably!

SCENE V

The preceding. QUEEN ISABEAU *with soldiers appears in the background.*

ISABEAU (*still behind the scene*):
  This is the way into the English camp!
RAIMOND: Woe's us! the foemen!
  (SOLDIERS *enter, as they enter notice* JOHANNA *and reel back terrified.*)
ISABEAU: Now! what halts the march!
SOLDIERS: God stand by us!
ISABEAU: A ghost affrightens you?
  Are you all soldiers? Cowards are you!—How?
  (*She presses through the others, steps forward and comes back, as she perceives the* VIRGIN.)
  What see I! Ha!
  (*Quickly composes herself and steps towards her.*)
              Surrender! Thou art now
  My prisoner.
JOHANNA: I am.
  (RAIMOND *flees with signs of desperation.*)
ISABEAU (*stepping back astonished*):
              Put her in chains!
  (*The* SOLDIERS *timidly approach the* VIRGIN, *she extends her arms and is fettered.*)
  Is that the Mighty One, the Terrible,

    Who scared away your troops as were they lambs,
    Who now her very self cannot protect?
    Doth she work wonders but, where one hath faith,
    And when a man meets her, become a woman?
    (to the VIRGIN*)*
    Wherefore departest thou thine host? Where is
    Count Dunois, thy knight and thy protector?
JOHANNA: I have been banned.
ISABEAU *(stepping back astonished):*
    What? How? Thou hast been banned?
    Art banned by Dauphin!
JOHANNA: Question not! I am
    Within thy power—now decide my fate.
ISABEAU:
    Art banned, since thou hast saved him from th' abyss,
    Hast placed the crown upon his head at Rheims,
    Hast made him Monarch over all of France?
    Art banned! Therein I recognize my son!
    —Lead her to camp. Display unto the army
    The dreaded ghost, before whom they so trembled!
    She a sorceress! Her only magic
    Is your delusion and your timid heart!
    She is a foolish maid, who sacrificed herself
    To save her King and now receives the King's
    Reward therefor.—Bring her to Lionel!
    The fortune of the Franks I send him bound.
    I'll follow soon.
JOHANNA: To Lionel! Here murder me
    At once, before thou sendest me to Lionel.
ISABEAU *(to the* SOLDIERS*):*
    Now harken to mine order. Hence with her!
    (Exits.)

SCENE VI

JOHANNA. SOLDIERS.

JOHANNA *(to the* SOLDIERS*):*
    Ye Englishmen, endure not, that alive

I from your hands escape! Avenge yourselves!
Draw forth your swords, submerge them in mine heart,
Drag me unsouled unto your General's feet!
Think, that 'twas I, who your most excellent
Hath murdered, who no pity bore for you,
Who made entire streams of English blood
To spill, who hath your brave, heroic sons
Deprived the day of joyous going home!
Now take a bloody vengeance! Murder me!
You have me now; not always may you me
So weak behold—
LEADER OF THE SOLDIERS:
    Do, what the Queen commanded you!
JOHANNA: Shall I
Become yet more unhappy, than I was?
O dreadful Saint! thine hand is so severe!
Hast thou thy grace towards me in full repealed?
No God appears, no angel is still here!
The wonders rest, the Heaven hath been sealed.
(*She follows the* SOLDIERS.)

SCENE VII

The French camp.

DUNOIS *between the* ARCHBISHOP *and* DU CHATEL.

ARCHBISHOP: Subdue your ominous ill temper, Prince!
Come with us! Turn again unto your King!
Do not forsake the universal cause
Within this moment, when we, once again
Oppressed, have need of your heroic arm.
DUNOIS: Wherefore are we oppressed? Wherefore arises
The enemy again? All had been done,
France was triumphant and the war was ended.
You have expelled the savioress—now save
Yourself! However I will not behold
The camp again, when she's no longer there.
DU CHATEL: Accept our better counsel, Prince. Dismiss

    Us not with such an answer!
DUNOIS: Silence, Du Chatel!
    I hate you, from you wish I nought to hear.
    You are the one, who first hath doubted her.
ARCHBISHOP: Who had not erred about her and would not
    Have wavered on this most unhappy day,
    When every sign against her testified!
    We were astonished, stupified; the blow
    Befell our hearts too violently—Who could
    In this alarming hour testing weigh?
    Now self-possession doth return to us:
    We see her, as she wandered in our midst,
    And we discover no reproach in her.
    We are confused, we fear that we have done
    A grave injustice. E'en the King feels rue,
    The Duke doth blame himself, La Hire is comfortless,
    And every heart enwraps itself in grief.
DUNOIS: She a deceiver! If the Truth desires
    To be embodied in a form that's visible,
    So must it bear her features in itself!
    If Innocence, Faith, Purity of heart
    Dwell anywhere on earth—upon her lips,
    Within her lucid eyes it must needs dwell!
ARCHBISHOP: May Heaven through a wonder intervene
    Into our midst and luminate this mystery,
    The which our mortal eye can't penetrate.
    Howe'er it be unraveled and resolved,
    One of the two have we been guilty of:
    Ourselves with hellish magic arms have we
    Defended—or a holy saint we've banned!
    And both call down the Heaven's penalty
    And wrath upon this most unhappy land!

SCENE VIII

A NOBLEMAN *to the preceding, hereafter* RAIMOND.

NOBLEMAN: A youthful shepherd asketh for thine
    Highness,

He urgently demands, to speak with thee,
He comes, he saith, from the Virgin—
DUNOIS: Hasten!
Bring him in here! He comes from her!
(NOBLEMAN *opens the door for* RAIMOND, DUNOIS
   hastens toward him.)   Where is she?
Where is the Virgin?
RAIMOND: Hail, my noble Prince,
And hail to me, that I this pious Bishop,
The holy man, the shield of the oppressed,
The father of th' abandoned, find with you!
DUNOIS: Where is the Virgin?
ARCHBISHOP: Tell it us, my son!
RAIMOND: My Master, she is no black sorceress!
By God and all the saints I do declare.
In error is the folk. The innocent
You've banned, whom God hath sent have you cast out!
DUNOIS: Where is she? Speak!
RAIMOND: I was her fellow traveler
Upon her flight into the Ardennes forest,
To me hath she her inmost there confessed.
In torture will I perish, may my soul
No share have in eternal happiness,
If she not pure is, Lord, of every guilt!
DUNOIS: The sun itself i' th' Heaven is not purer!
Where is she? Speak!
RAIMOND: Alas if God your heart
Hath altered—so make haste! so rescue her!
She is imprisoned by the Englanders.
DUNOIS: Imprisoned! What!
ARCHBISHOP: The most unhappy one!
RAIMOND: Within the Ardennes, where we sought for shelter,
Hath she been apprehended by the Queen
And then delivered into English hands.
O rescue her, who hath once rescued you,
From a most horrifying death!
DUNOIS: To arms! Arise! Sound the alarm! Roll the drums!

Lead all the folk into the fight! All France
Equip yourself! Your honor is extended,
The crown, and the palladium expended—
Set all your blood, set all your life at stake!
Free must she be, before the day is ended!
(*Exit.*)

SCENE IX

A watch-tower, above an opening.

JOHANNA *and* LIONEL, *to them* FASTOLF, *then* ISABEAU.

FASTOLF (*entering hastily*):
  The people can no longer be subdued.
  In rage they're urging, that the Virgin die.
  In vain is your resistance. Murder her
  And cast her head down from this tower's peak!
  Her flowing blood alone the host appeases.
ISABEAU (*comes*):
  They're laying ladders on, they're charging now!
  Come, pacify the people. Will you wait,
  Till in blind rage they fully overturn
  The tower and we're all destroyed therewith?
  You could not her protect—surrender her!
LIONEL: Let them attack! Let them in frenzy rage!
  This castle's firm, and underneath its wreckage
  I'll bury me, ere me their will compels.
  —Respond to me, Johanna! Be thou mine,
  And I shall thee protect against a world.
ISABEAU: Are you a man?
LIONEL: By thine own folk art thou
  Rejected, thou art free of every duty
  To thine unworthy fatherland. The cowards,
  Who once thee wooed, have now deserted thee,
  They ventured not to battle for thine honor.
  But I, against my people and thine own
  Avouch for thee.—Once thou didst let me think,

That my life to thee precious be! And then
I stood as foe opposed to thee in battle—
And now thou hast no friend but me!
JOHANNA: Thou art
The foe to me, the hated, of my people.
Nought can there common be 'tween thee and me.
Nor can I give thee love, but if thine heart
Inclines to me, so let it blessings bring
Unto our people.—Lead thine host away
From this the ground of mine own fatherland,
The keys to all the cities give to us,
Which you have conquered, pay back all the loot,
Release all of our prisoners, send hostages
O' th' holy covenant—so I to thee
Shall offer peace in mine own Monarch's name.
ISABEAU: Wilt thou in fetters furnish us with laws?
JOHANNA: Do it betimes, for thou must still do it.
France will never carry England's fetters.
Ne'er, never will that happen! Sooner will
It be a spacious grave for all your hosts.
Your very best have fallen now—reflect
Upon a safe return; all of your fame
Is surely lost, your power is undone.
ISABEAU: Could you endure this raving one's defiance?

SCENE X

The preceding. A CAPTAIN *comes hastily.*

CAPTAIN: Hie, General, hie, to post the host for battle!
The Franks advance now with their flying banners,
All of the valley flashes with their arms.
JOHANNA (*inspired*):
The Franks advance! Now, haughty England, out
Into the field! Now one must briskly fight!
FASTOLF: O senseless woman, thy delight restrain!
Thou wilt this day's conclusion not behold.

JOHANNA: My folk will be victorious, and I shall die—
  The valiant now require mine arm no more.
LIONEL: I ridicule these weaklings! We have them
  Before us scared away in twenty battles,
  Before this hero-maiden fought for them!
  All of the folk I do despise but one,
  And this one they have banished now.—Come, Fastolf!
  We will for them a second battle day
  At Crecy and Poitiers prepare.
  You, Queen, remain within this tower, guard
  The Virgin, till the action is decided.
  I'll leave you fifty knights for your protection.
FASTOLF: What? Shall we march against the enemy
  And leave this raging woman in the rear?
JOHANNA: A fettered woman frightens thee?
LIONEL: Give me
  Thy word, Johanna, not to free thyself!
JOHANNA: To liberate myself is my sole wish.
ISABEAU: Lay on her threefold chains. I'll guarantee
  My life, that she shall not escape from here.
  (She is fettered with heavy chains around her body and around her arms.)
LIONEL *(to* JOHANNA*)*:
  Thou willst it so! Thou forcest us! It rests with thee.
  France disavow! Bear England's banner now,
  And thou art free, and all these raging ones,
  Who now demand thy blood, will thee assist!
FASTOLF *(urgently)*:
  Away, away, my General!
JOHANNA: Spare thy words!
  The Franks now do advance, defend thyself!
  (Trumpets resound, LIONEL *hastens forth.)*
FASTOLF: You know, what you now have to do, my Queen!
  Doth luck declare itself against us, do
  You see, our folk are fleeing—
ISABEAU *(drawing a dagger)*:   Worry not!

She shall not live, to ever see our fall.
FASTOLF (*to* JOHANNA):
Thou know'st, what thee awaiteth. Now beseech
Good fortune for thy people's arms!

(*He exits.*)

SCENE XI

ISABEAU. JOHANNA.
SOLDIERS.

JOHANNA: I will!
Therein shall no one hinder me.—Now hark!
That is the war march of my folk! How brave
It ringeth to mine heart and victory-foretelling!
Destruction unto England! Triumph to the Franks!
Up, my brave comrades! Up! The Virgin's near
To you; she can't 'fore you as formerly
The banner carry—heavy shackles fetter her,
Yet free from out her prison soars her soul
Upon the pinions of your martial song.
ISABEAU (*to a* SOLDIER):
Climb up the tower there, which looketh toward
The field, and tell us, how the battle turns.
(SOLDIER *climbs up.*)
JOHANNA: Be brave, be brave, my folk! It is the final fight!
But this one triumph and the foe lies down.
ISABEAU: What seest thou?
SOLDIER: Already they have met.
A raging one upon a Barbary steed,
In tiger's fur, springs forth with men-at-arms.
JOHANNA: That is Count Dunois! Fresh, valiant fighter!
Thine is the triumph!
SOLDIER: The Burgundian
Attacks the bridge.
ISABEAU: Would that ten lances might

In his false heart now penetrate, the traitor!
SOLDIER: Lord Fastolf gives him manly opposition.
  They both dismount, they struggle man to man,
  The forces of the Duke and those of ours.
ISABEAU: See'st thou the Dauphin not? Dost thou the signs
  Of royalty not recognize?
SOLDIER: All is
  Confused in dust. I can distinguish nought.
JOHANNA: Had he *mine* eyes or did I stand above,
  The smallest thing would not elude my gaze!
  The wild hen I can reckon in its flight,
  The falcon I discern i' th' highest air.
SOLDIER: Along the trench there is a dreadful throng:
  The greatest, seems, the first to battle there.
ISABEAU: Doth wave our banner still?
SOLDIER: It flutters high.
JOHANNA: Could I but look through fissures of the wall,
  I would direct the battle with my gaze!
SOLDIER: Woe's me! What do I see! Our General is
  Encircled!
ISABEAU (*draws the dagger on* JOHANNA):
            Die, unhappy one!
SOLDIER (*quickly*):   He's freed.
  The valiant Fastolf in the rear lays hold
  O' th' foe—breaks into his most serried troops.
ISABEAU (*pulls back the dagger*):
  That spake thine angel!
SOLDIER: Triumph! Triumph! They're in flight!
ISABEAU: Who flees?
SOLDIER: The Franks, and the Burgundians flee,
  The field is covered with the fugitives.
JOHANNA: God! God! So much wilt thou me not forsake!
SOLDIER: A gravely wounded one is yonder led.
  Much people spring to help him, it's a prince.
ISABEAU: One of our own or one of France's own?
SOLDIER: They take his helmet off, Count Dunois is't.

JOHANNA *(seizes her chains with convulsive exertion)*:
And I am nothing but a fettered woman!
SOLDIER: See! Halt! Who wears the heavenly blue mantle,
Betrimmed with gold?
JOHANNA *(lively)*: That is my Lord, the King!
SOLDIER: His steed grows shy—it somersaults—it falls—
He wrenches working hard back to his feet—
(JOHANNA *accompanies these words with passionate movements.*)
Our forces now draw nigh in full career—
They now have reached to him—encircle him—
JOHANNA: O hath the Heaven not an angel more!
ISABEAU *(deridingly)*:
Now is the time! Now, Savior, save thyself!
JOHANNA *(falls on her knees, praying with violently passionate voice)*:
Hear me, O God, in this mine highest need!
To Thee on high, in hot imploring wish,
Unto Thy Heaven I commend my soul.
Thou canst the fibers of a spider's web
Make strong just like the cable of a ship,
'Tis nought for Thine omnipotence, to change
These bonds of brass into thin spider webs—
Thou willst, and so these chains will fall away,
This tower wall will crack in two—Thou didst
Help Samson, when he blind and fettered was
And bitter scorn of his proud enemies
Endured—On Thee entrusting did he seize
The pillars of his prison mightily
And bowed down low and overturned the structure—
SOLDIER: Triumph! Triumph!
ISABEAU: What is't?
SOLDIER: The Monarch is Imprisoned!
JOHANNA *(springs up)*:
So be gracious God to me!

(She hath seized her chains forcefully with both hands and broken them asunder. In the same moment she hurls herself upon the nearest standing soldier, rips his sword away from him and hurries out. All look after her with staring astonishment.)

SCENE XII

Preceding without JOHANNA.

ISABEAU *(after a long pause):*
  What was that? Did I dream? Where did she go?
  How did she break these hundred-weighted bonds?
  For all the world would I it not believe,
  Had I myself not seen it with mine eyes.
SOLDIER *(on the watch-tower):*
  How? Hath she wings? Or hath a stormwind led
  Her hence?
ISABEAU: Speak, is she down below?
SOLDIER: Amid
  The battle strideth she—Her course is quicker
  Than is my sight—Now is she here—now there—
  I see her at one time in many places!
  —She splits the multitude—All yield to her,
  The Franks now halt, they post themselves anew!
  —Woe's me! What see I! All our people cast
  Their weapons from themselves, our banners sink—
ISABEAU: What? Will she snatch sure victory from us?
SOLDIER: Straight to the Monarch doth she press—She hath
  Him reached—With force she drags him from the fight.
  —Lord Fastolf falls—The General is imprisoned.
ISABEAU: I will no further listen. Come down here.
SOLDIER: Escape, my Queen! You shall be overtaken.
  An armèd folk is charging at the tower.
  (He climbs down below.)

ACT V, SCENE XIII   THE VIRGIN OF ORLEANS

ISABEAU *(drawing the sword):*
  So fight, ye cowards!

SCENE XIII

Preceding. LA HIRE *with soldiers. At his entrance the people of the Queen extend their weapons.*

LA HIRE *(nears her respectfully):*
                Queen, submit yourself
  To the Almighty—All your knights have now
  Surrendered, all resistance is for nought!
  Accept my services. Command whereto
  You want to be escorted.
ISABEAU: Any place
  Is all the same, where I'll not meet the Dauphin.

(Hands over her sword and follows him with the soldiers.)

The scene is transformed into the battlefield.

SCENE XIV

Soldiers with flying banners fill the background. Before them the KING *and the* DUKE OF BURGUNDY; *in the arms of both princes lies* JOHANNA, *mortally wounded, without signs of life. They step forward slowly.* AGNES SOREL *rushes in.*

SOREL *(throws herself on the* KING'S *breast):*
  You are now freed—You live—I've you again!
KING: I have been freed—I am so for this price!
  (points to JOHANNA*)*
SOREL: Johanna! God! She dies!
BURGUNDY: She hath now ended!
  Behold an angel part! Behold, how she there lies,
  Painless and tranquil as a sleeping child!
  The peace of Heaven plays around her features.

> No breathing lifts her bosom more, yet life
> Can be discovered still in her warm hand.

KING: She is departed—She'll no longer waken,
> Her eye will see the earthly nevermore.
> Now soars she up there, a transfigured spirit,
> Beholds our pain no more and our remorse.

SOREL: She opens up her eyes, she lives!

BURGUNDY *(astonished):* Comes she
> Back to us from the grave? O'ercomes she death?
> She raises herself up! She stands!

JOHANNA *(stands entirely upright and looks around):*
> Where am I?

BURGUNDY: With thine own folk, Johanna! With thine own!

KING: Within thy friends' and thine own Monarch's arms!

JOHANNA *(after she looks at him long and fixedly):*
> No, I am not a sorceress! Indeed,
> I am not.

KING: Thou art holy as the angels,
> Yet our eyes were with darkest night bedecked.

JOHANNA *(looks around smiling brightly):*
> And am I really now among my folk
> And am no more rejected and despised?
> They curse me not, they kindly look on me?
> —Yes, now I recognize all clearly once again!
> That is my Monarch! That is France's banner!
> Yet mine own banner see I not—Where is it?
> Without my banner dare I not to come:
> It was entrusted to me by my Master,
> Before His throne I must needs lay it down—
> I may display it, for I bore it true.

KING *(with face turned away):*
> Give her the banner!
> *(It is given to her. She stands completely freely upright, the banner in her hand. The Heaven is illuminated by a rosy shine.)*

JOHANNA: Do you behold the rainbow in the air?

The Heaven opens up its golden gates:
I' th' choir of angels stands she gleaming there,
She holds th' eternal Son upon her breast,
Her arms she smiling stretches out to me.
What comes o'er me—Light clouds are lifting me—
The heavy armor doth to wingèd garments turn.
Upward—upward—The earth doth backward flee—
Brief is the pain, the joy shall be eterne!

(The banner falls away from her, she sinks down thereupon dead.—All stand for a long time in speechless emotion.—Upon a gentle beckon of the KING *all banners are gently let down upon her, so that she is entirely covered thereby.)*

The Poet of Freedom, Friedrich Schiller (1759-1805), and his beloved wife Charlotte (1766-1826). His works have continued to inspire republican movements to this day—witness the performance of Beethoven's Ninth Symphony, with Schiller's "Ode to Joy" in the fourth movement, in demonstrations from China's Tiananmen Square to the Berlin Wall.*

On November 9, 1989, the hated Berlin Wall was opened, and millions, young and old, hammered at the wall and danced on top of it.

Schiller Institute Chairman Helga Zepp-LaRouche with Norbert Brainin, principal violinist of the legendary Amadeus Quartet. Mr. Brainin gave a free all-Beethoven concert in Berlin, on December 17, 1989, sponsored by the Schiller Institute. The concert was attended by over 1,000 Germans, from East and West, whose love for classical culture has not been killed by decades of oppression.

Lyndon H. LaRouche, Jr. and his wife Helga Zepp-LaRouche, in November, 1988, at the Berlin Wall. LaRouche proposed a "Food for Peace" policy to bring about German reunification and development for the East bloc. One month later, he and six associates were sentenced to prison, framed up by the circles of Henry Kissinger and the Eastern Establishment, who prefer a "condominium" with Moscow and Beijing.

*Schiller's father, Johann Caspar Schiller, a professional military man, pictured here in Lieutenant's uniform.**

*Schiller's mother, Elisabeth Dorothea Schiller, née Kodweis, was born of an old, established family in Marbach, where Schiller too was born.**

Schiller's four children: Ernst Friedrich Wilhelm Schiller (1796-1841), Karl Friedrich Ludwig Schiller (1793-1857), Emilie Henriette Luise Schiller (1804-1872), and Karoline Luise Friederike Schiller (1799-1850).

SCHILLER'S FRIENDS... AND FOILS

Christian Gottfried Körner (1756-1831) and his wife Minna Stock, (1762-1843) whose marriage Schiller celebrated with his Love, Virtue, Friendship. *It was also with Körner, Schiller's best friend and most frequent correspondent, that the* Philosophical Letters *were composed.* *

Johann Wolfgang Goethe (1749-1832), Schiller's much-acclaimed contemporary, was, in fact, what Helga Zepp-LaRouche has called Schiller's "counter-pole." Schiller said of Goethe, in a letter to Körner on September 12, 1788: "And his entire character is different from mine from the outset, his world is not mine, and the way we think appears to be utterly different."*

Immanuel Kant (1724-1804), the hegemonic philosopher in Schiller's day. Schiller's theory of aesthetics was based upon a refutation of Kant's Critique of Judgment. *Kant, whose theories gave rise to German romanticism, rejected the idea that beauty could be objectively determined. Insisting that beauty is merely a matter of subjective taste, he denied the intelligibility and therefore the reproducibility of creativity, i.e., he denied that there is a science of the human mind and a science of the mind's ability to produce works of art. **

The cover of Schiller's literary magazine Thalia, *which he produced from 1786-1791, and as* New Thalia *from 1792-1794. Such works as* The Ghostseer *and* On Grace and Dignity *first appeared in this journal.**

*Source is Schiller National Museum, Marbach, Federal Republic of Germany, Friedrich Schiller: Eine Dokumentation in Bildern.

HOMAGE TO THE ARTS

A LYRICAL PLAY

*To Her Imperial Highness
The Princess of Weimar
Maria Paulovna
Princess of Russia
In respect Dedicated and
Performed at Weimar's Royal Theater
12 November 1804*

DRAMATIS PERSONÆ

FATHER	CHORUS OF COUNTRY
MOTHER	FOLK
YOUTH	GENIUS
MAIDEN	THE SEVEN ARTS

This "lyrical play," in which elements of Greek drama are combined with opera, was Schiller's last completed work. It was first performed at Weimar's Royal Theater on November 12, 1804, two days after Schiller's last birthday, for the wedding festival of Princess Maria Paulovna. Schiller wrote this piece in fourteen days, while on his deathbed. He directed that, when his collected works were published, *Homage to the Arts* be placed at the beginning of the poetry section. This was done in the first edition of his works, published by Cotta at Tübingen in the middle of April 1805.

The scene is an open rural region.

In its midst an orange tree, laden with fruits and adorned with ribbons. The country people are simply occupied, planting it in the earth, whilst the maiden and children hold it on both sides with a floral chain.

FATHER:
Flourish, flourish, blossoming tree
With the golden crown all fruited,
Which we from abroad uprooted
Plant now in our native lea!
With abundant fruit so luscious
Bow thine ever verdant branches!

ALL COUNTRY FOLK:
Flourish, flourish, blossoming tree
Striving for the heavens free!

YOUTH:
Grandly the golden fruit thou bearest
With the fragrant blooms unite!
Stand before the years' fierce tempest,
And endure the ages' flight!

ALL:
Stand before the years' fierce tempest,
And endure the ages' flight!

MOTHER:
Take him in, O holy Earth, O
Take the tender stranger in,
Leader of the speckled herds, O
Lofty field-god, nurse thou him!

MAIDEN:
Nurse him tender dryads sylvan,
Guard him, guard him, Father Pan!
And free oreads o' th' mountain,
That no weather shall e'er harm him,
Fetter all the tempests down!

ALL:
Nurse him, tender dryads sylvan,
Guard him, guard him, Father Pan!

YOUTH:
Smile on thee the ardent ether,
Ever clear and ever blue!
Sun, O give to him thy beaming,
Earth, O give to him thy dew!

ALL:
Sun, O give to him thy beaming,
Earth, O give to him thy dew!

FATHER:
Joy, O joy, a life reviving
May'st each wand'rer thou be giving;
For 'tis joy that planted thee.
Mayest thou with nectar pouring,
E'en the grandson be restoring,
And revived, may he bless thee!

ALL:
Joy, O joy, a life reviving
May'st each wand'rer thou be giving;
For 'tis joy that planted thee!

They dance in a colorful roundelay about the tree. The music of the orchestra accompanies them and passes gradually to a nobler mode, during which one sees GENIUS *in the background descending with the seven* GODDESSES. *The* COUNTRY FOLK *remove themselves toward both sides of the stage, whilst* GENIUS *steps to the middle, and the three plastic* ARTS *place themselves on his right, the four speaking and musical* ARTS *to his left.*

CHORUS OF THE ARTS:
From far off location,
We stride and we wander
From nation to nation,
From era to era,

For permanent home search the earth all about.
Fore'er to be dwelling
Where peace is compelling,
In silence creative,
In plenitude active,
We wander and search and we find it not out.

YOUTH:
See, who are they, who are nearing,
'Tis a host of godly mien!
Wond'rous, they're to me appearing,
Figures as we've never seen.

GENIUS:
Where the weapons are clanging
With ironish sound,
Where delusion and hate are hearts e'er entangling,
Where the people ever in error are wrangling,
Therefrom we turn fleeing and hurriedly bound.

CHORUS OF THE ARTS:
We hate the deceitful,
Who God are despising,
The upright and truthful
Of mankind we're seeking;
Where innocent customs
Us friendly receive,
There huts we will build us
And settle to live!

MAIDEN:
What all of a sudden!
What's happ'ning to me!
I'm drawn unto them with mysterious power,
The figures beloved, to me they're familiar,
Yet know I, I never before them did see!

ALL:
What all of a sudden!
What's happ'ning to me!

GENIUS:
> Ah, but still! There see I landsmen,
> And quite blessed they seem to be;
> Rich with garland and with ribbon,
> Festive is adorned the tree.
> —Are these not of joy the traces?
> Speak ye! What is happ'ning here?

FATHER:
> Herdsmen are we in these places,
> And a feast we're making here.

GENIUS:
> What's the feast? O herdsmen, tell us!

MOTHER:
> It is meant, our *Queen* to honor,
> The sublime, the gracious donor,
> Who to this our quiet dell
> For to bless us has descended
> From the high imperial hall.

YOUTH:
> She, who's by all charms attended,
> Good as the sun's beam to all.

GENIUS:
> Wherefore plant ye here this tree?

YOUTH:
> Ah, she comes from foreign land,
> And her heart doth gaze behind her!
> We would gladly like to bind her
> Here to the new fatherland.

GENIUS:
> Therefore plant ye here this tree
> In the earth its roots so deeply,
> That at home her Highness will be
> Here in the new fatherland?

MAIDEN:
>Ah, so many bondings tender
>To her land of youth do draw her!
>All she left behind her there,
>Paradise of childhood fair
>And the holy womb of mother
>And the mighty heart of brother
>And the sister's tender breast—
>How could *we* replace such measure?
>In all nature be there price
>For such joy or for such treasure?

GENIUS:
>Love doth reach too in the distance,
>Love to no one place is bound!
>As the flame doth not diminish,
>But ignited by its fire
>Yet another doth redound—
>What she precious there had taken,
>Is not for her left behind;
>She has love back there forsaken,
>Love she also here doth find.

MOTHER:
>Ah, from marble rooms she's striding,
>Out of Splendor's golden halls.
>Will her Highness to her liking
>Find it here, where o'er fields freely
>But the gold sun's laughter falls?

GENIUS:
>Herdsmen, to you 'tis not given
>To behold a heart so lovely!
>Know ye, an exalted mind
>*Places* greatness into living
>*Seeks* it not therein to find.

YOUTH:
>O stranger beauteous! Teach us to bind her,
>O teach us thou, how we could please her best!

So gladly would we fragrant garlands wind her
And lead her to our cottages to rest!

GENIUS:
A beaut'ous heart has soon its own home founded,
Creates itself, in silence, its own world.
And as the tree within the earth doth wind
With mighty roots and chain itself so firmly,
So twines the noble one, the excellent,
With his own deeds down into life as well.
So quickly are love's tender ribbons binding:
Where one finds joy, one's fatherland is finding.

ALL:
O beauteous stranger, say, how do we bind her,
The glorious one, to this our quiet pasture!

GENIUS:
It is already found, the tender band,
Not all to her is strange within this land:
Me and my train she'll soon be knowing,
When we're to her our identity showing.

(*Here* GENIUS *steps up to the proscenium, the seven* GODDESSES *do the same, so that they form a half-circle right at the front. In the moment, when they step forward, they unveil their attributes, which until now they have held hidden under their garments.*)

GENIUS (*toward the* PRINCESS):
I am the Genius who's Beauty creating,
And following me, is Art's lovely band.
We are what crowns all that mankind is making,
The palace and altar adorneth our hand.
Long dwelt we in thine imperial fam'ly,
And *she*, the glorious one, who gave thee birth,
She nursed us at the off'ring's fire holy
With purest hand at her home altar's hearth.
We've been following *thee*, by *her* assignment,
For but through us comes all joy to fulfillment.

ARCHITECTURE *(with a mural crown on her head, a
    golden ship in her right hand):*
  Thou saw'st *me* on the Neva stream throned!
  Thy great ancestor called me to th' North up there,
  And there I built for him a second Rome;
  Through me 'twas it an emperor's throne to bear.
  A paradise of greatness and of glory
  Arose beneath my magic rod's display.
  Now roaring is the din of life so merry,
  Where foretimes just a somber fog did lay;
  The proud armada with its masts' expansion
  Doth scare the ancient Belt within his ocean mansion.

SCULPTURE *(with a Victoria statue in her hand):*
  Me too hast thou so often seen with wonder,
  The earnest sculptress o' th' ancient Pantheon.
  A boulder have I—it will stand forever—
  Impressed its great heroic form upon.
  And this Victoria, which is my creation,
  (showing the Victoria)
  Thy lofty brother swings in his strong hand;
  It flies along 'fore *Alexander's* weapons,
  He did with it his army ever band—
  I can from clay but lifeless figures fashion,
  He shapes from savages a civil nation.

PAINTING *(with pallet and brush):*
  Me too, sublime one! won't thou be mistaking
  The gay creatress of the forms illusory.
  With life it flashes, and the color's blazing
  Upon my cloth with glowing energy.
  I know how fondly to deceive the senses,
  Yes, through the eyes deceive I e'en the heart;
  With the beloved's imitating brushes
  I sweeten oft the longing's bitter smart.
  They who themselves toward north and south
      departed,
  They still have *me*, and are not fully parted.

HOMAGE TO THE ARTS

POETRY:
>No bonds hold me, I brook no limitation,
>Free soar I through all spaces undeterred,
>My vast and boundless kingdom is Conception,
>And my bewingèd instrument's the Word.
>What moves itself on earth and in the heaven,
>What nature deep in secrecy enframes,
>Must be to *me* unsealèd and unhidden,
>For nought the free poetic might constrains;
>Yet nought more beaut'ful's found, as long my choice be,
>Than in the beaut'ful form—the soul of beauty.

MUSIC *(with the lyre)*:
>The pow'r of tones, which from the strings is welling,
>Thou playest mightily, it well thou ken'st,
>What's the deep bosom with foreboding swelling,
>Is in my tones alone in full expressed;
>Upon thy senses plays a lovely magic,
>As forth my stream of harmonies doth flow,
>The heart would break apart in sweetness tragic,
>And from the lips the soul desires to go,
>And my tone ladder set I down, I bear thee
>Upon it upward to the highest beauty.

DANCE *(with cymbals)*:
>The lofty godliness, it rests in earnest stillness,
>With quiet mind it would perceivèd be;
>While Life prefers to move in sumpt'ous fullness,
>Youth would express itself, would joyous be.
>By Beauty's bridle Joy am I commanding,
>Which fain would gentle bound'ries overstep,
>To pond'rous body zephyr wings I'm lending,
>Proportion set I in the dance's step.—
>What moves itself, I with my staff am guiding,
>The beauteous gift is Grace that I'm providing.

DRAMA *(with a Janus mask)*:
>In Janus mask let me 'fore thee be plying,

For here the joy and here the pain's expressed:
All mankind wavers 'twixt delight and crying,
And with the solemn also weddeth jest.
With all its depths and all its heights displayèd
Am I unfurling Life before thy glance.
When thou hast seen the great world play portrayèd,
So thou returnest to thyself enhanced;
For he who in his mind the whole addresses,
For him the strife within his breast then passes.

GENIUS:
And all of us, who 'fore thee have appearèd,
The lofty Arts' divine and holy band,
We at thy service, Princess, stand preparèd;
But ask it, thou, and quick at thy command,
As did the lyre's tones at th' Theban jetty
The senseless stone with life itself endow—
Unfolds itself to thee a world of beauty.

ARCHITECT:
The columns shall themselves in columns row.

SCULPTURE:
The marble melt beneath the hammer's whirring.

PAINTING:
Upon the canvas Life afresh be stirring.

MUSIC:
The stream of harmonies for thee be singing.

DANCE:
The lively roundelay shall thee be ringing.

DRAMA:
The world shall play to thee upon this scaffolding.

POETRY:
The Phantasie her mighty wings unfolding,
Shall charm thee up into celestial fields!

PAINTING:
And as from out of sunbeams shining builds

Itself the rainbow's beauteous ring of colors,
So shall we with our beautiful joint striving,
The lofty Beauty's seven holy numbers,
Thee, glorious one, Life's tapestry be weaving!

ALL ARTS *(embracing):*
For from the strength of beautiful joint striving
Arises, active, first the truly living.

William Ferguson

HISTORY

THE HISTORY OF THE REVOLT OF THE UNITED NETHERLANDS AGAINST SPANISH RULE

INTRODUCTION

TRANSLATED BY SUSAN JOHNSON

One of the most remarkable among the events of state, which have made the sixteenth century the most splendid in the world, seems to me the establishment of the Netherlands' freedom. If the glittering deeds of glory-seeking and a destructive appetite for power lay claim to our admiration, how much more so an event, where an oppressed humanity struggles for its noblest rights, where the good cause is paired with unaccustomed powers, and the resources of

---

Schiller's great historical account of the Revolt of the Netherlands was first published at the end of October 1788, in Leipzig. Schiller undertook this historical study as background to writing his dramatic poem *Don Carlos, Infante of Spain* (written between 1785 and 1787), a fictional account of the political intrigues surrounding the history of the Revolt of the Netherlands and its relation to the Spanish court. This *Introduction* stands by itself as one of Schiller's finest explications of the principles of republican statecraft. The Schiller Institute plans to publish a new English translation of the full historical work in a later volume.

resolute desperation triumph over the fearsome arts of tyranny in unequal combat. Great and comforting is the reflection, that against defiant usurpations by monarchic force, in the end a remedy is still at hand, that their most calculated designs against human freedom can be spoiled, that a bold-hearted resistance can bend low even the outstretched hand of a despot, heroic perseverance can finally exhaust his terrifying resources. Never did this truth pierce me so vividly as the history of that memorable revolt, which severed the United Netherlands forever from the Spanish crown—and on that account, I regarded it as not unworthy of the effort to set before the world this beautiful memorial of common citizens' strength, to awaken in the breast of my reader a joyful sense of his own individual self, and to give a new incontestable example, of what human beings can dare to hazard for the cause, and what they may accomplish by uniting together.

It is not the extraordinary or heroic in this event, which incites me to describe it. The world's annals have stored up comparable undertakings, which appear still bolder in design, still more brilliant in execution. Many states fall to their ruin with a more magnificent convulsion, with a loftier bound others arise. Likewise, one may expect here no superlative, colossal men, none of the astonishing deeds, which the history of bygone times presents to us in such profuse abundance. Those times are past, those men are no more. In the feeble lap of refinement we have let the energies slacken, which that era exerted and made essential. With dejected admiration we now gaze astonished at these images of giants, as an enervated old fellow at the manly games of youth. Not so in the history at hand. The populace, which we see making its appearance here, was the most peaceable in this part of the world, and less than all its neighbors capable of that heroic spirit, which gives to even the most insignificant action a higher impetus. The force of circumstances surprised them with their own strength and required of them a transitory greatness, which they were never supposed to have and perhaps will never have again.

It is therefore precisely the lack of heroic greatness, which makes this event singular and instructive, and if others set themselves the goal, of showing the superiority of genius to accident, I present here a portrait, in which necessity created genius and accidents made heroes.

Were it ever allowed, to weave a higher providence into human affairs, this history would be the place; so contrary it seems to reason and all experience. Philip II, the mightiest sovereign of his time, whose dreaded superiority of strength threatens to devour all Europe, whose treasures surpass the combined riches of all Christian kings, whose fleets command all the seas; a monarch, whose hazardous objectives many armies serve, armies, which, hardened through long and bloody wars and a Roman discipline, inspired by a defiant national pride and inflamed by the memory of well-fought victories, are thirsting for honor and booty, and move under the audacious genius of their leaders as obedient limbs—this dreaded man, sacrificing himself to an obstinate design, *one* mission the tireless labor of his long reign, all these formidable resources directed to one single purpose, which in the evening of his days he must surrender unfulfilled—Philip II, in a struggle with a few weak nations, which he cannot finish!

And against which nations? Here, a peaceable folk of fishermen and shepherds, in a forgotten corner of Europe, which they were still laboriously wresting from the ocean flood-tide; the sea their workshop, their wealth, and their plague, an independent poverty their highest good, their fame, their virtue. There, a good-natured, well-bred commercial folk, luxuriating in the sumptuous fruits of a blessed diligence, watchful over laws, which were their benefactors. In the fortunate leisure of prosperity, they abandon the anxious sphere of sheer necessities and learn to thirst after higher gratification. The new truth, whose gladdening dawn now breaks over Europe, throws a germinal beam into these favorable regions, and joyfully the free citizen welcomes the light, shunned by sad oppressed slaves. It incites him to test, with a cheerful bravado which readily accompanies material abundance and liberty, the authority of old accustomed opinions, and to break an ignominious fetter. The heavy scourge of despotism hangs over him, an arbitrary force threatens to tear down the pillars of his good fortune, the custodian of his laws becomes his tyrant. Simple in his statecraft as in his manners, he makes bold to display an old, unused treaty and admonish the lord of both Indies on behalf of natural law. A name decides the entire outcome of things. In Madrid they termed rebellion, that which in Brussels was called merely, a legitimate action; the grievances of Brabant required a politically artful intermediary; Philip II sent them an executioner, and the unleashing of the war was accomplished. An unparalleled tyranny assails life and property. The desperate citizen, left a choice between two kinds of death, chooses the nobler one on the battlefield. A wealthy, lavish people loves peace, but it becomes warlike, when it becomes poor. Now it ceases to tremble for a life, which is to lack everything that made it desirable to preserve. The fury of revolt grips the remotest provinces; trade and commerce come to a halt; the ships vanish from the harbors, the artisan from his workplace, the peasant from the wasted fields. Thousands flee to distant lands, thousands of victims fall on the bloody scaffolds, and fresh thousands hasten thither; divine, then, must be a doctrine, which can be so joyously died for. Still lacking is the final consummating hand—the illumined, initiating spirit, who would seize this great political moment and raise the offspring of accident to the plane of wisdom.

William the Silent consecrates himself, a second Brutus, to the great desire for freedom. Risen above a timorous self-concern, he renounces duties to the throne, the violation of which is punishable, magnanimously divests himself of his princely existence, descends to a voluntary poverty, and is nothing more than a citizen of the world. The just cause is wagered on the gaming-table of battle; but scraped-together hirelings and peaceable farmers cannot withstand the formidable onslaught of an experienced war machine. Twice he leads his disheartened army against the tyrant, twice they, but not his courage, abandon him. Philip II sends as many reinforcements, as the inhuman greed of his intermediary was making into paupers. Fugitives, cast out of their fatherland, seek a new one on the sea, and on the ships of their enemy seek satisfaction of their vengeance and their hunger. Now corsairs become maritime heroes, a navy assembles out of pirate vessels, and a republic rises up from morasses. Seven provinces all break their fetters: a new youthful state, mighty through union, through its flooding by water, and through desperation. A solemn decree of the nation deposes the tyrant from the throne, the Spanish name disappears from all laws.

Now is an act accomplished, which no longer finds forgiveness; the republic becomes frightened, because she can no longer retreat. Factions rip apart her union, even her dreadful element, the sea, conspiring with her oppressor, threatens an early grave for her tender beginning. She feels her forces succumb to the superior power of the enemy, and throws herself supplicatingly before Europe's mightiest thrones, in order to give away a sovereignty, which she can no longer protect. At last, with difficulty—so contemptibly did this nation-state begin, that even the avarice of foreign kings disdained its young blossoms—she presses her dangerous crown upon a stranger. New hopes refresh her sinking spirit, but destiny gave her a betrayer in this new paternal guardian of the nation, and at the urgent point, when the relentless foe already storms the gates, Charles of Anjou violates the liberty to whose protection he was called. An assassin's hand, besides, tears the helmsman from the rudder, her fate seems sealed, with William of Orange all her redeeming angels fled—but the ship flies ahead in the storm, and the pulsing sails require the pilot's help no longer.

Philip II sees the fruit lost of a deed, which cost him his royal honor and perhaps the secret pride of his unavowed consciousness. Stubbornly and precariously freedom struggles with despotism; murderous battles are fought; a shining array of heroes succeeds one another on the field of honor;

Flanders and Brabant were the school, that trained the field commanders of the coming century. A long, devastating war tramples the yield of the open countryside, victor and vanquished bleed to death, while the emerging maritime state attracted fleeing industry to itself and on the ruins of its neighbors raised up the splendid edifice of its greatness. For forty years endured a war, whose happy conclusion did not rejoice Philip's dying sight, which blotted out one paradise in Europe and created a new one on its ruins—which devoured the bloom of martial youth, enriched an entire continent, and made the possessor of gold-rich Peru a poor man. This monarch, who, without oppressing his realm, might expend nine-hundred tons of gold, who extorted yet far more through tyrannical artifices, heaped a debt of a hundred and forty million ducats on his depopulated realm. An irreconcilable hatred of freedom devoured all these treasures and fruitlessly consumed his royal life; but the Reformation flourished under the devastation of his sword, and out of citizens' blood the new republic raised its victorious flag.

This extraordinary turn of events seems to border on a miracle; but many things combined, to break the power of this king and to cast favor on the progress of the young state. Were the whole weight of his strength fallen on the United Provinces, there was no salvation for her religion, her liberty. His own ambition came to the rescue of her weakness, as it compelled him, to divide his strength. The costly policy of hiring traitors in every cabinet of Europe, the subsidies for the League in France, the uprising of the Moors in Grenada, the conquest of Portugal, and the opulent construction of the Escurial, at last exhausted his seemingly immeasurable treasures and prevented him from acting with spirit and energy in the field. The German and Italian troops, which only the hope of booty had lured under his flag, now angrily mutinied, because he could not pay them, and faithlessly deprived their leader of their effectiveness at the decisive moment. These formidable instruments of oppression now turned their dangerous strength against the

King himself and vented their hostile rage in the provinces that remained loyal to him. That ill-fated mobilization of arms against Britain, on which he, like a frenzied gambler, staked the whole power of his kingdom, completed his collapse; with the Armada perished the tribute of both Indies and the best of the Spanish breed of heroes.

But to the same extent that Spanish power spent itself, the republic won fresh life. The gaps torn by the new religion, the tyranny of the Inquisition, the raging plunder of the soldier rabble, and the ravages of a long wearisome war without intermission in the provinces of Brabant, Flanders, and Hainault, which were the garrisons and storehouses of this costly war, naturally rendered it each year more difficult to maintain and replenish the armies. The Catholic Netherlands had already lost one million citizens, and the trampled fields no longer nourished their ploughmen. Spain itself could spare few more men. These regions, taken unawares by a sudden prosperity, which gave rise to idleness, had greatly declined in population and could not long maintain these exportations of men to the New World and the Netherlands. Few among them saw their fatherland again; these few had left it as youths and now came back as exhausted old men. Gold having become more common made soldiers more and more expensive; the prevailing impulse toward effeminate indulgence raised the price of the opposite virtues. Matters stood quite otherwise with the rebels. All the thousands, which the viceroy's inhuman cruelty had driven from the southern Netherlands, the Huguenot war from France, and the coercion of conscience from other regions of Europe, all were theirs. Their recruiting-ground was the entire Christian world. The fanaticism of the persecutors, as of the persecuted, worked in their behalf. The fresh inspiration of a newly proclaimed doctrine, vengefulness, hunger, and hopeless misery drew adventurers from all quarters of Europe under their flags. Everything which was won for the new doctrine, which was suffered at the hands of the despot or still to be feared of him in the future, made the destiny of this new republic as it were its own. Every mortification undergone at a tyrant's hands, bestowed a citizen's right in Holland. Men hastened toward a country, where freedom raised its gladdening flag, where respect and safety and revenge on her oppressors were assured to fugitive religion. When we consider the confluence of every people in today's Holland, who upon entering her territory regain their human rights, what must it have been then, when all the rest of Europe still groaned under a mournful oppression of spirit, when Amsterdam was well-nigh the sole free port of entry to all opinions? Many hundreds of families found safety for their wealth in a country which the ocean and domestic concord protected with equal power. The republican army was at full strength, without the necessity of dismantling the plough. Amidst the stir of arms bloomed industry and trade, and the tranquil citizen enjoyed in advance all the fruits of liberty, which would be first contended for with foreign blood. At the very time when the republic of Holland was still struggling for her existence, she advanced the borders of her territory across the ocean and quietly built up her East Indies thrones.

Still more, Spain conducted this costly war with dead, infertile gold, which never returned into the hand which gave it away, yet raised the price of all necessities in Europe. The treasure-chambers of the republic were industry and commerce. Time diminished Spain's resources, multiplied the republic's. To precisely the extent that the resources of the imperial government exhausted themselves through the long continuance of the war, the republic began for the first time to actually reap its harvest. It was a husbanded, remunerative sowing, which gave late, but hundredfold returns; the tree, from which Philip broke himself fruits, was a felled trunk and did not again bear green.

Philip's adverse destiny willed that all the treasure, which he squandered toward the downfall of the provinces, helped to enrich those very provinces. That uninterrupted outflow of Spanish gold had spread wealth and luxury through all of Europe; Europe, however, received her increased requirements for the most part from the hands of the Netherlands, which commanded the trade of the entire known world and determined the price of all goods. Even during this war Philip could not prevent the republic of Holland from trading with his own subjects, indeed he could not even wish to do so. He himself defrayed for the rebels the costs of their defense; precisely the war, which was meant to destroy them, increased the sale of their goods. The monstrous outlay for his fleets and armies flowed for the most part into the treasury of the republic, which was allied with the commercial centers of Flanders and Brabant. What Philip set in motion *against* the rebels, operated indirectly *for* them. All the immeasurable sums, which a forty-year war devoured, were poured into the casks of the Danaïdes* and disappeared into a bottomless depth.

The sluggish course of this war did the King of Spain as much harm, as it brought the rebels advantages. His army was largely put together out of the remainder of those victorious troops, who under Charles V had already gathered their laurels. Age and long service entitled them to rest; many among them, enriched by the war, impatiently wished themselves back at home, to end in comfort a toilsome life. Their former zeal, their heroic fire and manly discipline slackened to the same degree, that they believed themselves to have discharged their duty and honor, and began at last to reap the fruits of so many campaigns. Additionally, troops which were accustomed to vanquish any resistance through the fierceness of their attack, could not help wearying of a war, which was conducted less with men than with elements, which exercised one's patience more than it satisfied the lust for fame, in which the combat was less against danger than against hardship and scarcity.

Neither their individual courage nor their long experience of warfare could prove useful to them in a country, whose peculiar conditions often gave even the most cowardly native advantages over them. Lastly, on foreign soil *one* defeat injured them more, than *many* victories over an enemy, on his own territory, could profit them. With the rebels the case was exactly the opposite. In such a tedious, long-drawn-out war, where no decisive battle took place, the weaker adversary was ultimately compelled to learn from the stronger, small defeats accustomed him to danger, small victories fueled his confidence. At the opening of the civil war the republican army hardly dared to show themselves to the Spanish in the field; the war's long duration trained and hardened them. As the royal army became weary of success, the rebels' self-confidence rose along with their better martial training and experience. At last, after half a century, master and pupil, unvanquished, parted as equal combatants.

Further, during the entire course of this war, the side of the rebels acted with more cohesion and unity than the side of the King. Before the former lost their first commander, the royal administration of the Netherlands had passed through no fewer than five different hands. The irresolution of the Princess of Parma imparted itself to the cabinet in Madrid and allowed it within a short time to wander through nearly all maxims of statecraft. The Duke of Alba's unbending harshness, the leniency of his successor Requesens, Don Juan of Austria's cunning deceit and malice, and the energetic Caesarian bent of the Prince of Parma, gave this war just as many contrary directions, while the plan of the rebellion, in the single head where it dwelt clear and vivid, always remained the same. The greater evil was, that the maxims for the most part missed the moment, in which they might be applied. At the beginning of the unrest, when the preponderance was manifestly still on the side of the King, when a swift resolve and manly steadiness could still suffocate the rebellion in its cradle, the reins of government were allowed to wobble feebly to and fro in the hands of a woman. After the uprising became an actual explosion, the strength of the rebel factions and of the King was more balanced, and a clever flexibility alone could avert the impending civil war, the viceroyship fell to a man who at this post lacked precisely this single virtue. So watchful an observer as William the Silent missed none of the advantages which the faulty policy of his opponents gave him, and with quiet diligence he slowly advanced toward the object of his great undertaking.

But why did Philip II not himself appear in the Netherlands? Why would he rather exhaust the most improbable remedies, simply in order not to attempt the sole thing, which could not strike amiss? To break the arrogant power of the nobility, there was no more natural expedient than the presence of the ruler in person. By the side of majesty every private dimension of greatness could not but sink, every other aspect of authority expire. Instead of the truth flowing through so many contaminated channels slowly and obscurely toward the distant throne, so that deferred measures of resistance allowed time for an action of heedlessness to ripen into an action of deliberate judgment, his own penetrating gaze would have distinguished truth from error; not his humanity, but cold statecraft alone would have saved the realm a million citizens. The nearer their source, the more forceful would be his edicts; the thicker on their target, the weaker and more disheartened the blows of the uprising. It requires infinitely more, to inflict to his face the evil, one may well venture against an absent enemy. The rebellion seemed at first to tremble at its own name and decked itself for a long time in the clever subterfuge of taking under its protection the cause of the sovereign against the arbitrary usurpations of his governor. Philip's appearance in Brussels would have put an end to this juggler's trick at once. Now the rebels would be obliged to live up to their false pretenses, or throw off the mask and condemn themselves through their true character of violence. And what relief for the Netherlands, had his presence spared them only that evil, which was heaped upon them without his knowledge and against his will! What gain for himself, had it served toward nothing further, than to watch over the use of the immeasurable sums, which, raised illegally for the requirements of the war, disappeared into the thieving hands of his stewards! What his proxies had to compel through the unnatural device of terror, would have been wholeheartedly forthcoming to his majesty. What made those proxies into objects of horror, would have earned him fear at most; for the abuse of hereditary power oppresses less painfully than the abuse of delegated power. His presence would have saved thousands, if he were simply nothing more than a thrifty despot; if he were not even *that*, the dread of his person would have preserved for him a territory, which was lost through hatred and scorn for his instruments.

Just as the oppression of the people of the Netherlands became an urgent affair to all men conscious of their rights, one might think, that the insubordination and revolt of this people would be a rallying-call to all princes, to protect their own privileges by protecting their neighbor's. But this time, envy of Spain triumphed over political sympathy, and the leading powers of Europe, more or less publicly, took the side of freedom. Emperor Maximilian II, although obligated to the Spanish house through ties of relationship, gave it just cause for the accusation of having favored the rebels' party in secret. Through the offer of his mediation he tacitly granted their grievances a degree of justification, which would surely encourage the rebels to insist upon them all the more resolutely. Under an emperor honestly devoted to the Spanish court, William of Orange would have had difficulty drawing so many troops and funds from Germany. France, without openly and formally breaking the peace, placed a prince of the blood at the head of the Netherlands' rebellion; the latter's operations were carried out for the most part with French funds and troops. Elizabeth of England simply wreaked a justified revenge and retaliation, when she protected the insurgents against their legitimate overlords, and if her frugal assistance only sufficed at most to avert the total ruin of the republic, this was infinitely much, at a point when hope alone could extend their exhausted courage. With these two powers Philip still stood at the time in a peace compact, and both became traitors to him. Between the strong and the weak, candid honesty is often no virtue; he who is feared, rarely gains advantage from the finer ties which bind equal with equal. Philip had himself banished truth from political intercourse, himself dissolved morality between kings, and made deception the deity of the cabinet. Without ever taking pleasure in his ascendancy, he was obliged his whole life through to contend with the envy he awakened in others. Europe let him suffer for misusing a power, whose full use in fact he had never possessed.

If, weighed against the inequality of the two combatants, which at first glance is so astonishing, one takes into consideration all accidents, which were inimical to the first and favorable to the other, this event's supernatural aspect disappears, but the extraordinary aspect remains—and one has found a just metric, to estimate these republicans' own credit for achieving their freedom. Yet one should not think, that the undertaking itself was preceded by such a precise calculation of forces, or that, as they entered upon this uncertain sea, the republicans were already acquainted with the shore on which they afterward landed. In the intent of its originators the action did not appear so developed as it ultimately stood in its accomplishment, any more than the perpetual division of the faith appeared before Luther's mind, when he stood up against the sale of indulgences. What a difference between the modest procession of those beggars in Brussels, who supplicate for a more humane treatment as for a boon, and the dreadful majesty of a free state, which treats with kings as its equals and within less than a century disposes of the throne of its former tyrant! The unseen hand of fate led forth the spent arrow in a higher trajectory and a wholly different direction than the bowstring had given it. In the womb of fortunate Brabant was born the freedom, which, torn from its mother as a newborn child, was to bless despised Holland. But the undertaking itself ought not appear to us as a lesser one because it turned out otherwise than it was intended. The individual works, polishes, and forms the rough stone, which the era brings his way; to him belong the moment and the place, but accident drives world history. If the passions, which during this event actively manifested themselves, were but not unworthy of the work they served unawares—if the forces, which they helped put into effect, and the particular actions, from whose linkage the event wondrously sprang up, were but in themselves noble forces, beautiful and great actions, then the event is great, interesting, and fruitful for us, and we are at liberty to marvel over the bold offspring of accident, or to elevate our admiration to a higher understanding.

The history of the world is self-consistent, like the laws of nature, and unitary, like the individual soul of man. The same conditions bring back the same phenomena. On just this soil, where now the Netherlands defy their Spanish tyrants, fifteen hundred years earlier their forefathers, the Batavi and Belgae, struggled with their Roman counterparts. In the same way as the Netherlanders were unwillingly subjected to a proud ruler, abused in the same way by rapacious satraps, they threw off their chains with like defiance and sought their fortune in just as unequal combat. The same conqueror's pride, the same ardor of a nation, in the Spaniards of the sixteenth century and in the Romans of the first, the same valor and manly training in both armies, the same terror inspired by their battle formations. There as here we see stratagem contend against superior strength, and perseverance, supported by unity, wear out a monstrous force, which has weakened itself through division. There as here, private enmity arms the nation; a single individual, born for his time, reveals to it the dangerous secret of its powers and leads its mute grief to a bloody manifesto. "Confess, Batavi!" Claudius Civilis addresses his fellow citizens in the sacred grove, "are we still treated by these Romans as allies and friends, or not instead as servile subjects? We are handed over to their prefects and governors, who, when our plunder, our blood, has satiated them, are replaced by others, who simply renew the same violent atrocities under other names. If it finally happens, that Rome sends us an inspector general, he oppresses us with a swaggering and costly entourage and an even more insufferable pride. The conscriptions approach once again, which tear children from parents, brothers from brothers forever, and deliver our vigorous youth over to Roman lechery. Now, Batavi, is the moment ours. Never did Rome lie prostrate as now. Let not this *name* 'legions' pursue you in terror; their camps contain nothing but old men and booty. We have footsoldiers and horsemen. Germany is ours, and Gaul would fain throw off its yoke. Let Syria serve them, and Asia, and the East, which needs kings! There are still those among us who were born before tribute was paid to the Romans. The gods side with the bravest." Solemn sacraments consecrate their conspiracy, like that of the Gueux League; like the latter, it hides itself cunningly in the cloak of submissiveness, in the majesty of a great name. The cohorts of Civilis swear an oath on the Rhine to Vespasian in Syria, as the compromise was sworn with Philip II. The same field of combat produces the same plan of defense, the same recourse for desperation. Both entrusted their foundering fortunes to a friendly element; in similar distress Civilis saves his island—as fifteen centuries after him William of Orange the city of Leyden—through an artificial flood. The valor of the Batavi exposes the impotence of the ruler of the world, as the beautiful courage of their descendants exhibits to all of Europe the decline of Spanish power. The same fertility of mind in the military leaders of both times allowed the war to persist with equal stubbornness and to show an almost equally doubtful outcome; but we note one difference, nevertheless: the Romans and Batavi made war humanely, for they did not make war on behalf of religion.[1]

Notes

* *Translator's note:* In Greek legend, the forty-nine daughters of the King of Argos, who killed their husbands at their father's command, were condemned in Hades to pour water into broken containers forever.

1. *Author's note:* Tacitus, *Histories*, books IV, V.

AESTHETICS AND PHILOSOPHY

LOVE, VIRTUE, FRIENDSHIP

TRANSLATED BY GABRIELE KARLS CHAITKIN

Five thousand years ago today, Zeus had invited the immortal gods to Olympus for a banquet. When all were seated, a dispute arose among the three daughters of Jupiter. *Virtue* wanted to go before *Love*, *Love* did not want to give way to *Virtue*, and *Friendship* maintained her position before both. All Heaven was thrown into commotion, and the quarrelling goddesses went before the throne of Saturn.

"There is only *one* nobility at Olympus," exclaimed the son of Chronos, "and only *one* law, whereby one judges the gods. He is first, who creates the happiest men."

"I have won," shouted *Love*, triumphant. "Even my sister *Virtue* cannot give her favorite any greater reward than *I*, and Jupiter and all present immortal gods may affirm that I spread delight."

"And how long does your rapture endure?" *Virtue* earnestly interrupted her. "Whom I protect with my invincible shield, laughs at dreadful Fate, to whom even the immortals pay homage. If *you* boast with the example of gods, so can I, too—the son of Saturn is mortal, as soon as he is not virtuous."

Schiller sent this fable on August 7, 1785 as a wedding present to his lifelong friend Christian Gottfried Körner and Körner's new wife, Minna Stock. *Love, Virtue, Friendship* is Schiller's only extant fable.

Friendship stood at a distance, and kept silent.

"And you, no word, my daughter?" called Jupiter, "what greatness will you offer your favorite?"

Nothing to all this answered the goddess, and secretly wiped away a tear from her blushing cheek. "I am left alone, when they are happy, but they only long for me, when they suffer."

"Reconcile yourselves, my children," spoke now the father of the gods. "Your quarrel is the most beautiful, which Zeus has ever mediated, but none of you has lost it. My manly daughter, *Virtue*, will teach her sister *Love* constancy, and *Love* will not bless any favorite, which *Virtue* has not led to her. But between both of you steps *Friendship*, and guarantees to me the eternity of this bond."

PHILOSOPHICAL LETTERS

TRANSLATED BY WILLIAM F. WERTZ, JR.

Preamble

Reason has its epochs, its destinies, like the heart, but its history is far more rarely treated. One seems to be satisfied therewith, to develop the passions in their extreme, their aberrations and consequences, without taking into consideration, how exactly they cohere with the intellectual system of the individual. The universal root of moral degeneration is a one-sided and wavering philosophy, so much the more dangerous, because it blinds the beclouded reason with an appearance of lawfulness, truth, and conviction, and just for this reason is held less in bounds by the inborn moral feeling. An enlightened understanding, on the other

---

The *Philosophical Letters* were published by Schiller in the March 1786 edition of *Thalia*, Schiller's journal of poetry and philosophical writings. The idea for the letters arose earlier, during Schiller's academic years. The poem *Friendship*, which is quoted in part in the letters, originally appeared in an anthology of his poems in the year 1782 and was referred to as coming from the letters of Julius to Raphael, a yet unpublished fictional work.
Although the letters are represented as a fiction, the *Theosophy of Julius*, which is the centerpiece of the correspondence, clearly reflects the philosophical outlook of the young Schiller. The role of Raphael was assumed by Schiller's friend Christian Gottfried Körner. The beginning of the first letter from Raphael was appar-

hand, also ennobles the sentiments—the head must form the heart.

In an epoch like the present one, where facilitation and spread of reading so astonishingly enlarge the thinking part of the public, where the happy resignation to ignorance begins to make room for a *half* enlightenment and only a few still wish to *remain there*, where the *accident of birth has cast them down*, it seems not to be so entirely unimportant to call attention to certain periods of awakening and progressing reason, to correct certain truths and errors, which are connected to morality and can be a source of felicity and misery, and, at the very least, to indicate the concealed reefs on which proud reason has already run aground. We arrive at truth only rarely other than through extremes—we must first exhaust the error—and often the nonsense, before we work ourselves up to the beautiful goal of tranquil wisdom.

Some friends, inspired by an equal warmth for the truth and moral beauty, who have united upon entirely different pathways in the *same* conviction and now survey with more tranquil glance the already traveled course, have joined in the plan, to develop several revolutions and epochs of thought, several excesses of the pondering reason in the portrait of two young men of unequal character, and to place

---

ently written by Körner, and the second letter from Raphael, which is the concluding letter of the correspondence, was definitely written by Körner and not Schiller.

Although Schiller printed the final letter by Körner in *Thalia*, it did not appear in the first printing, nor in subsequent printings. This letter was apparently part of a plan by Schiller to continue the letters beyond the *Theosophy of Julius*, but this plan was never carried out beyond Körner's final letter. This letter is therefore included in this translation for its historical interest, but should not be read as a direct philosophical statement by Schiller. It in no way contradicts the view, that the *Theosophy of Julius* and the poem *Friendship* reflect the youthful philosophical outlook of the Poet of Freedom.

them before the world in the form of an exchange of letters. The following letters are the beginning of this attempt.

The opinions which will be presented in these letters, can therefore also only be respectively true or false, just so, as the world is mirrored in this one's soul and no other. The pursuit of the letter exchange will show how these one-sided, often exaggerated, often contradictory assertions finally are resolved in a universal, purified, and firmly grounded truth.

Skepticism and free-thinking are the feverish paroxysms of the human spirit and must, through the very same unnatural concussion, which they cause in well-organized souls, at last help fortify the health. The more blinding, the more seducing the error, that much more the triumph for truth, the more tormenting the doubt, the greater the invitation to conviction and firm certainty. However, to express this doubt, this error, was necessary; the knowledge of the disease had to precede the cure. The truth loses nothing, if a passionate youth misses it, just as little as virtue and religion, if a scoundrel renounces them.

This had to have been said in advance, in order to specify the point of view from which we wish the following exchange of letters to be read and judged.

JULIUS TO RAPHAEL

In October.

Thou art gone, Raphael—and the beautiful nature sinks below, the leaves fall yellow from the trees, a thick autumn fog lies like a pall over the deserted fields. Alone I wander through the melancholy region, call out thy name aloud and am wroth, that my Raphael does not answer me.

I have survived thy last embraces. The sad rush of the carriage, which transported thee away, was at last silenced in mine ear. I, the fortunate one, had already piled up a charitable hill of earth over the joys of the past, and now thou standest up like thy departed spirit anew in these regions, and announcest thyself to me at each favorite site of our walks. These rocks have I ascended at *thy* side, at thy side I wandered through this immeasurable perspective. In the black sanctuary of this beech grove we first devised the bold ideal of our friendship. Here it was, where we for the first time unrolled the genealogical tree of the spirit and Julius found in Raphael such a close relative. Here is no spring, no thicket, no hill, where some memory of departed happiness did not take aim at my tranquility. Everything, everything has conspired against my recovery. Wherever I but tread, I repeat the anxious scene of our separation.—

What hast thou made of me, Raphael? What has in a short time become of me! Dangerous great man! that I never had known or never lost thee! Hasten back, come back upon the wings of love, or thy tender planting is past. Couldst thou venture with thy gentle soul, to abandon thy work just begun, still so far from its completion? The founding pillars of thy proud wisdom totter in my brain and heart, all the magnificent palaces, which thou didst construct, collapse, and the worm, crushed to death, writhes whimpering under the ruins.

Blessed paradisiacal time, when with eyes bound, I still staggered through life like a drunk—when all my forwardness and all my wishes turned back once again to the boundaries of my fatherly horizon—when a serene sunset caused me to have a presentiment of nothing higher than a beautiful day in the morrow—when only a political newspaper reminded me of the world, only the funeral bell of eternity, only ghost stories of being called to account after death, when I still trembled before a devil and all the more heartily clung to the Divinity. I *felt* and was happy. Raphael has taught me to *think*, and I am on the way to weep over my creation.

Creation? —No, that is indeed only a sound without meaning, which my reason may not permit. There was a time, when I knew of nothing, when no one knew of me, therefore one says, I was not. That time is no longer, therefore one says, that I be created. However, one now also knows nothing more of the millions, who were present centuries ago, and yet one says, they are. Whereupon ground we the right, to affirm the beginning and to deny the end? The cessation of thinking beings, one asserts, contradicts infinite Goodness. Did this infinite Goodness then originate first with the creation of the world? —If there had been a period, when there were still no spirits, was infinite Goodness thus indeed ineffective for an entire preceding eternity? If the structure of the world is a perfection of the Creator, so did He indeed lack a perfection before the creation of the world? However, such an assumption contradicts the idea of the perfect God, therefore there was no creation—Where have I gotten to, my Raphael?— Terrible fallacy of my conclusions! I give up the Creator, so soon as I believe in a God. Wherefore do I need a God, if I suffice without the Creator?

Thou hast stolen the belief from me, which gave me peace. Thou hast taught me to despise, where I worshipped. A thousand things were so venerable to me, before thy sad wisdom undressed them to me. I saw a crowd of people stream toward the church, I heard their inspired devotion unite in a brotherly prayer—twice did I stand before the bed of death, saw twice—powerful wonderwork of religion!—the hope of heaven triumph over the horror of annihilation and kindle the fresh light beams of joy in the dimmed eyes of the dying. Godly, yes godly must the doctrine be, I called out, which the best among men acknowledge, which so powerfully triumphs and so wonderfully comforts. Thy cold wisdom extinguished my enthusiasm. Just as many, thou didst say to me, once thronged around the Statue of Armenius and to Jupiter's temple, just as many have just as joyfully ascended the stake to honor their Brahma. What thou findest so abominable in heathenism, shall that prove the divinity of thy doctrine?

Believe none but thine own reason, thou didst further say. There is nothing more holy than the truth. What reason discerns, is the truth. I have thee obeyed, have all opinions sacrificed, have, like that desperate conqueror, set fire to all my ships, when I landed on this island, and destroyed all hope of return. I can never again reconcile myself with an opinion, which I once ridiculed. My reason is now all to me, my only guarantee for divinity, virtue, immortality. Woe to me from now on, if I meet this only guarantor in a contradiction! if my respect for its conclusions sinks! if a broken thread in my brain shifts its course! —My happiness is from now on entrusted to the harmonious rhythm of my sensorium. Woe to me, if the strings of this instrument give a false sound in the critical periods of my life—if my convictions waver with my pulse beat!

JULIUS TO RAPHAEL

Thy theory has flattered my pride. I was a prisoner. Thou hast led me out into the day, the golden light and the immeasurable open air have delighted mine eyes. Before, I was satisfied with the modest reputation of being called a good son of my house, a friend of my friends, a useful member of society, thou hast transformed me into a citizen of the universe. My wishes had not yet encroached upon the rights of the great. I tolerated those fortunate ones, because beggars tolerated *me*. I did not blush to envy a part of the human species, because there was yet a greater part remaining, which I had to lament. Now I learned for the first time, that my pretensions to enjoyment were as weighty as those of my remaining brothers. Now I realized, that a layer above this atmosphere I was worth exactly as much and as little as the rulers of the earth. Raphael cut all bonds of agreement and of opinion in two. I felt myself entirely free—for reason, Raphael said to me, is the only monarchy in the world of spirits, I carried my imperial throne in my brain. All things in heaven and upon the earth have no worth, no valuation, except so much as my reason concedes them. The entire creation is mine, for I possess an unchallengeable full power, to enjoy it fully. All spirits—one step below the most perfect Spirit—are my fellow brothers, because we all obey *one* rule, to pay homage to *one* Supreme Master.

How sublime and magnificent this announcement sounds! What a store for my thirst of knowledge! but—unfortunate contradiction of nature—this free upward-striving spirit is woven into the rigid, unchangeable clockwork of a mortal body, mixed up with its small requirements, yoked to its small destiny—this god is banished into a world of worms. The enormous space of nature is opened to his activity, but he may only not think two ideas at the same time. His eyes carry him up to the sunny goal of the Divinity, but he himself must first creep toward Him inertly and laboriously through the elements of time. To exhaust one enjoyment, he must give up for lost every other; *two* unrestricted desires are too great for his small heart. Every newly acquired joy costs him the sum of all the previous ones. The present moment is the tomb of all of the past ones. A shepherd's rendezvous is an intermittent pulse beat in friendship.

Wherever I but look, Raphael, how limited is man! How great the distance between his pretensions and their fulfillment!—Oh yet envy him his beneficent sleep. Wake him not. He was so happy, until he began to question, whither he had to go, and whence had come. Reason is a torch in a prison. The prisoner knew nothing of the light, but a dream of freedom appeared over him like a lightning flash in the night, which leaves it darker behind. Our philosophy is the unhappy curiosity of Oedipus, who did not slacken his search, until the horrible oracle was solved.

Mayest thou never discover who thou art!

Does thy wisdom compensate me, for what it has taken from me? If thou hadst no key to Heaven, why didst thou have to lead me away from the earth? If thou didst know in advance, that the way to wisdom led through the terrible abyss of doubt, why didst thou venture the peaceful innocence of thy Julius upon this dubious design?

>   —If to the good,
>   Which I intend to do, there borders all
>   Too near what's very bad, so I would rather
>   Not do the good—

Thou hast torn down a cottage which was inhabited, and founded a magnificent dead palace upon the spot.

Raphael, I claim my soul from thee. I am not happy. My courage is gone. I despair of mine own strength. Write me soon. Only thy healing hand can pour balsam on my burning wound.

RAPHAEL TO JULIUS

A happiness such as ours, Julius, without interruption, were too much for a human lot. This thought quite often pursued me in the full enjoyment of our friendship. What then embittered my bliss was curative preparation, for alleviating my present condition. Hardened in the rigorous school of resignation, I am still more susceptible to the comfort of seeing in our separation a small sacrifice, in order to earn from fate the joys of our future union. Thou didst not yet know until now what *privation* be. Thou dost suffer for the first time—

And yet is it perhaps a benefit for thee, that I was just now torn from thy side. Thou hast to survive an illness, from which thou canst only recover through thine own self alone, in order to be safe from any relapse. The more deserted thou feel'st thyself, the more thou wilt summon all healing power in thyself; the less thou receivest momentary alleviation from deceptive palliatives, the more certain wilt thou succeed in rooting out the evil at its foundation.

That I have roused thee from thy sweet dreams, I do not yet regret, even if thy present condition is unpleasant. I have done nothing except accelerate a crisis, which, to such souls as thine, sooner or later is inevitably imminent and in which everything depends thereon, in which period of life it is endured. There are situations in which it is terrible, to despair at truth and virtue. Woe to him, who, in the storms of passion, has to fight with the subtleties of a caviling reason. What this means I have felt myself in its entire extent, and, in order to preserve thee from such a destiny, nothing remained left to me, but to neutralize this unavoidable epidemic through *inoculation*.

And what more favorable moment could I have chosen, my Julius! In the full strength of youth thou stoodst before me, body and spirit in the most glorious bloom, oppressed by no cares, fettered by no passion, to succeed *freely* and *strongly* in the great fight, whereof the sublime peace of *conviction* is the prize. Truth and error were not yet interwoven in thine interest. Thine enjoyment and thy virtues were independent of both. Thou didst require no deterring images to pull thee back from base debaucheries. The feeling for noble joys had made these disgusting to thee. Thou wert *good* from *instinct*, from undesecrated moral grace. I had nothing to fear for thy morality, if a structure collapsed on which it was not grounded. And yet thine apprehensions did not yet frighten me. Whatever may inspire in thee a melancholy temper, I know thee better, Julius.

Ungrateful one! Thou dost decry reason, thou forgetest, what joys it has already awarded to thee. Even hadst thou been able to escape the addiction to doubt for thine entire life, so was it a duty for me, not to withhold pleasures from thee, of which thou wert capable and worthy. The step, whereon thou stoodst, was not worthy of thee. The path, on which thou didst climb upward, offered thee compensation for everything that I robbed from thee. I still remember with what delight thou didst bless the moment, when the bandage fell from thine eyes. That warmth, with which thou didst grasp the truth, has perhaps led thine all-devouring imagination to the abyss, before which, terrified, thou drawest back shuddering.

I must trace the course of thine inquiries, in order to discover the sources of thy complaints. Thou hast otherwise written up the results of thy reflections. Send me these papers, and then I will answer thee.—

JULIUS TO RAPHAEL

This morning I root through my papers. I find a lost composition again, drawn up in those happy hours of my proud enthusiasm. Raphael, how entirely different do I find everything now! It is the wooden stage of the theater, when the lighting is gone. My heart sought a philosophy, and imagination substituted her dreams. The warmest was to me the true.

I search for the laws of the spirit—swing myself up to the infinite, but I forget to prove that they really exist. A bold assault of materialism collapses my creation.

Thou wilt read through this fragment, my Raphael. Would that thou dost succeed in kindling once again the extinct sparks of my enthusiasm, to reconcile me again with my genius—but my pride has sunk so deeply that even Raphael's applause will hardly raise it up again.

THEOSOPHY OF JULIUS

The world and the thinking being

The universe is a thought of God. After this ideal mental image stepped over into reality and the engendered world fulfilled the design of its Creator—permit me this human presentation—so is the vocation of all thinking beings, to find once again the first design in this existing whole, to seek out the rule in the machine, the unity in the composition, the law in the phenomenon and to pass backward from the structure to its founding design. Therefore, for me there is a single appearance in nature, the thinking being. The great composition, which we name the world, remains noteworthy to me now, only because it is present to indicate to me symbolically the manifold expressions of that being. Everything in me and outside of me is only the hieroglyph of a power, which is similar to me. The laws of nature are the ciphers, which the thinking being joins together, to make itself understandable to the thinking being—the alphabet, by means of which all spirits converse with the most perfect spirit and with themselves. Harmony, truth, order, beauty, excellence give me joy, because they place me into the active condition of their inventor, of their possessor, because they betray to me the presence of a rational, feeling Being and let me divine my relationship with this Being. A new experience in this realm of truth, gravitation, the discovered circulation of the blood, the natural system of Linnaeus, signify to me originally the same as an antique, dug up at Herculaneum—both only the reflection of one spirit, a new acquaintance with a being similar to me. I confer with the infinite through the instrument of nature, through the history of the world—I read the soul of the Artist in his Apollo.

Wouldst thou convince thyself, my Raphael, so search backward. Each state of the human soul has some parable in the physical creation, through which it is indicated, and not artists and poets alone, but even the most abstract thinkers have drawn from this abundant warehouse. Lively activity we name fire, time is a stream, which rolls rapaciously forth, eternity is a circle, a mystery is wrapped in midnight, and the truth dwells in the sun. Yes, I begin to believe, that even the future destiny of the human spirit lies proclaimed in advance in the dark oracle of the physical creation. Each coming spring, which drives the shoots of plants out of the womb of the earth, gives me explanation of the uneasy riddle of death and refutes my anxious apprehension of an eternal sleep. The swallow, which we find benumbed in winter and in spring see come to life again, the dead caterpillar, which, rejuvenated as the butterfly, rises into the air, give us an excellent sensuous image of our immortality.

How noteworthy everything becomes to me now!—Now, Raphael, all is peopled round about me. There is for me no longer any solitude in the whole of nature. Where I discover a body, there I divine a spirit—Where I notice movement, there I conjecture a thought.

"Where no dead lies buried, where no resurrection will be," speaks Omnipotence indeed to me through His works, and so I understand the theory of an omnipresence of God.

Idea

All spirits are attracted by perfection. All—there are aberrations here, but no single exception—all strive after the condition of the highest free expression of their powers, all possess the common drive, to extend their activity, to attract all to themselves, to assemble in themselves, to make their own what they recognize as good, as excellent, as fascinating. Intuition of the beautiful, of the true, of the excellent is the instantaneous taking possession of these properties. Whichever condition we perceive, we enter into it ourselves. In the moment when we think of them, we are the proprietors of a virtue, the authors of an action, inventors of a truth, owners of a happiness. We ourselves become the perceived object. Let me be confused here by no ambiguous smile, my Raphael—this assumption is the basis whereupon I based all the following, and we must be agreed, before I have courage to complete my construction.

The inner feeling already tells everyone something similar. When we, for example, admire an act of generosity, of bravery, of intelligence, does not a secret consciousness stir here in our heart, that we were capable of doing the same? Does not the bright red, which at the hearing of such a story colors our cheeks, already betray that *our* modesty trembles at the admiration? that *we* become embarrassed over the praise, which the ennobling of our being must earn us? Yes, even our body in this moment attunes itself in the gestures of the acting man and shows clearly, that our soul has passed over into this condition. If thou wert present, Raphael, when a great event was related before a large assembly, didst thou not read in the narrator's face, how he himself awaited the incense, he himself consumed the applause, which was offered to his hero—and, if thou wert the narrator, didst thou never surprise thy heart in this happy deception? Thou hast examples, Raphael, how lively I can wrangle even with my heart's friend about the reading of a beautiful anecdote, of an excellent poem, and my heart has softly confessed to me, that I only begrudged thee the laurel, which passes over from the creator to the reader. A quick and intimate artistic feeling for virtue is universally held to be a great talent for virtue, just as one, on the contrary, bears no hesitation to question the heart of a man, whose head grasps moral beauty difficultly and slowly.

Do not object to me that, not infrequently, the opposing defect is found with the lively perception of a perfection, that a high enthusiasm for the excellent often *overcomes* even the villain, an enthusiasm of high Herculean greatness sometimes flames through even the weak. I know, for example, that our admired Haller, who unmasked in such a manly way the esteemed nothingness of vain honors, whose philosophical greatness I afforded so much admiration, that even he was not able to despise the even more vain nothingness of a knight's star medallion, which offended his greatness. I am convinced that, in the happy moment of the ideal, the artist, the philosopher, and the poet are really the great and good men, whose image they outline—however, this ennobling of the spirit is with many only an unnatural condition produced forcibly by a more lively boiling of the blood, a more rapid flight of the imagination, which, however, for that very reason, disappears as fleetingly as any other enchantment and delivers the heart all the more exhausted over to the despotic caprice of the base passions. All the more exhausted, I say—for a universal experience teaches, that the relapsing criminal is always the more furious, that the renegades of virtue recover all the more sweetly from the uncomfortable compulsion of repentance only in the arms of vice.

I wanted to prove, my Raphael, that it is our own condition, when we feel a strange one, that the perfection becomes ours at the moment wherein we awaken in ourselves a conception of it, that our pleasure in truth, beauty, and virtue is resolved at last in the consciousness of our own ennobling, our own enriching, and I believe I have proven it.

We have concepts of the wisdom of the highest Being, of His goodness, of His justice—but none of His omnipotence. To indicate His omnipotence, we help ourselves with the stepwise presentation of three successions: Nothing, His Will, and Something. It is waste and dark—God calls: Light—and it becomes light. Had we a real idea of His working omnipotence, so were we creators, as He.

Every perfection, therefore, which I perceive, becomes mine own, it gives me joy, because it is mine own, I desire it, because I love myself. Perfection in nature is no property of matter, but rather of the spirit. All spirits are happy through their perfection. I desire the happiness of all spirits, because I love myself. The happiness, which I present to myself, becomes my happiness, therefore I desire, to awaken these presentations, to multiply and to elevate them—therefore, I desire to extend happiness all around me. What beauty, what excellence, what enjoyment I bring forth outside me, I bring forth within myself; that which I neglect, destroy, I destroy within myself, I neglect within myself—I desire the happiness of others, because I desire mine own. Desire for the happiness of others we name benevolence, *love*.

Love

Now, best Raphael, let me look around. The height has been scaled, the fog has fallen, as in a blossoming landscape I stand in the midst of the immeasurable. A purer sunlight has refined all my concepts.

Love therefore—the most beautiful phenomenon in the soul-filled creation, the omnipotent magnet in the spiritual world, the source of devotion and of the most sublime virtue—Love is only the reflection of this single original power, an attraction of the excellent, grounded upon an instantaneous exchange of the personality, a confusion of the beings.

When I hate, so take I something from myself; when I love, so become I so much the richer, by what I love. Forgiveness is the recovery of an alienated property—hatred of man a prolonged suicide; egoism the highest poverty of a created being.

When Raphael stole away from my last embrace, my soul was torn apart, and I cry at the loss of my more beautiful half. On that blessed evening—thou art acquainted with it—when our souls for the first time ardently came in touch, all thy great perceptions became mine own, I only asserted mine eternal property right upon thine excellence—prouder thereof, to love thee, than to be loved by thee, for the first had made me into Raphael.

> "Was't not this omnipotent desire,
> That in love's eternal happy fire
> Did our hearts unto each other force?
> Raphael, upon thine arm—delight!
> Venture I to th' spir'tual sun so bright
> Joyful on perfection's course.
>
> Happy! Happy! Thee have I thus found,
> Have from out of millions thee wound round,
> And from out the millions thou art *mine*.
> Let the savage chaos come once more,
> Let the atoms in confusion pour,
> For eternity our hearts entwine.
>
> Must I not from out thy flaming eyes
> Draw th' reflection of my paradise?
> But in thee I wonder at myself.
> Fairer doth th' fair earth to me appear,
> In the friend's demeanor shines more clear,
> Lovelier the Heav'n itself.
>
> Melancholy drops the tearful weight,
> Sweetly th' storm of passion to abate,
> In the breast of charity.
> Seeks not e'en the torturous delight,

Raphael, within thy spirit's sight,
A voluptuous grave impatiently?

Stood i' th' All o' creation I alone,
Do I dream of souls i' th' rocky stone,
And embracing them I kiss.
My complaints I moan into the sky
I enjoyed, the chasm did reply,
Fool enough, sweet sympathetic bliss."—

Love does not take place between equal sounding souls, but between harmonious ones. With pleasure I discern again my perceptions in the mirror of thine, but with fiery longing I devour the higher ones, which are lacking in me. *One* rule guides friendship and love. The gentle Desdemona loves her Othello for the dangers which he survived; the manly Othello loves her for the tears which she shed for him.

There are moments in life, when we are disposed to press to our bosoms every flower and every distant star, every worm and every higher spirit thought of—an embrace of the whole of nature like our beloved. Thou dost understand me, my Raphael. The man who has brought it so far, as to gather up all beauty, greatness, excellence in the small and great of nature and to find the great unity in this manifoldness, has already moved very much nearer to the Divinity. The entire creation dissolves his personality. If each man loved all men, so each individual possessed the world.

The philosophy of our time—I fear—contradicts this theory. Many of our thinking heads have made it their business, to mock this heavenly instinct away from the human soul, to efface the stamp of divinity and to dissolve this energy, this noble enthusiasm in the cold, deadening breath of a pusillanimous indifference. In the slavish feeling of their own degradation, they have resigned themselves to the dangerous enemy of benevolence, self-interest, to explain a phenomenon, which was too godlike for their limited hearts. Out of a scanty egoism they have spun their comfortless theory and have made their own limits into the measure of the Creator—Degenerate slaves, who decry freedom amidst the clang of their chains. Swift, who carried the reproach of folly up to the insult of mankind and at first wrote his own name on the pillory, which he erected for the whole species, even Swift could not inflict so deadly a wound upon human nature as these dangerous thinkers, who adorn their self-interest with every display of sagacity and genius and ennoble it into a system.

Why should the entire species suffer, if several members despair of their worth?

I admit it frankly; I believe in the reality of an unselfish love. I am lost, if it is not, I give up the Divinity, immortality, and virtue. I have no further remaining proof for these hopes, if I cease to believe in love. A spirit, which loves itself alone, is a swimming atom in the immeasurable *empty* space.

Sacrifice

But love has brought forth effects, which seem to contradict its nature.

It is thinkable, that I enlarge mine own happiness through a sacrifice, which I offer for the happiness of others—but also then, when this sacrifice is my life? And history has examples of such sacrifice—and I feel it lively, that it should cost me nothing, to die for Raphael's deliverance. How is it possible, that we regard death as a means to enlarge the sum of our enjoyments? How can the cessation of my existence agree with the enrichment of my being?

The assumption of an immortality lifts this contradiction—but it also distorts forever the high gracefulness of this appearance. Consideration of a rewarding future excludes love. There must be a virtue, which suffices even without the belief in immortality, which effects the same sacrifice even at the danger of annihilation.

It is indeed ennobling to the human soul, to sacrifice the present advantage for the eternal—it is the noblest degree of egoism—but egoism and love separate mankind into two highly dissimilar races, whose boundaries *never* flow into one another. Egoism erects its center in itself; love plants it outside of itself in the axis of the eternal whole. Love aims at unity, egoism is solitude. Love is the co-governing citizen of a blossoming free state, egoism a despot in a ravaged creation. Egoism sows for gratitude, love for ingratitude. Love gives, egoism lends—regardless in front of the throne of the judging truth, whether for the enjoyment of the next-following moment, or with the view toward a martyr's crown—regardless, whether the tributes fall in this life or in the other!

Think thee of a truth, my Raphael, which benefits the whole human species into distant centuries—add thereto, this truth condemns its confessor to death, this truth can only be proven, only be believed, if he dies. Think thee then of the man with the bright, encompassing, sunny look of genius, with the flaming wheel of enthusiasm, with the wholly sublime predisposition to love. Let the complete ideal of this great effect climb aloft in his soul—let pass to him in a faint presentiment all the happy ones, whom he shall create—let the present and the future press together at the same time in his spirit—and now answer thee, does this man require the assignment to an other life?

The sum of all these perceptions will become confused with his personality, will flow together into one with his I. The human species, of which he now thinks, is he himself. It is *one* body, in which *his* life, forgotten and dispensible, swims like a drop of blood—how quickly will he shed it for his health!

God

All perfections in the universe are united in God. God and nature are two quantities, which are perfectly alike.

The sum total of harmonic activity, which exists *together* in the divine substance, is in nature, the image of this substance, *scattered* in innumerable degrees and measures and steps. Nature (permit me this pictorial expression), nature is an infinitely divided God.

As in the prismatic glass a white stripe of light is split up into seven darker beams, the divine *I* has been refracted into countless perceiving substances. As seven darker beams melt together again in *one* bright stripe of light, out of the union of all these substances a divine Being would issue forth. The existing form of nature's structure is the optical glass, and all activities of the spirits only an infinite play of colors of that simple divine beam. If it pleased the Omnipotence one day, to smash this prism, so the dam between it and the world would collapse, all spirits would sink into *one* infinity, all accords flow into one another in *one* harmony, all brooks cease in *one* ocean.

The attractive power of the elements brought about the bodily form of nature. The attractive power of spirits, multiplied and continued into the infinite, had to lead at last to the annulment of that separation, or (may I express it, Raphael?) bring forth God. Such an attractive power is love.

Therefore love, my Raphael, is the ladder, whereby we climb aloft to divine likeness. Without laying claim thereto, unconsciously to ourselves, we aim thereat.

> "Lifeless groups are we, whene'er we hate,
> Gods, when lovingly we do relate,
> Yearning for the gentle shackles' force.
> Upward through the thousandfold gradation
> Of the countless spirits in creation,
> Does this urge divinely course.
>
> Arm in arm, e'er freer still and freer
> From barbarian to Grecian seer,
> Who unto the last Seraph is near,
> Of one mind in coiling dance we flow,
> Till there in the sea of everlasting glow
> Time and measure dying disappear.

> Friendless was the Lord o' th' World so great,
> Lack He felt, thus spirits did create,
> Mirrors blest of *His* felicity.
> Though the highest One no equal found,
> From the cup of all of being's round,
> Foams to Him Infinity."

Love, my Raphael, is the exuberantly growing *arcanum*, to produce again the dishonored *king* of gold from the plain chalk, to rescue the eternal from the ephemeral, and the great oracle of duration from the destroying blaze of time.

What is the sum of all the foregoing?

Let us *look into* excellence, so it becomes ours. Let us become intimate with the high idealistic unity, so we shall join ourselves to one another with brotherly love. Let us plant beauty and joy, so we harvest beauty and joy. Let us think clearly, so shall we love ardently. Be perfect, as your Father in heaven is perfect, says the founder of our belief. Weak humanity grew pale at this command, therefore He explained Himself more clearly: Love one another.

> "Wisdom with the sunlike view,
> Goddess great, step backward do,
> Yield the way to love.
> Who i' th' steep and starry sky
> Led thee like a hero nigh
> To the Godhead's room?
> Who unveiled the holy home,
> Showed to thee Elysium
> Through the breach o' th' tomb?
>
> Bid us enter did not *she*,
> Wished we immortality?
> Sought we too the spirits
> Without her the master?
> Love and Love alone doth lead
> To the Father of the seed,
> Love alone the spirits."[1]

Here, my Raphael, hast thou my reason's confession of belief, a fleeting outline of my undertaken creation. Just as thou findest here, the seed came up, which thou strewed thyself in my soul. Mock now or take joy or blush at thy student. As thou wishest—but this philosophy has ennobled my heart and beautified the perspective of my life. 'Tis possible, my best, that the entire scaffolding of my conclusions has been a non-existent vision—the world, as I paint it here, is real perhaps nowhere, except in the brain of thy Julius—perhaps, at the end of a thousand thousand years of that Judge, when the promised wiser man sits upon the seat, at the sight of the true original I shall blushingly tear into pieces my schoolboy design—All of this may transpire, I await it; then, however, even if the reality never once resembles my dream, the reality will surprise me all the more charmingly; all the more majestically. Should *my* ideas be more beautiful than the ideas of the eternal Creator? How? Should He tolerate it, that His sublime work of art lagged behind the expectations of a mortal connoisseur?— That is exactly the unique experiment of His great perfection and the sweetest triumph for the Highest Spirit, that even false conclusions and deception do not injure His acknowledgment, that all serpentine writhings of the unbridled reason at last strike in the straight direction of the eternal truth, at last all apostate arms of its stream run toward the same estuary. Raphael—what idea the Artist rouses in me, who distorts differently in a thousand copies, nevertheless in all the thousands remains self-similar, from whom even the devastating hand of a bungler cannot withdraw worship!

By the way, my representation could be thoroughly wrong, could be thoroughly illegitimate—still more am I convinced that it must necessarily be so, and nevertheless it is possible that all results of it become true. Our whole knowledge, as all wise men of the world agree, amounts in the end to a conventional deception, with which, however, the strictest truth can exist. Our purest concepts are in no way *images* of things, but rather merely their necessary determined and coexisting *signs*. Neither God, nor the human soul, nor the world is really that which we consider them. Our thoughts of these things are only the endemic forms, wherein the planet which we inhabit delivers them over to us—our brain *belongs* to this planet, and thus also the idioms of our concepts, which lie preserved therein. But the power of the soul is peculiar, necessary, and always self-similar: the arbitrariness of the materials, through which it expresses itself, changes nothing in the eternal laws, according to which it expresses itself, so long as this arbitrariness does not stand in contradiction with itself, so long as the sign remains thoroughly true to the thing designated. Thus, as the thinking power develops the relations of the idioms, these relations must also be actually present in the things. Truth, therefore, is no property of the idioms, but rather of the conclusions; not the similarity of the sign with the designated, of the concept with the object, but rather the agreement of these concepts with the laws of the thinking power. Just so does the theory of quantity make use of ciphers, which are nowhere present except on the paper, and finds therewith what is present in the real world. What similarity, for example, have the letters A and B, the signs ":" and "=," "+" and "−" with the fact that should be gained? —And yet the comet announced centuries before rises in the distant heaven, yet the expected planet steps before the disc of the sun. Upon the infallibility of his calculation, the world discoverer Columbus makes a risky bet with an unnavigated ocean, to seek the missing second half of the known hemisphere, the great island of Atlantis, which should fill out the gap in his geographical map. He found it, this island of his paper, and his reckoning was right. Would it have been less so, if a hostile storm had shattered his ships or had driven them back toward their home?—The human reason makes a similar calculation, when it measures the nonsensuous with the help of the sensuous, and applies the mathematics of its conclusions to the hidden physics of the *superhuman*. But the last test of its calculations is still lacking, for no traveller came back from that land, to tell of his discovery.

Human nature has its own limits, each individual his own. Respecting the former, we want to mutually comfort ourselves; the latter Raphael will grant to the boyhood of his Julius. I am poor in conceptions, a stranger in many areas of knowledge, which one assumes to be indispensible to investigations of this kind. I have belonged to no philosophical school and have read few printed writings. It may be, that here and there I substitute my fantasies for stricter conclusions of reason, that I present the boiling of my blood, the forebodings and wants of my heart for sober wisdom, also that, my dear friend, shall nevertheless not cause me to regret the lost moment. It is real gain for universal perfection, it was the foresight of the wisest spirit, that the erring reason should also populate even the chaotic land of dreams and make arable the barren ground of contradiction. Not the mechanical artist only, who polishes the rough diamond into the brilliant—also the other is valuable, who ennobles common stones till they approach the apparent dignity of the diamond. The industry in the forms can sometimes cause one to forget the massive truth of the material. Is not every exercise of the thinking power, every fine sharpness of the mind, a small step toward its perfection, and every perfection must have obtained existence in the complete world. Reality does not limit itself to the absolutely necessary: it encompasses also the conditionally necessary; every birth of the brain, every tissue of the wit has an undeniable citizen's right in this greater sense of creation. In the infinite design of nature no activity was to be left out, no degree of enjoyment was to be lacking to universal happiness. That great Housekeeper of His world, who lets no splinter fall unused, no gap be unpeopled, where still some enjoyment of life has room, who with the poison, which threatens man, satisfies vipers and spiders, who sends plantings into the dead province of decay, the small blossoms of voluptuousness, which can germinate in madness, still dispenses economically, who at last processes vice and folly into excellence and knew to spin the great idea of the world-ruling

Rome from the lechery of Tarquinius Sextus—This Inventive Spirit shall also not allow *error* to consume His great purpose and this wide-ranging world course to run wild in the soul of man and to lie empty of joy? Every facility of reason, even in error, increases the facility for conception of truth.

Let, dear friend of my soul, let me also contribute mine to the wide-ranging cobweb of human wisdom. The image of the sun is painted differently in the dewdrops of the morning, differently in the majestic mirror of the earth-girdling ocean! But shame to the turbid, cloudy swamp, which never receives it and never reflects it back. Millions of plants drink from the four elements of nature. *One* storage room is open for all; but they mix their sap in a million different ways, return it in a million different ways; the beautiful manifoldness announces a rich master of the house. There are four elements, wherefrom all spirits draw: their *I*, *Nature*, *God*, and the *Future*. All mix them in a million different ways, return them in a million different ways, but there is *one* truth, which, like a firm axis, goes commonly through all religions and all systems—"Draw nearer to the God, in whom you believe."

RAPHAEL TO JULIUS

That were then certainly bad, if there were no other means to quiet thee, Julius, than to reproduce in thee the belief in the first born of thy reflection. I have again found with inner pleasure these ideas, which I saw sprouting up in thee, in thy papers. They are worthy of a soul, such as thine, but here thou couldst and mayest not remain. There are joys for every age, and enjoyments for every degree of the spirit.

Difficult must it indeed have been for thee, to sever thyself from a system, which was so entirely created for the requirements of thine heart. No other one, I wager thereon, will ever again strike such deep roots in thee, and perhaps mayest thou be left entirely but to thyself, in order to become reconciled again sooner or later to thy favorite ideas. The weaknesses of the opposite systems thou wouldst soon observe, and then in their equal unprovability, prefer the one most worthy of being desired, or perhaps discover new grounds of proof to rescue at least that which is essential thereof, even if thou hadst to abandon some ventured assertions.

But all of this is not in my plan. Thou shalt arrive at a higher *freedom of the spirit*, where thou art no more in need of such expedients. This is of course not the work of a moment. The ordinary aim of the earliest education is subjugation of the spirit, and of all the feats of the art of education this almost always succeeds the first. Even thou, in all the elasticity of thy character, appearest determined to a willing submission to the domination of *opinions* before thousands of others, and this condition of being under age could last in thee all the longer, the less thou feelest the oppression thereof. Head and heart are in thee in the closest connection. The theory became of worth to thee through the teacher. Soon thou didst succeed, to discover an interesting side therein, to ennoble it according to the needs of thine heart, and in regard to the points, which had to be striking to thee, to becalm thyself through resignation. Attacks against such opinions thou didst despise, as rascally revenge of a slavish soul against the rod of the disciplinarian. Thou madest a show with thy fetters, which thou didst believe to carry of thine own free choice.

So I found thee, and it was a sorrowful sight, how thou wert so often hemmed in by anxious considerations in the midst of the enjoyment of thy most blossoming life, and in the expression of thy most noble powers. The consistency with which thou actest according to thy convictions, and the strength of the soul, which made every sacrifice light to thee, were double restrictions of thine activity and thy joys. Then I resolved to frustrate those bungling efforts, whereby one had sought to compel a spirit like thine into the form of everyday minds. Everything depended thereon, to make thee attentive to the worth of self-thinking, and to infuse thee with confidence in thine own powers. The result of thy first attempts favored my intention. Thine imagination was indeed more employed thereby, than thine acumen. Its presentiments compensated thee more rapidly for the loss of thy dearest convictions, than thou couldst expect from the snail's pace of cold-blooded research, which progresses stepwise from the known to the unknown. However, even this inspiring system gave thee the first enjoyment in this new field of activity, and I guarded myself more against destroying a welcome enthusiasm, which promoted the development of thy most excellent predisposition. Now the scene has changed. The return under the guardianship of thy childhood is obstructed forever. Thy way goes forward, and thou dost require no further sparing.

That a system such as thine could not endure the test of a strong criticism, may not surprise thee. All attempts of this kind, which resemble thine in boldness and breadth of extent, have no other fate. Also nothing was more natural, than that thy philosophical career began with thee individually, as with the human species as a whole. The *first* object, on which the human spirit of research attempted, was always—the universe. Hypotheses about the origin of the cosmos and the coherence of its parts had occupied the greatest thinkers for centuries, when Socrates called the philosophy of his times down from the heaven to the earth. But the boundaries of the wisdom of life were too narrow for the proud thirst for knowledge of his followers. New systems arose from the debris of the old. The acumen of later times roamed through the immeasurable field of possible answers to those ever-anew obtruding questions about the mysterious interior of nature, which could be uncovered through no human experience. Some indeed succeeded, to give the results of their reflections a color of certainty, completeness, and evidence. There are many juggling arts, whereby the vain reason seeks to escape the disgrace, not to be able to step beyond the bounds of human nature in the extension of its knowledge. Soon one believes to have uncovered new truths, when one takes apart a concept into the individual components, out of which it was first *capriciously* composed. Soon an imperceptible assumption serves as the basis of a chain of conclusions, whose gaps one knows how to slyly conceal, and the surreptitiously obtained conclusions are wondered at as high wisdom. Soon one accumulates one-sided experiences, in order to found an hypothesis, and conceals the contradictory phenomena, or one mistakes the meaning of words according to the requirements of the line of reasoning. And these are not only artifices for the philosophical charlatan, to deceive his public. Even the most honest, most unprejudiced researcher often employs similar means, without being conscious of it, to satisfy his thirst for knowledge, so soon as he once steps out of the sphere, in which alone his reason can legitimately enjoy the results of its activity.

After what thou hast formerly heard from me, Julius, these expressions must not surprise thee a little. And yet they are not the product of a skeptical whim. I can give thee an account of the grounds, whereon they rest, but hereto I would indeed have to send out in advance a somewhat dry examination into the nature of human knowledge, which I prefer to save for a time, when it will be a requirement for thee. Thou art not yet in that state of mind, where the humiliating truths of the limits of human knowledge can be of interest to thee. First make a trial of the system, which displaced in thee thine own. Examine it with the same impartiality and severity. Proceed just the same with the other theoretical structures, which have recently become known to thee; and if none completely satisfies all of thy demands, then the question will be forced upon thee: whether these demands were also really *just?*

"A disagreeable consolation," wilt thou say. "Resignation is therefore mine whole prospect after so many bright hopes? Was it indeed then worth the effort, to summon me to the full employment of my reason, in order to establish bounds to it right then, when it begins to become the most fruitful to me? Did I have to become acquainted with a higher enjoyment, only in order to feel doubly the pain of my limitations?"

And yet it is just this suppressing feeling, which I would so gladly put down in thee. To remove everything, which hinders thee in the full enjoyment of thine existence, to bring to life in thee, the germ of every higher inspiration— the consciousness of the nobility of thy soul—this is mine aim. Thou art awakened from the slumber, in which slavery rocked thee among strange opinions. But the measure of the greatness, whereto thou art determined, wouldst thou never fulfill, if thou didst squander thy strength in striving after an unattainable goal. Until now this might have passed, and was also a natural consequence of thy newly achieved freedom. The ideas, which had occupied thee formerly for the most part, necessarily had to give the first direction to the activity of thy spirit. Whether this be the most fruitful among all the possible ones, thine own experiences would have to inform thee sooner or later. My job was simply to accelerate, where possible, this moment.

It is an ordinary prejudice, to estimate the *greatness* of man according to the *matter* with which he is employed, not according to the *manner* in which he *works* upon it. But a higher Being certainly honors the *stamp of perfection* even in the smallest sphere, when in comparison He looks down with pity upon the vain attempt to survey the cosmos with the sight of an insect. Among all the ideas, which are contained in thine essay, I can grant thee from this least of all the proposition, that it be the highest determination of man, to divine the spirit of the Creator of the world in His work of art. Indeed, I also know no more sublime image than *art* to express the activity of the most perfect Being. But an important distinction thou dost appear to have overlooked. The universe is no *pure* impression of an ideal, like the completed work of a human artist. The latter rules despotically over the dead matter, which he uses to render sensuous his ideas. But in the divine artwork, the peculiar value of each of its components is cared for, and this preserving view, with which He appreciates every germ of energy even in the smallest creature, glorifies the Master just so much, as the harmony of the immeasurable whole. *Life* and *Freedom*, to the greatest possible extent, is the stamp of divine creation. It is never more sublime, than where it seems to be most short of its ideal. But even this higher perfection can not be grasped by us in our present limitation. We *survey* a too small part of the cosmos, and the resolution of the great abundance of dissonances is unachievable to our ears. Every step, which we climb up the ladder of being, will make us more susceptible of *this* enjoyment of art, but even then it certainly has its value only as a *means*, only insofar as it inspires us to similar activity. Lazy admiration of an unknown greatness can never be a higher merit. The nobler man is neither lacking in matter for his efficacy nor in the powers, to become himself a *creator* in his own sphere. And this vocation is also thine, Julius. Hast thou once recognized it, so will it never occur to thee again, to complain about the limits, which thy thirst for knowledge can not overstep.

And this is the moment, which I expect to see thee completely reconciled with me. First must the extent of thy powers become fully known to thee, before thou canst appreciate the value of its freest expression. Until then, be angry with me always, only do not despair of thyself.

Translator's Note
1. These two stanzas are excerpted by Schiller from his poem *The Triumph of Love*.

ON THE PATHETIC

TRANSLATION BY WILLIAM F. WERTZ, JR.

Representation of suffering—as mere suffering—is never the end of art, but, as means to its end, it is extremely important to the same. The ultimate end of art is the representation of the supersensuous, and the tragic art in particular effects this thereby, that it makes sensuous our moral independence of the laws of nature in a state of emotion. Only the resistance, which it expresses to the power of the emotions, makes the free principle in us recognizable; the resistance, however, can be estimated only according to the strength of the attack. Therefore, shall the *intelligence* in man reveal itself as a force independent of nature, so must nature have first demonstrated its entire might before our eyes. The *sensuous being* must profoundly and violently *suffer*; there must be pathos, therewith the being of reason may be able to give notice of his independence and be actively *represented*.

One can never know, whether *self-composure* is an effect of one's moral force, if one has not become convinced, that it is not the effect of insensitivity. It is not art, to become

---

Schiller began this essay in 1793, as part of his early study of the subject of the sublime. Together with its companion piece, *Of the Sublime*, it was first published in August of 1794, in the fourth issue of the *New Thalia*, and then later, together with the later essay *On the Sublime*, in the third part of *Smaller Prose Writings* in May 1801. It is a critical commentary on the writings of Immanuel Kant.

master of feelings, which only lightly and fleetingly sweep the surface of the soul; but to retain one's mental freedom in a storm, which arouses all of sensuous nature, thereto belongs a capacity of resisting that is, above all natural power, infinitely sublime. Therefore, one attains to representation of moral freedom only through the most lively representation of suffering nature, and the tragic hero must first have legitimized himself to us as a feeling being, before we pay homage to him as a being of reason, and believe in the strength of his soul.

Pathos is therefore the first and unrelenting demand upon the tragic artist, and it is permitted him, to carry the representation of suffering so far as it can be done, *without disadvantage to his ultimate end*, without oppression of moral freedom. He must, so to speak, give his hero or his reader the whole full load of suffering, because it remains otherwise always problematic, whether his resistance to the same is an act of the soul, something *positive*, and not rather merely something *negative* and a lack.

This latter is the case with the old French tragedy, where we extremely rarely or never receive a glimpse of *suffering nature*, but rather see mostly only the cold, declamatory poet or even the comedian walking on stilts. The frigid tone of declamation suffocates all true nature and their worshipped *decency* makes it altogether completely impossible for the French tragedians, to portray humanity in its truth. *Decency* everywhere, even if it is in its right place, falsifies the expression of nature, and yet art demands this relentlessly. Scarcely can we believe it of a French tragic hero, that he *suffers*, for he expresses himself about the state of his soul as the calmest man, and an incessant regard for the impression which he makes upon another, never permits him to leave nature in its freedom. The kings, princesses, and heroes of Corneille and Voltaire never forget their rank, even in the most violent suffering, and take off their *humanity* far sooner than their *dignity*. They resemble the kings and emperors in the old picture books, who go to bed along with their crowns.

How completely different are the *Greeks,* and those among the moderns, who have composed poetry in their spirit. Never is the Greek ashamed of nature, he leaves sensuousness its full rights and is, nevertheless, certain that he will never be subjugated by it. His deep and correct understanding lets him distinguish the accidental, which bad taste makes into the principal work, from the necessary; everything, however, which is not humanity, is accidental to man. The Greek artist, who has to represent a Laocoön, a Niobe, a Philoctetes, knows of no princes, no king, and no king's son; he adheres only to the man. For this reason, the wise sculptor casts away the clothing and shows us merely naked figures, although he knows quite well that this was not the case in real life. Clothes are to him something accidental, behind which the necessary may never be placed, and the laws of good manners or of physical need are not the laws of art. The sculptor ought and wishes to show us the *man,* and conceal the garments of the same; therefore he rightly casts them aside.

Just as the Greek sculptor casts off the useless and impeding load of garments, in order to make way for *human nature,* so the Greek poet releases his men from the just as useless and just as impeding compulsion of convenience, and from all frigid laws of good manners, which only make man artificial and conceal his nature. The suffering nature speaks truly, candidly, and deeply, penetrating to our hearts in Homeric poetry and in tragedy: all passions have a free play, and the rule of propriety holds no feeling back. The heroes are just as sensitive as others to the suffering of humanity, and that is just what makes them heroes, that they feel the suffering strongly and intimately, and yet are not thereby overpowered. They love life as ardently as we others, but this sentiment does not so much govern them that they can not give it up, if the duties of honor or of humaneness demand it. Philoctetes fills the Greek stage with his laments, the enraged Hercules himself does not suppress his pain. Iphigenia, designated for sacrifice, confesses with moving openness that she parts with the light of the sun with pain. Nowhere does the Greek seek his fame in dullness and indifference to suffering, but rather in *endurance* of it with all feeling for the same. The gods of Greece themselves must pay nature a tribute, so soon as the poet wishes to bring them nearer to humanity. The wounded Mars cries out in pain as loudly as ten thousand men, and Venus, scratched by a lance, climbs *weeping* to Olympus and foreswears all battles.

This tender sensitivity for suffering, this warm, candid nature, lying here true and open, which moves us so deeply and lively in Greek works of art, is a model of imitation for all artists and a law, which the Greek genius has prescribed for art. The first demand on man *nature* makes always and eternally, which never may be rejected; for man is—before he is something else—a feeling being. The second demand upon him *reason* makes, for he is a rational feeling being, a moral person, and it is duty for such, not to let nature rule over herself, but rather to rule over her. When *first nature's* interest has been served, and when *second reason* has asserted its, only then is it permitted to *good manners*, to make the third demand on man, to impose on him, in the expression both of his feelings and his convictions, regard for society and to appear—as a *civilized* being.

The first law of tragic art was representation of suffering nature. The second is representation of the moral resistance to suffering.

Emotion, as emotion, is something indifferent, and the representation of the same, viewed for itself alone, would be without aesthetic value; for, to repeat it once again, nothing that concerns merely sensuous nature, is worthy of representation. Hence, not only all merely relaxing (melting) emotions, but also all the *highest degrees*, of whatever emotion it may be, are beneath the dignity of tragic art.

The melting emotions, the merely tender feelings, belong to the province of the *agreeable*, with which beautiful art has nothing to do. They merely delight the senses through dissolution or relaxation and merely refer to the outer, not to the inner state of man. Many of our romances and tragedies, especially the so-called *dramas* (something between comedy and tragedy), and of the popular family portraits, belong in this class. They merely effect emptyings of the tear sac and a voluptuous easing of the vessels; but the spirit comes away empty, and the noble power in man is not at all strengthened thereby. Just so, says Kant, many a person feels himself *edified* by a sermon, wherewith, however, nothing at all has been *built up* in him. Also the music of the moderns seems preferably to aim only at sensuousness and flatters thereby the prevailing taste, which will be only pleasantly tickled, not affected, not strongly moved, not elevated. Everything *melting* is therefore preferred, and however great the noise is in a concert hall, so everyone becomes suddenly all ears, if a melting passage is performed. An expression of sensuousness, going as far as the animal, appears commonly in all faces, the drunken eyes swim, the open mouth is all desire, a voluptuous trembling seizes the whole body, the breath is quick and weak, in short, all the symptoms of intoxication appear; as clear evidence that the senses revel, the mind, however, or the principle of freedom, becomes prey to the violence of the sensuous impression. All these emotions, I say, are excluded from art by a noble and manly taste, because they please the *senses* alone, with which art has no intercourse.

However, on the other hand, all these degrees of emotion are also excluded, which merely *torment* the sense, without at the same time compensating the mind therefor. They oppress mental freedom through *pain* no less than others through *voluptuousness*, and for this reason can bring about abhorrence only, and no emotion which is worthy of art. Art must delight the mind and be pleasing to freedom. He who is prey to a pain, is merely a tormented animal, no longer a suffering man; for a moral resistance to life is absolutely demanded of man, by which the principle of freedom in him, the intelligence, can alone be made conscious.

For these reasons, those artists and poets who believe they achieve pathos merely through the *sensuous* force of the emotion and the most lively description of suffering understand their art very poorly. They forget that suffering itself can never be the *ultimate* end of the representation, and never the *immediate* source of pleasure, which we perceive in the tragic. The pathetic is only aesthetic, insofar as it is sublime. However, effects, which are merely inferred from a sensuous source and are grounded merely on the affection of the capacity of feeling, are never sublime, no matter how much force they may betray: for everything sublime derives *only* from reason.

A representation of mere passion (both of the voluptuous and the painful), without the representation of the supersensuous power of resistance, is called *common*, the opposite is called *noble*. *Common* and *noble* are concepts, which everywhere that they are employed, show a relation to the share or lack of share of the supersensuous nature of man in an action or in a work. Nothing is *noble*, but what springs *from* reason; everything, which sensuousness produces for itself, is *common*. We say of man, he acts *commonly*, if he merely follows the suggestions of his sensuous instinct; he acts *decently*, if he follows his instinct only with regard to the law; he acts *nobly*, if he follows reason alone, without regard to his instincts. We call a facial shape *common*, when it by no means makes recognizable the intelligence in man; we call it *expressive*, when the mind determined the features, and *noble*, when a pure mind determined the features. We call a work of architecture common, when it shows us no other than a physical end; we call it noble, when it, independent of all physical ends, is at the same time the representation of ideas.

Good taste therefore, I say, does not allow the representation of emotion, however powerful the mere physical suffering and physical resistance expressed, without making visible at the same time the higher humanity, the presence of a supersensuous capacity—and indeed for the already developed reason, because never is suffering in itself, only the resistance to suffering, pathetic, and worthy of representation. Therefore, all of the absolutely highest degrees of emotion are forbidden to both the artist and the poet; for all oppress the inner resisting force, or rather already presuppose the oppression of the same, because no emotion can attain its absolutely highest degree, so long as the intelligence in man still renders some resistance.

Now arises the question: Wherethrough does the supersensuous resistance force manifest itself in an emotion? Through nothing other than control or, more generally, through the combatting of emotion. I say of *emotion*, for sensuousness can also fight, however, that is no fight with emotion, but rather with the cause, which produces it—no moral, but rather a physical resistance, which the worm also expresses, when one treads on it, and the bull, when one wounds it, without for this reason arousing pathos. That the suffering man give his feelings an expression, that he remove his enemy, that he seek to bring the suffering limb to safety, he has in common with every animal, and already instinct undertakes this, without first inquiring of his will. That is therefore still no act of his humanity, that does not yet mark him as an intelligence. Sensuousness will indeed always combat its enemy, but never itself.

The fight with emotion is, on the contrary, a fight with sensuousness, and therefore presupposes something, which is distinct from sensuousness. Against the object, that makes him suffer, man can defend himself with the help of his understanding and his muscular strength; against suffering itself he has no other weapon than the ideas of reason.

These must therefore be found in the representation, or be awakened through it, where pathos shall occur. Now, however, ideas can not be represented in the proper sense and positively, because nothing can correspond to them in the intuition. However, they can be represented negatively and indirectly, if something is given in the intuition, for which we seek the conditions in *nature* in vain. Every phenomenon, whose ultimate foundation can not be derived from the world of the senses, is an indirect representation of the supersensuous.

Now how does art succeed thereto, to present something, which is above nature, without helping oneself to supernatural means? What sort of phenomenon must that be, which is accomplished through natural forces (for otherwise were it no phenomenon) and yet can not be derived from physical causes without contradiction? This is the problem; and now how does the artist solve it?

We must remind ourselves, that the phenomena, which can be perceived in a man in the state of emotion, are of two kinds. Either they are such as belong to him merely as animal, and as such merely follow natural law, without his will being able to master them or the independent force in him being able to have an immediate influence thereon. The instinct produces them immediately, and they blindly obey its laws. To this kind belong, for example, the organs of blood circulation, of respiration, and the entire surface of the skin. But also those organs, which are subject to the will, do not always await the decision of the will, but rather the instinct often sets them immediately into motion, there especially, where pain or danger threatens the physical state. So our arm indeed stands under the rule of the will, but when we unknowingly seize something hot, so is the drawing back of the hand certainly not a willful action, but rather the instinct alone accomplishes it. Yes still more. Speech is certainly something, which stands under the rule of the will, and yet instinct can also dispose even of this instrument and the work of the understanding at its pleasure, without first inquiring of the will, as soon as a great pain or only a strong emotion surprises us. Let the most composed stoic once see something most wonderful or unexpectedly terrible; let him stand thereby, when someone slips and is about to fall into an abyss, so will a loud cry, and indeed not simply an unarticulated sound, but rather an entirely distinct word, involuntarily escape him, and *nature* will have acted in him sooner than the *will*. This serves therefore as proof, that there are phenomena in man, which can not be ascribed to his person as intelligence, but merely to his instinct as a natural force.

There is, however, also a *second* type of phenomenon in him, which stands under the influence and under the rule of the will, or which one can at least consider as such, which the will may have been able to *prevent;* for which, therefore, the *person* and not the *instinct* had to be responsible. It belongs to the instinct, to attend to the interest of sensuousness with blind zeal, but it belongs to the person, to limit the instinct through regard for the law. The instinct in itself pays attention to no law, but the person has to take care, that the prescriptions of reason be infringed upon by no action of the instinct. So much is therefore certain, that instinct alone does not have to determine unconditionally all phenomena in man in an emotional state, but rather that a limit can be placed upon it through the will of man. If instinct alone determine the phenomena in man, so is nothing more present, that could recollect the *person*, and it is merely a natural being, therefore an animal, which we have before us; for every natural being under the rule of instinct is called an animal. Therefore, if the person shall be represented, so must some phenomena in man be found, which have either been determined in opposition to the instinct, or indeed not through the instinct. Already that they were not determined through the instinct, is sufficient to lead us to a higher source, so soon as we but realize, that the instinct would have determined them absolutely differently, if its power had not been broken.

Now we are able, to address the manner and way in which the supersensuous independent force in man, his moral self, can be brought in emotion into representation.— For this reason, namely, that all the parts which obey only nature, of which the will can dispose either never at all, or at least not under certain circumstances, betray the presence of suffering—those parts, however, which have escaped the *blind* power of the instincts and do not necessarily obey the law of nature, show only a small trace of this suffering or none at all, therefore appear free to a certain degree. In this disharmony now between those features, which are imprinted on the animal nature according to the law of necessity, and between those, which the self-acting mind determines, one discerns the presence of a *supersensuous principle* in man, which can place a limit upon the effects of nature, and is therefore thereby marked as distinct from the same. The merely animal part of man follows the law of nature and may therefore appear oppressed by the power of the emotion. In this part, therefore, the whole strength of suffering manifests itself, and serves, so to speak, as a measure by which the resistance can be estimated; for one can judge the strength of the resistance, or the moral power in man only by the strength of the attack. The more decisive and violent the emotion now expresses itself in the *field of animality*, without, however, being able to assert the same power in the field of humanity, the more this latter becomes known, the more the moral independence of man manifests itself gloriously, the more pathetic is the representation and the more sublime the pathos.[1]

In the statues of the ancients one finds this aesthetic principle made clear, but it is difficult to reduce to concepts and express in words the impression which the sensuous living view makes. The group of Laocoön and his children is an approximate measure for that, which the plastic art of the ancients was able to achieve in the pathetic. "Laocoön," Winckelman says in his *History of Art*, "is a nature in the highest pain, made in the image of a man, who seeks to assemble against the same the deliberate strength of the mind; and whilst his suffering swells up the muscles and tightens the nerves, the mind, armed with strength, steps forth on his buoyant brow and the breast rises through oppressed breath and through restraint of the expression of feeling, in order to hold and lock up the pain in itself. The anxious sigh, which he in himself and the breath to himself draws, empties the abdomen and makes the sides hollow, which lets us judge, so to speak, the movement of his bowels. His own suffering, however, seems to him to be less cause for alarm than the pain of his children, who turn their faces to the father and cry for help; for the paternal heart manifests itself in the melancholy eyes and compassion seems to swim in a turbid fragrance in the same. His face is lamenting, but not screaming, his eyes are turned toward higher help. The mouth is full of melancholy, and the sunken lower lip heavy from the same; in the over-drawn upper lip, however, the same is mixed with pain, which with a movement of displeasure, as over an undeserved unworthy suffering, ascends into the nose, makes the same swell, and manifests itself in the enlarged and upwardly drawn nostrils. Under the brow, the strife between pain and resistance, united as in a point, is formed with great truth; for whilst the pain drives the eyebrows into the heights, so the struggle against the same presses the upper eye flesh downward and against the upper eyelid, so that the same is almost entirely covered by the infringing flesh. Nature, which the artist could not beautify, he has sought to show more unfolded, strenuous, and powerful; here, wherein the greatest pain is placed, appears also the greatest beauty. The left side, in which the snake poured out its poison with furious bites, is that which seems to suffer the most intensely through the nearest sensation to the heart. His legs want to rise, in order to escape its evil; no part is at rest, yes, even the chisel strokes contribute to the import of a benumbed skin." [This statue appears in the picture section following page 306—ed.]

How true and fine is the fight of intelligence with the suffering of sensuous nature developed in this description, and how appropriately the phenomena given, in which are manifested animality and humanity, the compulsion of nature and the freedom of reason! Virgil, as is known, described this same scene in his *Aeneid*, but it did not lie in the plan of the epic poet, to dwell upon the mental state of Laocoön, as the sculptor had to do. In Virgil, the entire narrative is only a hazy work, and the purpose, for which it shall serve him, is sufficiently attained through the mere representation of the physical, without his necessarily having had to let us take a deep look into the soul of the suffering, since he wants to move us not so much with compassion as to penetrate us with terror. The duty of the poet was therefore in this respect merely negative, namely, not to drive the representation of suffering so far, that every expression of humanity or of moral resistance was lost thereby, because, otherwise, indignation and disgust inevitably had to ensue. He preferred therefore to keep to the representation of the *cause* of suffering, and found it good to enlarge in a detailed way on the dreadfulness of both serpents and on the rage with which they attack their battle victims, rather than on the feelings of the same. He only hurries quickly over these, because it had to be his concern to preserve unweakened the presentation of a divine judgment and the impression of terror. Had he, on the contrary, let us know so much of Laocoön's person, as the sculptor, so would the punishing deity no longer have been the hero in the action, but rather the suffering man, and the episode would have lost its purposefulness in respect to the whole.

One is acquainted with the Virgilian narrative already from Lessing's excellent commentary. But the purpose, for which Lessing employed it, was merely to make clear the limits of poetic and pictorial representation with this example, not to develop therefrom the concept of the pathetic. To the latter purpose, however, it seems to me no less useful, and may one permit me, to run through it once more in this regard.

> Ecce autem gemini Tenedo tranquilla per alta
> (horresco referens) immensis orbibus angues
> incumbunt pelago, pariterque ad littora tendunt;
> Pectora quorum inter fluctus arrecta jubaeque
> sanguineae exsuperant undas; pars caetera pontum
> pone legit, sinuatque immensa volumine terga.
> Fit sonitus spumante salo, jamque arva tenebant,
> ardentes oculos suffecti sanguine et igni,
> sibila lambebant linguis vibrantibus ora.
> —*Aeneid*, ii. 203-211

> Two snakes with endless coils, from Tenedos
> strike out across the tranquil deep (I shudder
> to tell what happened), resting on the waters,
> advancing shoreward side by side; their breasts
> erect among the waves, their blood-red crests
> are higher than the breakers. And behind,

the rest of them skims on along the sea;
their mighty backs are curved in folds. The foaming
salt surge is roaring. Now they reach the fields.
Their eyes are drenched with blood and fire—they burn.
They lick their hissing jaws with quivering tongues.
—*translation by Allen Mandelbaum*

The first of the three above-cited conditions of the sublime of power is here given: namely, a mighty natural force, which is aimed for destruction and mocks any resistance. That, however, this mighty force may be at the same time *terrible* and the terrible *sublime*, rests upon two different operations of the mind, that is upon two representations, which we self-actively produce in ourselves. Whilst *first* we compare this irresistable natural might with the weak capacity of resistance of the physical man, we recognize it as terrible, and whilst we *secondly* refer it to our will and call into our consciousness the absolute independence of the same from any natural influence, it becomes to us a sublime object. Both of these relations *we*, however, employ; the poet gave us nothing further than an object armed with strong power and striving for expression of the same. If we *tremble* before it, so it occurs simply, because we *think* ourselves or a creature similar to us in combat with the same. If we feel ourselves sublime by this trembling, so is it, because we ourselves are conscious, that we, even as a victim of this power, would have nothing to fear for our free selves, for the autonomy of the determinations of our will. In short, the representation up to here is merely contemplatively sublime.

> Diffugimus visu exsangues, illi agmine certo
> Laocoonta petunt. . .
> —*Aeneid*, ii. 212–213

> We scatter at the sight, our blood is gone.
> They strike a straight line toward Laocoön . . .
> *Mandelbaum*

Now is the mighty *given* at the same time as the terrible, and the contemplatively sublime passes over into the pathetic. We see it actually enter into combat with the impotence of man. Laocoön or we, the difference is only of degree. The sympathetic instinct startles the preservation instinct, monsters dart freely at—us, and all escape is in vain.

Now it depends no longer upon us, whether we want to measure this power with ours and refer it to our existence. This occurs without our contribution in the object itself. Our fear has not, as in the foregoing moment, a merely subjective ground in our mind, but rather an objective ground in the object. For do we at once recognize the whole for a mere fiction of the imaginative power, so do we nevertheless distinguish in this fiction a conception, which is communicated to us from outside, from another one, which we produce self-actively in ourselves.

The mind loses therefore a part of its freedom, because it receives from outside, what it produced previously through its self-activity. The conception of danger keeps an appearance of objective reality, and the emotion becomes earnest.

Were we now nothing but beings of sense, who follow no other than the instinct for preservation, so would we stop here and persist in a state of mere suffering. But something is in us, which takes no part in the affections of sensuous nature and whose activity is directed according to no physical conditions. To the extent that this self-acting principle (the moral predisposition) has been developed in a soul, the suffering nature will be left more or less room and will more or less self-activity remain in the emotion.

In moral souls the terrible (of the imaginative power) passes over quickly and easily into the sublime. So as the imagination loses its freedom, so reason asserts its own; and the mind *only extends itself all the more inward, whilst it finds outward limits*. Knocked out of all entrenchments, which can procure physical protection for the being of sense, we throw ourselves into the impregnable citadel of our moral freedom and win nothing else thereby but an absolute and unending safety, whilst we give up for lost a merely comparative and precarious rampart in the field of the phenomenon. But, precisely because it must have come to this physical distress, before we seek the assistance of our moral nature, so can we purchase this high feeling of freedom not otherwise than with suffering. The common soul merely stops at this suffering and feels in the sublime of pathos no more than the terrible; an independent mind, on the contrary, takes just this suffering as a bridge to the feeling of his most glorious efficacy and knows how to produce from anything terrible something sublime.

> Laocoonta petunt, ac primum parva duorum
> corpora gnatorum serpens amplexus uterque
> implicat, ac miseros morsu depascitur artus.
> —*Aeneid*, ii. 213–215

> They strike a straight line toward Laocoön.
> At first each snake entwines the tiny bodies
> of his two sons in an embrace, then feasts
> its fangs on their defenseless limbs.
> *Mandelbaum*

It has a great effect, that the moral man (the father) is attacked sooner than the physical. All emotions are more aesthetical when from a second hand, and no sympathy is stronger, than that we feel for sympathy.

> Post ipsum auxilio subeuntem ac tela ferentem
> corripiunt.
> —*Aeneid*, ii. 216-217

> Next seize upon Laocoön himself,
> who nears to help his sons, carrying weapons.
> *Mandelbaum*

Now the moment is here, to place the hero as moral person in our esteem, and the poet seizes this moment.

From their description, we are acquainted with all the power and rage of the hostile monsters and know how all resistance is futile. Now were Laocoön merely a common man, so would he perceive his advantage and, like the remaining Trojans, seek his rescue in a rapid flight. But he has a heart in his bosom, and the danger to his children holds him back to his own destruction. Already, this unique trait makes him worthy of our entire compassion. At whatever moment the serpents would like to have seized him, it would have always moved and shaken us. However, that it occurs just in *the* moment, where he becomes worthy of our respect as father, that his demise is presented, so to speak, as the immediate consequence of the fulfilled paternal duty, of the tender concern for his children—this inflames our sympathy to the highest. He is it now, so to speak, himself, who gives himself up to destruction of his free choice, and his death becomes an act of the will.

* * *

In all pathos must therefore the sense through suffering, the mind through freedom, be interested. If it lacks a pathetic representation in an expression of suffering nature, so is it without *aesthetic* force, and our heart remains cold. If it lacks an ethical ground, so can it never be *pathetic* in all sensuous force and will inevitably incense our sentiment. Throughout all freedom of the mind must the suffering man always shine, throughout all suffering of humanity must always the independent or of-independence-capable mind.

In two ways, however, can the independence of the mind in the state of suffering manifest itself. Either *negatively:* if the ethical man does not receive the law from the physical and no causality over the *mind* is permitted to the *state;* or *positively:* if the ethical man *gives* the law to the physical and the mind exercises causality over the state. From the first arises the sublime of *disposition*, from the second the sublime of *action*.

A sublime of disposition is any character independent of fate. "A valiant spirit, in combat with adversity," says Seneca, "is an attractive spectacle even for the gods." Such a view the Roman Senate gives us after the disaster at Cannae. Even Milton's Lucifer, when he looks around himself in Hell, his future residence, for the first time, penetrates us, on account of this soul's strength, with a feeling of admiration.

> "Hail, horrors, hail.
> Infernal world, and thou, profoundest Hell;
> Receive thy new Possessor: one who brings
> A mind not to be chang'd by Place or Time.
> The mind is its own place, and in itself
> Can make a Heav'n of Hell. . . .
>   Here at least
> We shall be free," etc.

The reply of Medea in the tragedy belongs to the same class.

The sublime of disposition causes itself to be *seen*, for it rests upon coexistence; the sublime of action, on the contrary, causes itself only to be *thought*, for it rests upon succession, and the understanding is necessary, in order to derive suffering from a free decision. Therefore, only the first is for the plastic artist, because this one only can represent the coexisting happily; but the poet can extend himself over both. Even when the plastic artist has to represent a sublime *action*, he must transform it into a sublime disposition.

It is demanded of the sublime of action, that the suffering of a man not only have no influence on his moral constitution, but rather concisely, be the work of his moral character. This can be in two kinds of ways. Either mediately and according to the laws of freedom, when it *selects* the suffering out of respect for some duty. The conception of duty determines it in this case as *motive*, and its suffering is an *act of will*. Or immediately and according to the law of necessity, when he morally *atones* for a violated duty. The conception of duty determines it in this case as *power*, and his suffering is merely an *effect*. An example of the first Regulus gives us, when he, to keep his word, gives himself up to the Carthaginian desire for revenge; he would serve us as an example of the second, when he had broken his word and the consciousness of this guilt had made him miserable. In both cases, the suffering has a moral ground, only with the distinction that in the first case, he shows us his moral character, in the other, merely his determination thereto. In the first case, he appears as a morally great person, in the second, merely as an aesthetically great object.

This last distinction is important for the tragic art, and therefore deserves a more precise discussion.

A sublime object, merely in the aesthetical estimation, that man already is, who explains to us the dignity of the human determination through his *state*, even supposing, that we should not find this determination realized in his *person*. He becomes sublime in the moral estimation then, only when he behaves at the same time as a person according to this determination, if our respect bears not only on his capacity, but rather on the use of this capacity, if dignity is due not only to his predisposition, but rather to his actual behavior. It is entirely something different, if we turn our attention in our judgment to the moral capacity generally and to the possibility of an absolute freedom of the will, or if to the use of this capacity and to the reality of this absolute freedom of the will.

It is something entirely different, I say, and this difference lies, not perchance, in the judged objects only, rather it lies in the different manner of judgment. The same object can displease us in the moral estimation and be very attractive to us in the aesthetical. But even if it affords us satisfaction in both instances of judgment, so it produces this effect on both in an entirely different manner. It becomes not morally satisfying, by the fact that it is aesthetically useful, and not aesthetically useful by the fact that it satisfies morally.

I think, for example, of the self-sacrifice of Leonidas at Thermopylae. Judged morally, this action is a representation to me of the moral law, performed in total contradiction to instinct; judged aesthetically, it is a representation to me of the moral capacity, independent of every compulsion of instinct. This action *satisfies* my moral sense (reason); it *delights* my aesthetical sense (the imaginative power).

For this difference of my feelings in respect to the same objects I give the following ground.

As our being is divided into two principles or natures, so are our feelings also, according to these, divided into two entirely different kinds. As beings of reason, we feel approbation or disapproval; as sensuous beings, we feel pleasure or displeasure. Both feelings, of approbation and pleasure, are grounded upon a satisfaction; the former on satisfaction of a *claim*, for reason merely *demands*, but does not need; the latter on satisfaction of a *desire*, for sense only *needs*, and can not demand. Both, the demands of reason and the needs of the senses, relate to one another as necessity to need; they are therefore both contained under the concept of necessity; only with the difference, that the necessity of reason takes place without condition, the necessity of the senses only under conditions. For both, however, the satisfaction is contingent. Every feeling, both of pleasure and of approbation, is therefore ultimately grounded upon agreement of the contingent with the necessary. If the necessary be an imperative, so will be the approbation, if it be a need, so will the feeling be pleasure; both in so much the stronger degree, as the satisfaction is contingent.

Now, with every moral judgment there is an underlying requirement of reason, that it be made morally, and there exists an unconditional necessity, that we wish what is right. However, since the will is free, so is it (physically) contingent, whether we really do it. Now, if we actually do it, so this agreement of the contingent in the use of freedom with the imperative of reason receives approval or approbation, and indeed in so much higher degree, as the antagonism of the inclinations made *this* use of freedom more contingent and more doubtful.

On the contrary, with the aesthetical estimation, the object is referred to the *need of the imaginative power*, which can not *command*, only *desire*, that the contingent may agree with its interest. The interest of the imaginative power is however: to maintain itself in play *free of laws*. To this propensity for unboundedness, the moral obligation of the will, through which its object is assigned to it in the strictest way, is not in the least favorable; and since the moral obligation of the will is the object of the moral judgment, so one easily sees, that to judge in this way the imaginative power could not find profit. But a moral obligation of the will can be conceived only under the assumption of an absolute independence of the same from the compulsion of natural instincts; the *possibility* of morality, therefore, postulates freedom and consequently agrees herein with the interest of imagination in the most perfect manner. However, since imagination can not so prescribe through its need, as reason prescribes through its imperative to the will of the individual, so the capacity of freedom, referred to imagination, is something contingent and therefore, as agreement of contingency with the (conditionally) necessary, must awaken pleasure. If we therefore judge that act of Leonidas *morally*, so we consider it from a point of view, wherein its contingency strikes us in the eyes less than its necessity. If we, on the contrary, judge it *aesthetically*, so we consider it from a standpoint, wherein we imagine its necessity less than its contingency. It is the *duty* of every will, so to act, as soon as it is a free will; however, the fact that there is a freedom of the will, which makes it possible so to act, is a *favor* of nature in regard to that capacity, to which freedom is a need. If the moral sense—reason— therefore judge a virtuous action, so is the approval the highest that can ensue, because reason can never find *more* and seldom *as much,* as it demands. On the contrary, if the aesthetic sense, the imaginative power, judge the same action, so does a positive pleasure ensue, because the imagi-

ON THE PATHETIC

native power can never demand unanimity with its needs and therefore must be found surprised by the real satisfaction of the same, as by a happy accident. That Leonidas *actually made* this heroic resolution, we approve; that he *could* make it, thereat do we exult and are we delighted.

The distinction between both kinds of judgment strikes the eyes still more clearly, if one takes an action as the basis, in respect to which the moral and the aesthetical judgment turn out differently. Let me take the self-immolation of Perigrinnus Proteus at Olympia. Judged morally, I can not give this action approbation, insofar as I find unpure motives active thereby, for the sake of which the *duty* of self-preservation is set aside. Judged aesthetically, however, this action pleases me, and indeed it pleases me precisely, because it is evidence of a capacity of the will, to resist even the mightiest of all instincts, the instinct of self-preservation. Whether it was a pure moral sentiment or whether it was merely a more powerful sensuous inducement, which oppressed the self-preservation instinct in the schwärmer Peregrin, thereto I do not pay attention in the aesthetical estimation, where I abandon the individual, abstract from the relation of *his* will to the law of the will, and think of the human will in general, as a capacity of the species, in relation to all the power of nature. In the moral estimation, one has seen, self-preservation would be presented as a *duty*, therefore its violation offended; in the aesthetical estimation, on the contrary, it would be regarded as an *interest*, therefore its disregard pleased. In the latter kind of judgment is the operation therefore directly opposite, to that we perform in the first. There we place the sensuously limited individual and the pathologically affectable will opposite to the absolute law of the will and the infinite duty of the mind, here, on the contrary, we place the absolute *capacity* of the will and the infinite *power* of the mind opposite to the compulsion of nature and the limits of sensuousness. For this reason, the aesthetical judgment leaves us free, and elevates and inspires us, because already through the mere capacity to will absolutely, already through the mere predisposition to morality, we prove to have evident advantage over sensuousness, because already through the mere possibility to renounce the compulsion of nature, our need for freedom is flattered. Therefore, the moral judgment limits us and humbles us, because in every particular act of the will compared with the absolute law of the will, we find ourselves more or less at a disadvantage, and through the restriction of the will to a single manner of determination, which duty absolutely demands, the instinct for freedom of imagination is contradicted. There, we swing upward from the real to the possible, and from the individual to the species; here, on the contrary, we climb down from the possible to the real, lock up the species in the limits of the individual; no wonder, therefore, we enlarge ourselves with the aesthetical judgment, with the moral, on the contrary, feel narrowed and bound.[2]

From all of this results then, that the moral and the aesthetical judgment, far from supporting one another, rather stand in the way of one another, because they give two entirely different directions to the mind; for the lawfulness, which reason demands as moral judge, does not exist with the unboundedness, which the imaginative power desires as aesthetical judge. Therefore, an object will be precisely so much the less fit to an aesthetical use, as it is qualified for a moral one; and if the poet had nevertheless to select it, so will he do well, to treat it so, that the attention of our reason is not drawn to the *rules* of the will, but rather of our imagination to the *capacity* of the will. For his own sake, the poet must enter upon this path, for with our freedom is his realm at an end. Only so long as we look outside ourselves, are we *his;* he has lost us, as soon as we grasp into our own bosom. This happens inevitably, however, as soon as an object is no longer *regarded by us as a phenomenon,* but rather *judges over us as law.*

Even from the expressions of the most sublime virtue the poet can use nothing for *his* purpose, but that which in the same belongs to *force.* He does not trouble himself about the direction of the force. The poet, even if he places the most perfect moral model before our eyes, has no other end *and may have no other*, than to delight us through the contemplation of the same. Now, however, nothing can delight us, except what improves our subject, and nothing can delight us intellectually, except that which elevates our intellectual capacity. But how can the dutifulness of another improve our subject and augment our intellectual force? That he *really* fulfills his duty, rests upon an accidental use, which he makes of his freedom and which, for that very reason, can prove nothing for *us*. It is merely the *capacity* for a similar dutifulness, which we share with him, and whilst we also perceive in his capacity that of ours, we feel our intellectual force elevated. It is therefore merely the conceived possibility of an absolutely free will, whereby the actual exercise of the same pleases our aesthetical sense.

Still more will one be convinced thereof, when one considers, how little the poetic force of the impression, which moral characters and actions make upon us, depends on their *historical reality*. Our pleasure in ideal characters loses nothing through the recollection, that they are poetic fictions, for it is the *poetic*, not the historical truth, upon which all aesthetical effect is grounded. The poetic truth does not exist in that something has actually occurred, but rather in that it could occur, therefore in the inner possibility of the matter. The aesthetical force must therefore already lie in the conceived possibility.

Even in real occurrences of historical persons the existence is not the poetic, but rather the capacity which has become known through its existence. The circumstance, that these persons actually lived and that these occurrences actually happened, can indeed very often increase our pleasure, but with a foreign addition, which is much more disadvantageous than conducive to the poetic impression. One has long thought to render a service to the poetry of our fatherland, when one recommended the treatment of national topics to poets. Thereby, it was said, Greek poetry became so overpowering to the heart, because it painted native scenes and eternalized native deeds. It is not to deny, that the poetry of the ancients, on account of this circumstance, accomplished effects of which the modern poetry can not boast—but do these effects belong to art and the poet? Woe to the Greek artistic genius, if it had nothing farther over the genius of the modern than this accidental advantage, and woe to the Greek artistic taste, if it first had to have been won through these historical connections in their works! Only a barbaric taste uses the prickle of private interest, in order to be enticed to beauty, and only the bungler borrows from matter a force, which he despairs to place in the form. Poetry should take its path not through the cold region of the memory, should never make learning into its interpreter, never self-interest into its intercessor. It should strike the heart, because it flows from the heart, and not aim at the citizen in the man, but rather at the man in the citizen.

It is fortunate, that the true genius does not give much heed to the pointers, which one sourly imparts to him, out of better opinion than competence; otherwise Sulzer and his successors would have given a very ambiguous form to German poetry. To educate man morally and to inflame national feeling in the citizen, is indeed a very honorable mission for the poet; and the Muses know it best, how closely the arts of the sublime and beautiful may cohere therewith. But what poetry quite excellently accomplishes indirectly, it would attain directly only very badly. Poetry never carries out a particular transaction in man, and one could select no more clumsy instrument, in order to see a particular mission, a detail, well cared for. Its sphere of activity is the totality of human nature, and merely, insofar as it influences the character, can it have influence upon its particular effects. Poetry can become to man, what love is to the hero. It can neither advise him, nor strike for him, nor otherwise do work for him; but it can educate him as a hero, it can summon him to deeds and to all that he should be, equip him with strength.

The aesthetical force, wherewith the sublime of sentiment and action seizes us, rests therefore in no way upon the interest of reason, that it *be done* rightly, but rather upon the interest of the imaginative power, that it *be possible* to do rightly, i.e., that no feeling, however powerful it may be, should be able to oppress the freedom of the mind. This possiblity lies, however, in every strong expression of freedom and force of will, and anywhere the poet merely meets these, there has he found a suitable subject for his representation. For *his* interest it is the same, from which class of characters, the bad or the good, he wishes to take his heroes, since the same measure of force, which is necessary for the good, very often can be required for consistency in the evil. How much more in aesthetical judgment do we attend to the force than to the direction of the force, how much more to freedom than to lawfulness, becomes already sufficiently evident therefrom, that we prefer to see force and freedom expressed at the cost of lawfulness, than lawfulness observed at the cost of force and freedom. As soon as cases occur, namely, where the moral law is coupled with impulses which threaten to carry away the will by their power, so the character gains aesthetically, if it can resist these impulses. A vicious person begins to interest us, as soon as he must risk his happiness and life, in order to put through his bad will; a virtuous person, on the contrary, loses our attention in the same proportion, as his happiness itself obliges his good behavior. Vengeance, for example, is incontestibly an ignoble and even base emotion. Nevertheless, it becomes aesthetic, as soon as it costs those who practice it, a painful sacrifice. Medea, whilst she murders her children, aims at Jason's heart with this action, but at the same time, she delivers a painful stroke to her own, and her vengeance becomes aesthetically sublime, as soon as we see the tender mother.

The aesthetical judgment contains more truth herein, than one ordinarily believes. The vices, which bespeak the strength of the will, evidently announce a greater predisposition for truly moral freedom than the virtues, which borrow a support from inclination, because it costs the consistent villain only a single triumph over himself, a single reversal of his maxims, in order to turn to the good all the consistency and dexterity of the will, which he lavished on the evil. Whence else can it come, that we thrust half-good characters from us with dislike and often follow the altogether wicked with shuddering admiration? Incontestibly the reason is, that in regard to the former, we give up even the possibility of the absolutely free will, and, on the contrary, in regard to the latter, perceive in every expression, that he can raise himself up to the whole dignity of humanity through a single act.

In the aesthetical judgment we are therefore not interested for morality in itself, but rather for freedom alone, and the former can please our imaginative power only insofar as it makes the latter visible. It is therefore evident confusion of boundaries, when one demands moral purposefulness in aesthetic things and, in order to extend the realm of reason, wishes to displace the imaginative power from its rightful domain. Either one will have to subjugate it entirely, and then all aesthetic effect has come to an end; or it will share its rule with reason, and then will not much indeed have been gained for morality. Whilst one pursues two different ends, one will run the danger of missing both. One will fetter the freedom of imagination through moral lawfulness and destroy the necessity of reason through the caprice of the imaginative power.

Author's Notes

1. Under the province of animality, I understand the whole system of those phenomena in man, which stand under the blind force of natural instinct and are completely explainable without the presupposition of freedom of the will; under the *province of humanity*, however, those which receive their laws from freedom. Now *is* emotion in the province of animality *lacking* in a representation, so does it leave us cold; on the contrary, *does* it *govern* in the province of humanity, so it disgusts us and makes us indignant. In the province of animality, the emotion must always remain

unresolved, otherwise the pathetic is missing; first in the province of humanity can the resolution be found. A suffering person, presented lamenting and weeping, will therefore move only weakly, for laments and tears resolve the pain already in the province of animality. Far more strongly does obstinate pain seize us, where we find no help in *nature,* but rather must take our refuge in something that lies beyond all nature; and precisely in this *reference* to *the supersensuous* lies pathos and tragic force.

2. This resolution, I remember incidentally, also explains to us the difference of aesthetic impression, which the Kantian conception of duty is wont to make on its different judges. A not-to-be-sneezed-at part of the public finds this conception of duty very humiliating; another finds it infinitely elevating for the heart. Both are right, and the reason for this contradiction lies merely in the difference of the standpoint, from which both view these objects. To do his bare duty, is certainly nothing great, and insofar as the best that we are able to perform, is nothing as fulfillment, and yet defective fulfillment is our duty, nothing inspiring lies in the highest virtue. But to do his duty nevertheless truly and persistently in all the limits of sensuous nature and to follow invariably the sacred law of the spirit in the fetters of matter, this is elevating to be sure, and worthy of admiration. Compared with the spiritual world, of course, nothing meritorious is in our virtue, and however much we would let it cost us, we will always *be good-for-nothing slaves;* compared with the world of sense, it is, on the contrary, an all the more sublime object. Insofar as we therefore judge the actions morally and refer them to the law of morals, we shall have little reason to be proud of our morality; insofar as we, however, look to the possibility of these actions and refer the capacity of our mind, that lies as the basis of them, to the world of phenomena, that is, insofar as we judge aesthetically, a certain self-reliance is permitted us, yes, it is even necessary, because we discover a principle in ourselves, that is great and infinite beyond all comparison.

ON THE SUBLIME

TRANSLATED BY WILLIAM F. WERTZ, JR.

"No man must must," says the Jew Nathan to the dervish, and this expression is true to a greater extent, than one might perhaps concede to the same. The will is the species character of man, and reason itself is only the eternal rule of the same. All nature acts according to reason; his prerogative is merely, that he act according to reason with consciousness and will. All other things must; man is the being, who wills.

Precisely for this reason is nothing so unworthy of man, as to suffer violence, for violence annuls him. Who does it to us, disputes nothing less than our humanity; who suffers it in a cowardly manner, throws away his humanity. But this claim to absolute liberation from all that is violence seems to presuppose a being, which possesses enough power, to drive away from itself any other power. If it is

---

It is not precisely known when Schiller began work on this essay, but it was first made public by him in 1801, appearing in the third part of *Smaller Prose Writings*. Schiller's two other major pieces on the subject of the sublime, *Of the Sublime* and *On the Pathetic*, the second of which appears in this volume, were written almost a decade before this piece, as early commentary on the philosophy of Immanuel Kant. This essay reflects Schiller's mature thinking on Kant, who devoted the better part of his *Critique of Judgment* to the question of the sublime, and Schiller's superceding of Kant's system.

found in a being, which does not maintain the uppermost rank in the realm of forces, so an unhappy contradiction arises therefrom between the instinct and the capacity.

Man finds himself in this case. Surrounded by numberless forces, which are all superior to him and play the master over him, he makes claim by his nature, to suffer from no violence. By his understanding he does indeed enhance his natural forces in an artificial manner, and up to a certain point he actually succeeds in becoming physically master over everything physical. For everything, the proverb says, there is a remedy, but not for death. But this single exception, if it actually is one in the strictest sense, would annul the whole notion of Man. By no means can he be the being, which wills, if there is even but a single case, where he absolutely must, what he does not will. This single terrible one, *which he merely must and does not will*, will accompany him as a ghost and, as is also actually the case among the majority of men, deliver him as a prey to the blind terrors of the phantasy; his boasted freedom is absolutely nothing, if he is bound even in a single point. Culture shall set man free and help him, to fulfill his entire notion. It will make him capable, therefore, of asserting his will, for man is the being, who wills.

This is possible in two kinds of ways. Either *actually*, when man opposes violence with violence, when he as nature rules over nature; or *ideally*, when he steps out of nature and so, in regard to himself, annihilates the concept of violence. What helps him to the first, is called physical culture. Man cultivates his understanding and his sensuous forces, in order to make the forces of nature according to their own laws either into instruments of his will or to secure himself before their effects, which he can not control. But the forces of nature can be ruled or be warded off only up to a certain point; beyond this point they withdraw from the power of man and subject him to theirs.

Now thus were his freedom done for, if it were capable of no other than physical culture. He ought, however, to be Man without exceptions, therefore, in no case suffer something *against* his will. Can he therefore no longer oppose to the physical forces a proportional physical force, so nothing else remains left to him, in order to suffer no violence, than: *to annul altogether a relation*, which is so disadvantageous to him and *to annihilate as a concept* the violence, which he must in fact suffer. To annihilate violence as a concept, however, is called nothing other, than to voluntarily subject oneself to the same. The culture, which makes him apt thereto, is called the moral.

The morally educated man, and only this one, is entirely free. Either he is superior to nature as power, or he is in harmony with the same. Nothing which it exerts upon him is violence, for before it comes up to him, it has already become *his own act*, and dynamic nature never even reaches him, because acting freely he retires from all that it can reach. This mentality, however, which morality teaches under the concept of resignation to necessity and religion, under the concept of submission to divine counsel, demands, if it shall be a work of free choice and reflection, already a greater clarity of thinking and a higher energy of the will, than man is characteristically accustomed to in active life. Fortunately, however, there exists in his nature only a moral predisposition, which can be developed through the understanding, but rather even in his sensuous rational, i.e., human nature, an *aesthetical* tendency thereto, which can be awakened through certain sensuous objects and cultivated through purification of his feelings into this ideal swing of the mind. I shall at present treat of this indeed ideal predisposition, according to its concept and being, which, however, even the realist displays clearly enough in his life, although he does not admit it into his system.

Indeed, the developed feelings for beauty already suffice thereto, to make us, up to a certain degree, independent of nature as a power. A mind which has been ennobled so far as to be more moved by the form than by the matter of things, and, without any regard to possession, to draw a free pleasure from the mere reflection upon the phenomenon's manner, such a mind carries in itself an inner fullness of life that can not be lost, and because it has no need to arrogate the objects in which it lives, so it is also not in danger, of being of the same. However, the appearance nevertheless ultimately wants to have a body, in which it appears, and so long as a need therefore even exists for a beautiful appearance, a need remains left for the existence of objects, and our satisfaction consequently is still dependent upon nature as a power, which commands over all existence. It is indeed something entirely different, if we feel a longing for beautiful and good objects or if we merely desire, that the existing objects be beautiful and good. The last can exist with the highest freedom of the soul, but the first not; that the existing be beautiful and good, we can demand; that the beautiful and good be existing, merely wish. That frame of mind, which is indifferent as to whether the beautiful and good and perfect exist, but with rigorous sternness desires, that the existing objects be good, beautiful, and perfect, is called preferably great and sublime, because it contains all realities of the beautiful character, without sharing its limits.

It is a distinguishing mark of good and beautiful, but at any time weak souls, always to insist impatiently upon the existence of their moral ideal and to be painfully affected by the hindrances to the same. Such men place themselves in a sad dependence upon chance, and it may always be predicted with certainty, that they will concede too much to the matter in moral and aesthetical things and will not pass the highest test of character and taste. Moral defectiveness ought not to infuse us with suffering and pain, which always bespeaks more an unsatisfied need than an unfulfilled demand. The latter must have a more vigorous emotion as companion and sooner strengthen and fortify the mind in its energy, than make it pusillanimous and unhappy.

There are two genii, which nature gave us as companions throughout life. The one, sociable and lovely, shortens the laborious journey for us through its lively play, makes the fetters of necessity light for us, and leads us amidst joy and jest up to the dangerous places, where we must act as pure spirits and lay aside everything bodily, as to cognition of truth and performance of duty. Here it abandons us, for only the world of sense is its province, beyond this its earthly wings can not carry it. But now the other one steps up, earnest and silent, and with stout arm it carries us over the dizzying depth.

In the first of these genii one recognizes the feeling of the beautiful, in the second the feeling of the sublime. Indeed, the beautiful is already an expression of freedom, but not that which elevates us above the power of nature and releases us from every bodily influence, but rather that, which we enjoy within nature as men. We feel ourselves free with beauty, because the sensuous instincts harmonize with the law of reason; we feel ourselves free with the sublime, because the sensuous instincts have no influence upon the legislation of reason, because the mind acts here, as if it stood under no other than its own laws.

The feeling of the sublime is a mixed feeling. It is a combination of *woefulness*, which expresses itself in its highest degree as a shudder, and of *joyfulness*, which can rise up to enrapture, and, although it is not properly pleasure, is yet widely preferred to every pleasure by fine souls. This union of two contradictory sentiments in a single feeling proves our moral independence in an irrefutable manner. For as it is absolutely impossible that the same object stand in two opposite relations to us, so does it follow therefrom, that *we ourselves* stand in two different relations to the object, so that consequently two opposite natures must be united in us, which are interested in the conception of the same in completely opposite ways. We therefore experience through the feeling of the sublime, that the state of our mind does not necessarily conform to the state of the senses, that the laws of nature are not necessarily also those of ours, and that we have in us an independent principle, which is independent of all sensuous emotions.

The sublime object is of a double description. We refer it either to our *power of comprehension*, and succumb in the attempt to form for ourselves an image or a concept of it; or we refer it to our *vital power,* and consider it as a power before which those of ours vanish into nothing. But although in the one as in the other case we preserve the painful feeling of our limits through its instigation, so we do not, however, flee it, but rather are attracted by it with irresistible force. Would this be quite possible, if the limits of our imagination were at the same time the limits of our power of comprehension? Would we want to be reminded quite gladly of the all-powerfulness of the forces of nature, if we had not still something in reserve, other than what can become a prey to them? We delight in the sensuous-infinite, because we can think, what the senses no longer grasp and the understanding no longer comprehends. We are inspired by the terrible, because we are able to will, what the instincts abhor and reject, what they desire. We gladly allow the imagination to find its master in the realm of phenomena, for it is ultimately, however, only one sensuous force, which triumphs over another sensuous one, but nature in all of its limitlessness can not attain to the absolute greatness in us ourselves. We gladly submit to the physical necessity of our well-being and our existence, for that reminds us precisely, that it has no command over our principles. Man is in its hand, but the will of man is in his own.

And thus has nature even employed a sensuous means, to teach us, that we are more than merely sensuous; thus did she even know to utilize sensations, to lead us to the track of this discovery, that we are not in the least subjected slavishly to the violence of the sensations. And this is an entirely different effect, than can be produced by the beautiful—namely by the beautiful of reality, for in the ideally beautiful even the sublime must be lost. In the beautiful, reason and sensuousness harmonize, and only on account of this harmony does it have attractiveness for us. Through beauty alone would we therefore eternally never learn, that we are determined and able to prove ourselves as pure intelligences. In the sublime, on the contrary, reason and sensuousness do not harmonize, and precisely in this contradiction between both lies the charm wherewith it seizes our soul. The physical and the moral man are separated here from one another most sharply; for exactly in such objects, where the first only feels its limits, does the other have the experience of its *force* and is elevated infinitely precisely through that which presses the other to the ground.

A man, I will assume, shall possess all of the virtues, whose union makes up the *beautiful character*. He shall find his pleasure in the practice of justice, beneficence, temperance, constancy, and faithfulness; all the duties, whose performance circumstances prescribe to him, shall become light play to him, and fortune shall make no action hard for him, whereto his philanthropic heart may ever summon him. To whom will this beautiful harmony of the natural instinct with the prescriptions of reason not be enchanting, and who could refrain from loving such a man? But can we think ourselves quite secure, in all affection for the same, that he really is virtuous, and that there is virtue in general! If this man had only aimed at agreeable sensations, so could he, without being a fool, absolutely not act otherwise, and he would have to hate his own advantage, if he wished to be vicious. It can be, that the source of his actions is pure, but he must settle that with his own heart; *we* see nothing thereof. We see him do not more, than also the simply clever man had to do, who makes pleasure his god. The world of sense, therefore, explains all the phenomena of his virtue, and we have no need at all, to look beyond the same for a reason for it.

This same man shall, however, suddenly fall into a great misfortune. One shall deprive him of his possessions, one shall ruin his good name. Illnesses shall throw him onto a painful bed, death shall tear away from him everything which he loves, everything in which he trusts, shall forsake him in his distress. In this condition, let one seek him again and demand of the unhappy one the practice of the same virtues, for which the happy one had formerly been so prepared. Does one find him in this event still entirely the same; has poverty not reduced his beneficence, ingratitude his obligingness, pain his equanimity, his own misfortune his sympathy with another's happiness; does one notice the transformation of his circumstances in his figure, but not in his conduct, in the matter, but not in the form of his behavior—then one indeed no longer makes do with an explanation from the *concept of nature* (according to which it is absolutely necessary, that the present as effect is grounded upon something past as its cause), because nothing can be more contradictory, than that the effect remain the same, when the cause has been transformed into its contrary. One must therefore renounce every natural explanation, must give up altogether deriving the conduct from the condition, and must shift the grounds of the first out of the physical world order into an entirely different one, to which reason can indeed fly with its ideas, the understanding, however, can not grasp with its concepts. This discovery of the absolute moral capacity, which is bound to no natural condition, gives to the melancholy feeling, whereby we are seized at the sight of such a man, the completely peculiar, inexpressible charm, in respect to which no pleasure of the senses, however ennobled it may be, can contest with the sublime.

The sublime, therefore, procures for us an exit from the sensuous world, wherein the beautiful would gladly always keep us imprisoned. Not gradually (for there is no transition from dependency to freedom), but rather suddenly and through a shock, does it tear the independent spirit away from the net, wherewith the refined sensuousness ensnared him, and which binds so much the more tightly, the more transparently it is spun. However much it has gained over man through the imperceptible influence of a rather soft taste—even if it has succeeded in penetrating, in the seducing veil of spiritual beauty, into the innermost seat of moral legislation and there poisoning the holiness of maxims at its source, so is a single sublime emotion often enough to tear up this web of deceit, to give back to this fettered spirit its entire elasticity all at once, to give it a revelation of its true destination, and to impose a feeling of its dignity, at least for a moment. Beauty in the form of the goddess Calypso has enchanted the valiant son of Ulysses, and, through the power of her charms, she holds him for a long time imprisoned upon her island. For long he believes he is paying homage to an immortal deity, since he lies only in the arms of voluptuousness—but a sublime impression seizes him suddenly in the form of Mentor: He remembers his better destiny, throws himself into the waves, and is free.

The sublime, like the beautiful, is poured out lavishly through all of nature, and the sensibility for both is placed in all men; but the germ thereto develops unequally, and must be helped to it by art. Already the aim of nature requires, that we hasten toward beauty from the first, although we flee before the sublime; for beauty is our nurse in the childish age and should lead from the rude state of nature to refinement. But, although she is our first love and our sensibility is first unfolded for the same, so has nature nevertheless provided therefor, that it matures more slowly and the formation of the understanding and the heart awaits first its full development. Did taste attain its full maturation, before truth and morality were planted in our heart in a better way than can occur through it, so would the world of sense remain eternally the limit of our endeavors. We would neither go beyond it in our concepts, nor in our sentiments, and what the imaginative power can not represent, would also have no reality for us. But, fortunately, it already lies in the ordering of nature, that the taste is, however, the last to ripen, although it blossoms first among all the capacities of the mind. In this interval, enough time is gained to cultivate a wealth of concepts in the head and a treasure of principles in the breast and, then also to develop, especially out of reason, the sensibility for the great and sublime.

So long as man was merely a slave of physical necessity, had found no exit yet from the narrow circle of need, and did not yet divine the high *demonic* freedom in his breast, so could *incomprehensible* nature only remind him of the limits of his conceptual power, and *decaying* nature only of his physical impotence. He therefore had to pass by the first with pusillanimity and turn away from the other with fright.

But, scarcely does free contemplation make room for him against the blind rush of the forces of nature, and scarcely does he discover in this deluge of phenomena something permanent in his own being, than the wild masses of nature round about him begin to speak to his heart an entirely different language; and the relative greatness outside of him is the mirror, wherein he perceives the absolute greatness within himself. Fearless and with thrilling pleasure, he now nears these frightful phantoms of his imaginative power and intentionally summons the entire force of this capacity, to represent the sensuous-infinite, in order, even if it succumbs in this attempt, to feel all the more lively the superiority of his ideas over the highest which sensuousness can provide. The view of unlimited distance and incalculable heights, the wide ocean at his feet and the greater ocean above him, snatch his mind away from the narrow sphere of the real and the oppressive imprisonment of physical life. A greater measure of estimation is held before him by the simple majesty of nature, and, surrounded by its great forms, he no longer endures the small in his way of thinking. Who knows how many luminous thoughts or heroic resolutions, which no prison study and no society saloon would have brought into the world, this courageous struggle of the soul with the great spirit of nature did not already bring forth during a walk—who knows if it is not attributed in part to a more seldom intercourse with this great genius, that the character of city dwellers turns so willingly to the paltry, stunted, and withered, when the spirit of the nomad remains as open and free as the firmament beneath which he encamps.

Not only the unattainable for the conceptual power, the sublime of quantity, but also the incomprehensible for the understanding, *the confusion*, can serve as a representation of the supersensuous and give the soul a buoyancy, so soon as it passes into greatness and announces itself as a work of nature (for otherwise it is contemptible). Who does not rather linger in the spirited disorder of a natural landscape, than in the spiritless regularity of a French garden? Who does not rather admire the wonderful fight between fertility and destruction on Sicily's fields, does not rather feast his eye on Scotland's wild cataracts and misty mountains, Ossian's great nature, than admire in tight-laced Holland the sour victory of patience over the most obstinate elements? No one will deny, that in Batavia's pastures better care is taken of the physical man than beneath the spiteful crater of Vesuvius, and that the understanding, which wants to comprehend and arrange, profits by a regular farm garden far more than by a wild natural landscape. But man has a further need than to live and to ensure his well-being, and even another destiny than to comprehend the phenomena round about him.

What makes the wild bizarreness in physical creation so attractive to the traveler of perception, precisely that discloses to a soul capable of inspiration, even in the dubious anarchy of the moral world, the source of a quite peculiar pleasure. Admittedly, he who enlightens the great housekeeping of nature with the needy torch of the *understanding* and always aims only thereat, to dissolve its bold disorder in harmony, he can not be pleased in a world where raving accident seems to rule more than a wise plan and, by far in the majority of cases, merit and fortune stand in contradiction to one another. He desires that, in the great course of the world, everything be ordered as in a good household, and should he miss this lawfulness, as it can indeed not be otherwise, so nothing remains left to him, other than to await from a future existence and from another nature the satisfaction, which remains due to him from the present and past. If, on the contrary, he willingly gives up wanting to bring this lawless chaos of phenomena under a unity of cognition, so does he amply win on another side, what he gives up for lost on this. Just this complete want of a purposeful connection among this throng of phenomena, whereby they become excessive and useless for the understanding, which must keep to this form of connection, makes it an all the more suitable symbol for pure reason, which finds its own independence of the conditions of nature represented in just this wild unboundedness of nature. For if one takes all the connections of a row of things under oneself, so has one the concept of independence, which surprisingly harmonizes with the pure reason's concept of freedom. Under this idea of freedom, which it takes from its own medium, reason therefore embraces, in a unity of thought, what the understanding can combine in no unity of cognition, submits through this idea to the infinite play of the phenomena, and asserts therefore its power at the same time over the understanding as a sensuously conditioned capacity. Should one now remember, what value it must have for a being of reason, to become conscious of his independence of natural laws, so one comprehends how it occurs that men of sublime bent of mind can hold out for compensation, through this idea offered to them of freedom, for every disappointment of cognition. Freedom, with all of its moral contradictions and physical evils, is for noble souls an infinitely more interesting spectacle than prosperity and order without freedom, where the sheep patiently follow the shepherd and the self-commanding will is degraded to the subservient part of a clockwork. The latter makes man merely into a spirited product and a more fortunate citizen of nature; freedom makes him into the citizen and co-ruler of a higher system, where it is infinitely more honorable, to occupy the nethermost place, than to command the ranks in the physical order.

Considered from this point of view, and *only* from this one, world history is to me a sublime object. The world, as historical object, is at bottom nothing other than the conflict of natural forces amongst one another and with the freedom of man, and history reports to us the result of this contest. So far as history has come up to now, it has far greater deeds to relate of nature (as which all emotions in man must be counted), than of the independent reason, and the latter has been able to assert its power only through single exceptions of the law of nature in a Cato, Aristides, Phocion, and similar men. Does one but approach history with great expectations of light and knowledge—how severely is one there deceived! All well-meant attempts of philosophy to bring into agreement that which the moral world *demands*, with that which the real *affords*, are disproved by the evidence of experience, and as pleasantly as nature conforms in its *organic kingdom* to the regulative principles of judgment or seems to conform, so ungovernably does it tear off the bridle in the kingdom of freedom, wherein it would gladly imprison the spirit of speculation.

How entirely otherwise, if one gives up *explaining* it, and makes thus its incomprehensibility itself the standpoint of judgment. Precisely the circumstance that nature, considered on a large scale, mocks all rules which we ascribe to it through our understanding; that in its self-willed free movement it crushes into the dust the creations of wisdom and of chance with equal heedlessness; that it sweeps away with it into *one* destruction the important just as the insignificant, the noble just as the common; that it preserves here a world of ants, there its glorious creation, man, it holds in its giant arms and smashes; that it often wastes its most toilsome acquisitions in a light-minded hour and often builds onto a work of folly for centuries—in a word: this defection of nature on a large scale from the rules of cognition, to which it submits in its particular phenomena, makes evident the absolute impossibility of explaining *nature itself* through the *laws of nature* and of applying *to* its kingdom, what applies *in* its kingdom and the mind is therefore driven irresistibly from the world of phenomena into the world of ideas, from the conditioned into the unconditioned.

The terrible and destructive nature leads us much further still than the sensuous-infinite, as long, namely, as we remain merely free observers of the same. The sensuous man, to be sure, and sensuousness in the rational one, fear nothing so much as to quarrel with this power, which has to rule over well-being and existence.

The highest ideal, toward which we strive, is to remain in good agreement with the physical world as the guardian of our felicity, without being compelled therefore, to break with the moral, which determines our dignity. Now, however, as everyone knows, it is not always feasible to serve both masters, and even if (an almost impossible case) duty should never come into conflict with need, so does natural necessity nevertheless enter into no agreement with man, and neither his force nor his skill can secure him against the malice of the fates. Happy is he therefore, if he has learned to endure what he can not change, and to surrender, with dignity, what he can not save! Cases can occur, where fate scales all ramparts upon which he grounded his safety, and nothing further remains left to him, than to escape into the holy freedom of the spirit—where there is no other means, than to wish to calm the instinct of life—and no other means to resist the power of nature, than to anticipate it and, through a free annulment of all sensuous interest, before a physical power does it, morally to kill the physical body.

Now sublime emotions and a frequent intercourse with destructive nature strengthen him thereto, both there, where it shows him its ruinous might merely from a distance, and also where it actually expresses it against his fellow man. The pathetic is an artificial misfortune, and like the true misfortune, it places us in *direct contact* with the spiritual law, that rules in our bosom. However, the true misfortune selects its man and its time not always well: it often surprises us defenseless and, what is even worse, it often *makes* us *defenseless*. The artificial misfortune of the pathetic, on the contrary, finds us in full armament, and because it is merely imagined, so the independent principle in our soul gains room, to assert its absolute independence. Now, the more frequently the mind renews this deed of self-action, the more the same becomes a skill to him, he gains an all the greater advantage over the sensuous instinct, so that he is at last able then, if from the imagined and artificial misfortune an earnest one comes, to treat it as an artificial one and—the highest swing of human nature!—to resolve the actual suffering into a sublime emotion. The pathetic, one can therefore say, is an inoculation against unavoidable fate, whereby it deprives it of its malignancy and the assault of the same is led to the strong side of man.

Therefore, away with the false understanding forebearance and the careless, overindulged taste, which throws a veil over the earnest face of necessity and, in order to place itself in the favor of the senses, *invents* a harmony between well-being and good conduct, of which no traces appear in the real world. Let evil destiny show itself to us face to face. Not in the ignorance of the danger surrounding us—for this must ultimately cease—only in the *acquaintance* with the same is there salvation for us. To this acquaintance we are now helped by the terrible, glorious spectacle of all destructive and *again* creative and again destructive alteration—of the now slowly undermining, now swiftly invading ruin, we are helped by the pathetical portraits of humanity wrestling with fate, of the irresistible flight of good fortune, of deceived security, of triumphant injustice, and of defeated innocence, which history establishes in ample measure and the tragic art through imitation brings before our eyes. For where were those, who, with a not entirely neglected moral predisposition, can read of the tenacious and yet futile fight of Mithridates, of the collapse of the cities of Syracuse and Carthage, and can dwell on such scenes, without paying homage to the earnest law of necessity with a shudder, momentarily reining in his desires and, affected by this eternal unfaithfulness of everything sensuous, striving in his bosom after the persevering? The ability to feel the sublime is therefore one of the most glorious predispositions in the nature of man, which, both because of its origin from the independent capacity of thinking and of the will, deserves our *attention*, and also because of its influence upon moral man, deserves the most perfect development. The beautiful is merely well-deserved of *man*, the sublime of the *pure demon* in him; and because it is once our determination, even in all sensuous limitations to conform to the law book of the pure mind, so must the sublime be added to the beautiful, in order to make the *aesthetical education* a complete whole and to enlarge the sensibility of the human heart to the entire extent of our determination, and therefore also beyond the world of sense.

Without the beautiful, there would be continual strife between our natural determination and our rational determination. On account of the endeavor, to satisfy our *intellectual* vocation, we would neglect our *humanity* and, all moments taken as departure from the world of sense, we would remain constant strangers in this sphere of activity once assigned to us. Without the sublime, beauty would make us forget our dignity. In the relaxation of an uninterrupted enjoyment, we would forfeit vigor of *character* and, fettered indissoluably to this *accidental form of existence*, lose sight of our unchangeable determination and our true fatherland. Only when the sublime is wedded with the beautiful, and our receptivity for both has been cultivated in equal measure, are we perfected citizens of nature, without for this reason being its slaves and without frittering away our rights as citizens in the intelligible world.

Now, indeed, nature already establishes for itself alone objects in quantity, in respect to which the receptivity for the beautiful and the sublime may be exercised; but man is, as in other cases, so also here, served better at second hand than at first and would prefer to receive a matter prepared and selected by art, than draw laboriously and scantily from an impure spring. The imitative creative instinct, which can endure no *impression*, without immediately striving after lively *expression*, and perceives in every beautiful or great form of nature a challenge to wrestle with it, has the great advantage over the same, to be able to treat that as main object and as a distinct whole, which nature— if it does not throw it down unintentionally—in the pursuit of an end lying near to it, takes along in passing. If nature *suffers violence* in its beautiful organic structures, either through the deficient individuality of the matter or through the effect of heterogeneous forces, or if it *exercises violence* in its great and pathetic scenes and acts as a power upon man, though it can become aesthetical only as an object of free contemplation, so is its imitator, plastic art, fully free, because it separates all accidental limitations from its object, and leaves even the mind of the beholder free because it imitates only the *appearance* and not the *reality*. However, as the whole charm of the sublime and beautiful lies only in the appearance and not in the contents, so does art have all the advantages of nature, without sharing her fetters with her.

THOUGHTS CONCERNING THE USE OF THE COMMON AND BASE IN ART

TRANSLATED BY NED NORRIS

Common is everything, which does not address the soul, and stimulates nothing other than a sensuous interest. There are indeed thousands of things, which already are common through their material or contents; but since the commonness of the material can be ennobled by its treatment, so we concern ourselves only with what in art is common in form. A common mind will profane the most noble material by a common treatment; a great mind and a noble soul, on the contrary, will know how to ennoble the common, specifically, in that he ties it into something spiritual and discovers in it an aspect of greatness. Thus, an historian of a common stamp will report to us the most insignificant doings of a hero just as carefully as his most sublime feats and will dwell just as long on his family tree, his dress, his household affairs, as on his projects and undertakings. His greatest deeds he will so relate, that no one sees them as

---

Schiller published this essay first in May 1802, in the fourth part of his *Smaller Prose Writings*. It belongs to the writings on the question of artistic theory from the winter of 1792–93, together with Schiller's writings on the question of the sublime.

what they are. Conversely, an historian of spirit and nobility of soul, will lay an interest and a content in the private life and the most unimportant actions of his hero, which make them important. In fine art, the Dutch painters have shown a common taste, the Italians a noble and great taste, the Greeks yet more so. The latter went always toward the ideal, discarded every common trait, and chose, also, no common material.

A portrait painter may treat his subject commonly or greatly. Commonly, if he depicts the accidental just as carefully as the necessary, if he neglects the great, and painstakingly details the small; greatly, if he knows how to discover the most interesting, separates the accidental from the necessary, only hints at the small and details the great. Greatly, however, is nothing but the expression of the soul in actions, gestures and postures.

A poet treats his material commonly, if he details unimportant actions but passes over important ones. He treats it greatly, if he combines it with the great. Homer knew how to treat very fleetingly the shield of Achilles, although the construction of a shield, as regards its materials, is something very common.

Yet a step below the common is the *base,* which is different from the former, in that it is not merely something *negative,* not merely a lacking of the spiritual and noble, but indicates something *positive,* a coarseness of feeling, bad morals and contemptible intentions. The common evidences merely a lack of an excellence, which is desired; the base, the want of a quality, which may be demanded of everyone. So is, for example, revenge, wherever it may be found, and however it may be expressed, something common, because it evidences a lack of magnanimity of spirit. However, one especially discerns a base revenge, if the person who perpetrates it, uses despicable means of gratification. The base always denotes something coarse and vulgar; however, a person of higher birth and better morals may also think and behave commonly, if he possesses mediocre abilities. A person behaves commonly, who is mindful

THE COMMON AND BASE IN ART

only of his own advantage, and insofar as he stands opposed to the noble person, who is able to forget himself, in order to provide a pleasure for another. The same person, however, would act basely, if he pursued his advantage at the cost of his honor and thereby would not even respect the law of decency. The common is therefore opposed to the noble; the base at the same time to the noble and decent. To surrender to every passion without any resistance, to satisfy every desire, without bridling oneself by the rules of decency, much less by those of morality, is base, and betrays a base soul.

Also in works of art one may fall into the base, not merely by choosing base subjects, which the sense of decency and propriety excludes, but also in treating them basely. One treats a subject basely, if one either draws attention to that side of it, which decency bids us conceal, or if one gives it an expression, which leads to base secondary conceptions. In the life of the greatest man, base actions occur, but only a base taste will bring them out and portray them.

One finds paintings from sacred history, where the Apostles, the Virgin and Christ himself have an expression, as if they had been snatched up out of the most common rabble. All such performances show a base taste, which gives us justification, to infer a coarse and vulgar mode of thinking by the artist himself.

There are indeed cases, where the base, even in art, may be permitted; namely, where it should cause laughter. Also, a person of fine morals may amuse himself at times, without displaying a corrupt taste, with the crude, but true expression of nature and with the contrast between morals of the refined world and of the rabble. The drunkenness of a man of rank, wheresoever it may appear, would cause displeasure; but a drunken post-horseman, sailor and barrowman make us laugh. Jokes, which would be intolerable from a person of education, give us pleasure in the mouth of the vulgar. Of this genre are many of the scenes of Aristophanes, which, however, at times overstep these boundaries and are definitely unacceptable. For that reason, we delight in parodies, where the sentiments, manner of speech and actions of the common people are foisted upon the same distinguished persons, whom the poet has treated with all dignity and decency. As soon as the poet lays out something merely to laugh at, and wishes nothing more, than to amuse us, then we may allow him the base, only he must never cause indignation or loathing.

He causes indignation, if he brings in the base, where we simply cannot forgive it, with persons, namely, of whom we are justified in demanding more refined morals. If he treats it contrarily, he violates either the truth, because we would rather take him for a liar, as wish to believe that persons of education might actually behave so basely; or, refined persons offend our sense of morals, and cause our indignation, which is even worse. Quite different is farce, where between the poet and the observer there is an unspoken understanding, that one does not expect truth. In farce, we exempt the poet from all fidelity of description, and he receives a license, so to speak, to deceive us. For here, the comical is based directly upon its contrast with the truth; it may, however impossibly, be at once true and opposite to the truth.

There are also in the serious and tragic, a few rare cases, where the base may be employed. Then, however, it must cross over into the frightful, and the momentary offense against taste must be resolved by a strong employment of emotion, and therefore be devoured, as it were, by a higher tragic effect. Theft, for example, is something absolutely base, and whatever may bring our heart to forgive a thief, however much he may have been misled to it by the press of circumstances, he is thus marked with an indissoluble brand, and aesthetically he always remains a base object. Taste forgives here even less than morality does, and its tribunal is more strict, because an aesthetic object is also accountable for all secondary ideas, which, at its instigation, are made active in us, while, in contrast, the moral judgment abstracts from all chance.

A person who steals would accordingly be a highly reprehensible object for any poetic representation of serious content. If, however, this person is, at the same time, a murderer, then he is indeed yet more reprehensible morally, but aesthetically he becomes thereby more useful again by a degree. Those who debase themselves (I speak here always of the aesthetic mode of judgment only) by an infamous act, can be lifted up again in some measure through a crime and be restored in our aesthetic evaluation. This divergence of the moral judgment from the aesthetic is significant and deserves notice. One may discern various causes for it. *Firstly*, I have already stated, that, because the aesthetic judgment depends upon the imagination, also all secondary conceptions, which are stimulated in us by an object, and stand in a natural relation with the same, flow into this judgment. If these secondary conceptions are of a base sort, then they debase the main object unavoidably.

Secondly, in the aesthetic judgment, we look to strength, in the moral, to lawfulness. Lack of strength is something contemptible, and every action that causes us to infer it, is so likewise. Every timid and cringing act is repugnant to us, due to the lack of strength that it betrays. On the contrary, a devilish act, so long as it displays strength, may please us aesthetically. An act of thievery, however, displays a sneaking, cowardly mode of thinking; an act of murder has at least the appearance of strength. At least, the degree of our interest, that we attach to it aesthetically, agrees with the degree of strength, which is thereby expressed.

Thirdly, in a severe and terrifying offense, we are drawn away from the quality of the same and made conscious of its frightful consequences. The stronger emotion suppresses then the weaker. We look not backward, into the soul of the perpetrator, but forward to his destiny, at the effects of his act. As soon as we begin to tremble, any tenderness of taste falls silent. The primary impression fills our soul fully, and the accidental, secondary ideas, on which the base really depends, disappear. Thus, the theft by the young Ruhberg, in the *Crime of Ambition*, is not repugnant on the stage, but truly tragic.—The poet has developed the conditions with much skill, so that we are carried along and do not get a breathing space. The horrible misery of his family, and especially his father's distress are topics, which lead our whole attention away from the perpetrator and toward the results of his act. We are far too much in an emotional state, to get involved in the conception of shame, wherewith the thievery would be branded. In short: the base is concealed by horror. It is peculiar, that this actually committed theft by young Ruhberg is not so much repugnant as the merely unfounded suspicion of a theft in another play. Here a young officer is unjustly accused of taking a silver spoon, which is subsequently found. The base is here merely imagined, merely a suspicion, and yet it does irreparable damage, in our aesthetic conception, to the innocent hero of the piece.

The reason is, because the assumption, that a person could behave basely, shows no sure view of his morality, since the laws of propriety require, that one be regarded as a man of honor so long as he does not demonstrate the contrary. If one credits him therefore with something contemptible, then it appears as if he had given cause even once to the possibility of such mistrust, although the baseness of an unfounded suspicion is actually on the side of the accuser. The hero of the cited piece suffers even more harm, in that he is an officer and in love with a lady of education and social standing. With both of these predicates, the predicate of thievery makes an entirely frightful contrast, and it is impossible for us, not to momentarily recall, when he is with his lady, that he might have had the silver spoon in his pocket. The greatest misfortune in it is, that he does not surmise the suspicion that rests upon him; for were this to be so, as an officer he would demand bloody satisfaction. The results then would go over into the frightful, and the base disappear.

Further one must differentiate the base of sentiment from the base of action and of condition. The first is beneath all aesthetic dignity, the latter may most often exist with it very well. Slavery is base; but a slavish sentiment in a state of freedom is contemptible, a slavish occupation, without such a sentiment, on the contrary, is not; much more may the base of condition, united with highness of sentiment, cross over into the sublime. Epiktet's master, who struck him, behaved basely, and the stricken slave showed a sublime soul. True greatness shines out from a base fate only the more gloriously, and the artist should not fear to introduce his hero even in a contemptible covering, only so long as he is assured, that he has command of the expression of the inner value.

But what may be allowed the poet is not always permitted to the painter. The former merely brings his object before the imagination, the latter, on the other hand, directly before the senses. Therefore, not only is the impression of the painting more vivid than that of the poem, but the painter can not make the internal so visible with his natural strokes, as the poet with his arbitrary symbols, and yet only the internal can reconcile us with the external. When Homer presents us with his Ulysses in beggar's rags, it is up to us how much we want to picture this image to ourselves and how long we wish to dwell on it. In no case, however, is it vivid enough, to be unpleasant or offensive to us. If, however, the painter or indeed yet the actor, wanted to imitate Ulysses faithfully to Homer, we would turn away from it in disgust. Here we don't have the intensity of the impression under our control. We must look at what the painter shows us, and may not so easily beat back the repugnant secondary ideas, which are brought into our memory thereby.

ON THE NECESSARY LIMITS IN THE USE OF BEAUTIFUL FORMS

TRANSLATED BY SUSAN JOHNSON

The misuse of the beautiful and the presumptions of the imagination, where she possesses only executive force, also to seize the legislative for herself, have inflicted so many injuries in life as well as in the learned sciences, that it is of no slight importance, to precisely determine the limits, which are put to the use of beautiful forms. These limits already lie in the nature of the beautiful, and we may simply recall, *how* taste expresses its influence, in order to be able to determine, *how far* it may extend that influence.

The effects of taste, taken altogether, are, to bring man's sensuous and intellectual powers into harmony and to unite them in an intimate alliance. Where, accordingly, such an intimate alliance between reason and the senses is fitting and legitimate, there taste is to be granted an influence. If, however, there are instances, where, be it in order to attain

---

This essay is a companion piece to *On the Moral Use of Aesthetic Manners*, also translated in this volume. Schiller published a first draft of this essay under the title *On the Necessary Limits of the Beautiful, Especially in Discourse on Philosophical Truths*, in the September 1795 issue of *Die Horen*. After several more drafts, the essay was published under this title, in the second part of *Smaller Prose Pieces*, in August of 1800.

a purpose, or be it in order to satisfy a duty, we must perform action free of any sensuous influence and as pure beings of reason, where accordingly the bond between mind and substance must be momentarily suspended, there taste has its limits, which it dares not overstep, without either thwarting a purpose, or making us deviate from our duty. Instances of such a kind do actually exist, however, and they are already prescribed to us by our destiny.

Our destiny is, to gain knowledge, and out of knowledge to act. To both belong an ability to exclude the senses from that which the mind performs, because in all cognition the process of perceiving, and in all moral volition the carnal appetites, must be abstracted away.

When we *cognize*, then we conduct ourselves *actively*, and our attention is directed toward a *subject*, toward a relationship between mental image and mental image. When we *perceive*, then we conduct ourselves *passively*, and our attention (if one can thus term its opposite something which is not any conscious action of the mind) is merely directed toward our *condition*, insofar as that is altered through a received impression. Because we merely perceive and not cognize the beautiful, in so doing we pay no heed to any relationship it has to other objects, we do not refer its mental image to other mental images, but instead to our perceiving self. *In* the beautiful subject we experience nothing, but *of* it we experience an alteration of our condition, of which the perception is the expression. Our knowledge is therefore not widened through judgments of taste, and no cognition is gained through the perception of beauty, not even one of beauty. Where, accordingly, cognition is the purpose, taste, at least directly and without mediation, can do us no service; rather, cognition is excluded, precisely so long as beauty occupies us.

But then of what use, one will object, is a tasteful wording of concepts, if the purpose of the discourse, which surely can be no other than to bring forth cognition, is thereby rather hindered than assisted?

Toward convincing the understanding, the beauty of the wording can of course contribute just as little as the tasteful arrangement of a meal to the satiety of the guests, or the outer elegance of a person to the judgment of his inner worth. But, just as in the former case through the beautiful ordering of the table the appetite is aroused, and in the latter case through the commendable in external things attention to the person as a whole is awakened and whetted, so through an enticing presentation of truth we are put into a favorable temper, to open our soul to her, and the obstacles in our souls are drawn away, which otherwise would have opposed the difficult pursuit of a long and rigorous train of thought. It is never the content, which gains victory through the beauty of form, and never the understanding, which taste assists in the course of cognition. The content must commend itself without mediation in its own stead, to the understanding, while the beautiful form speaks to the imagination, and coaxes her with an appearance of freedom.

But even this blameless indulgence toward the senses, which one allows oneself merely in the *form*, without thereby altering anything in the *content*, is subject to great reservations, and can be totally contrary to purpose, depending upon the mode of cognition and the degree of conviction, which one has in mind in conveying one's thoughts.

There is a *scientific* knowledge, which rests upon clear concepts and recognized principles, and a *popular* knowledge, which bases itself upon more or less developed feelings. What is often very conducive to the latter, can flatly contradict the former.

In the first case, where one seeks to effect a rigorous conviction based on principles, it is not accomplished, by propounding the truth merely *regarding the content*, but instead *the test* of truth must be contained as well in the form of the discourse. This, however, can only mean that not merely the content, but also its exposition, must accord with the laws of thought. With the same rigorous necessity, under which the concepts join in the understanding, they must also fit together in the discourse, and the continuity in the presentation must correspond to the continuity in the idea. Now, however, that freedom which is granted to the imagination during cognition, contends against the rigorous necessity, by which the understanding links judgment with judgment and inference with inference. The imagination, in conformity with her nature, always strives toward intuitions, i.e. toward complete and thoroughly determined mental images, and is unceasingly bent on presenting the universal in a particular case, limiting it in space and time, making the concept into an individual being, giving the abstract a body. Moreover, she loves *freedom* in her combinations, and recognizes thereby no other law than the accident of spatial and temporal linkage; for this is the only connection, which remains among our mental images, when we think away everything which is concept, everything, which internally binds them. Exactly the reverse, the understanding occupies itself only with *partial representations* or concepts, and its effort is bent on differentiating characteristics in the living totality of an intuition. Because it links things *according to their internal relationships*, which can only be discovered through differentiation, so the understanding is able to *connect*, only insofar as it first *divides*, i.e., only through partial representations. The understanding observes rigorous *necessity and lawfulness* in its combinations, and it is only the constant connection of concepts through which it can be satisfied. This connection is, however, destroyed each time, as soon as the imagination inserts *entire* mental images (particular cases) into this chain of abstractions, and mixes into the rigorous necessity of objective linkage the accident of temporal linkage.[1] It is hence unavoidably necessary, that where one cares only about rigorous consistency in thinking, the imagination disavow her arbitrary character, and learn to subordinate and sacrifice to the requirements of the understanding her strivings toward the greatest possible sensuousness in mental images and the greatest possible freedom in linking those images. For that reason, the discourse must already be prepared to knock down that striving of the imagination, through exclusion of everything individual and sensuous, and to set bounds to her restless poetic instinct, through exclusion of everything individual and sensuous, and, through precision of expression as well as through lawfulness in the sequence of development to set bounds to her arbitrariness in making combinations. Of course, she will not subject herself to this yoke without resistance, but one reasonably relies here too on some self-denial, and on an earnest resolve by the listener or reader, for the sake of the subject matter not to mind the difficulties, which are inherent in the form.

Where, however, such resolve cannot be presupposed, and where one can have no reason to hope that interest in the content would become strong enough, to inspire courage for this effort, then one admittedly will be obliged to renounce imparting a scientific cognition, in order, however, to gain somewhat more freedom with respect to the discourse. One relinquishes in this case the form of science, which exerts too much force against the imagination and can be made acceptable only through the importance of its purpose, and chooses the form of beauty, which, independent of all content, is already commended through her very self. Because the subject matter does not wish to defend the form, the form must plead for the subject matter.

Popular instruction comports with this freedom. Inasmuch as the popular speaker or popular author (a term, under which I include those who do not exclusively direct themselves to men of learning) does not speak to an audience which is prepared in advance, and does not select his reader as the others do, but must take them where he finds them, so he can presuppose only the universal *conditions of thinking* and only the universal impulse to attentiveness among them, but yet no special *skill in thinking*, no acquaintance with precise concepts, no interest in precise subjects. Therefore, he also can not allow matters to depend upon whether the imagination of those whom he wishes to instruct, may link the proper meaning with his abstractions, and provide a content for the general concepts, to which the scientific discourse confines itself. In order to proceed safely, he therefore prefers to give the intuitions and particular cases *all at once,* to which those concepts refer, and leaves it to the understanding of his reader, to form the concept out of this material on the spur of the moment. The imagination will thus certainly be far more brought into play in popular discourse, but nevertheless always merely *reproductively* (reconstituting received mental images), not however *productively* (manifesting its self-developing power). The particular cases or intuitions are, for the immediate purpose, much too strictly premeditated, and, for the use that is to be made of them, much too precisely arranged for the imagination to be able to forget that she acts merely *in the service of the understanding.* The discourse, to be sure, keeps somewhat closer to life and to the sensuous world, but it does not yet lose itself in them. Thus, the presentation is still always simply *didactic,* for, in order to be beautiful, it still lacks the two most eminent characteristics: *sensuousness in expression* and *freedom in movement.*

The presentation becomes *free,* when the understanding indeed determines the connection of ideas, but with lawfulness concealed in such a way, that the imagination thereby seems to act completely arbitrarily, and simply to follow the accident of temporal linkage. The presentation becomes *sensuous,* when it conceals the general in the particular, and surrenders to the imagination the living image (the *entire* representation), where the concern is only the concept (the partial representation). The sensuous presentation is, thus, considered from the one side, *rich,* because where only *one* determination is required, it gives a complete image, a totality of determinations, an individual being; it is however, considered from another side, once again *confined* and *impoverished,* because it affirms only of an individual being and of a single case, what is to be understood of a whole domain. Hence, it truncates the understanding precisely to the extent that it presents the

THE USE OF BEAUTIFUL FORMS 287

imagination in excess; for the more complete in content a mental image is, the smaller its compass.

The interest of the imagination is, in varying its objects at will; the interest of the understanding is, to link its objects with rigorous necessity. Much as these two interests seem to contest with each other, nevertheless there exists between them a point of union, and to discover this, is the actual merit of the beautiful mode of writing.

In order to satisfy the imagination, the discourse must have a material element or *body*, and this consists of the intuitions from which the understanding isolates the single characteristic or concepts; for, however abstractly we are inclined to think, nevertheless it is in the end always something sensuous which underlies our thought. The imagination desires only to leap across, from intuition to intuition, unbound and unregulated, and to tie itself down to no other connection than the sequence of time. If, therefore, the intuitions, which give the corporeal element to the discourse, stand in no objective state of linkage with one another, if they seem instead to hold their own as independent links and as proper totalities subsisting for themselves, if they reveal the total disarray of a playful imagination obedient only to itself, then the word-form has aesthetic freedom, and the want of improvisation is satisfied. Such a depiction, one could say, is an *organic* product, where not only is the totality alive, but also the individual parts have their own specific life; the simply scientific or scholarly presentation is a *mechanical* work, where the parts, lifeless with regard to their own self-subsistence, impart to the whole an artificial life through their congruity with each other.

In order on the other side to satisfy the understanding and bring forth knowledge, the discourse must have an intellectual element, *meaning*, and this it receives through the concepts, by means of which those intuitions are referred to one another and joined into a whole. Now, if the closest connection occurs among these concepts, as the intellectual element of the discourse, while the intuitions corresponding to them, as the sensuous element of the discourse, seem to come together merely through an arbitrary play of the imagination, then the problem is solved, and the understanding is appeased through lawfulness, as the imagination is cajoled through lawlessness.

If one investigates the magical power of the beautiful use of words, one will always find it contained in this sort of happy relation between external freedom and internal necessity. The *individualizing* of the objects and the figurative or *non-literal expression*, contribute most to this freedom of the imagination: the former, in order to heighten sensuousness, the latter, in order to produce it, where it does not exist. Inasmuch as we represent the species through an individual being, and present a general concept in a particular case, we cut from the imagination the shackles which the understanding has placed on her, and give her full authority, to prove herself creatively. Constantly striving toward exhaustiveness of determinations, she now receives and makes use of her right, to complete at her pleasure the image given to her, to quicken it, to reconstitute it, follow it in all its relations and transformations. She is allowed for the moment to forget her subordinate rôle, and act as a despotic autocrat, because through rigorous internal coherence it is sufficiently assured, that she can never entirely escape the bridle of the understanding. Non-literal expression drives this freedom still further, in that it couples together images, which as regards their content are quite different, but join in concert under a higher concept. Now, because the imagination would hold onto the content, the understanding on the other hand to that higher concept, the former makes a leap just where the latter observes the most consummate continuity. The concepts develop themselves according to the *law of necessity*, but according to the *law of freedom* they pass over the imagination; the thought remains the same, only the medium varies, that presents it. So the eloquent writer creates out of anarchy itself the most splendid order, and erects on ever-shifting ground, on the stream of the imagination which always flows forth, an enduring structure.

THE USE OF BEAUTIFUL FORMS

If one compares the scientific, the popular, and the beautiful use of words, it becomes evident that all three do convey the thought at hand, with equal faithfulness regarding its substance, and thus all three assist us to a cognition, but that the nature and degree of this cognition are markedly different in the case of each one. The beautiful writer represents for us the subject, of which he treats, as *possible* and *desirable*, rather than being able to convince us of its reality or even of its necessity; for his idea proclaims itself merely as an arbitrary creation of the imagination, which by itself is never in a position, to vouch for the reality of its notions. The popular writer arouses in us the belief, that something is *actually* the case, yet he brings things no further; for he indeed makes the truth of that proposition felt, but not absolutely certain. Feeling, however, can no doubt teach what *is*, but never, what *must be*. The philosophical writer elevates that belief to conviction, for he proves from indubitable foundations, that something is *necessarily* the case.

If one proceeds from the principles above, then it will not be hard, to assign each one of these three different forms of diction its due place. Taking everything into consideration, it can be accepted as a rule, that where not merely the result, but at the same time the demonstration of proof is concerned, the scientific mode of writing deserves preference, and where in general only the result is concerned, the popular and beautiful modes deserve preference. *At what point,* however, popular expression should cross over into the beautiful, is decided by the greater or lesser degree of interest, which one has to presuppose and to engender.

Genuine scientific expression puts us (more or less, according to whether it is more philosophic or more popular) in *possession* of a cognition; beautiful expression *lends* us the same merely for momentary enjoyment and use. The first gives us—if I may be allowed the comparison—the tree together with the root, but of course we must wait patiently, until it blooms and bears fruit; beautiful expression plucks for us merely the flowers and fruits thereof, but the tree, that bore them, is not ours, and when they are withered and consumed, our wealth has disappeared. Now, absurd as it would be, to pluck the mere flowers or fruits for someone who wants to have the tree itself planted in his garden, it would be just as nonsensical, to offer to someone who just now longs only for a piece of fruit, the tree itself with its forthcoming fruits. The point speaks for itself, and I simply note, that beautiful expression suits the professorial chair as little as the schoolroom style suits the *beau monde* and the rostrum.

He who is learning, accumulates for later purposes, and for a future use; hence, the teacher has to take care, to *make him* into the *complete proprietor of the knowledge* which he imparts to him. Nothing is ours, however, except what is given over to the understanding. The orator, on the contrary, intends a quick use, and has to satisfy a current need of his public. His interest is, therefore, to make *practical* the knowledge which he disseminates, as quickly as he can, and this he attains most securely, when he delivers the knowledge to the *senses*, and prepares it for *perception*. The teacher who takes charge of his public only conditionally, and is justified in presupposing that they already have the temper of mind that is required for assimilating the truth, addresses himself simply to the *object* of his discourse, whereas, on the contrary, the orator, who dares not make any preconditions regarding his public, and must first win their favor, has to address himself at the same time to the *subjects*, to whom he wants to appeal. The former, whose public was already there and is coming back again, needs merely to deliver fragments, which do not make up a totality until combined with the preceding lectures; the latter, whose public constantly varies, comes unprepared, and perhaps never returns, must *complete* his task at every lecture, each of his performances must be a totality per se and contain its full elucidation.

Hence, it is no wonder, if an ever-so-thorough dogmatic lecture has no success in polite society and at the pulpit, and an ever-so-ingenious beautiful lecture bears no fruits at the professor's chair—when the *beau monde* leaves writings in the academic sphere unread which are epoch-making in academic worlds, and the scholar ignores works which edify men of the world, and are devoured with eager appetite by all fanciers of the beautiful. Either can gain admiration in the circle, for which it is destined; indeed, in intrinsic value, both can be perfectly equal, but it would mean demanding the impossible, if a work that taxes the thinker is to serve at the same time as child's play for the mere dilettantish aesthete.

On this basis, I hold it to be damaging, when writings are chosen for the instruction of youth, in which scientific matters are dressed up in beautiful form. Here I speak not at all of such writings where the content is *sacrificed* to the form, but of truly excellent writings, which withstand the strictest objective test, yet do not contain this test in their form. It is true, one attains with such writings the goal of being read, but always at the expense of the more important goal of why one wants to be read. The understanding is always exercised during these readings only in its accord with the imagination, and therefore never learns to separate form from matter, and act as a pure faculty. And yet, the sheer exercise of the understanding is surely a principal factor in the instruction of youth, and depends, in most cases, more on the thinking itself than on the thought. When one wants an undertaking to be well executed, let him take care, not to announce it as a game. Rather, the mind must already be put into a state of tension through the form of treatment, and pushed forward with a certain force from passivity toward activity. The teacher should in no way conceal from his student the rigorous lawfulness of the method, but rather make him attentive toward it and, where possible, eager for it. The student ought to learn to pursue an objective, and, for the sake of the objective, also to submit to a difficult means. In good time he shall strive after the nobler pleasure, which is the reward of exertion. In scholarly discourse, the senses are utterly repudiated, in beautiful discourse, their interest is attracted. What will be the consequence of this? One devours such a writing, such an amusement, with interest, yet, if one is asked about the outcome, then one is hardly in a position to give an accounting thereof. And very naturally so! For the concepts enter the soul in undivided masses, and the understanding cognizes only where it differentiates; the soul conducts itself passively rather than actively during the reading, and the mind possesses nothing, but what it does.

This remains true, merely for the beautiful of an ordinary sort and the ordinary manner of perceiving the beautiful. The truly beautiful grounds itself on the most rigorous determinateness, on the most scrupulous abstraction, on the highest internal necessity; but this determinateness must rather let itself be found, than forcibly issue forth. The highest lawfulness must be there, but it must appear as Nature. Such a production will give the understanding complete satisfaction, as soon as it is studied, yet just because it is truly beautiful, it does not obtrude its lawfulness, it does not appeal to the understanding *in particular*, but speaks as a pure unity to the harmonious totality of the person, as Nature to Nature. An ordinary critic finds it perhaps empty, scanty, far too little defined; exactly that offends him, wherein consists the triumph of the depiction, the complete dissolution of the parts into a pure whole, because he only knows how to differentiate and only has a sense of the particular. Certainly in philosophical presentations, the understanding, as the faculty of differentiation, should be gratified, and provided with specific results; this is the purpose that in no way may be slighted. If, however, the writer, through the most rigorous internal determinateness, has seen to it that the understanding must find these results necessary, as soon as it merely comes upon them; yet, not satisfied with this alone, and urged by his nature (which always acts as a harmonic unity, and where it loses this unity through the business of abstraction, quickly restores it), he re-connects that which was severed, and through the unified summoning of sensuous and intellectual powers, constantly lays claim to the entire person, then he has not actually so much written poorly, as he has come closer to the highest perfection. The ordinary critic, admittedly, who without a sense of that harmony always insists only upon the particular, who in St. Peter's itself would seek out only the cambers supporting this artificial firmament, will scarcely be grateful that the writer made for him a double labor; for such a man must of course first *translate* him, if he wants to comprehend him, as the mere naked understanding, stripped of all power of depiction, must first convert into its language the beautiful and harmonious in Nature as in Art, and dissect it, in short, as the schoolboy in order to read, must first learn to spell. But the depictive writer never receives the law from the narrowness and impoverishment of his readers. He goes toward the ideal he bears within himself, untroubled, who chances to follow and who remains behind. Many will remain behind; for so rare it is, even merely to find thinking readers, it is infinitely rarer, to encounter readers, who can think representationally. Such a writer will, in the nature of things, therefore incur the disfavor of those, who only intuit and only perceive, for he sets them the sour task of thinking—as of those, who only think, for he demands of them, what for them is quite impossible, to compose in a lively manner. Because, however, both are only very imperfect representatives of a more universal and more authentic humanity, which demands harmony of those two undertakings throughout, so their opposition means nothing; rather, their verdicts confirm for him, that he attained what he sought. The abstract thinker finds the writer's content thought out, and the intuitive reader his mode of writing lively; both approve, therefore, what they grasp, and only miss, what exceeds their faculties.

Such a writer is, however, for just this reason utterly unqualified, to make an ignorant person acquainted with the subjects that he treats, or, in the most essential sense of the word, to *teach*. Fortunately, he is also not necessary for that purpose, because there will never be a lack of subjects for the instruction of students. The teacher in the most rigorous sense must address himself to impoverishment; he proceeds from the premise of incapacity, where, on the contrary, the author described above demands already a certain integrity and development from his reader or listener. In return, however, his effect does not confine itself to imparting mere dead concepts, he seizes the lively with lively energy and makes himself master of the whole person, his understanding, his feeling, his will alike.

If it were found detrimental for thoroughness of cognition, to indulge the demands of taste in the course of actual learning, it is in no way maintained thereby, that the development of this faculty in the student is premature. Quite the contrary, one ought to encourage him, and cause him to convey his schoolroom knowledge by the method of lively depiction. As soon as the former has been observed, the latter can have nothing other than useful consequences. Certainly one must already have mastered a truth to a high degree, to be able to leave behind without danger the form in which it was found; one must possess a large understanding, not to lose one's object, even in the free play of imagination. He who relays his knowledge to me in academically correct form, indeed convinces me, that he grasped it accurately and knows how to demonstrate it; but he who at the same time is capable of conveying it in a beautiful form, proves not only that he is qualified to widen his knowledge, he proves as well, that he has assimilated it into his nature, and is able to represent it in his action. For the results of thinking, there is no other path to the will and into life, than through the self-active power of development. Nothing except what is already living action *in ourselves*, can come to be so *outside ourselves*, and it is with the mind's creations as with organic developments; only from the flowers does the fruit come forth.

If one reflects, how many truths already took living effect as internal intuitions long ago, before philosophy demonstrated them, and how impotent oftentimes remain the demonstrated truths for the feelings and the will, then one recognizes, how important it is for practical life, to follow this hint from Nature, and transform the cognitions

THE USE OF BEAUTIFUL FORMS

of science once more into living intuitions. Only in this way is one in a position, to allow even those, whose nature as yet prohibits them from traveling the unnatural path of science, to take a share in the treasures of wisdom. Beauty performs here with regard to cognition just what she performs in the sphere of morality with regard to the manner of action; she unites men in results and in substance, who never would have been united in form and in principles.

The other sex, in accordance with its nature and its beautiful destiny, is never able or permitted to share *science* with the masculine sex, but through the medium of representation she can share with him the *truth*. The man submits to an offense against his taste, if only the internal content renders compensation to the understanding. Ordinarily, he is all the more pleased, the more harshly the determinateness issues forth, and the more purely the inner essence abstracts itself from the appearance. But the woman does not forgive the richest content for neglected form, and the whole inner construction of her being gives her a right to this rigorous demand. This sex, which, even if she did not rule through beauty, would already have to be called the fair sex, because she is ruled by beauty, takes everything that presents itself to her, before the tribunal of perception, and that which does not plead its case or even offends the bench, is a lost cause in her view. To be sure, through this channel the material of truth only can be passed on, but not the truth itself, which is inseparable from its proof. Yet fortunately she requires only the material of truth, in order to reach her highest perfection, and the exceptions hitherto apparent, can not excite the wish, that they might become the rule.

Therefore the undertaking, which Nature did not merely neglect but prohibited in the other sex, the man must shoulder doubly, if he otherwise wishes to meet the woman on the same footing in this weighty area of existence. He will accordingly seek, as much as he possibly can, to move across from the realm of abstraction, where *he* rules, into the realm of imagination and perception, where the woman is at the same time exemplar and judge. Inasmuch as he can install in the feminine mind no perennial plantings, he will seek to produce as many flowers and fruits as possible on his own field, in order to replenish all the more often the fast-shriveling supply in the other, and will seek to be able to maintain, there, where no natural harvest ripens, an artificial one. Taste improves—or conceals—the natural difference of mind between the sexes, it nourishes and ornaments the feminine mind with the produce of the masculine, and allows the charming sex to perceive where it has not thought, and enjoy, where it has not labored.

To taste, therefore, under the restrictions of which I previously made mention, is indeed entrusted the form of conveying cognition, but under the emphatic condition that it not violate the content. It should never forget, that it executes an order from the outside, and is not conducting its own business. Its entire share should be confined to putting the soul in a temper favorable to cognition; but, in all things which affect the subject matter, it should presume to no authority whatever.

If it does the latter—if it elevates to the uppermost *its* law, which is nothing other than to please the imagination, and gratify in contemplation—if it applies this law not merely to the *treatment*, but also to the *subject matter*, and not merely arranges, but chooses the material according to the standard of that law, then it not only oversteps its commission, but betrays it, and debases the object, which it was to faithfully deliver to us. Now it is no longer asked, what things *are*, but how best they recommend themselves to the senses. Rigorous consistency of thought, which was to have been simply concealed, is thrown away as a burdensome shackle, perfection is sacrificed to acceptability, the truth of the part to the beauty of the whole, inner essence to outer impression. Where, however, the content must be governed by the form, there is no content at all; the depiction is empty, and instead of having increased one's knowledge, one has merely played an entertaining game.

THE USE OF BEAUTIFUL FORMS

Authors, who possess more wit than understanding and more taste than scientific learning, only too often make themselves guilty of this fraud, and readers who are accustomed more to feeling than to thinking, show themselves only too eager to indulge them. In general it is hazardous, to give taste its full cultivation before one has trained the understanding as a pure capacity of thought, and enriched the mind with concepts. For inasmuch as taste always looks to the treatment alone, and not to the subject, where it is the sole judge, all objective differences among things disappear. One becomes indifferent to reality, and in the end puts all value on form and appearance.

Hence the spirit of superficiality and frivolity, which one very often sees predominating in such ranks and circles, which otherwise not unjustly pride themselves on the highest refinement. To introduce a young man into this circle of the *Graces*, before the *Muses* have released him as being of age, must of necessity become corrupting to him, and without fail, exactly that which gives the pure young man his outer perfection, makes the unripe one into a fop.[2] Substance without form is, to be sure, only a half-possession, for the most splendid knowledge is lying in a mind, which knows not how to give it any shape, buried like dead treasures. Form without substance, on the contrary, is only the shadow of a possession, and all artistic skill in expression is of no use, to one who has nothing to express.

If, accordingly, fine culture is not to lead into this false path, then taste must determine only the outer shape, reason and practical knowledge, however, must determine the inner essence. If sense-impression is made the supreme judge, and objects are simply referred to perception, then the human being never comes out of servitude to material substance, then his mind will never grow clear, then, in short, he loses just as much in freedom of reason, as he grants *in excess* to the imagination.

The beautiful already makes its effect in the sheer process of being observed, the true wishes to be studied. Thus, he who would merely exercise his sense of beauty, contents himself, even where study is positively necessary, with superficial observation, and wishes merely to play intelligently, even where exertion and earnestness are required. Through mere observation, however, nothing is ever won. He who wishes to do something great, must deeply penetrate, sharply distinguish, manifoldly connect, and resolutely persevere. Even the artist and poet, although both work solely on behalf of contemplative pleasure, can succeed in making their works playfully delight us only through an exacting and no less than stimulating process of study.

This seems to me to be as well the unerring touchstone, by which one can distinguish the mere dilettante from the true artistic genius. The seductive attraction of the great and beautiful, the fire with which it ignites the youthful imagination, and the semblance of ease with which it deceives the senses, have already persuaded many a one without skill, to seize the palette or the lyre, and to gush out in shapes or tones, that which was aroused in him. In his head, dark ideas ferment like an emerging universe, which make him believe, that he is inspired. He takes the darkness for profundity, the wild for the potent, the indeterminate for the infinite, the meaningless for the transcendental—and how he flatters himself with his labor! Yet the connoisseur's judgment won't confirm this testimonial of warm self-love. With unaccommodating criticism he destroys the deception of the schwärming formative power, and lights his way down into the deep shaft of learning and experience, where, concealed from everything profane, the source of all true beauty springs up. If then genuine powers of genius slumber in the questioning youth, certainly at the outset his modesty will hesitate, but the courage of true talent will soon urge him on to make a trial. If Nature fitted him out as a plastic artist, he studies the human structure under the knife of the anatomist, *climbs into the lowest depths, in order to be true on the surface,* and investigates the entire species, in order to prove his claim to the individual. If he is a born poet, he eavesdrops on mankind in his own breast, in order to comprehend its endlessly changing play on the wide stage of the world, subjugates arrogant fantasy to the discipline of taste, and lets the sober understanding survey the banks, through which the stream of inspiration shall rush. To him it is well understood, that greatness only springs up out of the plain, insignificant thing, and, grain of sand by grain of sand, he assembles the wonderful structure, which now deceptively takes hold of us in a single impression. If, on the contrary, nature has merely stamped him as a dilettante, difficulty chills his impotent zeal, and he either abandons, if he is modest, a road toward which self-deception pointed him, or, if he is not, he belittles the great ideal in accordance with the small span of his ability, because he is not in a position, to extend his ability in conformity with the great standard of the ideal. The genuine artistic genius is accordingly always to be recognized, in that he maintains, amidst the most ardent feeling for the whole, coolness and assiduous patience for the particular, and, in order to make no rupture in perfection, prefers to sacrifice enjoyment to completeness. To the mere dilettante, the laboriousness of the means spoils the end, and he would like to be as comfortable in the producing as in the contemplating.

What follows was originally a separate essay, On the Danger of Aesthetic Manners.

Up to now, the disadvantages for thinking and for judgment have been spoken of, which arise from an exaggerated sensitivity to beauty of form and from over-extended aesthetic demands. Of far greater significance, however, are these very usurpations on the part of taste, when they have the *will* as their object; for it is something entirely different, whether the exaggerated proclivity for the beautiful hinders the enlargement of our knowledge, or whether it corrupts the character and makes us violate our duties. Belletristic arbitrariness in thinking is indeed something very *wrong*, which must obscure the understanding; but precisely this arbitrariness applied to maxims of the will, is something *wicked,* and must unfailingly corrupt the heart. And to this dangerous extreme aesthetic refinement inclines a man, as soon as he *exclusively* entrusts himself to the sense of beauty, and makes taste the absolute legislator of his will.

The moral destiny of the person demands complete independence of the will from all influence of sensuous impulses, and taste, as we know, labors unceasingly, to make the bond between reason and the senses ever more intimate. Now, thereby it admittedly causes the appetites to ennoble themselves and to become more in accord with the demands of reason, but even from this, great danger for morality can eventually arise.

That is to say, because in aesthetically refined men the imagination *even in its free play is guided by laws,* and because the senses submit to taking no enjoyment without the assent of reason, therefore the reciprocal duty is quite easily required of reason, *to be guided in the earnestness of its law-giving according to the interest of the imagination,* and not to command the will without the assent of the sensuous instincts. The moral obligation of the will, which nevertheless remains in force entirely without conditions, is surreptitiously regarded as a contract, which binds one party only so long as the other fulfills it. The *accidental* accord of duty with inclination is ultimately established as a *necessary* condition, and so morality is poisoned at its source.

How the human character little by little falls into this corruption, can be made comprehensible in the following way.

So long as man is still a savage, so long as his impulses simply extend to material objects, and an egoism of the coarser sort guides his action, sensuousness can be dangerous to morality only through its *blind strength,* and can oppose the precepts of reason simply as a force. The voice of justice, of restraint, of humaneness is drowned out by the louder-speaking appetites. He is dreadful in his revenge, because he takes offense dreadfully. He robs and murders, because his lusts are still too powerful for the weak bridle of reason. He is a raging beast toward others, because natural instinct still bestially rules himself.

If, however, he exchanges this wild state of nature for the condition of refinement, if taste ennobles his impulses, if he points out to them worthier objects in the moral universe, if he tempers their raw outbreak through the precept of beauty, then it can occur, that these very impulses, which up to now were frightful only *through their blind force*, become, through an appearance of *dignity* and through a *usurped authority* of morality of character, far more dangerous still, and under the mask of innocence, nobility, and purity exert a far worse tyranny against the will.

The man of taste voluntarily withdraws from the coarse yoke of instinct. He subjugates his impulses at his pleasure to reason, and condescends to let the objects of his appetites be determined by the reflective mind. The more frequently now the circumstance repeats itself, that the moral and the aesthetic judgment, the moral feeling and the feeling of beauty, meet in the same object and concur in the same verdict, the more reason will incline, to take such a very *etherealized* impulse for one of *its own*, and finally to transfer to it the rudder of the will with unconstrained authority.

So long as a possibility is still at hand, that inclination and duty meet in the same object of desire, this *representation* of the moral feeling through the feeling of beauty can cause no positive harm, although, strictly speaking, nothing is gained thereby for the morality of the particular actions. But the case changes greatly, when sensibility and reason have a different interest—when duty bids a type of conduct that shocks taste, or when taste sees itself drawn to an object, which reason, as moral judge, is compelled to condemn.

That is to say, necessity now suddenly enters, to set against one another the claims of the moral and aesthetic senses, which were mingled well-nigh inextricably in such a long-standing pact, to determine their mutual rights, and to ascertain the true power-holder in the heart. Yet such a continuous delegation of authority has sunk him into oblivion, and the long habituation, to obey at once the promptings of taste and in so doing to find them good, perforce gained surreptitiously for taste the appearance of a right. Given the *irreproachability,* with which taste administered its supervision over the will, it could not fail that a certain *respect* was conceded to its utterances, and this respect is just what inclination, with insidious dialectic, now asserts against the duty to conscience.

Respect is a feeling, which can be experienced only for the law and what conforms to the law. What can demand respect, makes claim to unconditional homage. The ennobled inclination, which has been able to stealthily obtain respect for herself, therefore wishes to no longer be *subordinate* to reason; she wishes to be *co-ordinate* with it. She wishes not to be taken for a perfidious subject, who rebels against her sovereign; she wishes to be regarded as a potentate, and deal with reason as moral law-giver, on a footing of equality. The scale thus stands level, as she alleges, with regard to rights, and how greatly is it not to be feared that self-interest may tip the balance!

Among all inclinations which stem from the feeling of beauty, and are the property of cultivated souls, none recommends itself so greatly to the moral feeling, as the ennobled affect of love, and none is more fertile in sentiments which correspond to the true dignity of man. To what heights does love not carry human nature, and what divine sparks is she not often able to strike even from ordinary souls! By her holy fire is every selfish inclination consumed, and scarcely can principles themselves more purely preserve the chastity of the soul, than love guards the nobility of the heart. Often, where the former were still struggling, has love already gained them the victory, and through its all-powerful energy precipitated decisions from which mere duty on the part of weak humankind would have demanded in vain. Who, indeed, should mistrust a state of feeling, which so powerfully takes under its protection the excellent in human nature, and so victoriously contests the hereditary enemy of all morality, egotism?

THE USE OF BEAUTIFUL FORMS

But one ought not cross swords with this commander, if one is not already safeguarded by a better one. It must eventually occur, that the object of our love is unhappy, that she is unhappy on account of us, that it depends upon us, through sacrificing some moral scruples, to make him or her happy. "Should we let her suffer, in order to keep a pure conscience? Is this permitted by the feeling-state, a state unselfish, magnanimous, altogether yielding toward its object, altogether self-oblivious in respect to its object? It is true, it goes against our conscience, to make use of the immoral means, whereby she can be helped—but is that called *loving*, if amidst the pain of the beloved, one still thinks of himself? Thus we are more apprehensive for ourselves, after all, than for the object of our love, because we would rather see her unhappy, than be so ourselves through the reproaches of our conscience?" It is with such sophistry that this feeling-state knows how to make the moral voice in us contemptible, *as an arousal of egotism,* when it runs counter to love's own interest, and to represent our moral dignity *as a component of our happiness*, which we can divest at will. If our character is not firmly secured through good principles, then will we act shamefully at every swing of an overexcited imagination, and believe that we are waging a glorious victory against our egotism, while, quite the reverse, we are its despicable victim. In the well-known French novel, *Liaisons Dangereuses,* one finds a very striking example of this trick, which love plays on an otherwise pure and beautiful soul. The wife of the president of Tourvel is tricked into unfaithfulness, and now she seeks to quiet her agonized heart with the thought, that she sacrificed her virtue to generosity.

It is the so-called partial duties which the sense of beauty prefers to take under its protection and not seldom asserts against the absolute duties. Inasmuch as they submit far more to the caprice of the subject, and at the same time throw off a gleam of meritoriousness, they recommend themselves to the taste disproportionately more, than the absolute duties, which unconditionally govern with stricter compulsion. How many men allow themselves, to be unrighteous, in order to be magnanimous! How many there are, who, in order to do good to an individual, violate the duty toward the whole, and conversely; who pardon an untruth sooner than an indelicacy, an injury to humanity sooner than to their honor, who, in order to expedite the perfection of their mind, ruin their body, and, in order to adorn their understanding, degrade their character. How many there are, who do not shrink even from a crime, if by that means a praiseworthy end stands to be attained, who pursue an *ideal of political bliss through all the horror of anarchy, tread laws into the dust, in order to clear the way for better things, and do not scruple to hand over the present generation to misery, in order to secure the happiness of the ones to follow.* The ostensible unselfishness of certain virtues gives them a gloss of purity, which makes them bold enough to defy duty to its face, and on many a man his fantasy plays the strange trick, that he wishes to be beyond morality and more rational than reason.

The man of refined taste is, in this regard, capable of a moral perversion, from which the raw son of nature, through his very rawness, is safeguarded. For the latter, the disparity between that, which the senses require, and that, which duty commands, is so marked and so glaring, and his appetites have so little of the intellectual or spiritual, that even if they *rule* him ever so despotically, they can never ingratiate themselves into his esteem. Thus, if overwhelming sensuality incites him to a wrong action, then he can indeed succumb to temptation, but he will not conceal from himself, that he *did wrong,* and will render homage to reason even at the same moment, when he acts against its precept. The refined pupil of art, on the contrary, will not have it said that he falls from virtue, and in order to put his conscience at rest, he prefers to *belie* it. He would certainly like to yield to his appetite, but without thereby sinking in his own estimation. How then does he accomplish this? He overturns in advance the higher authority, which opposes his inclination, and before he transgresses the law, he calls into doubt the authority of the legislator. Are we to believe, that a perverse will could so pervert the understanding? All dignity, to which an inclination can make claim, she possesses thanks only to its accordance with reason, and now she is as deluded as she is bold, even to presume this dignity in her conflict with reason, yes, even to make use of it against the authority of reason.

So dangerously can it turn out for morality of character, when between the sensuous and moral impulses, which only in the ideal realm and never in reality can be perfectly at one, an excessively intimate partnership holds sway. Certainly in this partnership sensuousness risks nothing, inasmuch as it possesses nothing, which it would not have to give up, as soon as duty speaks and reason demands sacrifice. For reason, however, as moral legislator, all the more is risked, if she allows herself to be *granted* by the inclination, that which she could *demand* from it; for under the semblance of *voluntariness*, the feeling of *obligation* can easily be lost, and a gift can be withheld, if one day sensuousness should find its delivery inconvenient. It is therefore incomparably safer for morality of charcter, if the representation of the moral feeling through the sense of beauty is at least momentarily suspended, if reason more often gives orders *at once, without mediation*, and shows the will its true sovereign.

Hence one quite rightly says, that genuine morality proves itself only in the school of adversity, and continuous happiness easily becomes a barrier to virtue. I call him happy, who, in order to find enjoyment, does not need to do wrong, and in order to act rightly, does not need to renounce. The uninterruptedly happy man thus never sees duty face to face, because his legitimate and well-regulated inclinations always *anticipate* the command of reason, and no temptation to breach the law recalls the law to his mind. Governed solely by the sense of beauty, reason's regent in the sensuous world, he will go to his grave, without experiencing the dignity of his destiny. The unhappy man, on the contrary, if he is at the same time a virtuous one, enjoys the sublime privilege, of *unmediated* intercourse with the divine majesty of the law, and inasmuch as *his* virtue is succored by no inclination, of proving the freedom of divine inspiration while still a man.

Author's Notes

1. A writer, who cares only about scientific rigor, will for that very reason avail himself of *examples* very unwillingly and very sparingly. What holds true of the universal with perfect truth, suffers qualifications in any special case; and inasmuch as in any special case circumstances are found, which are accidental with respect to the general concept thereby to be presented, so it is always to be feared, that these accidental relations are carried along into that general concept, and rob something of its universality and necessity.

2. Herr Garve, in his insightful comparison of *bourgeois* and *aristocratic manners* in Part I of his *Essays, etc.* (a writing which I dare presume will be in everyone's hands), among the prerogatives of the aristocratic young man has imputed as well his precocious competence to intimacy with fashionable society, from which the bourgeois is already excluded by birth. But whether this privilege, which from the standpoint of outer and aesthetic cultivation is indisputably to be considered an advantage, could also be called a benefit from the standpoint of the inner cultivation of the aristocratic young man, and thus of the totality of his education, of this, Herr Garve has not told us his opinion, and I doubt, whether he would be able to justify such a claim. As much as is to be gained in this way in form, must thereby be neglected in substance, and if one reflects, how much more easily form occasions a content, than content a form, then the burgher is not likely to very much envy the nobleman this prerogative. Of course, if the arrangement is henceforth to continue, that the bourgeois *works*, and the aristocrat *keeps up appearances*, then one can choose no more convenient means thereto, than precisely this difference in education, but I doubt, whether the aristocrat will forever tolerate such a division.

This statue of Jeanne d'Arc stands in the center of Paris. A simple maiden from Lorraine, her life and heroic leadership on behalf of the nation of France are the subject of Schiller's The Virgin of Orleans.

A militant statue of Jeanne d'Arc in front of the French Hospital in the Chinatown district of Los Angeles. Statues of Jeanne d'Arc can be found in almost every major American city.

A U.S. government advertising poster from World War I. Jeanne d'Arc was the symbol of the patriotic American woman.

Leonardo da Vinci's Annunciation. Schiller's Johanna was divinely inspired by God through the Virgin Mary, whose banner she carried. This is the reason Schiller gave the name The Virgin of Orleans to his play.

Brief Is The Pain, The Joy Shall Be Eterne
by L. van Beethoven

Ludwig van Beethoven (1770-1827), a great admirer of Schiller's, personally identified with Jeanne d'Arc, as represented in Schiller's play. The most poignant reflection of this is the composer's canonical setting of the last line of The Virgin of Orleans: "Brief is the pain, the joy shall be eterne"—a sentiment which Beethoven, who overcame immense adversity to be a creative genius, certainly shared with the maiden from Lorraine.

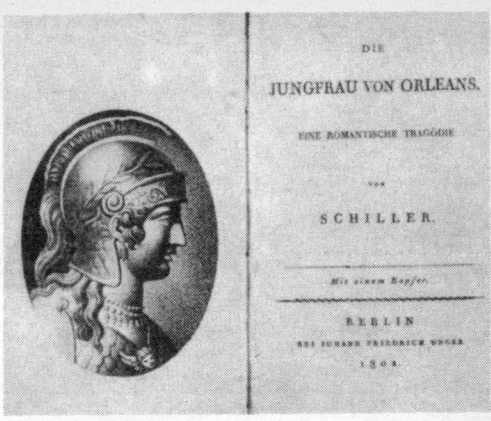

Cover of Unger's 1802 publication of Schiller's The Virgin of Orleans: A Romantic Tragedy.*

Playbill for the opening night of The Virgin of Orleans *in Leipzig, September 11, 1801. Leipzig is the home of the movement for liberty which sparked the downfall of the Communist government in East Germany in 1989.**

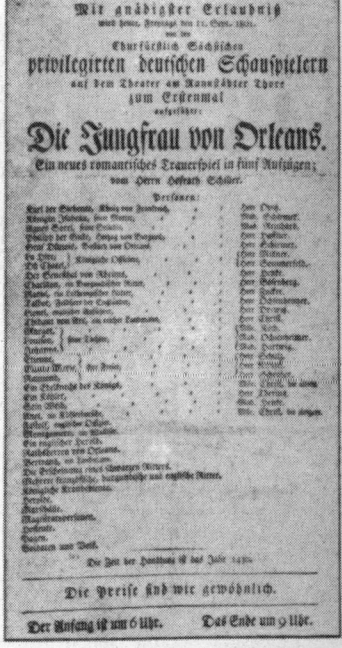

Models of the principal actors in The Virgin of Orleans *from the Museum Exposition at the Château de Culan, Cher, France.*

Drawing of the armor of Jeanne d'Arc, on display at the Jeanne d'Arc Museum in Orleans, France. Note that Jeanne d'Arc's banner has the word "Maria" written upon it, and the traditional fleur de lis, *symbolizing France.*

In his On the Pathetic, *Schiller analyzes this statue of* Laocoön: *"The group of Laocoön and his children is an approximate measure for that, which the plastic art of the ancients was able to achieve in the pathetic."* Laocoön group in the Vatican Museum, Rome.

Participants in a 1985 poetry competition sponsored by the Schiller Institute. The Institute's publication of three volumes of English translations of the works of Friedrich Schiller is helping to spark a renaissance in the dramatic arts in the West.

*Source is Schiller National Museum, Marbach, Federal Republic of Germany, Friedrich Schiller: Eine Dokumentation in Bildern.

ON NAÏVE AND SENTIMENTAL POETRY

TRANSLATED BY WILLIAM F. WERTZ, JR.

There are moments in our life, when we dedicate a kind of love and touching respect to nature in its plants, minerals, animals, landscapes, just as to human nature in its children, in the morals of country folk and of the primeval world, not because it is pleasing to our senses, not even because it satisfies our understanding or taste (the opposite can often occur in respect to both), but rather merely *because it is nature*. Every fine man, who does not altogether lack feeling, experiences this, when he walks in the open, when he lives upon the land or tarries beside monuments of ancient times, in short, when he is surprised in artificial relations and situations with the sight of simple nature. It is interest, not seldom elevated to need, which lies at the foundation of many of our fancies for flowers and animals, for simple

---

This treatise first appeared in three segments with other writings: in 1795 in the November issue of *Die Horen*, under the title *On the Naïve;* in the December 1795 issue of *Die Horen*, under the title *The Sentimental Poet;* and in the January 1796 issue of *Die Horen*, under the title *Conclusion of the Treatment of the Naïve and Sentimental Poet, Including Some Remarks on a Characteristic Difference Between the Men Concerned*. In the second part of his *Shorter Prose Writings*, which appeared in August 1800, Schiller gave this piece its final title, *On Naïve and Sentimental Poetry*.

gardens, for walks, for the country and its inhabitants, for many products of remote antiquity, etc.; provided, that neither affectation nor an accidental interest in it be in play. This kind of interest in nature takes place, however, only under two conditions. First, it is entirely necessary, that the object which infuses us with the same, be *nature* or certainly be held by us therefor; second, that it (in the broadest meaning of the word) be *naïve*, i.e., that nature stand in contrast with art and shame her. So soon as the last is added to the first, and not before, nature is changed into the naïve.

Nature in this mode of contemplation is for us nothing other than voluntary existence, subsistence of things through themselves, existence according to its own unalterable laws.

This conception is absolutely necessary, if we should take interest in such phenomena. If one could give to an artificial flower by means of the most perfect deception, the appearance of nature, if one could carry the imitation of the naïve in morals up to the highest illusion, so would the discovery, that it be imitation, completely destroy the feeling of which we are speaking.[1] From this it is clear, that this kind of pleasure in regard to nature is not aesthetical, but rather moral; for it is produced by means of an idea, not immediately through contemplation; also, it by no means depends upon the beauty of forms. What would even a plain flower, a spring, a mossy stone, the chirping of birds, the buzzing of bees, etc., have in itself so charming for us? What could give it any claim upon our love? It is not these objects, it is an idea represented through them, which we love in them. We love in them the quietly working life, the calm effects from out itself, existence under its own laws, the inner necessity, the eternal unity with itself.

They *are* what we *were;* they are what we *ought to become* once more. We were nature as they, and our culture should lead us back to nature, upon the path of reason and freedom. They are therefore at the same time a representation of our lost childhood, which remains eternally most dear to us; hence, they fill us with a certain melancholy. At the same time, they are representations of our highest perfection in the ideal, hence, they transpose us into a sublime emotion.

But their perfection is not their merit, because it is not the work of its choice. They afford us, therefore, the entirely peculiar pleasure, that they, without shaming us, are our model. A constant divine appearance, they surround us, but more refreshingly than dazzlingly. What constitutes their character is precisely that which is lacking in ours to be complete; what distinguishes us from them is precisely that which is missing in them to be divine. We are free, and they are necessary; we change, they remain the same. But only when both are united with one another—when the will freely obeys the law of necessity, and with all change of the imagination reason maintains its rule, does the divine or the ideal issue forth. We therefore perceive *in them* eternally that which is missing from us, but after which we are required to strive, and which, although we never attain it, we nevertheless may hope to approach in an infinite progress. We perceive *in ourselves* an advantage, which is wanting in them, but of which they can partake either never at all, such as those lacking in reason, or not other than if they go *our* way, such as in childhood. They provide us accordingly with the sweetest enjoyment of our human nature as idea, although they must necessarily humble us in regard to every *determined state* of our human nature.

Since this interest in nature is grounded upon an idea, so can it appear only in souls, which are susceptible to ideas, i.e., in moral ones. By far the majority of men merely affect it, and the universality of this sentimental taste to our times, which is expressed, especially since the appearance of certain writings, in sentimental journeys, such gardens, walks, and other fancies of this kind, is yet by no means proof of the universality of this manner of perception. Nevertheless, nature will always express something of this effect even on those most lacking in feeling, because the *predisposition* to morality, which is common to all men, is already sufficient thereto and we are all driven to it *in the idea*, irrespective of how great the distance of our own *acts* is from the simplicity and truth of nature. This sentimentality in respect to nature is especially strongly and most universally expressed at the instigation of such objects, which stand in a close connection with us and bring nearer to us the retrospective view of ourselves and the *unnatural* in us, as for example, with children or childlike nations. One errs, if one believes, that it be merely the conception of helplessness, which sees to it that we dwell on children with so much emotion in certain moments. That may perhaps be the case in respect to those, who in the face of weakness are accustomed never to feel something other than their own superiority. But the feeling of which I speak (it takes place only in quite peculiar moral dispositions and is not to be mistaken for that which the joyous activity of children arouses in us), is more humiliating than favorable to self-love; and if, indeed, an advantage comes thereby into view, so is this by no means on our side. Not because we look down upon the child from the height of our force and perfection, but rather because, from the *limitation* of our condition, which is inseparable from the *determination*, which we have once obtained, we *look up* to the boundless *determinability* in the child and to his pure innocence, we fall into emotion, and our feeling in such a moment is too evidently mixed with a certain melancholy than that this source of the same were mistaken. In the child, the *predisposition and determination* is represented, in us the *fulfillment*, which always remains infinitely far behind the former. Hence, the child is to us a vivid representation of the ideal, not indeed of the fulfilled, but of the commissioned, and it is therefore by no means the conception of its poverty and limits, it is quite to the contrary the conception of its pure and free force, its integrity, its infinity, which moves us. To the men of morality and feeling, a child will for that reason be a *sacred* object, an object namely, which through the greatness of an idea annihilates every greatness of experience; and which, whatever it may lose in the judgment of the understanding, gains again in the judgment of reason in ample measure.

Precisely from this contradiction between the judgment of reason and of understanding, issues forth the quite peculiar phenomenon of the mixed feeling, which the *naïve* way of thinking excites in us. It combines the *childlike* simplicity with the *childish;* through the latter it exposes a vulnerable point to the understanding and calls forth that smile, whereby we make known our *(theoretical)* superiority. So soon, however, as we have reason to believe, that the childish simplicity be simultaneously a childlike one, that consequently the source thereof be not want of understanding, no incapacity, but rather a higher *(practical)* strength, a heart full of innocence and truth, which out of inner greatness disdains the help of art, so is the former triumph of the understanding past, and the mockery of simpleness passes over into admiration of simplicity. We feel ourselves compelled to esteem the object, at which we previously have smiled, whilst we at the same time cast a look into ourselves, to lament that we are not similar to the same. So arises the quite peculiar phenomenon of a feeling, in which joyous mockery, respect, and melancholy flow together.[2] It is required of the naïve, that nature bring forth the victory thereof over art,[3] it do this either against the knowledge and will of the person or with complete consciousness of the same. In the first case, it is the naïve of *surprise* and amuses; in the other, it is the naïve of *conviction* and is moving.

With regard to the naïve of surprise, the person must be *morally* capable of denying nature; with regard to the naïve of conviction, he may not be, nevertheless, we may not think of him as *physically* incapable thereof, if it shall produce a naïve impression upon us. Hence, the actions and conversations of children give us the pure impression of the naïve only so long as we do not remember their inability for art, and in general, only consider the contrast between their naturalness and artificiality in us. The naïve is a *childlikeness, where it is no longer expected,* and precisely for that reason, can not be attributed to real childhood in the strictest sense.

In both cases, however, with regard to the naïve of surprise as with regard to that of conviction, nature must be right, art, however, wrong.

First, the concept of the naïve is completed through this latter determination. Emotion is also nature, and the rule of decency is something artificial; yet the triumph of emotion over decency is by no means naïve. On the contrary, should the same emotion triumph over affectation, over false decency, over dissimulation, so bear we no hesitation to call it naïve.[4] It is therefore required, that nature triumph over art, not through its blind violence as *dynamical*, but rather through its form as *moral* greatness, in short, not as *need*, but rather as *inner necessity*. Not the insufficiency, but rather the *inadmissibility* of the latter must procure the victory of the form; for the former is want, and nothing which originates from want can produce respect. Indeed, it is with regard to the naïve of surprise, always the superiority of emotion and a *want* of reflection, which makes nature recognizable; but this want and that superiority still do not entirely constitute the naïve, but rather merely provide the occasion, so that nature *follows unhindered its moral nature*, i.e., the law *of harmony*.

The naïve of surprise can only fall to man, and indeed only to man, insofar as, in this moment, he is no longer pure and innocent nature. It supposes a will, which does not agree with that which nature does by its own hand. Such a person, if one brings him to his senses, will be alarmed about himself; the naïvely *minded*, on the contrary, will be surprised at the men and at their astonishment. Since, therefore, here not the personal and moral character, but rather merely the natural character set free by emotion confesses the truth, so we attribute to man no merit for this sincerity, and our laughter is well-deserved derision, which is held back through no personal high estimation of the same. Since, nevertheless, it is here still the sincerity of nature, which breaks through the veil of falsehood, so is contentment of a higher kind combined with the malicious enjoyment of having caught a man; for nature in contrast to affectation, and truth in contrast to deceit must excite respect every time. We therefore also feel in respect to the naïve of surprise a really moral pleasure, although not in regard to a moral character.[5]

With regard to the naïve of surprise, we indeed always respect nature, because we must respect the truth; with regard to the naïve of conviction, we, on the contrary, respect the *person* and therefore enjoy not merely a moral pleasure, but also on account of a moral object. In the one as in the other case, nature is *right*, that it speaks the truth; but in the latter case, nature is not merely right, but rather the person has *honor* as well. In the first case, sincerity of nature always disgraces the person, because it is involuntary; in the second, it always redounds to the merit of the person, even supposing, that that which it declares, may bring him disgrace.

We ascribe a naïve conviction to a man, if, in his judgment of things, he overlooks their artificial and affected relations and keeps merely to simple nature. Everything which can be judged thereof within healthy nature, we require of him and only release him absolutely from that which presupposes a removal from nature, be it either in thinking or feeling, at least knowledge of the same.

If a father relates to his child, that this or that man languishes in poverty, the child goes thence and carries his father's purse to the poor man, so is the action naïve; for healthy nature would act out of the child, and in a world where healthy nature would rule, it would have been completely right so to proceed. It sees only the need and the nearest means to satisfy it; such an extension of the right of property, whereby a part of mankind can perish, is not grounded in mere nature. The action of the child is therefore a humiliation of the real world, and our heart confesses that also, through the pleasure which it feels over this action.

If a man without knowledge of the world, but otherwise of a good sense, confesses his secrets to another, who deceives him, but knows how to skillfully dissemble and lends him through his sincerity itself the means to injure him, so do we find that naïve. We laugh at him, but can nevertheless not keep from esteeming him highly on that account. For his trust in others springs from the honesty of his own inner convictions; at least, he is only naïve insofar as this is the case.

The naïve way of thinking can accordingly never be a property of a corrupted man, but rather belongs only to children and childlike-minded men. These latter often act and think naïvely in the midst of the artificial relations of the great world; they forget out of their own beautiful human nature, that they have to do with a corrupt world, and conduct themselves even in the courts of kings with an ingenuousness and innocence as one finds only in the world of shepherds.

It is, besides, not at all so easy, to distinguish the childish innocence from the childlike always correctly, whilst there are actions, which hover on the outermost boundaries between both, and with which we are left absolutely in doubt, as to whether we should laugh at the simpleness or esteem highly the noble simplicity. A very noteworthy example of this kind one finds in the history of the government of Pope Adrian VI, which Mr. Schröckh has described for us with the thoroughness and pragmatic truth characteristic of him. This Pope, a Netherlander by birth, administered the pontificate in one of the most critical moments for the hierarchy, when an embittered party laid bare the weak points of the Roman Church without any forbearance, and the opposite party was interested in the highest degree in concealing them. What the truly naïve character, if indeed such a one strayed onto the chair of the holy Peter, had to do in this case, is not the question; but indeed, how far such a naïveté of conviction might be compatible with the role of a Pope. It was, after all, this, which placed the predecessors and successors of Adrian in the least embarrassment. With uniformity, they followed the once-adopted Roman system, to concede nothing anywhere. But Adrian actually had the upright character of his nation and the innocence of his former position. From the narrow sphere of the learned he was elevated to his sublime post, and even in the height of his new honors, had not become untrue to that simple character. The abuses in the Church moved him, and he was much too honest, to dissimulate publicly, what he confessed in silence. In consequence of this way of thinking, he allowed himself in the *instruction*, which he gave to his legate in Germany, to be misled into confessions, which had hitherto been heard from no Pope and ran directly contrary to the principles of this court: "We know well," he said among other things, "that for many years many abominations have taken place on this holy chair; no wonder, if the sick condition of the head has been handed down to the members, of the Pope to the prelates. We all have deviated, and for a long time there has been none among us, who would have done something good, not even one." Again elsewhere, he orders the legates to explain in his name, that he, Adrian, may not be blamed for that which was done by the Popes before him, and that such debaucheries, even when he had lived in a low station, had always displeased him, etc. One can easily conceive, how such a naïveté in the Pope may have been received by the Roman clergy; the least of which he was considered guilty, was, that he had betrayed the Church to the heretics. This most imprudent step of the Pope would, however, be worthy of our complete respect and admiration, if we could only convince ourselves, that it had really been naïve, i.e., that it would have been wrested from him merely through the natural truth of his character, without any regard to the possible consequences, and that he would have done it no less, if he had understood the impropriety committed in its entire extent. But we have some reason to believe, that he did not regard this step as so impolitic at all, and in his innocence went so far as to hope to have won something very important to the advantage of his Church through his flexibility. He did not imagine merely having to take this step as an honest man, but rather, being able to take responsibility for it also as Pope, and whilst he forgot, that the most artificial of structures could only be absolutely supported by a continued denial of the truth, he committed the unpardonable error of adhering to instructions applied in an entirely contrary situation, which would have been valid in a natural circumstance. To be sure, this alters our judgment very much; and although we can not renounce our respect for the honesty of the heart, from which this action flows, so is this latter not a little weakened by the reflection, that nature in art and the heart in the head would have had a too weak adversary.

Every true genius must be naïve or it is not genius. Its naïveté alone makes it genius, and what it is in the intellectual and the aesthetical, it can not deny in the moral. Unaware of the rules, the crutches of weakness, the taskmaster of perversity, guided only by nature or instinct, its protecting angel, it walks calmly and safely through all the snares of false taste, in which, if it be not so prudent as to avoid it already from the distance, the non-genius will be unfailingly ensnared. It is only given to the genius, to be always at home outside the known and to *enlarge* nature, without *going beyond* it. Indeed, the latter sometimes happens to the great geniuses, but only because these have their fanciful moments, when protecting nature abandons them, because the power of example overpowers them, or the corrupted taste of their time leads them astray.

The most complicated problems the genius must solve with unpretentious simplicity and facility; the egg of Columbus holds good for judgment of genius. Thereby alone does it legitimize itself as genius, that it triumphs over complicated art through simplicity. It does not proceed according to known principles, but rather according to sudden ideas and feelings; but its sudden ideas are inspirations of a God (everything that healthy nature does is divine), its feelings are laws for all times and for all generations of men.

The childlike character, which the genius imprints on it works, it shows also in its private life and its morals. It is *bashful*, because nature is always so; but it is not *decent*, because only corruption is decent. It is *intelligent*, for nature can never be the opposite; but it is not *cunning*, for only art can be that. It is *true* to its character and its inclinations, but not so much because it has principles, as because nature, in all its oscillations, always returns to its last place, always brings back the old wants. It is *modest*, yes shy, because genius always remains a mystery to itself; but it is not anxious, because it does not know the dangers of the road on which it walks. We know little of the private life of the great geniuses; but even the little, which has been preserved for us, for example of Sophocles, of Archimedes, of Hippocrates, and in modern times of Ariosto, Dante, and Tasso, of Raphael, of Albrecht Dürer, Cervantes, Shakespeare, of Fielding, Sterne *et al.*, confirms this assertion.

Yes, what seems to be still far more difficult, even the great statesman and general, so soon as they are great through their genius, will display a naïve character. I wish to mention here among the ancients only Epaminondas and Julius Caesar, among the moderns only Henry IV of France, Gustavus Adolphus of Sweden, and Czar Peter the Great. The Duke of Marlborough, Turenne, Vendôme all show us this character. To the other sex, nature has assigned its greatest perfection in the naïve character. After nothing does the womanly desire to please strive so much as after the *appearance of the naïve;* sufficient proof, even if we were to have no other, that the greatest power of the sex reposes in this property. But, because the ruling principles in the education of woman lie in eternal strife with this character, so is it to the woman, in the moral, just as difficult as to the man, in the intellectual, to preserve this magnificent gift of nature with the advantages of a good education; and the *woman*, who ties this naïveté of manners with a skillful behavior in regard to the great world, is just as deserving of high respect as the learned man, who combines the freedom of thought characteristic of genius with all the strictness of the school.

From the naïve way of thinking flows in a necessary manner also a naïve expression, as much in words as movements, and it is the most important ingredient of grace. Genius expresses its most sublime and deepest thoughts with this naïve grace; they are divine sayings from the mouth of a child. If the scholastic understanding, always anxious before error, nails its words like its concepts to the cross of grammar and logic, is hard and rigid, in order not to be indeterminate, uses few words, in order not to say too much, and prefers to take force and sharpness from the thoughts, that therewith it not cut the incautious, so does genius give to its own with a single happy stroke of the brush an eternally determined, firm, and yet entirely free outline. If there the sign remains eternally heterogenous and alien to the signified, so here, as through an inner necessity, the language springs forth from the thoughts and is so much one with the same, that even under the bodily envelope the spirit appears as denuded. Such a manner of expression, where the sign completely vanishes in the signified, and where the language, so to speak, leaves the thought which it expresses naked, since the other can never represent it, without simultaneously veiling it, is it, that one calls preferably ingenious and inspired in style.

Free and natural, like genius in its intellectual works, the innocence of the heart expresses itself in its living intercourse. As is known, in social life one has gotten away from the simplicity and rigorous truth of expression, in the same proportion as from the simplicity of inner convictions, and the easily wounded guilt, just like the easily seduced imaginative power, have made necessary an anxious decency. Without being false, one often speaks differently than one thinks; one must make circumlocutions, to say things; one can only cause pain to a sickly self-love, only bring danger to a corrupted imagination. An ignorance of these conventional laws, combined with natural sincerity, which despises any crookedness and any appearance of falsehood (not coarseness, which dispenses with them, because they are burdensome to it), produce in the intercourse a naïve of expression, which consists therein, to name things, which one either may not signify at all or only artificially, with their right names and in the shortest way. The ordinary expressions of children are of this kind. They excite laughter through their contrast with manners, yet one will always confess in one's heart, that the child is right.

The naïve of conviction can indeed, taken properly, be attributed also only to the man as a being not absolutely subject to nature, although only insofar as pure nature still acts out of him; but, through an effect of the poetizing, imaginative power, it is frequently transferred from that having reason to that devoid of reason. So we often attribute to an animal, a landscape, a structure, yes, to nature in general, a naïve character, in contrast to the capricious and to the fanciful concepts of man. This, however, always demands, that we lend a will in our thoughts to that devoid of will, and take notice of the strict regulation of the same, according to the law of necessity. The discontentment over our own ill-employed moral freedom and over the moral harmony absent in our conduct, leads to such a frame of mind, in which we address that which is devoid of reason as a person and, as if it really would have had to struggle against the temptation to do the opposite, make its eternal uniformity into a merit, envy its peaceful behavior. It suits us well in such a moment, that we hold the prerogative of our reason to be a curse and an evil and, on account of the vivid feeling of the imperfection of our actual performance, ignore doing justice to our predisposition and destiny.

We see then in nature devoid of reason only a fortunate sister, who remained behind in the maternal home, out of which we stormed in the high spirits of our freedom into foreign parts. With painful desire we long to return thence, so soon as we've begun to experience the distress of culture and hear in the foreign country of art, the moving voice of the mother. So long as we were merely children of nature, we were happy and perfect; we have become free and have lost both. Therefrom originates a twofold and very unequal longing for nature, a longing for its *happiness*, a longing for its *perfection*. The sensuous man laments only the loss of the first; the moral one can mourn only for the loss of the other.

Therefore, ask thyself well, sentimental friend of nature, whether thy indolence yearns for its repose, whether thy offended morality for its harmony? Ask thyself well, when art is loathsome to thee and abuses in social life impel thee to inanimate nature in solitude, whether it is its deprivations, its burdens, its hardships, or whether it is its moral anarchy, its capriciousness, its disorder, which thou detestest in it? Into these thy spirit must plunge with joy, and thy compensation must be the freedom itself, from which they flow. Thou canst well assume for thyself the calm happiness of nature as thine aim in the distance, but only that which is the reward of thy dignity. Therefore, nothing of complaints about the aggravations of life, about the inequality of conditions, about the pressure of relations, about the insecurity of possession, about ingratitude, oppression, persecution; all the *evils* of culture must thou submit to with a free resignation, must respect them as the natural conditions of the only good; only the *evil* of the same must thou deplore, but not merely with careless tears. Rather take care, that thou actest pure thyself amidst these defilements, free amidst this slavery, constant amidst this ill-humored change, lawful amidst this anarchy. Fear not before the confusion outside of thee, but before the confusion in thee; strive for unity, but seek it not in uniformity; strive for repose, but not through equilibrium, not through a standstill of thy activity. This nature, which thou enviest in that which is devoid of reason, is worthy of no respect, of no longing. It lies behind thee, it must eternally lie behind thee. Abandoned by the ladder, which bore thee, no other choice is now still left to thee, than to seize the law with free consciousness and will or to fall without hope of rescue into a bottomless depth.

But when thou hast been consoled over the lost *happiness* of nature, so let its *perfection* serve thine heart as a model. Dost thou step out of thine artificial circle to it, does it stand before thee in its great repose, in its naïve beauty, in its childlike innocence and simplicity—then tarry beside this image, cultivate this feeling, it is worthy of thy most glorious humanity. Let it no longer occur to thee, to want to *exchange places* with it, but take it into thyself and strive to wed its infinite advantage with thine own infinite prerogative and to produce the divine from both. Let it surround thee like a lovely *idyl*, in which, out of the confusion of art, thou always findest thyself once more, with which thou dost gather courage and new confidence in thy course and in thy heart dost kindle anew the flame of the *ideal*, which is extinguished so easily in the storms of life.

If one remembers the beautiful nature, which surrounded the ancient Greeks; if one reflects how intimately this people under its happy sky could live with free nature, how much closer its mode of conception, its manner of feeling, its morals lay to simple nature, and what a faithful impression of the same its poetic works are, so must the remark appear strange, that one meets among the same so few traces of the *sentimental* interest, which we moderns can take in natural scenes and in natural characters. The Greek is indeed in the highest degree exact, faithful, detailed in description of the same, but yet no more and with no more excellent interest of the heart, than he is also in description of a suit, a shield, armor, house furniture, or any mechanical product. He seems in his love for the object to make no distinction between that which is through itself, and that which is through art and through the human will. Nature seems more to interest his understanding and his curiosity than his moral feeling; he does not adhere to the same with intimacy, with sentimentality, with sweet melancholy as we moderns. Indeed, whilst he personifies and deifies it in its individual phenomena and represents its effects as actions of free being, he annuls the calm necessity in it, through which it is precisely so attractive to us. His impatient imagination leads him beyond it to the drama of human life. Only the living and free, only characters, actions, fates, and morals satisfy him, and if *we* can wish in certain moral dispositions, to give up the advantage of our freedom of the will, which exposes us to so much conflict with ourselves, so much disquiet and confusion, for the involuntary, but calm necessity of that which is devoid of reason, so, directly the opposite, is the imagination of the Greeks occupied with commencing human nature already in the inanimate world and there, where a blind necessity rules, giving influence to the will.

Whence indeed this different spirit? How comes it, that we, who in everything that nature is, are so infinitely far surpassed by the ancients, precisely here pay homage to nature in a higher degree, can adhere to it with intimacy and embrace even the lifeless world with the warmest feeling? Hence comes it, because nature with us has disappeared from humanity and we encounter it again in its truth only outside this, in the inanimate world. Not our greater *conformity to nature*, quite the opposite, the *repulsiveness to nature* of our relations, conditions, and morals impels us, to obtain a satisfaction in the physical world to the awakening instinct for truth and simplicity, which, like the moral predisposition, out of which it flows, lies incorruptible and ineradicable in all human hearts, which is not to be hoped for in the moral. For this reason is the feeling, wherewith we adhere to nature, so closely related to the feeling, wherewith we lament the age which has fled, of childhood and childlike innocence. Our childhood is the single unmutilated nature, which we still encounter in cultivated humanity, hence it is no wonder, when every footprint of nature out of us leads us back to our childhood.

Very much otherwise was it with the ancient Greeks.[6] With these, culture did not degenerate so far, that nature was abandoned over it. The entire structure of social life was erected upon feelings, not upon a concoction of art; their mythology itself was the inspiration of a naïve feeling, the birth of a joyful imaginative power, not of subtilizing reason, like the ecclesiastical beliefs of modern nations; since, therefore, the Greek had not lost nature in humanity, so could he also not be surprised by it outside of the latter and could have no such pressing need for objects, in which he found it again. At one with himself and happy in the feeling of his humanity, he had to stop with the latter as his maximum and take pains to make all else approach the same; while *we*, at variance with ourselves and unhappy in our experiences of humanity, have no more pressing interest, than to fly away from the same and to remove from our sight such an unsuccessful form.

The feeling, of which we are here speaking, is therefore not that which the ancients had; it is rather of the same kind as that which we *have for the ancients*. They felt naturally; we feel the natural. It was doubtless a totally different feeling, which filled Homer's soul, when he caused his divine sow-herd to entertain Ulysses, than what moved the soul of young Werther, when he read this song after a tedious social gathering. Our feeling for nature resembles the feeling of the sick for health.

Just as nature gradually begins to vanish from human life as *experience* and as the (acting and feeling) *subject*, so do we see it rise in the poetical world as *idea* and as *object*. That nation, which had simultaneously carried it the farthest in unnaturalness and in reflection upon it, first must needs have been moved the strongest by the phenomenon of the *naïve* and given a name to the same. This nation, so far as I know, was the French. But the perception of the naïve and the interest in the same is of course much older and dates already from the beginning of the moral and aesthetical corruption. This alteration in the manner of feeling is for example already extremely striking in Euripides, if one compares the latter with his predecessors, especially Aeschylus, and yet the former poet was the favorite of his time. The same revolution is also evidenced among the ancient *historians*. Horace, the poet of a cultivated and corrupt age, praises the calm happiness in his *Tibur*, and one could call him the true founder of this sentimental kind of poetry, just as he is in the same a not yet surpassed model. Also in Propertius, Virgil, *et al.*, one finds traces of this manner of feeling, less with Ovid, in whom the fullness of heart is lacking for it and who painfully misses in his exile at Tomes the happiness, which Horace so gladly did without in his *Tibur*.

The poets are everywhere, according to their concept, the *guardian* of nature. Where they can no longer entirely be the latter and already experience in themselves the destructive influence of capricious and artificial forms, or indeed have had to struggle with the same, then will they appear as the *witnesses* and the *avengers* of nature. They will either *be* nature, or they will *seek* the lost nature. Therefrom arise two entirely different kinds of poetry, through which the entire province of poetry is exhausted and measured out. All poets, who are really such, will, according to the time in which they flourish, or as accidental circumstances have influence upon their general education and upon their passing dispositions of mind, belong either to the *naïve* or to the *sentimental*.

The poet of a naïve and spirited young world, as also he, who approaches nearest to him in the age of artificial culture, is austere and prudish, like the virginal Diana in her forests; without all intimacy he flees from the heart, which seeks him, from the desire, which wishes to embrace him. The dry truth, wherewith he treats his object, appears not seldom as insensibility. The object possesses him entirely, his heart lies not like a base metal directly under the surface, but rather wishes to be sought like gold in the depths. Like the deity behind the world edifice, so does he stand behind his work; he is the work, and the work is he; one must be no longer worthy, or not be master, or be tired of the first, in order even to inquire after him.

So appears, for example, Homer among the ancients and Shakespeare among the moderns: two most different natures, separated by the immeasurable distance of time, but just in this character trait perfectly one. When I, at a very early age, first became acquainted with the latter poet, his coldness revolted me, his insensibility, which allowed him to jest in the highest pathos, to disturb the heart-rending scene in *Hamlet*, in *King Lear*, in *MacBeth*, etc., through a fool, which allowed him now here to stop, where my feeling would hasten away, now there cold-heartedly to carry forth, where the heart would so gladly stand still. Through the acquaintance with modern poets misled, to seek at first in the work of the poet to encounter *his* heart, to reflect mutually *with him* on his object, in short, to see the object in the subject, it was unbearable to me, that the poet could never here be seized and would never converse with me. For some years, he had my full reverence and was my study, before I learned to take a liking to his individual. I was not yet able to understand nature at first hand. I could only bear it through the image reflected by the understanding and arranged by the rules, and for this reason the sentimental poets of the French and also the German, from the year 1750 to approximately 1780, were precisely the right subjects. After all, I am not ashamed of this child's judgment, since the aged critic passed a similar one and was naïve enough to publish it to the world.

The same thing also occurred to me with Homer, with whom I became acquainted in a still later period. I remember now the remarkable passage in the sixth book of the *Iliad*, where Glaucus and Diomed strike at one another in combat and, after they are recognized as guest and host, give presents to one another. With this moving portrait of the piety, with which the laws of *hospitality* were observed even in war, can be compared a description of *chivalrous generosity* in Ariosto, where two knights and rivals, Ferragus and Finaldo, the latter a Christian, the former a Saracen, after a violent fight and covered with wounds, make peace and, to overtake the fugitive Angelica, mount the same horse. Both examples, however different they may otherwise be, are nearly the same as one another in regard to the effect on our heart, because both paint the beautiful triumph of morals over passion and move us through the naïveté of convictions. But how completely different do the poets undertake the description of this similar action. Ariosto, the citizen of a later world and one which has gotten away from the simplicity of morals, can not conceal his own astonishment, his emotion in his relating of this incident. The feeling of the distance of the former morals from those which characterize his age, overwhelms him. He all at once abandons the painting of the object and appears in his own person. One knows the beautiful stanza and has always admired it as excellent:

> Not far has gone Rinaldo, when he sees
> Before him leaping his fierce steed: "Now still,
> Baiardo mine, hold fast thy fleeing pace,
> To be without thee does me too much ill."
> But deaf to him, and quickening his race,
> The steed flies from him further. Fit to kill,
> Rinaldo follows, raging for his plight.
> Now let's pursue Angelica in her flight.[7]
> *Orlando Furioso*, canto i, stanza 32
> *translation by Nora Hamerman*

And now the ancient Homer! Hardly does Diomed learn from Glaucus's, his adversary's, story, that the latter is, from the time of their fathers, the guest and host of his family, so he plants his lance in the earth, converses in a friendly manner with him and agrees with him, that they will in the future avoid one another in combat. But let us hear Homer himself:

> "Thus, then, I am for thee a faithful host in Argos, and thou to me in Lycia, when I shall visit that country. We shall, therefore, avoid our lances meeting in the strife. Are there not for me other Trojans or brave allies to kill when a god shall offer them to me and my steps shall reach them? And for thee, Glaucus, are there not enough Achaeans, that thou mayest immolate whom thou wishest? But let us exchange our arms, in order that others may also see that we boast of having been hosts and guests at the time of our fathers." Thus they spoke, and, rushing from their chariots, they seized each other's hands, and swore friendship the one to the other.
> Alexander Pope's *Iliad*, vi 264–287

Hardly would a *modern* poet (at least hardly one, who is such in the moral sense of this word) even have waited as far as here, to attest to his joy in this action. We would pardon him all the more easily, since our heart also comes to a standstill in the reading of it, and willingly distances itself from the object, in order to look into itself. But no trace of all of this in Homer; as if he had been reporting something which occurs every day, indeed, as if he himself bore no heart in his bosom, he continues in his dry truthfulness:

> Then the son of Saturn blinded Glaucus, who, exchanging his armor with Diomed, gave him golden arms of the value of one hecatomb, for brass arms only worth nine beeves.[8]
> Pope's *Iliad*, vi 234–236

Poets of this naïve kind are no longer in their proper place in an artificial age. They are also hardly possible any more in the same, at least in no other way possible, than if they *run wild* in their age and are saved by a favorable fate from the mutilating influence of the same. From society itself they can never and not at all come; but out of the same they appear sometimes, but more as strangers, at which one wonders, and as uneducated sons of nature, at whom one feels angry. However beneficent these phenomena are for the artist, who studies them, and for the genuine connoisseur, who understands how to appreciate them, so little do they thrive on the whole and in their century. The seal of the ruler rests upon their brow; we, on the contrary, want to be rocked and carried by the Muses. By the critics, the true constables of taste, they are hated as *border-disturbers*, whom one would rather oppress; for even Homer may have been merely indebted to the force of a more than thousand-year testimony, that these judges of taste allow him; also it becomes hard enough to them, to assert their rules against his example, and his authority against their rules.

The poet, I said, *is* either nature, or he will *seek* it. The former produces the naïve, the latter the sentimental poet.

The poetic spirit is immortal and can not be lost from humanity; it can not otherwise be lost than simultaneously with the same and with the predisposition to it. For though man departs through the freedom of his imagination and his understanding from the simplicity, truth, and necessity of nature, so not only does the road to the same always stand open to him, but a more powerful and indestructible instinct, the moral, also drives him back incessantly to it, and precisely with this instinct does the poetical capacity stand in the closest relationship. Thus, the latter is also not lost simultaneously with the natural simplicity, but rather only works in another direction.

Even now, nature is the only flame, on which the poetic spirit feeds; from it alone it draws all its power, to it alone it speaks even in the artificial, in the man engaged in culture. To produce any other kind is foreign to the poetical spirit; hence, to speak parenthetically, all so-called works of wit are entirely falsely called poetic, although we for a long time, misled by the authority of French literature, have mixed them therewith. Nature, I say, is even now in the artificial state of culture, whereby the poetical spirit is powerful; only it now stands in an entirely different relation to the same.

So long as man is still pure, it is understood, not coarse nature, he acts as an undivided sensuous unity and as an harmonizing whole. Sense and reason, receptive and self-acting capacity, have not yet been separated in their operations, much less do they stand in contradiction with one another. His feelings are not the formless play of chance, his thoughts not the contentless play of conceptual power; from the law of *necessity* emerges the former, from *reality* emerges the latter. If man be encountered in the state of culture, and has art laid its hand upon him, so is this *sensuous* harmony annulled in him, and he can only express himself still as moral unity, i.e., as striving toward unity. The agreement between his feeling and thinking, which *actually* took place in the former state, exists now merely *ideally*; it is no longer in him, but rather outside of him, as a thought, which should first be realized, no longer as a fact of life. Should one now apply the concept of poetry, which is nothing other *than to give humanity its most complete expression possible,* to both of these states, so it ensues, that there in the state of natural simplicity, where man still acts with all his powers at one time, as an harmonious unity, where therefore all his nature expresses itself completely in reality, the poet must *imitate the real* as completely as possible—that, on the contrary, here in the state of culture, where that harmonious cooperation of its entire nature is merely an idea, *the poet must* elevate reality to the ideal or, what amounts to the same, *represent the ideal.* And these are also the only two possible ways, in which the poetic genius can in general express itself. They are, as one sees, extremely different from one another, but there is a higher concept, which embraces both, and it should not be at all surprising, if this concept coincides with the idea of humanity.

Here is not the place to pursue further the thought, which only a separate exposition can place in its full light. Whoever, however, only knows how to make a comparison between ancient and modern poets,[9] according to the spirit and not merely according to accidental forms, will be easily convinced of the truth of the same. The former move us through nature, through sensuous truth, through living presence; the latter move us through ideas.

The latter path, which the modern poets take, is after all the same, that man generally must pursue individually and as a whole. Nature makes him one with himself, art divides and disunites him, through the ideal he returns to unity. However, because the ideal is an infinity, which he never attains, so can the cultivated man never become perfect in *his* type, as the natural man can indeed become in his. He must needs, therefore, be infinitely inferior to the latter in respect to perfection, if attention is paid merely to the relation, in which both are to their type and to their maximum. Should one, on the contrary, compare the types themselves with one another, so it appears, that the end toward which man *strives* through culture, is infinitely superior to that which he *attains* through nature. The one receives its value, therefore, through absolute attainment of a finite, the other obtains it through the approach to an infinite greatness. However, because only the latter has *degrees* and makes *progress,* so is the relative value of man who is engaged in culture, taken as a whole, never determinable, although the same viewed individually is at a necessary disadvantage in respect to that, in which nature acts in its full perfection. However, insofar as the final end of humanity can not otherwise be attained than by this progress and the latter cannot otherwise progress, than whilst he is cultivated and consequently passes into the former, so is there no question, to which of the two the advantage is due in regard to this final end.

The same, which is said here of the two different forms of humanity, can also be applied to these two forms of poets, who correspond to them.

For this reason, one must needs have compared ancient and modern—naïve and sentimental—poets with one another either not at all or only under a common higher concept (there is really one such). For, of course, if one has first abstracted one-sidedly a specific notion of poetry from the ancient poets, so is nothing easier, but also nothing more trivial, than to belittle the moderns in regard to it. If one only calls poetry, that which acted uniformly in all times on simple nature, so can it not otherwise be, than that one will have to contest the name of poet in the modern poets precisely in their most peculiar and most sublime beauty, because precisely here they only speak to the pupil of art and have nothing to say to the simple nature.[10] He whose disposition is not already prepared to go beyond reality into the realm of ideas, for him the richest content will be empty appearance and the highest poetic flight exaggeration. It can occur to no one of reason, to wish to place in that, wherein Homer is great, any of the moderns by his side, and it sounds laughable enough, when one sees a Milton or Klopstock honored with the name of a modern Homer. Just so little, however, will any of the ancient poets and least of all Homer, in that which characteristically distinguishes the modern poets, be able to be held in comparison with the same. The former, I would like to say, is powerful through the art of limitation; the latter is so through the art of the infinite.

And exactly therefrom, that the strength of the ancient artist (for what has been said here of the poet, can, under the restrictions which are self-evident, be in general also extended to the fine artist) consists in limitation, is explained the great advantage, which the plastic art of antiquity asserts over that of modern times, and in general the unequal proportion of value, in which modern poetry and modern plastic art stand in regard to both kinds of art in antiquity. A work for the eye finds its perfection only in the limitation; a work for the imaginative power can also attain it only through the unlimited. In plastic works, his superiority in ideas accordingly helps the modern little; here is he obliged to *determine in space* the image of his imaginative power with the greatest precision and, consequently, be measured with the ancient artist precisely in this property, wherein the latter has his incontestible advantage. In poetical works it is otherwise, and if the ancient poets triumph equally also here in the simplicity of forms and in that which is sensuously representable and *corporeal*, so can the moderns leave them behind again in the wealth of the matter, in which what is unrepresentable and unspeakable, in short, in that which one calls mind in works of art.

Since the naïve poet merely follows simple nature and feeling and is confined merely to imitation of reality, so can he also only have a single relation to this object, and there is, in *this* regard, no choice of treatment for him. The different impression of naïve poetry rests (provided that one disregards everything that belongs to the content and views that impression only as the pure work of the poetic treatment), rests, I say, merely in the different *degree* of one and the same mode of perception; even the difference in the external forms can make no alteration in the quality of that aesthetical impression. The form may be lyrical or epic, dramatic or descriptive: we can indeed be moved more weakly and more strongly, but (so soon as abstracted from the matter) never in a different way. Our feeling is universally the same, entirely from *one* element, so that we are able to distinguish nothing therein. Even the distinction of languages and age changes nothing here, for just this pure unity of their source and their effect is a characteristic of naïve poetry.

It is entirely different with the sentimental poet. The latter *reflects* on the impression, which the objects make in him, and only on this reflection is the emotion grounded, in which he himself is moved and moves us. The object is here connected with an idea, and only in this connection does his poetical force rest. The sentimental poet is therefore always concerned with two conflicting conceptions and feelings, with reality as limit and with his idea as the infinite, and the mixed feeling, which he arouses, will always testify to this two-fold source.[11] Therefore, since here a plurality of principles occurs, so does it depend upon which of the two is *predominant* in the feeling of the poet and in his representation, and consequently a difference in the treatment of it is possible. For now arises the question, whether he dwells more on the reality, or more on the ideal, or whether he wants to achieve the former as an object of aversion, or the latter as an object of inclination. His representation will therefore be either *satirical* or it will (in a broader sense of this word, which will be explained afterward) be *elegiac*; every sentimental poet will adhere to one of these two modes of feeling.

The poet is satirical, if he takes as his object the distance from nature and the contradiction of reality with the ideal (in the effect upon the soul, both result in the same). This he can, however, perform both earnestly and with passion as well as sportively and with cheerfulness, according as he dwells either in the domain of the will or in the domain of the understanding. The former occurs through the *punishing* or *pathetic*, the latter through *sportive* satire.

Taken strictly, the aim of the poet agrees neither with the tone of punishment nor that of amusement. The former is too serious for play, which poetry should always be; the latter is too frivolous for the earnestness, which should be the basis of all poetical play. Moral contradictions necessarily interest our heart and these deprive the soul of its freedom, and yet all personal interest, i.e., all reference to a need, should be banished from poetical emotions. Contradictions of the understanding, on the contrary, leave the heart indifferent, and nevertheless the poet deals with the highest desires of the heart, with nature and the ideal. It is hence no small problem for him, not to violate in pathetic satire the poetical form, which consists in the freedom of play, not to miss in the sportive satire the poetical contents, which must always be the infinite. This problem can only be solved in a single way. The punishing satire obtains poetical freedom, whilst it passes over into the sublime; the laughing satire receives poetical content, whilst it treats its theme with beauty.

In satire, the real as deficiency is placed in opposition to the ideal as the highest reality. It is after all not at all necessary, that the latter be expressed, if the poet only knows how to awaken it in the soul; but this must he do absolutely or he will not act poetically at all. The real is therefore here a necessary object of aversion; but, whereon everything here depends, this aversion itself must necessarily originate again from the opposing ideal. It could, that is, also have a merely sensuous source and be grounded solely on need, with which the real quarrels; and frequently enough, we believe we feel a moral indignation in respect to the world, when merely the antagonism of the same to our inclination embitters us. It is this material interest, which the common satirist brings into play, and because he does not at all fail to take this road, to move us in our emotion, so he believes he has our heart in his power and is master in the pathetic. But any pathos from this source is unworthy of poetry, which moves us only through ideas and may only take the road to our heart through reason. Also this impure and material pathos will always be apparent through a preponderance of passion, and through a painful preoccupation of the soul, since, on the contrary, true poetical pathos is recognizable in a preponderance of self-activity and in a mental freedom, which persists even in a state of emotion. Should the emotion originate, that is, from the ideal opposed to the real, so is any hemmed-in feeling lost in the sublimity of the ideal, and the greatness of the idea, by which we are filled, elevates us above all restrictions of experience. In the representation of revolting reality, everything depends accordingly thereon, that the necessary be the basis, upon which the poet or the narrator lays out the real, that he know how to dispose our mind for ideas. Should *we* but take an elevated position in judgment, so does it not matter at all, if the object remains deep and low beneath us. When the historian Tacitus describes to us the profound decay of the Romans of the first century, so is it a lofty spirit, who looks down on the low, and our frame of mind is truly poetic, because only the height, whereupon he himself stands and to which he knew to elevate us, renders his object low.

The pathetic satire must therefore flow at all times from a frame of mind, which is deeply permeated by the ideal. Only a ruling instinct toward harmony can and may produce that deep feeling of moral contradiction and that glowing indignation against moral perversity, which in a Juvenal, Swift, Rousseau, Haller, and others becomes enthusiasm. The same poets would and must needs have composed with the same success also in touching and tender types, if accidental reasons had not given their souls in early life this definite direction; they have partly also actually done it. All of those named here lived either in a degenerate age and had a dreadful experience of moral corruption before their eyes, or their own fates have strewn bitterness in their souls. Also, the philosophical mind, when it separates with unrelenting strictness the appearance from being and penetrates into the depths of things, inclines the soul to this severity and austerity, with which Rousseau, Haller, and others paint reality. But these external and accidental influences, which always act restrictively, may at most only determine the direction, never provide the content of the enthusiasm. The latter must on the whole be the same and, free of any external need, flow forth from a glowing instinct for the ideal, which is absolutely the only true calling to the satirical as in general to the sentimental poet.

If the pathetic satire suits only *sublime* souls, so can mocking satire only succeed in a *beautiful* heart. For the former is already preserved from frivolity by its earnest theme; but the latter, which may only treat a morally indifferent matter, would inevitably fall into it and lose any poetical dignity, if the treatment did not here ennoble the content and the *subject* of the poet were not to substitute for his object. But it is not bestowed on the beautiful heart, to impress a perfect image of itself independent of the object of its action on each of its expressions. The sublime character can make itself known only in individual victories over the resistance of the senses, only in certain moments of flight and of momentary exertion; in the beautiful soul, on the contrary, the ideal acts as nature, therefore uniformly, and can therefore appear also in a state of rest. The deep sea appears the most sublime in its movement, the clear brook the most beautiful in its calm course.

It has repeatedly been a matter of dispute, which of the two, tragedy or comedy, deserves to be ranked above the other. If the question is merely, which of the two treats the more important object, so is there no doubt, that the former has the advantage; however, should one want to know, which of the two requires the more important subject, so would the decision more likely prove to be for the latter.— In tragedy, very much occurs already through the theme, in comedy, nothing occurs through the theme and everything through the poet. Now, since the matter never comes into consideration in the judgment of taste, so must of course the aesthetical value of these two kinds of art stand in inverse proportion to their material importance. The object carries the tragic poet, the comic, on the contrary, must support his in the aesthetical height through his subject. The former may take a flight, which is not exactly such a great matter; the other must remain the same, he must already *be* there and be at home there, whereto the other does not succeed without a vault. And that is precisely it, wherein the beautiful character is distinguished from the sublime. In the former, all greatness is already contained, it flows unconstrained and effortless from its nature, it is, according to its ability, an infinity in every point of its course; the other can be stretched and elevated to all greatness, it can through the force of its will be torn from every condition of limitation. The latter is therefore only free by fits and starts and only with effort, the former is so with ease and always.

To bring forth and to nourish in us this freedom of mind, is the beautiful task of comedy, just as tragedy is assigned, to help reestablish mental freedom on an aesthetical path, when it has been violently annulled by an emotion. In tragedy, mental freedom must therefore be annulled artificially and as an experiment, because it demonstrates its poetic force in the restoration of the same; in comedy, on the contrary, care must be taken, that it never come to this annulment of mental freedom. Therefore, the tragic poet always treats his theme practically, the comic poet his always theoretically, even when the former (as Lessing in his *Nathan*) would have the fancy to treat a theoretical, the latter, a practical matter. Not the domain from which the theme is taken, rather the forum, before which the poet brings it, makes the same tragic or comic. The tragedian must be on his guard against tranquil reasoning and always interest the heart; the comedian must guard against pathos and always entertain the understanding. The former, therefore, displays his art through constant excitement, the latter through constant prevention of passion; and this art is naturally in both cases so much the greater, the more the theme of the one is of an abstract nature and that of the other is inclined to the pathetic.[12] If, therefore, tragedy sets out from a more important point, so must one concede, on the other hand, that comedy aims at a more important end, and it would, if it were to achieve it, make all tragedy superfluous and impossible. Its end is identical with the highest toward which man struggles, to be free of passion, always clearly, always calmly to look around himself and into himself, to find everywhere more accident than fate, and to laugh more at absurdity than to be angry at wickedness or to weep.

As in active life, so it also often occurs in poetic representations, that mere light-mindedness, agreeable talent, joyful good nature are mistaken for beauty of the soul, and since the common taste is in general never elevated above the agreeable, so is it to such *elegant* minds an easy thing, to usurp that glory, which is so difficult to deserve. But there is an infallible test, by means of which one can distinguish the facility of the natural from the facility of the ideal, just as the virtue of temperament from the true morality of character, and this is, when both are attempted in a difficult and great object. In such a case, the elegant genius falls infallibly into insipidity, just as the virtuous by temperament into the material; the true beautiful soul, on the contrary is just as certain to pass over into the sublime.

So long as Lucian merely chastises absurdity, as in the *Wishes*, in the *Lapithas*, in *Jupiter Tragödus*, etc., he remains a mocker and pleases us with his joyful humor; but an entirely different man emerges from him in many passages of his *Nigrinus*, his *Timon*, his *Alexander*, when his satire also strikes at moral depravity. "Unhappy wretch," so he begins in his *Nigrinus* the revolting picture of Rome at that time, "why forsakest thou the light of the sun, Greece, and that happy life of freedom and cam'st here to this turmoil of splendid subservience, of services and banquets, of sycophants, flatterers, poisoners, legacy-hunters and false friends? etc." On such and similar occasions must the lofty earnestness of feeling be evident, which must underlie all play, if it shall be poetical. Even through malicious jests, wherewith both Lucian as well as Aristophanes mistreated Socrates, a serious reason shines forth, which avenges the truth against the sophist and does combat for an ideal, which it merely does not always express. Also the first of the two has justified this character against all doubt in his Diogenes and Demonax; among the moderns, what great and beautiful character does Cervantes not express at every worthy occasion in his Don Quixote! What a glorious ideal must not have lived in the soul of the poet, who created a Tom Jones and a Sophonisba! How the laughter of Yorik, so soon as he wishes, can so greatly and so powerfully move our souls! Also in our Wieland I discern this earnestness of feeling; even the wanton play of his humor inspires and ennobles the grace of the heart; even in the rhythm of his song it imprints its stamp, and never does he lack the power to soar, as soon as it is wanted, to carry us aloft to the highest.

No such judgment can be made of the Voltairean satire. Indeed, it is also in the case of this author only the truth and simplicity of nature, whereby he sometimes moves us poetically, whether it be, that he actually attains it in a naïve character, as many times in his *Ingènu*, or that he seeks and avenges it as in his *Candide*, etc. Where neither of the two is the case, he can indeed amuse us as a witty mind, but certainly not move us as a poet. But everywhere, too little earnestness underlies his mockery, and this makes his vocation as a poet justly suspect. We always encounter only his understanding, not his feeling. No ideal appears under his flimsy veil and hardly anything absolutely fixed in this eternal motion. His wonderful multiplicity of external forms, far from proving anything in behalf of the inner fullness of his spirit, rather bears critical witness thereagainst, for regardless of all these forms, he has not even found *one*, wherein he could have impressed a heart. One must therefore almost fear, it was in this rich genius only the poverty of heart, which determined his vocation as satire. Were it otherwise, so would he have had to step by chance on his long road out of this narrow rut. But in all the so-great variety of matter and of external form, we see this inner form return in eternal, needy monotony, and, despite his voluminous career, he has nevertheless not accomplished the circle of humanity in himself, which one finds passed through with joy in the above-mentioned satirists.

Should the poet so oppose nature to art and the ideal to the real, that the representation of the first predominates and the pleasure in the same becomes the ruling feeling, so do I call him *elegiac*. Also, this type has, like satire, two classes under it. Either is nature and the ideal an object of sadness, when the former is represented as lost, the latter as unattained, or both are an object of joy, whilst they are conceived as real. The first gives *elegy* in the narrower, the other the *idyl* in the broadest sense.[13]

Like indignation in the pathetic, and like mockery in sportive satire, so may sadness in elegy flow only from an enthusiasm awakened by the ideal. Thereby alone does the elegy receive poetical content, and every other source of the same is completely beneath the dignity of poetry. The elegiac poet seeks nature, but in its beauty, not merely in its agreeableness, in its agreement with ideas, not merely in its compliance to need. The sadness over lost joys, over the golden age which has disappeared from the world, over the happiness of youth, of love, etc., which has fled away, can only then become the matter for elegiac poetry, if those conditions of sensuous peace are conceived at the same time as objects of moral harmony. For this reason, I can not as a whole consider as a poetical work the mournful songs of Ovid, which he strikes up from his place of exile by the Black Sea, however moving they are, and however many passages they have of the poetical. There is much too little energy, much too little spirit and nobility in his pain. Need, not inspiration, pours forth those laments. There breathes therein, although no common soul, yet the common frame of mind of a noble spirit, which his fate trampled to the ground. Indeed, if we remember, that it is Rome and the Rome of Augustus, for which he mourns, so we pardon the son of joy his pain; but even glorious Rome with all of its blessings is, if the imaginative power does not first ennoble it, merely a finite greatness, therefore an unworthy object for poetry, which, elevated above all that reality erects, rightly mourns only for the sake of the infinite.

The content of the poetical lament can therefore never be an external, at all times only an internal ideal object; even when it mourns over a loss in reality, it must first transform it into an ideal. In this reduction of the limited to an infinite consists the true poetical treatment. The external matter is therefore always indifferent in itself, because poetry can never employ it, as it finds it, but rather it only gives it poetical dignity through that which it itself makes of it. The elegiac poet seeks nature, but as an idea and in a perfection, in which it has never existed, although he weeps over it as something that has existed and now is lost. When Ossian tells us of the days, which are no more, and of the heroes, who have disappeared, so has his poetical power transformed these pictures of his memory of long ago into the ideal, these heroes into gods. The experiences of a particular loss have become extended into the idea of universal transitoriness, and the deeply moved bard, whom the image of omnipresent ruin pursues, soars up to heaven, in order to find there in the course of the sun an emblem of the imperishable.[14]

I turn immediately to the modern poets of the elegiac type. Rousseau, as poet and as philosopher, has no other tendency than to either seek nature or to avenge it in art. According as his feeling dwells either on the one or the other, we find him now moved elegiacally, now inspired to Juvenalian satire, now as in his *Julia,* transported into the sphere of the idyl. His compositions have indisputable poetic merit, since they treat the ideal; only he does not know how to employ the same in a poetical manner. His earnest character, no doubt, lets him never descend into frivolity, but also does not permit him to be elevated up to poetic play. Now yoked by passion, now by abstraction, he seldom or never achieves aesthetical freedom, which the poet must maintain over his matter, must communicate to his reader. Either it is his sickly sensibility, which rules over him and drives his feelings to the point of being painful; or it is the force of his thinking, which places fetters on his imagination and, through the strictness of the concept, annihilates the grace of the portrayal. Both properties, whose intimate reciprocity and union properly constitutes the poet, are found in this author in an unusually high degree and nothing is lacking, other than that they also manifest themselves actually united with one another, that his self-activity be joined more to his feeling, that his susceptibility be joined more to his thought. Therefore, even in the ideal, which he erects from human nature, too much regard is given to the limits of the same, too little to its capability and a want of physical *repose* is everywhere more visible therein than of moral *harmony*. It is owing to his passionate sensibility, that he, in order to be rid of that struggle in human nature as soon as possible, prefers to see the same led back to the spiritless uniformity of his initial condition, rather than to see that struggle ended in the spirited harmony of a completely accomplished education, that he prefers not to let art begin at all, rather than await its completion, that he prefers to place the goal lower and prefers to lower the ideal, in order to attain it the more quickly, in order to attain it more safely.

Among Germany's poets of this type I wish to mention here only Haller, Kleist, and Klopstock. The character of their poetry is sentimental; they move us through ideas, not through sensuous truth, not so much because they themselves are nature, as because they know how to enthuse us for nature. What, however, is true *in general* of the character of these, as well as of all sentimental poets, does not of course exclude in any way the capability to move us *in particular* through naïve beauty: without this, they would not be poets overall. It is only not their proper and prevailing character, to receive with a calm, simple, and easy sense and to represent in the same manner, that which is received. Involuntarily, imagination anticipates the intuition, the thinking power the perception, and one closes eyes and ears, in order to sink contemplatively into oneself. The soul can endure no impression, without immediately paying attention to its own play and, through reflection, placing before and outside itself, what it has in itself. We receive in this way never the object, only what the reflecting understanding of the poet made from the object, and even then, if the poet himself is this object, if he wishes to represent his feelings, we do not experience his condition immediately and at first hand, but rather as the same is reflected in his soul, what he has thought about it as spectator of himself. When Haller mourned the death of his spouse (one knows the beautiful song) and begins as follows:

> Soll ich von deinem Tode singen?
> O Mariane, welch ein Lied!
> Wann Seufzer mit Worten ringen
> Und ein Begriff den andern flieht, u.s.f.

> Must I needs of thy dying sing?
> O Marian, what a refrain!
> When sighs with words are struggling
> And one idea the other flees, etc.

so do we find this description strictly true, but we also feel, that the poet does not properly communicate his feelings to us, but rather his thoughts about it. He also moves us for this reason far more weakly, because he himself must have already been very much cooled down, in order to be a spectator of his own emotion.

Already, the mostly supersensuous matter of Hallerian and also part of the Klopstockian compositions excludes them from the naïve type; so soon, therefore, as this matter should be treated poetically, so must it, since it assumes no bodily nature and consequently can not be an object of the sensuous intuition, pass over into the infinite and be elevated to an object of the spiritual intuition. In general, only in this sense can didactic poetry be conceived without internal contradiction; for, to repeat it once more, poetry only possesses these two domains: either it must stay in the world of sense, or it must stay in the world of ideas, since it can absolutely not thrive in the realm of concepts or in the world of understanding. Yet, I confess, I know no poem of this kind, neither from ancient nor modern literature, which would have brought the concept, which it treats, either purely and completely down to the individual or up to the idea. The ordinary case, when it still goes happily, is that the two are alternated, such that the abstract concept dominates and that the imaginative power, which ought to govern in the poetical domain, is merely permitted to serve the understanding. The didactic poem, wherein the thought itself were poetic and it would also remain so, is still awaited.

What is said here in general of all didactic poems, is true also of the poems of Haller in particular. The thought itself is not a poetical thought, but the execution is so sometimes, now through the use of images, now through the flight towards the ideal. Only in the last quality do they belong here. Force and depth and a pathetical earnestness characterize this poet. His soul is enkindled by an ideal, and his glowing feeling for truth seeks, in the silent Alpine valleys, the innocence which has disappeared from the world. Deeply touching is his lament; with energetic, almost bitter satire, he draws the perplexities of the understanding and heart, and with love, the beautiful simplicity of nature. Only in this picture, the concept predominates overly much, just as in himself the understanding plays master over feeling. Therefore, he *teaches* generally more than he *represents*, and represents generally with more forceful than lovely strokes. He is great, daring, ardent, sublime; however, he is seldom or never elevated to beauty.

In idea content and in depth of mind, Kleist is far inferior to this poet; in grace he might excel him, if we did not otherwise impute to him, as sometimes occurs, a want on the one side as a strength on the other. Kleist's feeling soul delights most in the sight of country scenes and manners. He gladly flees the empty noise of society and finds in the bosom of inanimate nature the harmony and peace, which he misses in the moral world. How touching is his longing for peace![15] How true and feeling, when he sings:

> Ja Welt, du bist des wahren Lebens Grab.
> Oft reizet mich ein heißer Trieb zur Tugend'
> Vor Wehmut rollt ein Bach die Wang' herab,
> Das Beispiel siegt, und du, o Feu'r der Jugend.
> Ihr trocknet bald die edlen Tränen ein.
> Ein wahrer Mensch muß fern von Menschen sein.

> Yes world, thou art the grave of the true life.
> An ardent instinct charms me oft to virtue,
> In sadness does a brook roll down my cheeks,
> Example wins, and thou, O fire of youth.
> You presently dry up these noble tears.
> A man who's true must distant be from men.

But, if his poetic instinct has led him out of the confining circle of relations into the spirited solitude of nature, so do the anguished image of the age and also unfortunately its fetters pursue him even here. What he flees is in him, what he seeks is eternally outside of him; never can he overcome the evil influence of his century. Be his heart ardent, his imagination energetic enough, so as to animate the dead forms of the understanding through representation, so does cold thought once again kill the living creation of poetic force, and reflection disturb the secret work of sentiment. His poetry is indeed as colorful and resplendent as the spring, of which he sang, his imagination is lively and active; yet one would sooner call it variable than rich, sooner playful than creative, sooner restlessly progressive than concentrative and formative. Traits succeed traits quickly and exuberantly, but without concentrating into an individual, without becoming full with life and rounded into form. So long as he merely composes lyrically and merely dwells on scenic portraits, partly the greater freedom of the lyrical form, partly the more arbitrary nature of the matter lets us overlook this deficiency, whilst we here in general desire represented the feelings of the poet more than the object itself. But the defect becomes only all too noticeable, when he presumes, as in his *Cisseis and Paches* and in his *Seneca*, to represent men and human actions; because here the imaginative power sees itself enclosed between firm and necessary limits and the poetic effect can only issue forth from the *object*. Here he becomes poor, tedious, meager, and frosty to the point of being unendurable; a warning example for all who, without an inner vocation from the field of musical poetry, lose their way climbing into the region of the plastic. In a related genius, Thomson, the same human mistake is made.

In the sentimental type and especially in the elegiac part of the same, few of the modern and still fewer of the ancient poets would be compared with our Klopstock. What is always to be attained only in the field of ideality, outside the limits of living form and outside the region of individuality, is performed by this musical poet.[16] Indeed, one would do him a great injustice, if one wanted to entirely deny to him that individual truth and vitality, with which the naïve poet describes his object. Many of his odes, many separate traits in his dramas and in his *Messiah* represent the object with striking truth and in beautiful enclosure; here especially, where the object is his own heart, has he demonstrated not seldom a great nature, a charming naïveté. Only *his* strength does not lie herein, only this property would not be sustained throughout the whole of his poetical sphere. Just as in the *musical* poetical view according to the above-given determination, the *Messiah* is a magnificent creation, so does it still leave much to be desired in the *plastic* poetical, where one expects determined forms and forms *determined for the intuition*. Perhaps in this poem the figures would be determined enough, but not for the intuition; only abstraction has created them, only abstraction can distinguish them. They are good examples as concepts, but not individuals, not living forms. It is left far too much to the imaginative power, which the poet ought to apply, and which he ought to command through the universal determination of his forms, in what manner it wishes to sensualize these men and angels, these gods and Satan, this heaven and this hell. There is an outline given, within which understanding must necessarily conceive them, but no firm limit is established, within which the imagination must necessarily represent them. What I say here of the characters, is true of everything, which in this poem is or ought to be life and action, and not only in this epic, but also in the dramatic poetry of our poet. For the understanding, all is excellently determined and bounded (I wish to recall here only his Judas, his Pilate, his Philo, his Solomon in the tragedy of this name), but it is much too formless for the imaginative power, and here, I confess it freely, I find this poet not in his sphere at all.

His sphere is always the realm of ideas, and he knows how to lead everything that he treats over into the infinite. One might say, from everything that he treats, he strips away the body, in order to turn it into spirit, just as other poets dress everything spiritual with a body. Almost every pleasure which his compositions yield must be obtained through an exercise of the thinking power; all feelings, which he, and indeed so intimately and powerfully, knows how to arouse in us, stream forth from supersensuous sources. Hence, this earnestness, this force, this buoyancy, this depth, which characterize everything which comes from him; hence also the eternal tension of the mind, in which we are kept in reading the same. No poet (except perhaps Young, who demands more therein than he, but without compensating for it, as he does) could be less adapted to be the favorite and to be the companion through life than precisely Klopstock, who always only leads us out of life, always only calls the spirit to arms, without refreshing the senses with the calm presence of an object. Chaste, other-worldly, incorporeal, holy, like his religion, is his poetic muse, and one must confess with admiration, that, if he wanders sometimes into these heights, yet never has he sunk down therefrom. For this reason, I acknowledge without concealment, that I am somewhat anxious for the mind of the same, who can really and without affectation make this poet his favorite book, a book namely, in which one can harmonize with every situation, to which one can return from every situation; also, I would think, one would have seen in Germany enough fruits of his dangerous authority. Only in certain exalted dispositions of mind can he be sought and felt; for this reason he is also the idol of youth, although by far not their happiest choice. The youth, who always aspires beyond life, who flees all form and finds every limit too narrow, wanders about with love and delight into infinite spaces, which are opened to him by this poet. When then, the youth becomes a man and returns from the realm of ideas into the limits of experience, so is much lost, much of this enthusiastic love, but nothing of the respect, which one owes to such a unique phenomenon, to such an extraordinary genius, to such a greatly ennobled feeling, which the German in particular owes to such a high merit.

I called this poet great chiefly in the elegiac kind, and scarcely will it be necessary, to justify this judgment in particular further. Capable of every energy and master of the entire sphere of sentimental poetry, he can shake us now through the highest pathos, now rock us in heavenly sweet sensations; but to a lofty, spirited melancholy his heart is predominantly inclined, and however sublime his harp, his lyre may sound, so shall the melting tones of his lute always resound more truly and deeply and movingly. I refer to that purely disposed feeling, whether it would not give up everything bold and strong, all fictions, all magnificent descriptions, every model of oratorical eloquence in the *Messiah*, all glimmering comparisons, wherein our poet is so superbly excellent, in exchange for the tender sentiments, which are manifest in the elegy *To Ebert*, in the glorious poem *Bardalus*, *The Tombs Opened Early*, the *Summer's Night*, the *Lake of Zurich*, and many others of this kind. Thus is the *Messiah* dear to me as a treasure of elegiac feelings and ideal depictions, although it satisfies me less as representation of an action and as an epic work.

Perhaps I should, before I leave this area, also recall the merits of Uz, Denis, Gessner (in his *Death of Abel*), Jacobi, Gerstenberg, Höltz, De Göckingk, and several others of this kind, which all move us through ideas and, in the above-established sense of the word, have been composed sentimentally. But my goal is not to write a history of German poetry, but rather to make clear what was said above through some examples from our literature. I wanted to show the different roads, which ancient and modern, naïve and sentimental poets take to the same goal—that, if the former move us through nature, individuality and lively *sensuousness*, the latter through ideas and a high spirituality demonstrate a just as great, although not so extensive, power over our minds.

In the preceding examples, one has seen how the sentimental poetical spirit treats a natural subject matter; but one could also be interested to know, how the naïve poetical spirit deals with a sentimental subject matter. This problem seems to be completely new and of an entirely special difficulty, since in the ancient and naïve world, such a *matter* is not found, in the modern, however, the *poet* would be lacking thereto. Nevertheless, the genius has also set this task for himself and solved it in a wonderfully happy way. A character, who embraces an ideal with glowing feeling and flees reality, in order to strive for an infinite devoid of being, he, who incessantly seeks outside himself, what is in himself, to whom only his dreams are the real, his experiences are always only limits, who finally sees in his own existence only a limit and tears even this away, as stands to reason, in order to penetrate to true reality—this dangerous extreme of the sentimental character has become the subject matter of a poet, in whom nature acts more faithfully and more purely than in anyone else, and who is among the modern poets perhaps least removed from the sensuous truth of things.

It is interesting to see, with what a happy instinct all that gives nourishment to the sentimental character is pressed together in *Werther:* schwärmerish unhappy love, sensibility for nature, religious feeling, a spirit of philosophical contemplation, finally, in order to forget nothing, the dark, formless, melancholy Ossianic world. Does one add thereto, how little reality is presented pleasingly, rather on the contrary, how hostilely, and how everything unites from outside to drive the tormented man back into his ideal world, so does one see no possibility, how such a character could have been rescued from such a circle. In the *Tasso* of the same poet, the same contrast reappears, although in entirely different characters; even in his latest *romance*, as in his first, the poetic mind is opposed to the matter-of-fact common sense, the ideal to the real, the subjective manner of presentation to the objective—but with what variety! Even in *Faust* we meet the same contrast again, admittedly, as even the subject matter required this, on both hands more coarsely and materialized; it is worthwhile to attempt a psychological explanation of this character, specified in four such different kinds.

It has been observed above, that the merely light and jovial disposition, if an inner fullness of ideas does not underlie it, does not at all serve as a vocation to sportive satire, though it is liberally taken therefor in ordinary judgment; just as little does mere tender soft-heartedness and melancholy provide a vocation for elegiac poetry. Both lack the energetic principle of true poetic talent, which must enliven the subject matter, in order to produce the truly beautiful. Products of this tender kind can accordingly only melt us and, without refreshing the heart and engaging the mind, can only flatter sensuousness. A continued propensity to this mode of feeling must necessarily eventually enervate the character and sink it into a state of passivity, from which no reality at all can issue, either for external or internal life. Accordingly, one has been quite right, to persecute with unrelenting mockery this evil of *sentimentality*[17] and of *whining character*, which began to take the upper hand about eighteen years ago in Germany, through the misrepresentation and servile imitation of several excellent works, although the indulgence, which one is inclined to demonstrate toward the not much better copies of these elegiac caricatures, toward the facetious character, toward heartless satire and spiritless temper,[18] displays clearly enough, that the zeal against it does not come from an entirely pure basis.

Upon the balance of true taste the one weighs as little as the other, because both lack the aesthetic content, which is contained only in the intimate union of the spirit with the matter and in the united relation of a production to the capacity of feeling and to the capacity of ideas.

One has scoffed at Siegwart and his cloister story, and the *Travels into Southern France* are admired; yet both productions have an equally great claim to a certain degree of appreciation and an equally small one to unconditional praise. True, although excessive feeling gives value to the first romance, a light humor and a sharp fine intelligence gives value to the second; but just as the one totally lacks the sobriety of mind, which befits it, so does the other lack the aesthetical dignity. The first becomes, in the face of experience, a little ridiculous, the other becomes, in the face of the ideal, almost despicable. Now, since the truly beautiful must be in harmony, on the one hand, with nature and, on the other, with the ideal, so can the one as little as the other claim to be called a beautiful work. Nevertheless, it is natural and reasonable, and I know it from my own experience, that the romance of Thummel is read with great pleasure. Since it offends only such requirements, which originate from the ideal, which consequently have not been expressed by the greatest part of the readers at all and by the better not directly in such moments when one reads romances, but, on the contrary, fulfills other requirements of the mind and of the body to an unusual degree, so must and will it remain justly a favorite book of our and all times, when one writes aesthetical works only in order to please, and merely reads in order to obtain enjoyment.

But does not poetical literature exhibit even classical works, which seemed to offend the lofty purity of the ideal in a similar manner and seemed to be very much removed through the materiality of their contents from that spirituality, which is demanded here of every aesthetical work of art? Whatever the poet, the chaste apprentice of the Muses, may be permitted, should that not be allowed to the novelist, who is only his half-brother and still moves the world so much? I may all the less avoid this question, since there are masterpieces both in the elegiac as well as in the satirical division, which have the appearance of seeking and commending an entirely different nature, than that of which this essay speaks, and of defending the same, not so much against bad, as against good morals. Either, therefore, must these poetic works needs be rejected, or the concept delineated here of elegiac poetry be assured to be much too arbitrary.

Might not what the poet can be permitted, it is said, be overlooked in the prose narrator? The answer is already contained in the question: what is allowed the poet, can demonstrate nothing for him, who is not one. In the concept of the poet itself, and only in this, lies the basis of that freedom, which is a merely contemptible license, so soon as it can not be derived from the highest and most noble, which constitutes him.

The laws of decency are alien to innocent nature; only the experience of corruption has given rise to them. So soon, however, as that experience has once been undergone and natural innocence has disappeared from morals, so are they sacred laws, which a moral feeling may not infringe upon. They are held true in an artificial world with the same justice, as the laws of nature reign in the world of innocence. But precisely that, indeed, constitutes the poet, that he annuls everything in himself, that recalls an artificial world, that he knows how to establish nature once again in its original simplicity. Has he, however, done this, so is he emancipated by this alone from all laws, through which a seduced heart secures itself against itself. He is pure, he is innocent, and what is permitted to innocent nature, is also to him; and thou, thou who read'st or hear'st him, art no longer innocent, and canst thou not become so again even for a moment through his purifying presence, so is it *thy* misfortune and not his; thou forsakest him, he has not sung for thee.

Therefore, as to these kinds of freedoms, the following can be established.

Firstly: only nature can justify them. They may not, therefore, be a work of choice and of intentional imitation; for we never forgive the will, which is always directed according to moral laws, for showing favoritism to sensuousness. They must therefore be naïveté. In order, however, to be able to convince us, that they actually are this, we must see them supported and accompanied by everything else, which is likewise grounded in nature, because nature is to be known only by the strict consistency, unity, and uniformity of its effects. We only permit a heart, which abhors all kinds of artifice in general and therefore also there, where it is useful, to be emancipated from it there, where it is oppressed and curtailed; we permit only a heart, which submits to all fetters of nature, to make use of the freedoms of the same. All the other feelings of such a man must consequently bear the stamp of naturalness in itself; he must be true, simple, free, open, sensitive, straightforward; all dissembling, all cunning, all caprice, all petty self-seeking must be banished from his character, all traces thereof from his works.

Secondly: Only *beautiful* nature can justify freedoms of this kind. They, therefore, ought not to be a one-sided outbreak of the appetites; for everything which originates from mere poverty is contemptible. These sensuous energies must therefore issue forth from the totality and from the fullness of human nature. They must be *humanity*. But in order to be able to judge, that the totality of human nature, and not merely a one-sided and common want of sensuousness summons them, we must see the totality represented, of which they constitute a particular feature. In itself, the sensuous mode of feeling is something innocent and indifferent. It displeases us, therefore, only as a man, because it is animal and is evidence of a lack of truly perfect humanity in him: it offends us therefore as a poetic work, because such a work makes claim to please us, therefore deems us capable of such a lack. However, should we see in the man, who is surprised thereby, human nature act in all its other capacities, should we find in the work, wherein one has taken freedoms of this kind, all the realities of human nature expressed, so is this basis for our displeasure removed, and we can take pleasure with an embittered joy in the naïve expression of true and beautiful nature. The same poet, therefore, who dares allow himself, to make us accomplices in such base human feeling, must know, on the other hand, how to carry us aloft to everything, which is humanly great and beautiful and sublime.

And so would we have indeed found the measure, to which we can subject every poet with certainty, who takes some liberties against decency and drives his freedom in the representation of nature up to this limit. His production is common, base, objectionable without any exception, so soon as it is *cold* and so soon as it is *empty*, because this demonstrates a source of intention and of a common want and a desperate appeal to our appetites. It is, on the contrary, beautiful, noble, worthy of applause without regard to all objections of frigid decency, so soon as it is naïve and unites intellect with heart.[19]

If one says to me that, under the measure given here, most French stories of this kind and the happiest imitations of the same in Germany would not succeed—that this might also in part be the case with many productions of our most graceful and most spirited poet, even his masterpieces not excepted, so would I have nothing to answer thereto. The verdict itself is by no means new, and I only bring forward here the grounds of a judgment, which long since has been pronounced by every delicate feeling on these matters. Precisely these principles, however, which seem perhaps all too rigorous in regard to the former writings, might, in regard to some other works, perhaps be found to be too liberal; for I do not deny, that the same grounds, upon which I hold to be completely inexcusable the seductive paintings of the Roman and German Ovid, just as those of a Crebillon, Voltaire, Marmontel (who is called a moral story-teller), Lacroix, and many others, reconcile me with the elegies of the Roman and German Propertus, indeed even with many of the decried productions of Diderot; for the former are only witty, only prosaic, only lascivious, the latter are poetic, human and naïve.[20]

Idyl

It remains for me to say some words about this third species of sentimental poetry, a few words only, for a detailed development of the same, which it preferably demands, remains reserved for another time.[21]

The poetical representation of an innocent and happy humanity is the universal concept of this kind of poetry. Because this innocence and this bliss seemed incompatible with the artificial relations of grand society and with a certain degree of education and refinement, so have the poets removed the scene of the idyl from the crowds of civic life to the simple pastoral state and given the same its place in the infancy of humanity *before the beginning of culture*. However, one understands well, that these determinations are merely accidental, that they do not come into view as the end of the idyl, but merely as the most natural means to the same. The end itself is everywhere, to represent man in the state of innocence, i.e., in a condition of harmony and of peace with himself and the outside.

But such a state occurs not merely before the beginning of culture, rather it is also that which culture, if only it shall have everywhere a determined tendency, intends as its final end. The idea alone of this state and the belief in the possible reality of the same can reconcile man with all the evils, to which he is subjected on the path of culture, and were it merely a chimera, so would the complaints of those be perfectly well founded, who decry grand society and the cultivation of the understanding as merely an evil and pass off the abandoned state of nature for the true end of man. For the man who is engaged in culture, it is therefore of infinite importance to obtain sensuous confirmation of the practicability of this idea in the world of sense, of the possible reality of this state, and as real experience, far from nourishing this belief, rather refutes it constantly, so also here, as in so many other cases, the capacity for poetry comes to the aid of reason, in order to bring this idea into intuition and to realize it in a particular case.

Indeed, this innocence of the pastoral state is also a poetic conception, and the imaginative power had therefore to be proven creative also there; but outside of the fact that the problem there was far simpler and easier to solve, so the particular features were already to be found in experience itself, which it only needed to select and join in a whole. Under a happy sky, in the simple relations of the initial state, nature is easily satisfied with a limited knowledge, and man does not become brutal, until he is distressed by want. All peoples, who have a history, have a paradise, a state of innocence, a golden age; yes, every individual man has his paradise, his golden age, which he remembers with more or less enthusiasm, according as he has more or less of the poetic in his nature. The experience itself, therefore, offers sufficient traits to the picture of which the pastoral idyl treats. For this reason, however, the latter remains always a beautiful, an elevating fiction, and the poetic power has really worked in the representation of the same in behalf of the ideal. For to the man, who has once diverged from the simplicity of nature and has been delivered over to the dangerous guidance of his reason, it is of infinite importance, to contemplate once again the legislation of nature in a pure exemplar, to be able to be purified once again of the depravities of art in this faithful mirror. But there is a circumstance thereby, which very much reduces the aesthetic value of such compositions. Planted *before the beginning of culture*, they immediately exclude with prejudice all advantages of the same and according to their nature, find themselves in a necessary struggle with the same. They therefore lead us backward *theoretically,* whilst they lead us *practically* forward and ennoble us. Unfortunately, they place the goal *behind* us, *toward* which they should however *lead* us, and therefore can inspire us with the sad feeling of a loss, not with the joyous feeling of hope. Because they achieve their end only through annulment of all art and only through simplification of human nature, so do they have the highest merit for the *heart*, but all too little for the *mind*, and their uniform circle is brought to an end too quickly. Hence, we can only love them and seek them, when we are in need of calm, not when our powers strive after movement and activity. They can only give a *cure* to the infirm soul, but no *nourishment* to the healthy; they can not enliven, only assuage. All the art of poets has not been able to remedy this defect, grounded in the nature of the pastoral idyl. Indeed, this kind of poem does not lack in enthusiastic admirers, and there are sufficient readers, who are able to prefer an *Amyntus* and a *Daphnis* to the greatest masterpieces of the epic and dramatic muse; but in such readers, it is not so much the taste as the individual need, that passes judgment on works of art, and their judgment can consequently not come into consideration here. The reader of mind and feeling indeed does not fail to recognize the value of such compositions, but he feels himself infrequently drawn to the same and is satiated earlier by them. In the precise moment of need, they act all the more powerfully therefor; but the truly beautiful should never need to wait for such a moment, but rather should produce it.

What I here criticize in the pastoral idyl, is after all true only of the sentimental; for the naïve can never be lacking in merit, since it is already contained *in the form itself*. That is, every kind of poetry must have an infinite merit, by which alone it is poetry; but it can realize this requirement in two different ways. It can be an infinite, as to form, if it represents its object *with all its limits*, if it individualizes it; it can be an infinite, as to matter, if it *removes all limits* from its object, if it idealizes it; therefore, either through an absolute representation or through representation of an absolute. The naïve poet takes the first road, the sentimental the second. The former can therefore not miss his value, so soon as he merely keeps faithful to nature, which is always completely limited, i.e., is infinite as to form. To the latter, on the contrary, nature stands in the way with its universal limitation, when he would place an absolute value in the object. The sentimental poet does not, therefore, understand his interest well, if he *borrows* his *objects* from the naïve poet, which are in themselves completely indifferent and become poetic only through the treatment. He thereby imposes on himself quite unnecessarily limits identical with the former, without, however, being able to carry out the limitation completely and to compete with the same in the absolute determination of the representation; he ought rather, therefore, to depart from the naïve poet precisely in the object, because he can only through the object win again from the latter, what the same has over him in respect to form.

In applying this to the pastoral idyls of the sentimental poet, so is it now made clear, why these compositions, with every display of genius and art, are completely satisfying neither to the heart nor to the mind. They have achieved an ideal and yet keep to the narrow, impoverished pastoral world, when they should have by all means selected either another world for the ideal, or another representation for the pastoral world. They are just so ideal, that the representation loses individual truth thereby, and are again just so individual, that the ideal value suffers therefrom. A shepherd of Gessner, for example, can not charm us as nature, not through the truth of imitation, for he is too ideal a being for that; just as little can he satisfy us as an ideal through the infinity of thought, for he is much too impoverished a creature for that. He will therefore please *up to a certain point all* classes of readers without *exception,* because he strives to unite the naïve with the sentimental and consequently gives satisfaction to a certain degree to the two opposite demands, which can be made of a poem; however, because the poet, in the effort to unite both, *does* not do *full justice* to either one, is neither wholly nature nor wholly ideal, so can he just for this reason not entirely stand up to a stringent taste, which is not able to pardon anything half-complete in aesthetical matters. It is strange, that this halfness extends as far as the language of the named poet, which wavers undecided between poetry and prose, as if the poet feared to depart too far from actual nature in metrical language, and to lose the poetical flight in the unmetrical. Milton's magnificent representation of the first human pair and of the state of innocence in Paradise affords a higher satisfaction; the most beautiful idyl known to me of the sentimental kind. Here is nature noble, spirited, simultaneously full of breadth and full of depth; the highest value of mankind is clothed in the most graceful form.

Therefore, even here in the idyl, as in all other poetical kinds, one must once and for all make a choice between individuality and the ideal; for to desire to satisfy both requirements at once, is, so long as one has not attained the end of perfection, the surest way to miss both at once. Should the modern feel the Greek spirit enough, to wrestle with the Greeks despite all the obstinacy of his matter, on their own field, namely in the field of naïve poetry, so may he do it entirely and do it exclusively and place himself apart from any requirement of the sentimental taste of his age. He would indeed attain his models with difficulty; between the original and happiest imitation will always remain a notable distance, but he is nevertheless certain on this road, to produce a truly poetic work.[22] On the contrary, should the sentimental poetic instinct carry him to the ideal, so would he pursue also this fully, in complete purity, and not stand still before reaching the highest, without looking behind him, to see if reality might also follow him. He would disdain the unworthy expedient of impairing the value of the ideal, in order to adapt it to human need, and to exclude the mind, in order to play more easily with the heart. He would not lead us backwards to our childhood, to make us buy with the most precious acquisition of the understanding a repose, which can last no longer than the slumber of our mental powers, but rather would lead us forward to our majority, in order to give us the higher harmony to feel, which rewards the combatant, which blesses the conqueror. He would take as his task an idyl, which realizes that pastoral innocence even in the subjects of culture and among all conditions of the most active, most ardent life, of the most extensive thought, of the most refined art, of the highest social refinement, which, in a word, leads the man, who can now no longer return to *Arcadia*, up to *Elysium*.

The concept of this idyl is the concept of a fully resolved struggle, both in the individual man as well as in society, of a free union of inclinations with the law, of a nature purified up to its highest moral dignity, in short, it is none other than the ideal of beauty, applied to real life. Its character consists therefore therein, that *all contradiction of reality with the ideal*, which would have furnished the matter for satirical and elegiac poetry, would be completely annulled and all strife of the feelings with the same would also cease. Repose were therefore the dominant impression of this kind of poetry, but the repose of perfection, not of laziness; a repose, which flows from the equilibrium, not from the standstill of powers, which flows from fullness, not from emptiness and is accompanied by the feeling of an infinite capacity.

But precisely because all resistance collapses, so will it become incomparably more difficult than in the two previous kinds of poetry to engender *movement*, without which no poetic effect can be conceived at all. There must be the highest unity, but it may take nothing from multiplicity; the soul must be satisfied, but without aspiration stopping on that account. The resolution of this question is properly what the theory of the idyl has to accomplish.

In regard to the relation of both kinds of poetry to one another and to the poetic ideal, the following has been established.

Nature has shown favor to the naïve poet, to act always as an undivided unity, to be in every moment a self-reliant and perfect whole and to represent men in reality, according to their full value. To the sentimental one it has lent the power, or rather imprinted a living instinct, to reestablish out of himself that unity, which has been annulled in him by abstraction, to complete humanity in himself and to pass from a limited state to an infinite.[23] To give human nature its full expression, is, however, the common task of both, and without that, they would not be able to be called poets at all; but the naïve poet has always the advantage of sensuous reality over the sentimental, whilst he achieves that as a real fact, which the other only strives to attain. And that is also what everyone experiences for himself, if he examines himself in the enjoyment of naïve poetry. He feels all the powers of his humanity active in such a moment, he requires nothing, he is whole in himself; without distinguishing anything in his feeling, he enjoys simultaneously his spiritual activity and his sensuous life. It is an entirely different disposition of mind, in which the sentimental poet puts him. Here he feels merely a living *instinct*, to produce harmony in himself, which there he really felt, to make a totality out of himself, to bring humanity in himself to a perfect expression. Hence, the mind is here in movement, it is stretched, it oscillates between contending feelings, while it is there calm, relaxed, one with itself and completely satisfied.

But if the naïve poet has it over the sentimental on the one side as to reality and brings that into actual existence, for which the latter can only awaken a living instinct, so has the latter in return the great advantage over the former, that he is able to give the instinct a *greater object* than the former has provided and could provide. All reality, we know, remains behind the ideal; everything existing has its limits, but thought is unlimited. Through this limitation, to which everything sensuous is subjected, the naïve poet also therefore suffers, while, on the contrary, the unconditioned freedom of the capacity for ideas is advantageous to the sentimental. The former, therefore, indeed realizes his task, but the task itself is something limited; the latter, indeed, does not entirely realize his, but the task is infinite. Also, everyone can be instructed on this by his own experience. From the naïve poet, one turns with ease and pleasure to the living presence; the sentimental will always put us out of tune, for a few moments, as regards real life. That is because our mind has here been expanded, so to speak, by the infinite idea beyond its natural measure, so that nothing existing can fill it any longer. We prefer to sink contemplatively into ourselves, where we find nourishment for the aroused instinct within the world of ideas, while there we instead strive forth from ourselves after sensuous objects. Sentimental poetry is the offspring of abstractedness and silence, and it also invites thereto; the naïve is the child of life, and it also leads back into life.

I have called naïve poetry a *favor of nature*, in order to observe that reflection has no share in it. It is a happy toss, in need of no improvement, if it succeeds, but also capable of none, if it fails. The entire work of the naïve genius is completed in feeling; here lies its strength and its limit. If he therefore has not *felt* at once poetical, i.e., not at once completely human, so can this lack be remedied no longer by art. Criticism can help him only to an examination of the defect, but it can place no beauty in its stead. Through its nature must the naïve genius do everything; through its freedom it is able to do little; and it will fulfill its concept, only so soon as nature acts in him by an inner necessity. Now everything is indeed necessary, which occurs by nature, and so is any even abortive product of naïve genius, from which nothing is more distant than arbitrariness; but constraint of the moment is one thing, the inner necessity of the whole another. Considered as a whole, nature is self-reliant and infinite; in each particular effect, it is, on the contrary, needy and limited. This holds good accordingly also in respect to the nature of the poet. Even the happiest moment, in which the same may be found, is dependent upon a preceding one; hence, only a conditional necessity can be attributed to him. But now the task falls to the poet, to make an individual state similar to the human whole, consequently to ground it absolutely and necessarily upon itself. From the moment of inspiration, every trace of a temporal need must therefore remain distant, and the object itself, as limited as it may be, should not limit the poet. One understands well, that this is possible only insofar as the poet already brings to the object an absolute freedom and fullness of capacity, and as he is able through practice, to embrace everything with all his humanity. However, he can obtain this practice only through the world in which he lives and by which he is immediately affected. Thus, the naïve genius stands in a state of dependence on experience, which the sentimental does not know. The latter, we know, first begins his operation there, where the former concludes his; his strength consists therein, to complete a defective object *out of himself* and to transport himself by his own power from a limited state to a state of freedom. The naïve poetical genius, therefore, needs assistance from the outside, while the sentimental nourishes and purifies himself from within himself; he must perceive a nature rich in forms, a poetical world, a naïve humanity around himself, since he has to complete his work in the sensuous frame of mind. Now should this assistance from the outside fail him, should he see himself surrounded by a spiritless matter, so can only one of two things happen. Either, if the species is predominant in him, he steps out of his particular *class* and becomes sentimental, in order to be only poetic, or, if his specific character gains predominance, he steps out of his *species* and becomes common nature, in order to remain only nature. The *first* might be the case with the most eminent sentimental poets in the ancient Roman world and in modern times. Born in another age, transplanted under another sky, they, who move us now through ideas, would have enchanted us through individual truth and naïve beauty. From the *second*, a poet would be able to be completely defended with difficulty, who in a common world can not abandon nature.

Actual nature, that is; but *true* nature, which is the *subject* of naïve compositions, can not be carefully enough distinguished from this. Actual nature exists everywhere, but true nature is all the more seldom, for an inner necessity of existence belongs thereto. Actual nature is an even common eruption of passion, it may even be true nature, but it is not a truly *human* nature; for this requires a share of the self-reliant capacity in every manifestation, the expression of which is every time dignity. Actual human nature is all moral baseness, but true human nature is hopefully not such; for the latter can never be other than noble. It is not to be overlooked, to what absurdities this confusion of actual nature with true human nature has led in criticism as in practice: what trivialities does one allow in poetry, yes extol, because they unfortunately(!) are actual nature: how one rejoices to see caricatures, which already cause one alarm in the actual world, carefully preserved in the poetic, and portrayed according to life. Of course, the poet may also imitate depraved nature, and this indeed brings with itself already the concept of the satirical; but in this case, his own beautiful nature must *carry over* into the object and the common subject matter not drag the imitator with it to the ground. Be he only, at least at the moment when he paints, himself true human nature, so does it not matter what he paints for us; but we can endure a faithful painting of reality absolutely only from such an one. Woe to us readers, if the caricature is reflected in the caricature, if the scourge of satire falls into the hands of those, whom nature determined to wield a much more earnest whip, if men, who, stripped of all that one calls poetic spirit, possess the ape's talent for common imitation, exercise it heinously and frightfully at the expense of our taste!

But even for the true naïve poet, I said, common nature can become dangerous; for ultimately that beautiful harmony between feeling and thinking, which constitutes the character of the same, is only an *idea*, which is never completely attained in reality; and even in the happiest geniuses of this class, receptivity will always predominate somewhat over self-activity. Receptivity, however, is always more or less dependent upon the external impression, and only a continuous activity of the productive capacity, which is not expected of human nature, could prevent matter from not sometimes exercising a blind violence over receptivity. So often, however, as this is the case, a common feeling emerges from a poetical one.[24]

No genius from the naïve class, from Homer down to Bodmer, has entirely avoided this reef; but, of course, it is the most dangerous to those who have to ward off a common nature from the outside, or who are savage through lack of discipline from inside. It is owing to the former, that even cultivated authors do not always remain free of platitudes and this already prevented many a splended talent from occupying the place to which nature had summoned him. The comic poet, whose genius lives mostly on real life, is just for that reason most exposed to platitude, as also the example of Aristophanes and Plautus and almost all of the later poets shows, who have followed in the footsteps of the same. How deeply does not even the sublime Shakespeare sometimes let us sink, with what trivialities do not Lope De Vega, Molière, Regnard, Goldoni torment us, into what mire does not Holberg drag us down? Schlegel, one of the most spirited poets of our fatherland, in whose genius it does not lay, that he not shine among the first of this species, Gellert, a truly naïve poet, just like also Rabener, Lessing himself, if I may name him differently here, Lessing, the cultivated pupil of criticism and such a watchful judge of his own self—how do they not suffer, more or less, for the spiritless character of nature, which they chose as the subject matter of their satire. Of the most *recent* authors of this kind I name none, since I can except none of them.

And not enough, that the naïve poetic spirit is in danger of coming all too near to common reality—through the ease, with which it is expressed, and through just this greater approximation to real life, it encourages the common imitator, to try his hand in the poetical field. Sentimental poetry, though from another side dangerous enough, as I will hereafter show, at least keeps *this* crew at a distance, because it is not everyone's concern to rise to ideas; but naïve poetry brings them to the belief, that mere feeling, mere humor, mere imitation of actual nature would constitute the poet. But nothing is more perverse, than when the insipid character considers trying to be lovable and naïve—that which ought to hide itself in all the veils of art, in order to conceal its repulsive nature. Hence then also the unspeakable platitudes, which the Germans let be sung under the title of naïve and sportive songs, and with which they are accustomed to assure themselves quite endlessly around a well-occupied table. Under the permit of good humor, of feeling, one tolerates these paltry concerns—but a humor, a feeling, which one can not carefully enough banish. The muses of the Pleisse in particular form a peculiarly pitiful chorus here, and they are answered by the muses of the Seine and the Elbe in no better harmony.[25] So insipid are these jests, so pitiful is the passion heard on our tragic stage, which, instead of imitating true nature, achieves only the spiritless and ignoble expression of the real, so that after such a banquet of tears we feel precisely as if we had paid a visit to hospitals or had read Saltzmann's *Human Misery*. It is yet much worse in satirical poetry and in comic romance in particular, which already in their nature lie so close to common life and hence it stands to reason, like every frontier post, should be just in the best hands. In truth, he has the least vocation, to become the *painter* of his time, who is the *creature* and the *caricature* of the same; but as it is something so easy, to hunt up some comical character, were it also only *a fat man*, among his acquaintances and to sketch a caricature with a coarse pen on paper, so sometimes the sworn enemies of all poetic genius also feel the tickling, to bungle in this province and to amuse a circle of worthy friends with a beautiful offspring. A purely disposed feeling will of course never be in danger of confusing these productions of a common nature with the spirited fruits of naïve genius; but it is just this pure disposition of feeling which is lacking and, in most cases, one merely wants to have a need satisfied without the mind making a claim. The concept, as falsely understood as it is in itself true, that one *refreshes* oneself in works of beautiful spirit, contributes its best to this indulgence, if one can indeed call it indulgence, when nothing higher is divined and the reader as well as the writer find their profit in the same manner. Common nature, that is, if it has been stretched, can be refreshed only in *inanity*, and even a higher degree of understanding, if it be not supported by a proportional culture of the feelings, rests from its business only in a spiritless sensuous enjoyment.

If the poetic genius must be able to rise with a free self-activity above all *accidental* limits, which are inseparable from every *fixed* condition, in order to attain human nature in its absolute capacity, so may it not, on the other hand, pass beyond the *necessary* limits, which the concept of human nature brings with it; for the absolute, but only within humanity, is his task and his sphere. We have seen, that the naïve genius is indeed not in danger of overstepping this sphere, but rather *not to realize it completely,* if it gives too much room to an external necessity or the accidental need of the moment at the expense of inner necessity. The sentimental genius, on the contrary, is exposed to danger, on account of the endeavor to remove all limits from it, to annul human nature altogether and not merely, as it may and should, to rise and to *idealize*, beyond every fixed and limited reality up to absolute possibility, but rather to pass even beyond possibility or to *schwärm*. This fault of *overstretching* is grounded precisely on the specific peculiarity of his behavior, as the opposite of *slackness* is on the peculiar mode of operation of the naïve. The naïve genius, that is, lets *nature* govern in itself without restriction, and since nature is always dependent and in need in its particular temporal expressions, so will the naïve feeling not always remain *exalted* enough, to be able to resist the accidental determinations of the moment. The sentimental genius, on the contrary, abandons reality, in order to ascend to ideas, to command his subject matter with free self-activity; since, however, reason according to its law always aspires to the unconditional, so will the sentimental genius not always remain *sober* enough, to keep itself uninterruptedly and uniformly within the conditions, which the concept of human nature carries with itself, and to which reason must here always remain bound even in its freest acts. This could occur only through a proportionate degree of receptivity, which is just as much overweighed in the sentimental poetical spirit by self-activity, as it overweighs self-activity in the naïve. Hence, if one sometimes misses mind in the creations of naïve genius, so will one often in the offspring of the sentimental inquire in vain after the *object*. Both, therefore, will fall, although in completely opposite ways, into the fault of *inanity;* for an object without spirit and a spiritual play without object are both a nothing in the aesthetical judgment.

All poets who draw their subject matter too one-sidedly from the world of thought and are driven to poetical images more by an inner fullness of ideas than by the urgency of feeling, are more or less in danger of going thus astray. Reason takes into consideration much too little the limits of the sensuous world in its creations, and thought is always driven further, than experience can follow it. Should it, however, be driven so far, that not only can no definite experience any longer correspond to it (for up to there the beautiful ideal may and must go), but rather that it runs counter to the conditions of all possible experience in general, and that consequently, in order to make it real, human nature would have to be altogether abandoned, then is it no longer a poetical, but rather an exaggerated thought—provided namely, that it has proclaimed itself to be representable and poetical; for if it has not done this, so is it already enough, if it only not contradict itself. Should it contradict itself, so is it no longer exaggeration, but rather *nonsense;* for what does not exist at all, that can also not exceed its measure. However, should it not at all proclaim itself to be an object for the imaginative power, so is it just as little an exaggeration; for mere thinking is limitless and what has no limit, can also not exceed. Therefore, only that can be called exaggerated, which wounds indeed not the logical, but rather the sensuous truth and nevertheless claims to be the latter. Hence, if a poet has the unhappy sudden thought, to select natures as the subject matter of his description, which are merely *superhuman* and *may* not be conceived otherwise, so can he be protected against exaggeration, only if he gives up the poetic and does not undertake again, to accomplish his object through the imaginative power. For were he to do this, so would either the latter confer its limits upon the object and make a limited *human* object out of an absolute one (what, for example, all Greek gods are and also ought to be), or the object would take its limits away from the imaginative power, i.e., it would annul it, wherein precisely lies exaggeration.

One must distinguish the exaggerated feeling from exaggeration in the representation; the discussion here is only of the first. The object of the feeling can be unnatural, but the feeling itself is nature and must accordingly lead also to the language of the same. If, therefore, the exaggerated in the feeling can flow from warmth of heart and a truly poetic predisposition, so the exaggerated in the representation is always proof of a cold heart and very often a poetical incapacity. It is therefore no fault, against which the sentimental poetical genius must be cautioned, but rather threatens only the mere imitator, who has no vocation to the same, hence, he in no way disdains the company of the insipid, spiritless, even the base. The exaggerated feeling is not totally without truth, and, as real feeling, it must also necessarily have a real object. Because it is nature, it therefore also admits of a simple expression and, coming from the heart, will also not miss the heart. However, since its object is not drawn from nature, but rather is brought forth one-sidedly and artificially through the understanding, so has it also only a logical reality, and the feeling is therefore not purely human. It is no delusion, that Heloise feels for Abelard, Petrarch for his Laura, Saint Preux for his Julia, Werther for his Charlotte, and that Agathon, Phanias, Peregrinus Proteus (I mean in Wieland) felt for their ideals; the feeling is true, only the object is artificial and lies outside of human nature. Had their feeling kept merely to the sensuous truth of the objects, so would it not have been able to take this flight; on the contrary, a merely capricious play of imagination without all inner value would not have been able to move the heart, for the heart is moved only by reason. This exaggeration, therefore, deserves reproof, not contempt, and who makes it, would do well to examine if he is not perhaps so clever out of heartlessness, so intelligent out of want of reason. Thus is also the exaggerated tenderness in respect to gallantry and honor, which characterizes the chivalrous romances, especially of Spain, thus is the unscrupulous delicacy, pushed to the point of preciousness, of the French and English sentimental romances (of the best kind) not only subjectively true, but also not without value viewed objectively; they are genuine sentiments, which really have a moral source and which are therefore only abominable, because they overstep the limits of human truth. Without this moral reality—how were it possible, that they could be imparted with such strength and intimacy, as experience however teaches? The same also holds true of moral and religious schwärmerei and of the exalted love of freedom and fatherland. Since the objects of these sentiments are always ideas and do not appear in external experience (for what, for example, moves the political enthusiast, is not what he sees, but rather what he thinks), so has the self-active imaginative power a dangerous freedom and can not, as in other cases, be sent back to its limits through the sensuous presence of its object. But neither man in general nor the poet in particular can withdraw from the legislation of nature, other than to place himself under the opposite legislation of reason; he may forsake reality only for the ideal, for freedom *must* be secured to one of these two anchors. But the road of experience to the ideal is so far and between them lies imagination with its unbridled caprice. It is hence unavoidable, that man in general, like the poet in particular, if he withdraws through the freedom of his understanding from the dominion of feeling, without being driven to it by the laws of reason, i.e., if he abandons nature out of mere freedom, so long as he *is without law*, is therefore given up as a prey to fancy.

Experience teaches, that both entire peoples as well as individual men, who have withdrawn from the safe guidance of nature, are actually in this condition, and just this also produces examples enough of a similar confusion in poetry.

Because the genuine sentimental poetic instinct, in order to be elevated to the ideal, must go beyond the limits of actual nature, so the non-geniune goes beyond every limit in general and persuades itself, as if the wild play of the imagination already constituted poetical inspiration. To the true poetic genius, who abandons reality only for the sake of the idea, this can never occur or only in moments when he has lost himself; then on the contrary, he can be led astray by his nature itself to an exaggerated mode of perception. He can, however, through his example lead others astray into fancy, because readers of lively imagination and weak understanding have in view only the liberties in him, which he takes with actual nature, without being able to follow him up to his lofty inner necessity. It happens to the sentimental genius here, as we have seen in respect to the naïve. Because the latter carries out everything that it does, through his nature, so the common imitator does not wish to consider his own nature a worse guide. Masterpieces of the naïve kind accordingly will ordinarily have as their followers the most insipid and most dirty copies of common nature, and the principal works of the sentimental a numerous army of fanciful productions, as this is easily verified in the literature of every people.

There are in regard to poetry two principles in use, which are completely correct in themselves, but in the sense, wherein one customarily takes them, directly annul one another. Of the first, "that poetry serve as a means of enjoyment and recreation," it has already been stated above, that it would be not a little favorable to inanity and platitudes in poetical representations; through the other principle, "that it serve the moral ennoblement of man," the exaggerated is taken under protection. It is not superfluous to examine somewhat more closely both principles, of which one so frequently speaks, so often entirely incorrectly lays out and so awkwardly applies.

We call recreation the transition from a violent condition to that which is natural to us. Everything here, therefore, depends on where we locate our natural condition, and what we understand as a violent one. If we locate the former solely in an unbounded play of our physical powers and in an emancipation from every constraint, so is every activity of reason, because it carries on a resistance against sensuousness, a violence, which occurs to us, and a mental repose, combined with sensuous movement, is the true ideal of recreation. If we, on the contrary, locate our natural condition in an unlimited capacity for every human expression and in the capability, to be able to dispose of all our powers with equal freedom, so is every separation and *isolation* of these powers a violent condition, and the ideal of recreation is the reestablishment of our natural totality after one-sided tensions. The first ideal is imposed solely through the want of *sensuous nature*, the second is through the independence of *human nature*. Which of these two kinds of recreation may and must poetry afford, should indeed not be a question in theory; for no one would want it to appear, as if he could be tempted to place the ideal of humanity after the ideal of animality. Nevertheless, the demands, which one is wont to make in real life on poetical works, are taken chiefly from the sensuous ideal, and in most cases—indeed, the *esteem* is not determined, which one shows these works, but rather the *inclination* decided and the *favorite* chosen according to the latter. The state of mind of the majority of men is, on the one side, straining and exhausting *work*, on the other, relaxing *enjoyment*. The former, however, we know, creates the sensuous need for mental rest and for a standstill of activity incomparably more pressing than the moral need for harmony and for an absolute freedom of activity, for above all things, *nature* must first be satisfied, before the mind can make a *demand;* the latter binds and cripples the moral instincts themselves, which had to express the former demand. Accordingly, nothing is more disadvantageous to the receptivity for the truly beautiful than these two only all too usual dispositions of mind among men, and this explains why so few of even the best have a correct judgment in aesthetical matters. Beauty is the production of harmony between mind and sense; it speaks to all the capacities of man at the same time and hence can be felt and appreciated only under the supposition of a complete and free use of all his powers. One must bring to it an open sense, an enlarged heart, a fresh and delicate spirit, one must have one's entire nature together, which is in no way the case with those, who are divided in themselves through abstract thinking, narrowed by small business formulas, enervated by straining attention. These indeed long for a sensuous matter, but not in order to pursue therein the play of their thinking power, but rather to suspend it. They would be free, but only from a burden, which fatigued their indolence, not from a limit, which curbed their activity.

Can one therefore still be astonished at the success of mediocrity and vacuity in aesthetical matters and at the revenge of weak spirits on the truly and energetically beautiful? They reckoned on recreation in the latter, but on a recreation for their need and for their poor concept, and they discover with annoyance, that an expression of power is now first demanded of them, to which even in their best moment, the capacity would be lacking to them. There, on the contrary, are they welcome, as they are; for as little power as they bring with them, so do they need still much less, to drain the spirit of its author. They are relieved here at once of the burden of thinking and their unyoked nature can indulge itself in the blessed enjoyment of nothingness on the soft pillow of *platitude*. In the temple of Thalia and Melpomene, just as it is with us, the beloved goddess is enthroned, receives the stupid learned man and the exhausted business man on her broad bosom and rocks the spirit in a magnetic sleep, whilst she warms the benumbed senses and swings the imaginative power in a sweet motion.

And why would one not overlook in common minds, what often enough is wont to befall even the best. The relaxation, which nature requires after any continuous strain and receives even when unrequested (and one is wont to save the enjoyment of beautiful works only for such moments), is so little favorable to the aesthetic power of judgment, that among the truly busy classes, there will be only extremely few, who can judge in matters of taste with certainty and, whereupon so much here depends, with uniformity. Nothing is more commonplace, than that learned men, in contrast to cultured men of the world, expose themselves as ridiculous in regard to the judgment of beauty, and that especially the art critics by profession are the laughing stock of all connoisseurs. Their neglected, now exaggerated, now crude feeling leads them falsely in the majority of cases, and even if in defense of the same they have apprehended something in theory, so can they form from it only *technical* (concerning the purposiveness of a work) but not *aesthetical* judgments, which must always embrace the whole and in respect to which, the feeling must therefore decide. If ultimately they would voluntarily renounce only the last and leave it be at the first, so might they always still be useful enough, since the poet in his inspiration and the feeling reader in the moment of enjoyment easily neglect the details. An all the more ridiculous spectacle is it, however, when these crude natures, which with all the painful labor in themselves lead at most to the education of a particular skill, set up their needy individualities as representative of universal feeling and in the sweat of their brow—pass judgment on the beautiful.

As we have seen, much too narrow limits are usually applied to the concept of *recreation*, because one is wont to refer it too one-sidedly to the mere want of sensuousness. On the contrary, a much too broad scope is usually given to the concept of *ennoblement*, which the poet should have in view, because one determines it too one-sidedly according to the mere idea.

According to the idea, the ennoblement goes on, that is, always to infinity, because reason is not bound in its requirements to the necessary limits of the world of sense and does not stand still sooner than in absolute perfection. Nothing, beyond which still something higher can be conceived, can give it pleasure; before its stern judgment, no want of finite nature is excused: it recognizes no other limits than of thought, and of the latter we know, that it ascends beyond all limits of time and space. Such an ideal of ennoblement, which reason delineates in its pure legislation, the poet can propose just as little to himself as his end, as that vulgar ideal of recreation, which sensuousness produces, since he should indeed set human nature free from all accidental limits, but without annulling its concept and displacing its necessary limits. What he ventures beyond these lines, is exaggeration, and he is seduced to the latter all too easily only through a falsely understood concept of ennoblement. But it is bad, that he can not indeed elevate himself to the true ideal of human ennoblement, without taking still a few steps beyond the same. In order, that is, to reach these, he must abandon reality, for he can, like any ideal, draw only from inner and moral sources. Not in the world which surrounds him, and in the turmoil of active life, only in his heart does he encounter it and only in the stillness of solitary contemplation does he find his heart. But this abstractedness from life will remove from sight not always only the accidental—it will remove more often even the necessary and unconquerable limits of human nature, and whilst he seeks the pure form, he will be in danger of losing all value. Reason will make its business much too insulated from experience, and what the contemplative mind has discovered on the calm path of thought, the active man will not be able to bring to fulfillment on the distressful path of life. So just that usually produces the schwärmer, which alone was able to fashion a wise man, and the advantage of the latter might indeed subsist less therein, that he has not become the former, than therein, that he has not remained one.

Since it can neither be left to the working part of men to determine the concept of recreation according to their need, nor to the contemplative part, to determine the concept according to their speculations, if the former concept shall not turn out too physical and the poetry too unworthy, the latter not too hyperphysical and the poetry too extravagant—but these two concepts, as experience teaches, shall govern the universal judgment on poetry and poetical works, so must we, in order to be able to lay them out, look around for a class of men, which, without working, is active and can idealize without schwärming; which unites in itself all realities of life with the least possible limits of the same and is carried by the stream of events without becoming the prey of the same. Only such a class can preserve the beautiful totality of human nature, which is momentarily disturbed by any work and constantly by a working life and in all that is purely human, can give laws to the universal judgment through its *feelings*. Whether such a class really exists, or rather whether that, which really exists under similar external relations, corresponds to this concept also in the internal, is another question, with which I am not here concerned. Should it not correspond to the same, so has it only itself to blame, since the opposite working class is least satisfied, to be looked upon as a victim of its vocation. In such a class of people (which I propose here, however, only as an idea and wish in no way to denote as a fact) would the naïve character therefore be united with the sentimental, so that each would keep the other from its extreme and, whilst the first would protect the soul from exaggeration, the other would secure it from relaxation. For ultimately, we must indeed confess, that neither the naïve nor the sentimental character, considered alone in themselves, entirely exhausts the ideal of beautiful humanity, that can issue forth only from the inner union of both.

Indeed, so long as one exalts both characters to the *poetical*, as we have also previously considered them, much is lost of the limits adhering to them and also their opposition always becomes less noticeable, in an ever higher degree they become poetical; for the poetical disposition is a self-reliant whole, in which all distinctions and all deficiencies disappear. But, precisely because it is only the concept of the poetical, in which both modes of feeling can coincide, so does their mutual difference and need become more noticeable in the same degree, as they put off the poetical character; and this is the case in common life. The more deeply they descend to this, the more they lose of their generic character, which brings them closer to one another, until finally in their caricatures only the specific character is left remaining, which sets them against one another.

This leads me to a very remarkable psychological antagonism among men in a self-cultivating century: an antagonism, which, because it is grounded radically and in the inner mental form, brings about a worse separation among men, than the accidental conflict of interests ever could bring forth; which deprives the artist and the poet of all hope to universally please and move, which, however, is his task; which makes it impossible for the philosopher, even if he has done everything, to universally convince, which, however, the concept of philosophy entails; which will never allow man in practical life to see his mode of action universally approved—in short, a contradiction, which is due to the fact, that no work of the mind and no action of the heart in one class can decisively thrive without precisely thereby incurring a verdict of condemnation in the other. This contradiction is without doubt so old as the beginning of culture and might hardly be settled before the end of the same, other than in particular rare subjects, which it is to be hoped there always were and will always be; but although this is also one of its effects, that it makes vain every attempt at its settlement, because no part will succeed in admitting a deficiency on its side and a reality on the other, so is it still always advantageous enough, to pursue such an important separation unto its final source and thereby to bring the true point of the conflict at least to a simpler formula.

One best attains the true concept of this contradiction, if one, as I just observed, abstracts from both the naïve as well as from the sentimental character, what both have that is poetical. There is nothing left remaining of the first, in regard to the theoretical, other than a sober spirit of observation and a firm devotion to the testimony of the senses, in regard to the practical, a resigned submission to the necessity (but not to the blind compulsion) of nature: an acquiescence, therefore, to that which is and which must be. There is nothing left remaining of the sentimental character other than (in the theoretical) a restless spirit of speculation, which presses to the unconditioned in all knowledge, in the practical a moral rigor, which persists in the unconditioned in actions of the will. Whoever is reckoned in the first class, can be called a *realist*, and whoever in the other, an *idealist*, by which names, however, one may be mentioned neither in the good nor in the bad sense, which one associates with metaphysics.[26]

Since the realist is defined by the necessity of nature, the idealist is determined by the necessity of reason, so must the same relation occur between both, which is encountered between the effects of nature and the actions of reason. We know nature, although an infinite greatness in the whole, appears dependent and needy in every individual effect; only in the totality of its phenomena does it express an independent great character. All individuality in it is only because of something else; nothing springs forth from itself, everything only from the preceding moment, in order to lead to a following one. But just this reciprocal relation of phenomena to one another secures the existence of each one through the existence of the other, and the constancy and necessity of the same is inseparable from the dependency of their effects. Nothing is free in nature, but also nothing is arbitrary in the same.

And the realist appears precisely so, both in his *knowledge* as well as in his *conduct*. To everything which exists conditionally, the circle of his knowledge and action extends; but he never brings it farther than to conditioned knowledge, and the rules, which he forms for himself from particular experiences, taken in all their strictness, are also valid only once; should he elevate the rules of the moment to a universal law, so will he plunge unfailingly into error. Hence, should the realist want to attain something unconditioned in his knowledge, so must he attempt it upon the same road, upon which nature becomes an infinite, namely upon the road of the whole and in the totality of experience. However, since the sum of experience is never fully accomplished, so is a comparative universality the highest that the realist achieves in his knowledge. In returning to similar cases, he builds his insight and hence will judge correctly in all that is in order; on the contrary, in all that is represented for the first time, his wisdom returns to its beginning.

What holds true of the knowledge of the realist, that also holds true of his *moral* action. His character has morality, but this lies, according to its pure concept, in no particular deed, only in the entire sum of his life. In any particular case, he will be determined by external causes and by external aims; only that those causes are not accidental, those aims not momentary, but rather flow subjectively from the natural whole and are related objectively to the same. The impulses of his will are therefore, indeed in the rigorous sense, neither free enough nor morally pure enough, because they have something other than the mere will as their cause and something other than the mere law as their object; but they are just as little blind and materialistic impulses, because this other is the absolute totality of nature, consequently something independent and necessary. So does the common human understanding, the superior portion of the realist, appear universally in the thinking and in the behavior. From the particular case he draws the rule of his judgment, from an inner feeling the rule of his action; but with happy instinct he knows how to separate from both everything momentary and accidental. With this method he proceeds excellently on the whole and will scarcely have to be reproached for a significant mistake; only he might not be able to make a claim to greatness and dignity in any particular case. The latter is only the prize of independence and freedom and thereof we see too few traces in his particular actions.

It is entirely different with the idealist, who takes his knowledge and motive from himself and from mere reason. If nature appears in its particular effects always dependent and limited, so reason places the character of independence and perfection at once in every particular action. It draws everything from itself and it relates everything to itself.

What occurs through it, occurs only for its own sake; an absolute greatness is every concept which it proposes, and every decision which it determines. And just so does the idealist also appear, so far as he correctly carries this name, in his knowledge as in his action. Not content with knowledge, which is valid under certain presuppositions, he seeks to press as far as truths, which presuppose nothing more and are the presupposition of all others. The philosophical insight only satisfies him, which leads back all conditioned knowledge to an unconditioned and secures all experience to the necessary in the human mind; the things, to which the realist submits his thinking, must be submitted to this thinking capacity. And he acts herein with complete authority, for if the laws of the human mind were not also at the same time the laws of the world, if reason ultimately were to stand also beneath experience, so would also no experience be possible.

However, he can not have brought it up to the absolute truths and yet not be benefitted much thereby in his knowledge. For everything of course stands ultimately under necessary and universal laws, but every particular is governed according to accidental and particular rules; and in nature everything is particular. He can therefore rule the whole with his philosophical knowledge and have gained nothing thereby for the particular, for the execution: yes, whilst he presses everywhere to the *highest* grounds, through which everything becomes possible, he can easily neglect the *nearest* grounds, through which everything becomes real; whilst he directs his attention everywhere to the universal, which makes the most different cases like to one another, he can easily neglect the particular, whereby they are distinguished from one another. He will therefore be able to *embrace* very much with his knowledge and, perhaps precisely for this reason, *grasp* little and often lose in insight, what he gains in overview. Hence is it that, if the speculative understanding despises the common for the sake of its *limitations*, the common understanding derides the speculative on account of its *vacuity;* for knowledge always loses in definite intrinsic value, what it gains in extent.

In the moral judgment, one will find in the idealist a purer morality in the particular, but far less moral uniformity in the whole. Since he is only an idealist insofar as he takes his ground of determination from pure reason, but reason is absolutely demonstrated in each of its expressions, so do his particular actions, so soon as they are in general only moral, bear the *entire* character of moral independence and freedom; and be there in general only in real life a truly moral deed, which would also remain so before a rigorous judgment, so can it be executed only by the idealist. But the purer the morality of his particular actions is, the more accidental is it also; for constancy and necessity is indeed the character of nature, but not of freedom. Not indeed, as if idealism could come into conflict with morality, which is contradictory, but rather because human nature is not at all capable of a consistent idealism. If the realist, even in his moral action, is calmly and uniformly subordinated to a physical necessity, so must the idealist soar, he must instantaneously exalt his nature, and he is able to do nothing, except insofar as he is inspired. Then, of course, he is also all the more able, and his behavior will show a character of loftiness and grandeur, which one seeks in vain in the actions of the realist. But real life is in no way prepared to awaken this inspiration in him, and still much less to nourish it uniformly. Compared with the absolutely great, from which he every time proceeds, the absolutely small of the particular case, upon which he has to apply it, causes entirely too large an interruption. Because his will is always directed according to the form toward the whole, so does he not want to direct it, according to the material, toward the fragment, and yet it is many times only insignificant effects, whereby he can demonstrate his moral conviction. So it happens then not seldom, that on account of the limitless ideal, he overlooks the limited case of application and, fulfilled by a maximum, neglects the minimum from which alone, however, everything great in reality arises.

Should one wish therefore to give the realist his due, so must one judge him according to the entire coherence of his life; should one wish to give the idealist his, so must one contain oneself to the particular expressions of the same, but one must first select from these. The common judgment, which so gladly decides according to the particular, will hence be indifferently silent about the realist, because his particular life actions provide just as little material for praise as for rebuke; about the idealist, on the contrary, it will always give rise to parties and be divided between rejection and admiration, because in the particular lies his deficiency and his strength.

It is unavoidable, that with such a great deviation in principles, both parties are in their judgment often directly opposed to one another and, even if they were to agree in the objects and results, shall be separated in their reasons. The realist will ask *for what purpose an object be good* and know to appraise the things according to what they are worth; the idealist will ask *whether they be good*, and appraise the things according to what they are worthy of. The realist does not know and think much of that, which has its worth and purpose in itself (the whole, however, always excepted); in matters of taste, he will speak in favor of enjoyment, in matters of morality, he will speak in favor of felicity, if he does not make this at once the condition of moral action; even in his religion, he does not willingly forget his advantage, only that he ennobles and sanctifies the same in the ideal of the *highest good*. What he loves, he will seek to bless, the idealist will seek to *ennoble* it. If accordingly, the realist aims at *prosperity* in his political tendencies, supposing that it should take something from the moral independence of the people, so will the idealist make *freedom* his aim at the risk of prosperity. The independence *of his condition* is to the former, independence *from his condition* is to the latter the highest goal, and this characteristic distinction is pursued through their mutual thinking and acting. Hence will the realist always demonstrate his liking thereby, that he *gives*, the idealist thereby, that he *receives;* through that which he sacrifices in his generosity, each discloses, what he treasures most. The idealist will requite the deficiency of his system with his individual and his temporal condition, but he does not esteem this sacrifice; the realist atones for the deficiency of his with his personal dignity, but he experiences nothing of this sacrifice. His system holds true to everything of which he has intelligence and toward which he feels a need—of what concern are goods to him, for which he has no presentiment and in which he has no belief? Enough for him, that he is in possession, the earth is his and there is light in his understanding, and contentment dwells in his breast. The idealist does not have quite so good a fate. Not enough, that he often falls out with fortune, because he neglects to make the moment into his friend, he falls out even with himself; neither his knowledge nor his action can give him satisfaction. What he demands from himself, is an infinite; but everything is limited that he does. This severity, which he shows toward himself, he does not even renounce in his conduct toward others. He is indeed generous, because he remembers less his own individual as opposed to others, but he is often unjust, because he just as easily overlooks the individual in another. The realist, on the contrary, is less generous, but he is more just, since he judges all things more *in their limitation*. The common, indeed even the base in thinking and acting he can pardon, only the capricious and the eccentric can he not; the idealist, on the contrary, is a sworn foe of all pettiness and insipidity and will reconcile himself with the extravagant and the enormous, if it only demonstrate a great capacity. The former shows himself as man's friend without even having a very high concept of man and of humanity; the latter thinks of humanity so highly, that he is in danger of despising man.

The realist for himself alone would never enlarge the circle of humanity beyond the limits of the world of sense, would never have made known the human spirit with its independent greatness and freedom; everything absolute in humanity is to him only a beautiful chimera and the belief therein not much better than a schwärmerei, because he perceives man never in his pure capacity, always only in a determined and therefore limited operation. But the idealist for himself alone would just as little have cultivated the sensuous powers and have developed man as a natural being, which is, however, an equally essential part of his destination and the condition of all moral ennoblement. The striving of the idealist goes much too far beyond the sensuous life and beyond the present; only for the whole, for eternity does he wish to sow and plant, and forgets that the whole is only the perfected circle of the individual, that eternity is only a sum of moments. The world, as the realist would like to constitute it round about himself and really does constitute it, is a well laid-out garden, wherein everything is of use, everything deserves its place and what does not bear fruit, is banished; the world in the hands of the idealist is a less useful nature, but one carried out in a greater character. To the former it does not occur, that man could still be here for something different, than to live well and contentedly, and that to this end, he must only send out roots, in order to force his stem into the heights. The latter does not reflect thereon, that he must first of all live well, in order to think uniformly well and nobly, and that the stem is also done for, if the roots fail.

If in a system something is left out, for which, however, an urgent and not to be avoided need is found in nature, so is nature satisfied only through an inconsistency in the system. Also, here both sides are due to such an inconsistency, and they demonstrate at once, if up to now it could be left still doubtful, the one-sidedness of both systems and the rich content of human nature. Of the idealist, I do not in particular need to first prove, that he must necessarily step out of his system, so soon as he aims at a definite effect; for all determined existence stands under temporal conditions and takes place according to empirical laws. In regard to the realist, on the contrary, it could appear doubtful, if he can not even by this time within his sytem satisfy all the necessary requirements of humanity. If one asks the realist: why dost thou what is right, and sufferest what is necessary? So will he in the spirit of his sytem answer thereto: because nature requires it so, because it must be so. But the question is still in no way answered therewith, for the discussion is not about what nature requires, but rather what man wills, for he can indeed also *not* will, what must be. One can also ask him again: why then willst thou, what must be? Why is thy free will subjected to this natural necessity, since it could just as well be opposed to it (although without result, which is also not the discussion here at all) and really is opposed to the same in millions of thy brothers? Thou canst not say, because all other natural beings are subjected to the same, for thou alone hast a will, indeed thou feelest, that thy subjection should be a voluntary one. Thou dost subject thyself therefore, if it occurs voluntarily, not to natural necessity itself, but rather to the *idea* of the same; for the former compels thee merely blindly, as it compels the worm; however, it can gain no hold upon thy will, since thou, though crushed by it, canst have another will. Whence dost thou, however, bring up this idea of natural necessity? Indeed not from the experience, which provides thee with only particular natural effects, but not with nature (as a whole), and only particular realities, but not with necessity. Thou goest therefore beyond nature and dost determine thyself idealistic, so often as thou willst either *act morally* or only not *suffer blindly*. It is therefore apparent, that the realist acts more worthily, than he grants according to his theory, just as the idealist thinks more sublimely, than he acts. Without admitting it to themselves, the former demonstrates, through the entire conduct of his life, the independence, the latter, through particular actions, the poverty of human nature.

To an attentive and impartial reader I will not first need to prove according to the picture given here (whose truth he can also acknowledge, who does not accept the result), that the ideal of human nature is distributed under both, but is attained fully by neither. Experience and reason both have their own rights, and neither one can encroach upon the domain of the other, without causing a bad consequence either for the internal or for the external conditions of man. Experience alone can teach us, what under certain conditions is, what under certain suppositions ensues, what must happen for definite purposes. Reason alone can, on the contrary, teach us what holds true without all conditions and what must necessarily be. Should we now presume to be able to decide something about the external existence of things with our mere reason, so do we merely engage in an empty game, and the result will lead to nothing; for all existence stands under conditions and reason determines unconditionally. However, let us determine an accidental event in respect to that which already involves the mere concept of our own being, so do we make ourselves into an empty game of chance, and our personality will lead to nothing. In the first case, it has therefore to do with the *worth* (the temporal value) of our life, in the second, with the *dignity* (the moral value) of our life.

Indeed, we have granted in the previous description a moral worth to the realist and to the idealist an experiential value, but merely insofar as both are not entirely consistent and the nature in them acts more powerfully than the system. Although, however, both do not entirely correspond to the ideal of perfect humanity, so is nevertheless the important distinction between the two, that the realist indeed satisfies the concept of reason in humanity in no particular case, however, also never contradicts the concept of understanding in the same, the idealist, on the contrary, comes nearer indeed in particular cases to the highest concept of humanity, however, not seldom remains under the lowest concept of the same. Now it depends, however, in the practice of life far more thereon, that the whole be *uniformly* humanly good, than that the particular be *accidentally* divine—and if, therefore, the idealist is a fit subject, to awaken a great concept in us of that which is possible for humanity and to inspire respect for its destiny, so can only the realist achieve it with constancy in experience and preserve the species in its eternal limits. The former is indeed a nobler, but a much less perfect being; the latter appears indeed universally less noble, but is on the other hand the more perfect; for the nobleness lies already in the demonstration of a great capacity, but the perfection lies in the conduct of the whole and in the actual deed.

What is true of both characters in their best meaning, that becomes yet more noticeable in their reciprocal *caricatures*. The true realism is more beneficent in its effects and less noble only in its source; the false is despicable in its source and in its effects somewhat less pernicious. The true realist, that is, submits indeed to nature and its necessity—but to nature as a whole, but to its eternal and absolute necessity, not to its blind and instantaneous *compulsion*. With freedom, he embraces and obeys its law, and he will always subordinate the individual to the universal; hence it can also not fail, that he will come to agree with the true idealist in the final result, however different is the road, which both take thereto. The common empiricist, on the contrary, submits to nature as to a power and with involuntary blind submission. His judgments, his endeavors are limited to the particular; he believes and understands only what he touches; he treasures only what improves him sensuously. He is accordingly also nothing further, than what the external impressions accidentally want to make out of him; his self-hood is oppressed, and as a man he has absolutely no worth and no dignity. But as an object he is still always something, he can still always be good *for something*. Even nature, to which he is delivered blindly, does not entirely let him sink; its eternal limits protect him, its inexhaustible assistance rescues him, so soon as he only gives up his freedom without all reservation. Although in this condition he knows of no laws, so do these nevertheless rule unrecognized over him, and however much his particular endeavors may lie in conflict with the whole, so will the latter know unerringly how to assert itself thereagainst.

There are men enough, indeed entire peoples, which live in this despicable condition, which exist merely through the grace of natural law, without all self-hood, and hence are also only good for something; but that they also only live and exist, proves, that this condition is not entirely valueless.

If, on the other hand, the true idealism is already unsafe and often dangerous in its effects, so is the false frightful in its. The true idealist abandons nature and experience only because he does not find here the unchangeable and unconditionally necessary, for which reason bids him to strive nevertheless; the visionary abandons nature out of mere caprice, in order to all the more unboundedly indulge in the obstinacy of desire and the whims of imaginative power. Not in the independence from physical, in the release from moral compulsion he places his freedom. The visionary renounces, therefore, not merely the human—he renounces all character, he is fully without law, he is therefore nothing at all, and is of no use at all. But, precisely because fancy is no extravagance of nature, but rather of freedom, and therefore originates out of a predisposition in itself worthy of respect, which is perfectible into infinity, so does it also lead to an infinite fall into a bottomless depth and can terminate only in a complete destruction.

Author's Notes

1. Kant, to my knowledge the first, who has begun to reflect expressly on this phenomenon, observes, that if we were to find the warbling of the nightingale imitated by a man to the highest deception and gave ourselves over to the impression of the same with complete emotion, all our delight would disappear with the destruction of this illusion. One should look at the chapter of intellectual interest on the beautiful in the *Critique of Aesthetic Judgment*. Whoever has learned to admire the author only as a great thinker, will joy, to encounter here a trace of his heart and be convinced through this discovery of the high philosophical vocation of this man (which absolutely requires both capacities combined).

2. Kant also distinguishes these three kinds of ingredients in the feeling of the naïve in a comment in the Analytic of the Sublime (*Critique of the Aesthetic Judgment*, p. 225 of the first edition), but he gives another explanation of it.

> Some combination of both (the animal feeling of pleasure and the mental feeling of respect) is found in *naiveté*, which is the breaking out of the sincerity originally natural to humanity in opposition to the art of dissimulation, which has become another nature. One laughs at the simplicity, which does not yet understand how to dissemble, and yet one is delighted with the simplicity of nature, which here thwarts that art. One expects the ordinary manner of utterance, which is artificial and devised carefully to make a beautiful show, and behold, it is the unspoiled innocent nature, which one does not expect to find and which, he who displays it, also did not think of disclosing. That the beautiful, but false show, which ordinarily has so much influence on our judgment, is here suddenly transformed into nothing, so that, as it were, the rogue in us is laid bare, produces the movement of the mind in two opposite directions, which at the same time shakes the body wholesomely. However, that something, that is infinitely better than all assumed manner, the purity of disposition (at least the tendency thereto), is not quite extinguished yet in human nature, mixes earnestness and high esteem with this play of the judgment. But because it is only a transitory phenomenon and the cover of the art of dissimulation is soon drawn over again, so there is mingled therewith a comparison, which is an emotion of tenderness, which, as play, quite readily can be combined with such a good-hearted laugh, and ordinarily is actually combined therewith, at the same time is wont to compensate him, who supplies the material therefor, for the embarrassment which results from not being wise after the manner of men.

I admit, that this mode of explanation does not entirely satisfy me, and indeed does not chiefly, because it asserts something about the naïve in general, that is most true of one species of the same, the naïve of surprise, of which I will speak later on. To be sure, it provokes *laughter*, if someone *exposes* himself through naïveté, and in many cases, this laughter may flow from a preceding expectation, which is dissolved into nothing. However, also the naïve of the noblest kind, the naïve of conviction, always provokes a *smile*, which, however, hardly has an expectation dissolved into nothing as its basis, but rather is only explained in general from the contrast of a certain behavior with the forms once accepted and expected. Also, I doubt whether the pity, which is mixed in the naïve of the last type in our feeling, is meant for the naïve person, and not rather for ourselves or rather for humanity in general, of whose decline we are reminded in such an occasion. It is too obviously a moral grief, which must have a nobler object, than the physical evil, by which uprightness is threatened in the ordinary course of the world, and this object cannot indeed be other than the loss of the truth and simplicity of humanity.

3. I should perhaps say quite briefly: *the truth over dissimulation*, but the concept of the naïve appears to me to include still something more, whilst simplicity in general, which prevails over affectation, and natural freedom, which prevails over stiffness, arouse a similar feeling in us.

4. A child is uneducated, if it acts in opposition to the precepts of a good education out of desire, frivolity, impetuosity, but it is naïve, if it is exempt from the mannerisms of an education devoid of reason, from the stiff postures of the dance master and the like, out of a free and healthy nature. The same also occurs in the naïve in a quite figurative sense, which arises through the passage from man to the senseless. No one will find the view naïve, if in a garden, which is attended badly, the weeds gain the upper hand, but it has something naïve, to be sure, if the free growth of the aspiring branches annuls the toilsome work of the shears in a French garden. So is it not at all naïve, if a trained horse performs his lesson poorly out of natural clumsiness, but it has something of the naïve, if it forgets the same out of natural freedom.

5. Since the naïve depends merely on the form, in which something is done or said, so does this property disappear from our eyes, so soon as the thing itself makes a predominate or quite contradictory impression through its causes or through its consequences. Through a naïveté of this type, a crime can also be discovered, but then we have neither the peace nor time, to direct our attention to the form of the discovery, and the horror over the personal character devours the pleasure in the natural. Just as the indignant feeling deprives us of the moral joy in the uprightness of nature, so soon as we experience a crime through a naïveté;

just so does the aroused compassion suppress our malicious joy, so soon as we see someone placed in danger through his naïveté.

6. However, also only with the Greeks; for it requires just such an active motion and such a rich fullness of human life, as surrounded the Greeks, to put life in the lifeless and to pursue the image of humanity with this eagerness. Ossian's human world, for example, was poor and monotonous; the lifelessness round about him was great, colossal, powerful, therefore intruded and asserted its rights even over men. In the songs of this poet, lifeless nature (in contrast to men) therefore steps forth much more as object of the feeling. While Ossian already also laments the decline of humanity, and, however small the circle of culture and its depravities was among his people, so the experience thereof was, however, just vivid and urgent enough, in order to frighten the sensitive moral singer back to the lifeless and, on account of his songs, to pour forth that elegiac tone, which makes them so moving and attractive for us.

7. *Orlando Furioso*. First song. Stanza 32.

8. From the classic English translation of Homer's *Iliad*, by Alexander Pope (1688–1744).

9. It is perhaps not superfluous to recall, that, if the modern poets are contrasted here to the ancients, not only the distinction of time but also the distinction of style is to be understood. We have also in the modern, indeed even in the most modern times, naïve compositions in all classes, although no longer the entirely pure type, and among the ancient Latin, indeed even Greek poets, sentimental compositions are not lacking. Not only in the same poet, also in the same work one frequently comes across both species combined; as, for example, in *The Sorrows of Young Werther*, and such productions will always be more effective.

10. Molière as naïve poet permitted it to depend on the verdict of his Maid, what should remain and be suppressed in his comedies; also, it were to have been wished, that the masters of the French Cothurn had now and then made this test with their tragedies. But I did not want to advise, that a similar test be ordained with the Klopstockian odes, with the most beautiful passages in the *Messiah*, in *Paradise Lost*, in *Nathan the Wise*, and many other pieces. Yet what am I saying? This test is actually ordained, and the Molièrian *Maid* argues the length and breadth indeed in our critical libraries, philosophical and literary annals and travel journals concerning poetry, art and the like, only, as

is fair, on German soil a little more tastelessly than on the French, and as is fit for the servant's hall of German literature.

11. Who pays attention in himself to the impression, which naïve compositions make on him, and is able to abstract therefrom the share, which is due thereby to the contents, will find this impression, also even in very pathetic objects, always joyful, always pure, always calm; in sentimental objects it will always be somewhat earnest and tense. That is, because in naïve representations, regardless of what they would treat, we always rejoice at the truth, at the living presence of the object in our imaginative power and also seek nothing more than these, in sentimental representations; on the contrary, we have to unite the conception of the imaginative power with an idea of reason and therefore fall into vacillation between two different conditions.

12. In *Nathan the Wise*, this has not occurred, here the frigid nature of the matter has cooled the entire work of art. But Lessing even knew, that he wrote no tragedy, and in a human manner, only forgot in his own endeavor the precept established in the *Dramaturgy*, that the poet is not authorized to apply the tragic form to another end than a tragic one. Without very substantial alterations, it would hardly have been possible to create this dramatic poem anew in a good tragedy; but with merely accidental alterations it might have supplied a good comedy. That is, the pathetic would have had to have been sacrificed to the last end, the argumentative to the first, and there is indeed no question, upon which of the two the beauty of this poem most depends.

13. That I employ the appellations satire, elegy and idyl in a broader sense than usually occurs, I shall hardly need to answer for with readers, who press deeply into the matter. My intention thereby is in no way, to disturb the boundaries, which the preceding observance has with good reason placed on satire and elegy as well as the idyl; I merely look at the *mode of perception* prevailing in these types of poetry, and it is indeed sufficiently known, that this can in no way be enclosed in those narrow boundaries. We are not moved elegiacally merely by the elegy, which is exclusively so called; also the dramatic and epic poets can move us in an elegiac manner. In the *Messiah*, in Thomson's *Seasons*, in *Paradise Lost*, in *Jerusalem Emancipated* we find several pictures, which are otherwise properly only idyl, elegy, satire. Just so, more or less, in almost every pathetic poem. That I, however, ascribe the idyl itself to the elegiac species, appears

rather to require a justification. One remembers, however, that the discussion here is only about that idyl, which is a species of sentimental poetry, to whose essence it belongs, that nature *is opposed* to art and the ideal to reality. Even be this not done expressly by the poet and he place the picture of uncorrupted nature or of fulfilled ideals pure and independent before our eyes, so is this opposition nonetheless in his heart and it is betrayed without his willing in every stroke of the brush. Indeed, were this not so, would the language, no doubt, of which he must avail himself, because it bears the spirit of the time in itself and would experience the influence of art, remind us of reality with its limits, culture with its affectation; indeed, our own heart would contrast the experience of corruption to the image of pure nature and would thus make the mode of perception in us elegiac, even if the poet had not aimed thereat. This latter is so unavoidable, that even the highest enjoyment, which the most beautiful works of the naïve kind from ancient and modern times afford the cultivated man, do not remain pure long, but rather sooner or later will be accompanied by an elegiac feeling. Finally, I observe further, that the division attempted here, precisely because it is grounded merely on the distinction in the mode of perception, should determine nothing at all in the division of the poems themselves and the derivation of poetical types; for since the poet, even in the same work, is in no way bound to this mode of perception, so can this division not be drawn therefrom, but rather must be drawn from the form of the representation.

14. Let one read, for example, the excellent poem entitled *Carthon*.

15. Let one look at the poem of this name in his works.

16. I say *musical*, in order to recollect here the double relationship of poetry with the musical art and with the plastic art. That is, according as poetry either imitates a definite *object*, as the plastic arts do, or according as it brings forth, as musical art, merely a definite *condition of mind*, without having need of a definite object therefore, can it be called *plastic* or musical. The latter expression refers therefore not merely to that, which in the poetry is music, actually and according to the material, but rather in general to all those effects of the same, which it is able to bring forth, without controlling the imaginative power through a definite object; and in this sense, I call Klopstock chiefly a musical poet.

17. "The propensity," as Mr. Adelung defines it, "for moving, gentle feelings *without rational intention* and beyond due *measure*." Mr. Adelung is very fortunate, that he feels only from intention and entirely only from rational intention.

18. One should indeed not spoil the paltry pleasure of certain readers and ultimately what is it to the critic, if there are people, who can be edified and made merry by the smutty wit of Mr. Blumauer. But judges of art should at least refrain from speaking of productions, with a certain respect, whose existence should justly remain a secret to good taste. Indeed, neither talent nor humor is to be mistakenly recognized therein, but it is all the more lamentable, that both are no longer purified. I say nothing of our German comedy; the poets paint the time in which they live.

19. With *heart*; for the merely sensuous glow of the picture and the luxuriant glow of the imaginative power still do not quite constitute it. Hence *Ardinghello* remains with all the sensuous energy and all the fire of Kolorit always only a sensuous caricature, without truth and without aesthetical dignity. Yet this curious production will always remain noteworthy as an example of the nearly poetical flight, which the *mere desire* is capable of taking.

20. If I name the immortal author of *Agathon*, *Oberon*, etc. in this company, so must I expressly explain, that I in no way want to have mistaken him for the same. His descriptions, even the most thoughtful from this side, have no material tendency (as a modern, somewhat thoughtless critic recently permitted himself to say); the author of *Love for Love* and of so many other naïve and genial works, in all of which a beautiful and noble soul is described with unmistakeable features, can not have such a tendency at all. But he appears to me to be pursued by the entirely peculiar misfortune, that such descriptions are made necessary by the plan of the poetry. The cold understanding, which devises the plan, demanded them from him, and his feeling seems to me so far removed from favoring them with preference, that I—in the execution itself believe the cold understanding can still always be recognized. And precisely this coldness in the representation is prejudicial to them in the judgment, because only the naïve feeling can justify such descriptions both aesthetically as well as morally. However, whether it is permitted to the poet, to expose himself in the devising of the plan to such a danger in the execution, and whether in general a plan can be poetical, which, I wish

just to admit this, can not be executed, without revolting the chaste feeling of the poet as well as of his reader and without making both dwell on the objects, from which an ennobled feeling so willingly distances itself—this is that which I doubt and concerning which I would gladly like to hear an intelligent judgment.

21. I must observe once more, that satire, elegy, and the idyl, just as they are laid down here as the only three possible types of sentimental poetry, have nothing in common with the three types of poetry, which one knows by these names, but the *mode of perception*, which is characteristic of the former as well as the latter. That there could be, however, outside the boundaries of naïve poetry, this threefold mode of perception and mode of poetry, consequently the field of sentimental poetry be measured completely through this dimension, can easily be deduced from the concept of the latter.

Sentimental poetry, that is, is distinguished from the naïve, in that it refers the real condition, in which the latter remains, to ideas and applies the ideas to the reality. It therefore always has to do, as has already been observed above, simultaneously with two conflicting objects, namely with the ideal and with experience, between which neither more nor less than just the three following relations can be conceived. Either it is the *contradiction* of the real conditions, or it is the *agreement* of the same with the ideal, which chiefly occupies the mind; or the latter is divided between both. In the first case, it is satisfied through the power of inner strife, *through the energetic movement;* in the other it is satisfied through the harmony of the inner life, *through the energetic rest;* in the third, strife *changes places* with harmony, rest changes places with movement. This threefold condition of perception gives rise to three different types of poetry, to which the employed appellations *satire*, *idyl*, *elegy* are completely suitable, as soon as one only recalls the frame of mind, to which the types of poetry occurring under this name move the mind, and abstracts from the means, whereby they effect the same.

Hence, whoever could still here question, in which of the three species I reckon the epic, the romance, the tragedy and others besides, would not have understood me at all. For the concept of these latter, as of *particular types of poetry*, is determined either not at all or not alone through the mode of perception; rather one knows, that such can be achieved in more than one mode of perception, consequently in several of the types of poetry laid down by me.

Finally, I observe here further, that if one is inclined to deem sentimental poetry, as is reasonable, to be a genuine type (not merely a variety) and an enlargement of true poetic art, in the determination of the poetic types, just as in general in all poetical legislation, which is still grounded always one-sidedly in the observance of ancient and modern poets, some regard must also be paid to it. The sentimental poet departs from the naïve in respects too essential for the forms, which the latter introduced, to be able to suit him everywhere without compulsion. Of course, it is here difficult to always correctly distinguish the exceptions, which the distinction of types requires, from the evasions which impotence permits itself, but so much does experience nevertheless teach, that in the hands of the sentimental poet (also of the most excellent), no single type of poetry has remained entirely that which it has been in the ancient, and that very often modern species have been achieved under the ancient name.

22. With such a work Mr. Voss has recently in his *Louise* not merely enriched, but also truly enlarged our German literature. This idyl, although not thoroughly free of sentimental influences, belongs entirely to the naïve species and strives through individual truth and genuine nature toward the best Greek models with remarkable success. Hence it can be compared with no modern poem from its division, which contributes to its high renown, but rather must be compared with Greek models, with which it shares the so remarkable advantage, to afford us a pure, definite and always equal pleasure.

23. For the scientifically examining reader I observe, that both modes of perception, considered in their highest concept, are related to one another as the first and the third categories, in that the latter always arises thereby, that one unites the first with its direct opposite. The opposite of naïve perception, namely, is the reflecting understanding, and the sentimental frame of mind is the result of the endeavor, *even under the conditions of reflection*, to recover the naïve perception according to the contents. This would occur through the fulfilled ideal, in which art encounters nature again. Should one pass through those three concepts according to the categories, so will one meet *nature* and the naïve frame of mind corresponding to it always in the first, *art* as

annulment of nature through the freely working understanding always in the second, finally the *ideal*, in which perfected art returns to nature in the third category.

24. How much the naïve poet depends on his object, and how much, indeed like everything, depends on his feeling, the ancient poetic art can give us the best illustrations. So far as nature is beautiful in them and outside them, they are the compositions of the ancients; on the other hand, should nature become common, so has the mind also dropped away from their compositions. Every reader of refined feeling must, for example, feel in their descriptions of feminine nature, of relations between both sexes and in particular of love a certain emptiness and satiety, which all truth and naïveté can not banish in the representation. Without discussing the word schwärmerei, which of course does not ennoble nature, but rather forsakes it, one will be permitted hopefully to presume, that nature in regard to that relation of the sexes and the emotion of love is capable of a nobler character, than the ancients have given it; also one knows the *accidental* circumstances, which stood in the way of the ennobling of those perceptions in them. That it was weakness, not inner necessity, that kept the ancients herein at a lower level, the example of more modern poets teaches, who have gone so much further than their predecessors, without however trespassing against nature. The discussion here is not of that which sentimental poets have known to make of this object, for these go beyond nature into the ideal, and their example can therefore prove nothing against the ancients; the discussion is merely about, how the same object is treated by truly naïve poets, how it is treated for example in *Sakontala*, in the minnesingers, in many courtly romances and courtly epics, how it is treated by Shakespeare, by Fielding and many others, even German poets. Here would the case for the ancients now have been, to spiritualize from inside out, through the subject, a matter from the outside too rough, to retrieve through reflection the poetic value, which has been lacking to the external perception, to complete nature through the idea, in a word, through a sentimental operation to make out of a limited object an infinite one. But they were naïve, not sentimental poetic geniuses; their work was therefore concluded with the external perception.

25. These good friends have taken very badly, what a reviewer has criticized in the *A.L.Z.* some years ago in Bürger's poetry, and the concealed rage, with which they rebel against the prickle,

ON NAÏVE AND SENTIMENTAL POETRY

seems to make known that they believe they are defending their own poetry with their concern for that poet. However, they are very much mistaken therein. The censure could be valid merely for a true poetic genius, who had been richly endowed by nature, but had neglected to develop that rare gift through his own culture. One may and must place such an individual under the highest standard of art, because he would have power enough in himself, to do the same, as soon as he earnestly wished to; but it were ludicrous and simultaneously cruel, to deal with people in a similar manner, of whom nature has not thought and who with every production that they bring to market, exhibit a perfectly valid testimony of poverty.

26. I observe, in order to prevent any misconstruction, that in this division I have not at all intended a choice between the two, consequently to cause support for the one to the exclusion of the other. Precisely this *exclusion*, which is found in experience, I oppose; and the result of the present reflections will be the proof, that only through the completely equal *inclusion* of both can the rational concept of humanity be satisfied. Besides, I take both in their most worthy sense and in the entire *fullness* of their concept, which can always only subsist with the purity of the same and with retention of their specific distinctions. Also it will appear, that a high degree of human truth is consistent with both and their deviations from one another cause a change indeed in the particular, but not in the whole, indeed according to the form, but not to the contents.

ON THE MORAL USE OF AESTHETIC MANNERS

TRANSLATED BY BRUCE DIRECTOR

The author of the essay, "On the Danger of Aesthetic Manners," in the eleventh issue of *Die Horen* of the past year, has correctly cast doubt on a morality, which is solely based on the feeling of the beautiful and has taste alone as its authority. But obviously, a lively and pure feeling for the beautiful has the happiest influence on the moral life, and this I will take up here.

When I attribute to taste the merit of contributing to the promotion of morality, my meaning can not at all be, that the interest, which good taste takes in an action, is able to make this action a moral one. Morality is never allowed to have another foundation than itself. Taste can promote morality of conduct, as I hope to prove in the present endeavor, but it can never itself, through its influence, produce something moral.

It is entirely the same case here with inner and moral freedom, as with external physical freedom; I act freely in the latter sense only, when I merely follow my will,

---

This essay is a companion piece to *On the Necessary Limits in the Use of Beautiful Forms*, also translated in this volume, and dates from Schiller's aesthetic work and writings from 1793. The essay first appeared in the middle of March 1796 in the third issue of *Die Horen* for that year.

independent of foreign influence. But as to the possibility of following my own will unrestrained, I can ultimately be indebted to a cause different from myself, as soon as it is accepted that this cause could have restrained my will. Just so, I can be indebted, ultimately, for the possibility to do good, to a cause different from my reason, as soon as this cause is thought of as a power which could have restrained my mental freedom. As one can therefore say quite well, that a man may obtain freedom from another, although freedom itself consists therein, that one be exempted from acting according to another; just as well, one can say that taste may help one to virtue, although virtue itself expressly brings with it, that one avail oneself thereby of no external assistance.

An action, therefore, does not at all cease to be called free, because, fortuitously, he who were able to restrain it keeps quiet, as soon as we but know that the actor followed merely his own will, without regard to any external one. Just so, for this reason, an inner action still does not lose the characteristic of a moral action, because, fortuitously, the temptations are lacking which could undo it, as soon as we but accept that the actor followed merely the expression of his reason, exclusive of an external motive. The freedom of an external action rests only on its direct origin in the will of a person, the morality of an internal action rests only on the direct determination of the will through the law of reason.

It can be more easy or more difficult for us to act as free men, accordingly as we knock against forces, which counteract our freedom and must be overcome. In this respect, there is gradation of freedom. Our freedom is greater, or at least more visible, when we assert it in the face of intense resistance of hostile forces; but it does not therefore cease, when our will finds no resistance, or when an external power intervenes and exterminates this resistance without our assistance.

The same is true with respect to morality. It may cost us more or less of a struggle to obey reason directly, accordingly as impulses are aroused within us, which conflict with its precepts, and which we must reject. In this respect, there is gradation in morality. Our morality is greater, or at least more striking, when we obey our reason directly, despite great impulses to the contrary; but it does not therefore cease, when no inducement to the contrary is found, or when something other than our will power enfeebles this inducement. In short, we act morally good, as soon as we but so act, because such an act is moral, and without first asking ourselves whether it is also pleasant; supposing even that a probability were present, that we might have acted otherwise, if it caused us pain or deprived us of pleasure.

Let it be granted out of respect for human nature, that no man could sink so low, as to prefer pure evil, simply because it is evil; rather that everyone without distinction would prefer the good, because it is good, if fortuitously it did not exclude the pleasurable or include the unpleasant. All immorality in reality appears, therefore, to arise from the collision of the good with the pleasurable or, what amounts to the same thing, from desire with reason; and to have as its source, on the one side, the strength of the sensual drive, and, on the other, the weakness of the moral will power.

Morality can therefore be promoted in two ways, just as it can be hindered in two ways. Either one must reinforce the side of reason and the power of good will, such that no temptation will be able to overcome it, or one must break the power of temptation, so that the weaker reason and the weaker good will may still be superior to it.

Indeed it could appear as if morality itself would win nothing through the latter operation, because no alteration occurs with the will, whose nature yet alone makes an action moral. That is, however, also in the assumed case not at all necessary, where one does not presuppose a bad will, which must be changed, only a good one, which is weak. And this weak good will achieves in this way the effect, which perhaps might not have happened, if stronger impulses had worked against it. But where a good will becomes the cause of an action, here real morality exists. Therefore, I have no hesitation to put forward the proposition, that that truly promotes morality, which eliminates the resistance of the inclination against the good.

The natural internal enemy of morality is the sensual drive, which, as soon as an object is held before it, strives for gratification, and as soon as reason demands something offensive to it, rebels against its precepts. This sensual drive is incessantly busy, to draw to its interest the will, which stands, however, under moral law and has an obligation to itself never to be found in contradiction with the claims of reason.

But the sensual drive does not recognize moral law, and wants its object realized through the will, despite what reason were to say of it. This tendency of the power of our desire, to directly command the will without any regard to a higher law, struggles with our moral destiny and is the strongest adversary which man has to fight in his moral conduct. To crude souls, lacking at the same time both moral and aesthetic education, desire gives the law directly, and they act merely according to the craving of the senses. To moral souls, to whom aesthetic education is lacking, reason gives the law directly, and it is merely with regard to duty, that it triumphs over temptation.

In aesthetically refined souls, there is still one more instance, which not seldom replaces virtue when it is lacking, and makes it easier when it is present. This instance is taste.

Taste demands moderation and decency, it abhors everything that is sharp, hard, and violent, and it is reverent towards everything that is light and harmoniously united. That we also hear the voice of reason in the storm of feeling and place a limit on the crude outbreaks of nature, demands of each civilized man, it is well known, good breeding, which is nothing other than an aesthetic law.

This constraint, which civilized man imposes on himself in the expression of his feelings, provides him with a degree of mastery over these feelings themselves, obtains for him at least a skill to interrupt the purely suffering condition of his soul through a self-initiated act, and to stop through reflection, the rapid transition of feelings into actions. But everything that breaks the blind power of the emotions still does not actually bring forth virtue (for this must always be virtue's own undertaking), but it makes room for the will to turn towards virtue. But this victory of taste over the raw emotion is not entirely a moral action, and the freedom, which the will wins here through taste, is still not entirely moral freedom. Taste liberates the soul from the yoke of instinct, only insofar as it guides it in its fetters; and whilst it disarms the first and obvious enemy of moral freedom, yet it not seldom remains itself, as the second remaining enemy, which under the cover of a friend, can be but all the more dangerous. That is, taste also governs the soul merely through the charm of pleasure—admittedly a nobler pleasure, because reason is its source—but where pleasure determines the will, morality still does not exist.

However, something great has been won by this interference of taste in the operations of the will. All these material inclinations and raw desires, which are so often stubbornly and ardently opposed to the practice of the good, are, through taste, expelled from the soul, and in their place, nobler and softer desires have been implanted therein, which relate to order, harmony, and perfection, and if they are not the same as the virtues, they nevertheless share an object with virtue. If, therefore, desire now speaks, it must endure a stringent examination before the sense of beauty; and if now reason speaks and demands actions of order, harmony, and perfection, it will find not only no opposition, but rather the liveliest agreement from the side of inclination. If we thus go through the different forms, under which morality can be expressed, we shall be able to reduce them all to these two. Either sensuousness creates motion in the soul, such that something happens or does not happen, and the will proceeds according to the law of reason; or reason creates motion in the soul, and the will obeys it, without asking the senses.

The Greek Princess Anna Komnena tells us of an imprisoned rebel, whom her father Alexis, while still a general of his predecessor, had been ordered to escort to Constantinople. On the way, as they were both yet riding together, Alexis desired to stop under the shade of a tree and recuperate from the heat of the day. Soon sleep overcame him; yet the other, for whom fear of his expected fate permitted no rest, remained awake. Whilst the one now lies in a deep sleep, the other catches sight of Alexis's sword, which has been hung on a tree limb, and he is tempted to set himself free by murdering his guardian. Anna Komnena leads us to understand, that she doesn't know what might have happened if Alexis had not fortunately awoken. Here now was a moral action of the first kind, where the sensual instinct had the first voice, and only then recognized reason as judge over it. Now had the former (the sensual instinct) triumphed over temptation out of mere respect for justice, there would be no doubt that he would have acted morally.

When the immortalized Duke Leopold of Braunschweig, standing on the banks of the rapid Oder, considered for himself, whether he should risk his life in the stormy stream so that he would have saved some unfortunate ones, who without him were helpless—and when he, I suppose the case, solely out of recognition of this duty sprang into the boat, which no one else would climb into, thus is there indeed no man who will deny that he acted morally. The Duke here found himself in the contrary situation to the previous one. Here the idea of duty came first, and before the drive for self-preservation was stirred to fight the rule of reason. But in both cases the will acted in the same manner: it followed reason directly, hence both of them are moral.

But will both cases still remain the same, when we allow the taste to have an influence on it?

Supposing, therefore, the first, who attempted to commit an evil act and out of respect for justice abstained from it, would have such an educated taste, that everything shameful and violent arouses in him an aversion, which nothing can overcome. So in the moment when the drive for self-preservation insists upon something shameful, the mere aesthetic sense will already reject it; it will not even, therefore, come before the moral forum—before the conscience—but will rather fall already in an earlier instance. But the aesthetic sense governs the will now merely through feeling, not through law. Therefore, this man denies himself the pleasurable feelings of a rescued life, because he cannot endure the adverse feeling of having committed a despicable act. Therefore, the entire business is already argued in the forum of feeling, and the conduct of this man, though it be legal, is morally indifferent—a merely beautiful effect of nature.

Supposing now, the other man, whose reason dictated to him to do something, and against which the natural instinct rebelled, would have likewise such a sensitive sense of beauty, in which everything that is great and perfect delights, so, at the same moment when reason makes its utterance, sensuousness also will go over to it, and he will do that with inclination, which, without this tender sensitivity for the beautiful, he would have to have done against inclination. But, because of that, will we consider him less perfect? Certainly not; for he acts naturally out of pure respect for the rule of reason, and that he obeys this rule with joy, can do no damage to the moral purity of this act. He is, therefore, morally just as perfect; on the other hand, he is by far more perfect physically, for he is a far more suitable subject for virtue.

Taste, therefore, gives the soul a suitable mood for virtue, because it removes the inclinations that hinder it, and arouses those which are favorable to it. Taste can not cause injury to true virtue, because, in all cases in which the natural instinct is the first stimulus, it has already dismissed before its tribunal, that which consciousness otherwise would have to have recognized, and, therefore, it is the cause, that amongst the actions of those who are governed by it, there are far more which are indifferent than are truly moral. For the excellence of men is not at all based on the greater sum total of individual rigorously-moral actions, but rather on the greater congruence of the entirety of man's natural tendency with moral law, and it is not conducive to a very high testimonial to a people or their age, when one hears so often in the same, about morality and individual moral acts; rather, one may hope that at the end of civilization, if one lets oneself think of such in general, little more will be spoken thereof. On the other hand, taste can be of positive use to true virtue, in each case where reason makes the first stimulation and is in danger of becoming overwhelmed by the stronger power of the natural instincts. In these cases, that is, taste disposes our sensuousness to the benefit of duty and, therefore, makes even a modest measure of moral will power measure up to the practice of virtue.

Now if taste, as such, in no case harms true morality, but in many more cases is obviously of use, so this circumstance must receive a great weight, that it is favorable in the highest degree to the legality of our behavior. Suppose now, that beautiful culture were able to contribute nothing at all to making us better-minded, it at least makes us fit to act, even without a true moral conviction, as if we had a moral conviction. Now it is true our actions do not at all matter before a moral tribunal, in so far as they are an expression of our convictions. But before the physical forum, and in the plan of nature, exactly to the contrary, our convictions do not matter insofar as they give rise to actions through which the purpose of nature is advanced. But now both world orders, the physical, in which powers govern, and the moral, in which laws govern, are so exactly calculable and intimately interwoven with each other, that actions, which are morally purposive according to their form, include at the same time a physical purposiveness in their content; and so, as the entire edifice of nature seems to exist only in order to make possible the highest of all purposes, which is the good, so does the good let itself be used again as the means, in order to keep the edifice of nature upright. The order of nature is therefore made dependent on the morality of our convictions, and we cannot transgress against the moral world, without at the same time bringing about confusion in the physical world.

If now human nature, as long as it remains human nature, is never to be expected to act without interruption and reversion, uniformly and constantly as pure reason and never offend against the moral order; if we must admit with all conviction to the necessity and the possibility of pure virtue, how very accidental the true practice of it is, and how little we are permitted to build upon the invincibility of our better principles; if we remember with this consciousness of our unreliability, that the edifice of nature suffers as a result of each of our moral lapses—if we call all this into memory, it would be the most wicked audacity to let the best of the world depend on this uncertainty of our virtue. Rather, from this arises an obligation for us at least to satisfy the physical world order by the content of our actions, even if we shall not please the moral order by the form of our actions—at least to pay as perfect instruments to the design of nature, that which we still owe as imperfect persons to reason, in order not to stand at the same time ignominiously before both tribunals. If we, therefore, wanted to make no arrangements for the legality of our behavior, because it is without moral worth, so could the world order be dissolved over it and, before we would finish our principles, all bonds of society would be broken. But, the more our morality is accidental, the more it is necessary to take precautions with respect to its legality, and a light-minded or proud neglect of this latter can be morally attributed to us. Just as an insane person, who foresees his approaching paroxysm, removes all knives and voluntarily offers himself to be bound, in order not to be responsible in a healthy state, for the crimes of his destroyed mind—similarly we are also obliged to bind ourselves through religion and aesthetical law, so that our passion does not injure the physical world in the periods of its rule.

I have not here unintentionally put religion and taste in a single class, because both have a common merit in respect to the effect, although not in respect to the internal worth, to serve as a surrogate for true virtue and to protect legality, where there is no hope of morality. Although that person, who would incontestably hold a higher place in the rank of the spiritual, who would have need of neither the charm of the beautiful nor the prospect of immortality in order to behave in accordance with reason, in every event, so the well known limits of mankind force even the most rigid moralist to diminish somewhat the severity of his system in its application, even though he may yield nothing in theory, and to attach the welfare of the human species, which would be badly attended to by our accidental virtue, for security's sake on the two strong anchors of religion and taste.

ON EPIC AND DRAMATIC POETRY

TRANSLATED BY EVELYN LANTZ

The epic and dramatic poets are both subject to universal poetic laws, especially the law of unity and the law of development; furthermore, they both treat similar subjects, and both can use all kinds of themes; their great essential difference lies, however, in that the epic poet presents the event as completely past, and the dramatic poet presents it as completely present. Would one derive the detail of the law, according to which both have to behave, from the nature of man, then one must always have in mind a rhapsodist and a mimic actor, both as poet, the former surrounded by his quietly hearkening circle, the latter by his impatiently onlooking and listening circle, and it would not be difficult to explain what is of most avail to each of these types of poetry, which subjects each especially chooses, which theme will be especially useful to each; I say especially: for

---

This essay, written in 1797 by Johann Wolfgang Goethe and Schiller, first appeared in 1827, after Schiller's death, in the first edition of six volumes of Goethe's *On Art and Antiquity*. It appeared again in 1829, as an appendix to *Correspondence between Schiller and Goethe in the Years 1794 to 1805*, in the third part of the *Letters* of the year 1797. It was written in the period when Schiller was working on the *Wallenstein* dramatic trilogy.

as I already observed at the beginning, neither can claim something for itself totally exclusively.

The subjects of the epic and tragedy should be purely human, important, and pathetic: The characters stand best at a certain level of culture, where self-activity is still left to its own resources, where one operates not morally, politically, or mechanically but rather personally. The myths from the heroic time of the Greeks were, in this sense, particularly favorable to the poet.

The epic poem especially presents personally limited activity, tragedy personally limited suffering; the epic poem presents man working outside himself: battles, journeys, every sort of undertaking, which requires a certain sensual breadth; tragedy presents the inwardly directed man, and the actions of the true tragedy need, for that reason, only little space.

I know of five kinds of themes:

1) *Progressive* ones, which advance the plot; drama especially makes use of these.

2) *Regressive* ones, which remove the plot from its goal; of these the epic poem almost exclusively makes use.

3) *Impeding* ones, which delay action or prolong the process; both poetic types make use of these to the greatest advantage.

4) *Reflexive* ones, through which that which has happened before the epoch of the poem, will be drawn upon.

5) *Anticipative* ones, which anticipate that which will happen after the epoch of the poem; both kinds are needed by the epic as well as the dramatic poet, in order to make his poem complete.

The *worlds*, which should be brought to view are common to both:

1) The *physical*, and indeed firstly the nearest to which the characters represented belong, and which surrounds them. In this, the dramatic poet generally is located in one place, the epic poet moves more freely in a larger locale; secondly, the more remote world, which I consider the

whole of nature. The epic poet, who generally employs the imagination, brings this world nearer through images, which the dramatic poet makes use of more sparingly.

2) The *moral* is completely common to both and will be represented most happily in its physiological and pathological simplicity.

3) The world of *chimeras, presentiments, appearances, accidents, and fates.* This is allowed to both, if only it is understood, that it would be brought in proximity to the sensual; whereby a special difficulty arises for the modern poets, because we do not easily find a replacement for the wonderful creatures, gods, fortune-tellers, and oracles of old, as much as it were desired.

Concerning the treatment of the whole, the rhapsodist, who presents what is completely past, will appear as a wise man, who, in quiet self-possession, surveys what has taken place; the purpose of his presentation will be to quiet the listeners, whereby they will listen to him protractedly and gladly, he will distribute their interest evenly, because he is not in a position to quickly balance an overly lively impression, he will refer backward and forward and wander at will; one will follow him everywhere, because he has only to do with the imaginative power, which generates images for itself, and which, to a certain degree, is indifferent to which kind it calls up. The rhapsodist should not appear himself as a higher being in his poem; he should, at the very best, read behind a curtain, so that one might abstract from all personality and only the voice of the muse would be believed to be heard in general.

The mimic actor, on the other hand, is exactly the opposite case; he represents himself as a definite individual, he wants one to participate exclusively with him and his closest surroundings, that one sympathize with the suffering of his soul and his body, share his predicaments, and forget oneself by way of him; certainly, he will also go to work in stages, but he can dare much livelier actions, because with sensuous presence, even more so the stronger impression can be destroyed by a weaker one. The onlooking listener by rights must remain in a constant sensuous exertion, is not allowed to elevate himself to reflection, he must passionately follow, his imagination is completely reduced to silence, one is allowed to make no claim upon it, and even what is narrated, must be as if it were graphically brought before one's eyes.